Development & Dispossession

The publication of this book was made possible, in part, by a generous grant
from The Brown Foundation, Inc., of Houston, Texas.

**School for Advanced Research
Advanced Seminar Series**

James F. Brooks
General Editor

Development & Dispossession

Contributors

Gregory V. Button
Department of Anthropology, University of Tennessee, Knoxville

Michael M. Cernea
Department of Anthropology, George Washington University

Dana Clark
International Accountability Project and Rainforest Action Network

Chris de Wet
Department of Anthropology, Rhodes University

Theodore E. Downing
Arizona Research Laboratories, University of Arizona

William F. Fisher
*International Development, Community, and Environment Program,
Clark University*

Carmen Garcia-Downing
Mel and Enid Zuckerman College of Public Health, University of Arizona

Barbara Rose Johnston
Center for Political Ecology, University of California, Santa Cruz

Satish Kedia
Department of Anthropology, University of Memphis

Dolores Koenig
Department of Anthropology, American University

Anthony Oliver-Smith
*Department of Anthropology, University of Florida, Gainesville,
and United Nations University Institute for Environment and Human Security*

Thayer Scudder
Department of Anthropology, California Polytechnic University

Development & Dispossession

The Crisis of Forced Displacement and Resettlement

Edited by Anthony Oliver-Smith

School for Advanced Research Press

Santa Fe

School for Advanced Research Press

Post Office Box 2188
Santa Fe, New Mexico 87504-2188
www.sarpress.sarweb.org

Co-director and Executive Editor: Catherine Cocks
Manuscript Editor: Kate Whelan
Designer and Production Manager: Cynthia Dyer
Proofreader: Amy K. Hirschfeld
Indexer: Sandi Frank
Printer: Cushing-Malloy, Inc.

Library of Congress Cataloging-in-Publication Data:

Development and dispossession : the crisis of forced displacement and resettlement / edited by
Anthony Oliver-Smith. – 1st ed.
     p. cm. – (School for advanced research advanced seminar series)
  Includes bibliographical references and index.
  ISBN 978-1-934691-08-3 (pa : alk. paper)
  1. Forced migration. 2. City planning–Social aspects. I. Oliver-Smith, Anthony.
  HV640.D48 2009
  307.2–dc22
                         2009002317

Cover illustration: Cover illustration: An elderly man sits beside his home, a shed built atop
demolished houses in Dachang Township, Chongqing Municipality, China, on May 14, 2006.
A town some 1,700 years old, Dachang was submerged in September 2006 as a result of the
construction of the Three Gorges Dam. In all, about 1.3 million people were relocated because
of the dam. Photo by China Photos/Getty Images, image no. 57611324..

Contents

Figures

Tables

Acknowledgments

The experience of participating in an advanced seminar at the School for Advanced Research (SAR) is generally considered one of the high points in the professional life of an anthropologist. To be able to discuss and debate the cutting-edge issues in one's field with a select group of colleagues, brought together from across the country and the world, for a week in the delightful atmosphere of "El Delirio" in Santa Fe is a rare privilege. I would like to thank SAR and its wonderful staff for affording our group that extraordinary opportunity to further our work. In doing so, not only have they performed a great service to us as researchers and activists, but also, we hope, the research and scholarship nourished by SAR will ultimately find some expression in improved policy and practice for the field of development-forced displacement and resettlement. I would also like to thank all the participants in the seminar for the energy and enthusiasm with which they embraced our task, for the insightful discussions, and, finally, for their superb essays. Although we may not always agree, we are a cordial group, most of whom have known one another for many years, sometimes working together, sometimes arguing opposing positions, but always respecting one another's efforts. Those efforts, put forth by all the seminar participants, are responsible for any merit this final product possesses.

Development & Dispossession

1

Introduction

Development-Forced
Displacement and Resettlement:
A Global Human Rights Crisis

Anthony Oliver-Smith

The displacement and resettlement of people and communities by large-scale infrastructural projects is one of the most bitterly contested issues in the field of development today. Publicly and, increasingly, privately funded development projects are estimated to displace more than fifteen million people a year (Michael Cernea, personal communication, September 2005). Capital-intensive, high-technology, large-scale projects convert farmlands, fishing grounds, forests, and homes into dam-created reservoirs, irrigation schemes, mining operations, plantations, colonization projects, highways, urban renewal, industrial complexes, and tourist resorts, all in the name of regional and national development. Aimed at generating economic growth and thereby improving general welfare, these projects have all too often left local people permanently displaced, disempowered, and destitute. Resettlement has been so poorly planned, financed, implemented, and administered that these projects generally end up being "development disasters." The process of displacement becomes a "totalizing" phenomenon, affecting virtually every aspect of life.

More people were involuntarily displaced in the twentieth century than in any other in recorded history. Adding to the wars and environmental havoc that uprooted millions was the global drive to develop. Despite sharing many similarities, displacement caused by development projects differs in important ways from the dislocation experienced by participants in voluntary relocation schemes, victims of natural and technological disasters, and refugees from civil and international conflicts. As in disasters and wars, people in DFDR (development-forced displacement and resettlement) are "pushed" to move rather than "pulled" or attracted by better possibilities elsewhere.[1] DFDR is entirely involuntary, despite the inducements devised to attract people to resettle voluntarily. Furthermore, although wars that turn people into refugees are the outcome of intentional decisions taken by political authorities, the general consensus is that wars should be avoided whenever possible. Large development projects, however, also the result of intentional decisions by authorities, are seen as positive steps that fit well within national ideologies of development. In effect, empowered by international standards granting the state the right to take property for national goals, such projects are justified by a cost-benefit analysis that assigns losses and gains on a political basis. Finally, unlike disasters and wars, there is no returning home after the situation has stabilized. DFDR is permanent. There can be no return to land submerged under a dam-created lake or to a neighborhood buried under a stadium or throughway. For this reason, the solutions devised to meet the needs of development-forced displacees must be durable, not contingency-based emergency strategies to meet immediate needs until people can return home (Guggenheim and Cernea 1993:3–4).

The problem of development-forced displacement and resettlement expresses the frequent tension between local and national development needs. In DFDR, society's need to develop its infrastructure to produce more energy, better water supplies, more efficient transportation systems, and more productive agriculture is balanced against the welfare of the local communities that face displacement and possible resettlement to make room for such projects. The DFDR costs borne by local people are measured against the benefits that the entire society will purportedly enjoy from a project's implementation.

In the phrase "development-forced displacement and resettlement," three basic ideas (development, displacement, and resettlement) are linked, but there has not always been, nor is there now, any necessary relationship between them. Development, obviously, can take place without displacement or resettlement. Many people displaced by development projects are never resettled and either succumb to the impacts of dislocation or find themselves consigned to the margins of society and the economy. Further, the vast majority of those displaced who do resettle suffer the outcomes of inadequately financed, poorly designed, and incompetently implemented resettlement projects that bear no resemblance to any honestly rendered interpretation of the concept of development. No necessary or inevitable linkage exists between development, displacement, and adequate, humane resettlement.

The trauma and hardships experienced by the displaced pose critical moral questions about the nature, scale, and ethics of such development models and practices (see de Wet, chapter 4, this volume). Generally, development as a goal of public policy aims at improving levels of well-being through enhancing productive capacity, based on the premise that greater production and income will filter through the system to increase general patterns of consumption. Enhanced productive capacity is posited on a principle of efficient use of resources to render maximum market value (Penz 1992:107). National governments and private developers assess that local users do not efficiently exploit resources and argue that large-scale projects will produce greater value, thereby enhancing levels of overall economic development. Projects that displace communities justify themselves ethically by the belief that greater value production increases consumption and welfare at all levels of society. When projects force people to resettle, the process may be defined in economic terms, but resettlement is fundamentally a political phenomenon, involving the use of power by one party to relocate another. Current trends suggest that development strategies will continue to promote large-scale projects that result in the resettlement of large numbers of people. The extent to which this kind of development can be carried out ethically, democratically, and effectively is an issue of considerable dispute.

For local people, often indigenous or minority groups and their allies in the global networks of social movements and NGOs (nongovernmental organizations), rights to land and other resources, self-determination, cultural identity, environmental protection, and more sustainable forms of development are central to the survival of their communities. Their claims emphasize the rights of the less powerful, the significance of cultural diversity, and the sustainability of environments over what they consider ecologically risky, economically questionable, and socially destructive projects (Oliver-Smith 2001). They point to the consistent failure of governments and private developers to adequately fund, plan, or train personnel for the complex tasks of DFDR, resulting in the impoverishment of the displaced. Deploying international covenants, they have actively broadened the agenda to include questions of human and environmental rights and justice in development, frequently converting their discourses of resistance into alternative models and strategies for socially responsible development.

A central issue in DFDR is the democratic character of the development process.

ANTHROPOLOGY AND DISPLACEMENT AND RESETTLEMENT RESEARCH, THEORY, AND PRACTICE

Anthropologists in the mid-twentieth century were among the first to recognize, report on, and work toward mitigating the serious impoverishment and gross violation of human rights occurring among populations resettled by development projects (Brokensha and Scudder 1968; Butcher 1971; Colson 1971; Hansen and Oliver-Smith 1982). Despite the participation of other disciplines, anthropology can reasonably claim to be the foundational discipline of the field of development-forced displacement and resettlement research. Because DFDR impacts virtually every domain of community life, anthropology's holistic approach well equips it to address the inherent complexity of the resettlement process. In DFDR, anthropology also has made the single strongest, tangible, and internationally documented and recognized contribution to development policy and practice over the past quarter century (Oliver-Smith 2005b).

Since the 1950s, anthropologists have spanned the entire field of DFDR in basic and applied research, policy formulation, theory building, evaluation, planning, implementation, and community- and NGO-based resistance movements. Anthropologists have helped to frame current DFDR debates concerning human and environmental rights, policy frameworks and guidelines, implementation, evaluation, the limits of state sovereignty, and the agendas of international capital (Colson 2003). Because of its central role in the field, anthropology has a responsibility to expand the array of approaches and methods addressing the current, intensified challenges presented by DFDR at the local community and project level, in national and international political discourse, and in the policy frameworks of multilateral institutions.

Research on displacement and resettlement emerged in the 1950s from the post-war concern for the welfare and fate of the enormous numbers of refugees and displacees in World War II. The pioneer document was Alexander Leighton's *The Governing of Men: General Principles and Recommendations Based on Experiences at a Japanese Refugee Camp* (1945). In 1952 Elizabeth Colson and Thayer Scudder (see Scudder, chapter 2, this volume) began long-term research on the social and ecological consequences of resettlement for the Gwembe Tonga, who were relocated by the construction of the Kariba Dam in what was to become Zambia (Colson 1971; Scudder 1973a; Scudder and Colson 1982). The topic also attracted interest elsewhere in Africa (Chambers 1970; Fahim 1983) and in Asia (Dobby 1952) and Latin America (Villa Rojas 1955) as post-war and subsequently post-colonial development efforts accelerated.

At roughly the same time, sociologists in the United States studied the displacement of urban neighborhoods by urban renewal and large-scale construction projects. Their research led to important perspectives on grief and mourning for lost homes among resettled people (Fried 1963; Gans 1962). In the 1960s, in efforts to develop greater conceptual understanding of the displacement and resettlement process, Chambers (1969) and Nelson (1973) proposed models for voluntary land-settlement projects in Africa and Latin America, respectively. The problems associated with DFDR provoked a response in the form of an organizational manual for resettlement from the UNFAO (United Nations Food and Agricultural Organization) (Butcher 1971).

In the 1970s the problems of people displaced by development projects were linked to those of people displaced by conflicts and natural disasters (Hansen and Oliver-Smith 1982). In that context, Scudder and Colson (1982), addressing the responses of dislocated peoples regardless of cause, proposed a stress-based, four-stage process of recruitment, transition, potential development, and incorporation (also see Scudder, chapter 2, this volume). As the pace of large-scale development and concomitant displacements accelerated, displacement and resettlement studies also expanded in the 1980s, focusing on the environmental and social impacts of large infrastructure projects, particularly dams. A key element in the growth of this concern about DFDR was the expansion of well-organized and widely publicized resistance movements in nations where projects were displacing and resettling many thousands of people, such as Brazil, India, Thailand, and Mexico. Resistance movements publicizing the many inadequacies of displacement and resettlement policies and practices moved DFDR to center stage in the debates about development and gained the attention of the general public and the research community alike (Fisher 1995 and chapter 8, this volume; Oliver-Smith 1994, 1996, 2006).

Following the lead of Colson and Scudder, studies stimulated by this massive increase in DFDR-affected peoples in the 1980s documented the social impacts and injustices of the displacement process, focusing on the stresses of dislocation and resettlement, the patterns of individual and group reaction, and the negative outcomes imposed on people in the resettlement process. DFDR research began to emerge in those nations in which large-scale infrastructural development processes were being funded by national, international, and multilateral sources. Along with international private consulting organizations, researchers produced a substantial "gray literature" of feasibility studies, project evaluations, and in-house reviews of policies and outcomes (for example, Rew and Driver 1986).

In similar fashion, anthropologists worked with NGOs to record the deficiencies of DFDR policy and the negative project impacts (for example, Aspelin and Coelho dos Santos 1981; Barabas and Bartolome 1973; Feit and Penn 1974). In India, researchers documented the displacement of hundreds of thousands with no resettlement at all by development projects (Fernandes and Thukral 1989). In Mexico, analysis of the displacement and relocation process for the Cerro de Oro Dam assessed the impacts as a process of "ethnocide" (Barabas and Bartolome 1973). Brazilian researchers also explored dam-induced, large-scale relocation and resettlement projects, particularly for indigenous and peasant populations in the Amazon region (Santos and de Andrade 1990; Sigaud 1986).

Researchers also pointed out the failure of governments and government agencies to adequately plan, fund, or train personnel for resettlement projects. Lack of consideration for the human rights of the people being affected and ignorance of the complexity and gravity of DFDR's impacts characterized the arrogance of authorities in many countries of both the developed and the developing worlds. Other researchers studied planning and implementation problems such as land replacement, social stress, differential gender-based effects, ideological impacts, legal issues, compensation problems, lack of participation in project planning and implementation by local people, problems experienced by host populations, failure to provide economic support, ecological impacts, and urban planning and housing.

Although much of this research focused on the negative outcomes, a number of investigators turned their attention to the question of successful resettlement in those relatively few cases where it could be claimed. Recognizing the difficulty inherent in establishing a set of criteria to measure success for such a multidimensional social process transpiring over many years, several researchers highlighted those projects that enjoyed partial success at one stage or another of development as beacons of light in the otherwise dismal record of DFDR (Partridge 1993).

A 2001 study by the World Bank's Operations Evaluation Department (OED) of five major bank-funded dam projects concluded that although better planning had occurred, the public agencies charged with resettlement implementation had not produced significant improvements. The study also found that income-restoration strategies, whether based on land for land or on other options, had not been successful generally. Success must be based on the borrower country's genuine commitment to the resettlement process as a development opportunity (Picciotto, van Wicklin, and Rice 2001). Another advance in dealing with the challenges of DFDR was provided by the Impoverishment Risks and Reconstruction (IRR) model. Developed by Michael Cernea, the IRR has become a significant tool for the prediction, diagnosis, and resolution of problems associated with DFDR (Cernea and McDowell 2000; see Scudder, chapter 2, this volume).

Generally, non-dam forms of DFDR, such as conservation, urban renewal, mining, public use complexes, transportation, and pipelines, have received less attention as causes of resettlement. As mentioned earlier, urban renewal (and, more recently, "gentrification") in the developed world has been closely examined since the 1950s (for example, Fried 1963; Gans 1962; Squires et al. 1987). With rapid urban growth in both the developed and the developing worlds, projects ranging from public use facilities (stadiums, conference centers, government complexes), to slum clearance, to major transportation redevelopment have displaced hundreds of thousands of people. Local authorities are increasingly employing eminent domain to transfer property to private developers in order to spur economic growth (Cauchon 2004; see Koenig, chapter 6, this volume).

Conservation-driven resettlement is also receiving increasing attention (Brechin et al. 2003; see Oliver-Smith, chapter 7, this volume). In 1980 the International Union for the Conservation of Nature (IUCN) published the World Conservation Strategy, which challenged the national park model and advocated the incorporation of local people into the conservation process—in Integrated Conservation and Development Projects (ICDP)—in order to benefit local people economically.

Dissatisfaction with the outcomes of such projects, however, has generated a more exclusionary strategy entailing the forced removal of people from their homelands, producing yet another variety of "environmental refugee" (Geisler and de Sousa 2001).

There is still considerable need for research on other forms of development-forced displacement, such as privately funded development projects. The significance of this form of research will only increase in the coming decade as privatization of previously publicly provided services increases. Some private-sector projects have developed their own resettlement plans and policies (Rio Tinto 2001). However, most privately funded development, such as the outcome of market factor speculation, presents significantly different problems for people affected by DFDR, in the disguised involuntary quality of market exchanges between parties of unequal power. Although private projects must agree to DFDR guidelines to get

World Bank guarantees for lower interest rates, other private-sector infra-structural initiatives that do not want or need the guarantees are free to subordinate the human and environmental rights of affected communities to corporate agendas and market logics.

DEVELOPMENT-FORCED DISPLACEMENT AND RESETTLEMENT AND APPLIED ANTHROPOLOGICAL PRACTICE

Anthropologists have spanned the entire field of DFDR in applied activities as diverse yet related as applied research, policy formation, evalu-ation, planning, implementation, and resistance. They have also played major roles in the development of appropriate policies within multilateral institu-tions such as the World Bank, the Inter American Development Bank, and the Asian Development Bank regarding the planning and implementation of resettlement projects that accompany infrastructural development. They have authored the guidelines for best practices and procedures that bor-rower nations must comply with. World Bank Operational Directive 4.30: Involuntary Resettlement (OD 4.30), written by applied anthropologist Michael Cernea, called for minimal resettlement; improvement or resto-ration of living standards, earning capacity, and production levels of local people; resettler participation in project activities; a resettlement plan; and valuation of and compensation for assets lost (World Bank 1990: 1–2). Although these guidelines have been an important step toward the partial reduction of damages, costs, and losses incurred by some resettled peoples, their implementation in borrower nations has been consistently problem-atic. A number of nations see the OD 4.30 guidelines as an infringement on national sovereignty. Furthermore, adoption of formal policies, either by the World Bank or by borrower nations, is no assurance of adequate implementation. In addition, the degree to which projects financed by pri-vate capital must adhere to these now modified guidelines and procedures established by the bank is far from clear. Most recently, World Bank policy and guidelines have been weakened regarding protection for indigenous peoples and other peoples lacking formal title to lands, making it easier to carry out resettlement and, in some circumstances, reducing the World Bank's responsibility for certain kinds of displacement and resettlement impacts (Clark 2002a:10–11).

Anthropologists working as consultants to international financial insti-tutions, among other kinds of organizations, have carried out assessments of policy frameworks, as well as the applied research necessary for better-informed planning and implementation of humane and developmentally oriented resettlement projects (Johnston and Garcia-Downing 2004; Partridge 1993; Rew, Fisher, and Pandey 2000). Anthropologists have also engaged in advocacy activities in behalf of affected communities. Working closely with groups and communities facing DFDR, anthropologists have joined in legally contesting the decisions and actions of international financial institutions, national and local governments, and private corporations (Johnston and Garcia-Downing 2004). Currently, anthropologists are taking leadership roles in many NGOs that work with affected communities to gain better conditions or to resist resettlement entirely. They are part of the larger community of activists and scholars keeping close watch on policy formulation in lending institutions to guard against the dilution or weakening of any policy relating to DFDR (Colchester 1994; Fox and Brown 1998; Waldram 1980).

Grassroots organizations, NGOs, and social movements resisting DFDR have also acquired legal personnel, expertise, and general knowledge that enable them to sue projects for violation of national civil and human rights law, as well as international accords. The growth of international human rights norms supplies a series of conventions and covenants that, although difficult to enforce in local circumstances, can be used to identify projects violating internationally accepted standards (see Fisher, chapter 8, and Clark, chapter 9, this volume). There are now much more active efforts to use these and other documents as means to achieve reparations for past injustices as well (Johnston 2000 and chapter 10, this volume).

THEORIZING DEVELOPMENT-FORCED DISPLACEMENT AND RESETTLEMENT

Theorizing DFDR as a problem in human social and cultural organization has been inextricably woven into applied concerns for developing approaches to deal with the dire needs of the affected people and their legal rights. Although some efforts toward theorizing voluntary resettlement had occurred, little theoretical work was done on DFDR until Thayer Scudder and Elizabeth Colson developed a model based on the concept of stress to describe and analyze the process of involuntary dislocation and resettlement (Scudder 2005a; Scudder and Colson 1982; see Scudder's elaborations on this model in chapter 2, this volume). They posited that three forms of stress result from involuntary relocation and resettlement: physiological, psychological, and sociocultural. These three forms of stress, referred to as "multidimensional stress," are experienced as affected people pass through the displacement and resettlement process. The process itself is represented as occurring in four stages: recruitment, transition, potential development, and handing over/incorporation. Scudder and Colson note that the potential development stage is often never reached in many DFDR projects because inept and inappropriate policy and implementation frequently trap people in perpetual transition.

At roughly the same time that Scudder and Colson were developing their model, an approach began in an emerging political ecology that focused on the linked ideas of vulnerability and risk. Terms initially employed in disaster research to understand the vast differences among societies in disaster losses, *vulnerability* and *risk* refer to the relationships between people, the environment, and the sociopolitical structures that make the conditions in which people live more prone to disasters. These concepts gained greater currency as Michael Cernea (1990) began to explore an approach that focused on the risks of poverty resulting from displacement by water projects. Eventually, he developed his well-known Impoverishment Risks and Reconstruction (IRR) approach to understanding (and mitigating) the major adverse effects of displacement. In this, he outlines eight basic risks to which people are subjected by displacement (Cernea 1996a, 1997; Cernea and McDowell 2000). The model rests on the three basic concepts of risk, impoverishment, and reconstruction. Cernea models displacement risks by deconstructing the "syncretic, multifaceted process of displacement into its identifiable, principle and most widespread components" (Cernea 2000a:19): landlessness, joblessness, homelessness, marginalization, food insecurity, increased morbidity, loss of access to common property resources, and social disarticulation (Scudder, chapter 2, this volume). He also notes a high probability that these risks will produce serious consequences in badly planned or unplanned resettlement.

Several refinements to the risk approach were developed by Dwivedi, who views risk as "a subjective calculation of different groups of people embedded differentially in political-economic and environmental conditions" (Dwivedi 1999:47). People facing DFDR must often cope with great uncertainty and a lack of information concerning their future, resulting in conditions of considerable stress, disorientation, and trauma (Dwivedi 1999:47). Indeed, most involuntary resettlement projects deprive people of control over fundamental features of their lives, as well as the necessary information to reestablish satisfactory control and understanding of the resettlement process or the changed circumstances of their lives. If people find that their understanding and control are diminished, then change will be characterized by conflict, tension, and, perhaps, active resistance. The often extremely negative, concrete impacts of resettlement projects on affected peoples compound the disorientation generated by the loss of control and understanding, creating motivation for resistance. Resistance is a reassertion of both a logic and a sense of control (Oliver-Smith 1996; Turner 1991).

NGOs, independent commissions, and other mediating institutions, in the ways they frame risk and uncertainties, have contributed to theorizing the challenges of DFDR. The World Commission on Dams (WCD) links risk with the concept of rights in advocating that an "approach based on 'recognition of rights' and 'assessment of risks' (particularly rights at risk)" be elaborated to guide future planning and decision making on dams (WCD 2000a:206). The global review of the WCD stressed the need to address the five values of equity, efficiency, participatory decision making, sustainability, and accountability as justification for the elaboration of a rights and risks approach to dam construction. Rights that were seen to be relevant in large dam projects included constitutional rights, customary rights, legislated rights, and property rights (of landholders and of developers and investors). In terms of purpose, rights pertain to material resources such as land, water, forests, and pasture or to spiritual, moral, and cultural resources such as religion, dignity, and identity (WCD 2000a:206).

Most recently, Chris de Wet, asking why resettlement so often goes wrong, sees two broad approaches to the question. First, the Inadequate Inputs approach argues that resettlement projects fail because they lack appropriate inputs, such as national legal frameworks and policies, political will, funding, pre-displacement research, careful implementation, and monitoring. The Inadequate Inputs approach optimistically posits that appropriate policies and practices can control and mitigate the risks and injuries of resettlement. The second approach, what de Wet calls the Inherent Complexity approach, identifies in resettlement a complexity that is inherent in "the interrelatedness of a range of factors of different orders: cultural, social, environmental, economic, institutional and political—all of which are taking place in the context of imposed space change and of local level responses and initiatives" (de Wet 2006:190). Moreover, these changes are taking place simultaneously in an interlinked and mutually influencing process of transformation. Further, these internal changes from the displacement process are also influenced by and respond to imposition from external sources of power, as well as initiatives of local actors. Therefore, the resettlement process emerges out of the complex interaction of all these factors in ways that are unpredictable and unamenable to a linear-based, rational planning approach.

De Wet suggests that a more comprehensive and open-ended approach than the predominately economic and operational perspective of the

Inadequate Inputs approach is necessary in order to understand, adapt to, and take advantage of the opportunities presented by the inherent complexity of the displacement and resettlement process. Some might see this perspective as unduly pessimistic, but the limited degree of control that authorities can exercise over a project creates a space for resettlers to take greater control over the process. The challenge thus becomes the development of policy that supports a genuine participatory and open-ended approach to resettlement planning and decision making (de Wet 2006).

ANTHROPOLOGY OF THE DISPLACED

Today, development planning and funding are rapidly changing, particularly regarding the roles of the public and private sectors, state–local relations, and social and environmental justice advocacy. Anthropology, building on the substantial work already done, needs to examine critically and participate in the evolving nature of the local–global politics of social and environmental advocacy to develop better understandings and approaches to the typical, as well as the novel, challenges that DFDR presents. For example, DFDR-affected peoples are developing innovative strategies to defend their rights in negotiations with the state and the global capital market by invoking international human rights covenants. Indeed, locally based resistance movements have, in some cases, provided an important corrective to or have completely halted seriously flawed projects (Oliver-Smith 2006). New sources and forms of political power have been emerging in supranational organizations, NGOs, and private institutions to support and expand the claims for disempowered subjects under the law (Clark, Fox, and Treakle 2003; Clark, chapter 9, this volume). DFDR-impacted communities provide a point of convergence for the human rights and environmental movements to create an arena for an expanded, international civil society across borders (Fisher 1995 and chapter 8, this volume). This convergence entails both a critique of development models that accept the necessity of relocating people and a questioning of the scale of development interventions that create major disruption for people, their way of life, and their environment. This critique explicitly espouses a reorientation toward more locally based, sustainable forms of development and a distancing from the ecological and human rights catastrophes resulting from development of an "industrialized nature" (Josephson 2002). Further, this discourse reassesses the extent of state sovereignty and invokes changes in global political culture.

The role of large infrastructural projects in the development process is now the focus of intense debate among powerful interests. On the one hand, national governments and private interests are redoubling their efforts to promote development projects with DFDR components but without significant legal and economic protection for increasing numbers of people and communities. Notwithstanding broad criticism, the practice of development today continues to favor large infrastructural expansion and economic growth over ecological and cultural concerns (Flyvbjerg, Bruzelius, and Rothengatter 2003; Josephson 2002). For example, the World Bank, nation-states, and industry associations have made recent efforts to reframe dams as environmentally benign, socially productive, efficient technologies. The World Bank now espouses a position favoring "high risk, high reward" projects. India's enormous river-linking scheme, for example, defies every major recommendation of the World Commission on Dams. Allegedly bowing to pressure from borrower nations that see their sovereignty threatened, the World Bank recently weakened its guidelines regarding both involuntary resettlement and protection of indigenous people affected by development projects (Downing and Moles 2002). Further, the activist community has become greatly concerned regarding the lack of clarity in the responsibilities of privately funded development projects to affected peoples.

On the other hand, these trends have been countered by initiatives from civil society that have produced significant steps toward policies and guidelines to limit projects and curb abuses. Such initiatives as the World Commission on Dams (2000b), the Extractive Industries Review (2003a), and the Equator Principles (2003) are aimed at creating what Jonathan Fox (2003:xii) has called "accountability politics" to ensure socially and environmentally responsible development. Pressure from civil society led the World Bank to create an inspection panel. The World Bank Inspection Panel gives people affected by bank-funded projects the opportunity to file complaints and request independent investigations regarding the bank's compliance with its own social and environmental guidelines. Although the panel's results since its creation in 1993 have been uneven, the inspection panel is another element in the quest for accountability (Clark, Fox, and Treakle 2003). Furthermore, gaining prior informed consent from people to be affected by projects (Goodland 2004) and strengthening the legal basis and procedures for payment of reparations for injuries and costs imposed on individuals and communities by projects have recently emerged as strategic priorities (Johnston 2000 and chapter 10, this volume). Because anthropology played a central role historically in documenting the problems and framing the debate on DFDR, the present context of rapidly evolving debate and conditions make it ever more urgent for the discipline to contribute further to the development of socially and environmentally responsible DFDR policy and practice in the future.

To that end, the advanced seminar "Rethinking Frameworks, Methodologies, and the Role of Anthropology in Development-Forced Displacement and Resettlement (DFDR)" met at the School of American Research (now the School for Advanced Research) in late September 2005. The assembled scholars focused on the known links between involuntary displacement and impoverishment, drawing on research over the preceding fifty years. The participants included anthropologists and activists working in the fields of economic development, medical anthropology, urban anthropology, ethics, conservation, nongovernmental organizations, and human rights. Questioning fundamental frameworks to generate alternative concepts and practical responses, the participants engaged DFDR issues such as human rights violations; compensation; environmental rights in conservation; reparations for displaced peoples; legal protections and international organizations; issues of free, prior, and informed consent; and theoretical syntheses in DFDR research. Because DFDR is a "totalizing" process, affecting virtually every aspect of life, to cover the topic comprehensively in one volume is impossible. Important topics that are not specifically discussed here include gender (Colson 1999; Koenig 1995), cultural heritage (Brandt and Hassan in press), and displacement by export processing zones (Free Trade Zones, Special Economic Zones), resistance to which has recently sparked so much violence in India. However, the seminar gained particular salience in view of its convening within three weeks of Hurricane Katrina on the Gulf Coast of the United States and the massive displacement and highly questionable resettlement of hundreds of thousands of citizens of New Orleans. To explore similarities, differences, and potential contributions of DFDR research to disaster-induced displacement, Gregory Button, a specialist in disaster research, was invited to join the group directly from his fieldwork with displaced hurricane victims at the Houston Astrodome. The seminar issued a Declaration on Disaster Recovery in response to the Katrina catastrophe, included as an appendix to this volume.

The first essay in this volume is by Thayer Scudder (chapter 2). His research on the problems of DFDR spans more than fifty years and focuses on the largely unrealized potential for social and cultural theory, as well as policy and practice that displacement and resettlement research represents. Development-forced displacement and resettlement presents the social sciences with a unique opportunity to develop important, policy-relevant theories as to how communities are impacted by and respond to complex development interventions. Because researchers can identify, before resettlement commences, development situations that will involve DFDR, they offer a quasi-laboratory context that allows long-term comparative research, starting with "benchmark" pre-resettlement studies. Four dimensions of DFDR are relevant to theory building: an increased rate of social change, resettlement's involuntary nature, resettlement as a byproduct of a different development initiative, and the complexity associated with DFDR. Calling for more systematic and longitudinal research, Scudder assesses the possibilities of theoretical synthesis between his and Colson's Four Stages model and Cernea's Impoverishment Risks and Reconstruction model by using both to analyze the impact of resettlement on the Gwembe Tonga by the Kariba Dam.

Michael Cernea's chapter 3 tackles the thorny issue of compensation for losses suffered by displaced and resettled peoples. He is particularly concerned with the reasons for the abject failure of so many resettlement projects to produce tangible benefits for displaced communities. Although states and international financial institutions have, for years, accepted the proposition that resettlement projects must be development projects in their own right, the record of dismal failures and concomitant pain and suffering for the displaced continues with depressing regularity. Cernea attributes this failure to flaws in the compensation principle and the accompanying intention to restore levels of well-being. Resettlement projects are consistently underfinanced because of a failure to understand the nature and extent of losses and needs, thus dooming displaced and resettled peoples to impoverishment. Drawing on economic theories of economic rent and concepts of property, Cernea proposes a variety of benefit-sharing strategies to address the lacking financial capacity of resettlement projects. To illustrate how such strategies can be used to address the inadequacies of resettlement financing and improve outcomes, he cites examples of successful outcomes through benefit sharing in Colombia, Brazil, China, Canada, Norway, and Japan.

Given the dismal outcomes for most peoples displaced and resettled by development projects, Chris de Wet (chapter 4) raises the question of how DFDR projects are approached in ethical terms and, further, of how to grapple with the ethical tensions arising out of such projects. De Wet poses the situation in which a choice has to be made between equally compelling but competing moral values within an ethical framework. In effect, he asks how we are to deal ethically with a development project that promotes human well-being for a generalized population at the cost of enormous deprivation and suffering for specific communities. The traditional use of cost-benefit analysis to weigh the gains for some against the pains of others is found wanting. However, he argues, blocking a project because it displaces and resettles people denies another population the benefits of the project. In some sense, decision makers find themselves having to trade off competing notions of good against each other, creating a situation in which it is impossible to apply an ethical approach consistently. In effect, de Wet finds that we are unable to create the moral space in which everyone can win. Development requiring resettlement thus displaces ethics, in turn requiring a general rethinking of the "very relationship between development and resettlement, and particularly what has been taken as self-evident in this relationship."

Dealing with perhaps the least well-studied or documented dimension of DFDR, Satish Kedia (chapter 5) presents the health consequences of hydroelectric dam projects for communities affected by dam sites and by displacement and resettlement. Such consequences are described as severe and wide-ranging. Kedia explores how dam construction impacts the health of populations residing in and around the construction area. He then discusses the health problems among displaced peoples affected by the Tehri Dam in northern India. Noting that the compensation policies for land losses were inadequate and poorly implemented, Kedia analyzes the impacts on the physical health of the displaced population caused by dam-created environmental changes, novel environmental threats and hazards in the resettlement site, the influx of eight thousand construction workers, declines in dietary intake, deterioration of water supplies, and changes in hygiene facilities and practices. The stresses engendered by the DFDR process were also the source of significant mental health consequences: most villagers suffered from insomnia, feelings of guilt, depression, and feelings of insecurity. Compounding this troubled mental state was their sense that sacred ancestors, gods, and spirits had been abandoned and that their illnesses and troubles derived from this weakening connection.

The increasing urbanization of the world, an outcome of massive migratory forces and processes, has led to almost unending urban construction as cities expand and renovate. Dolores Koenig (chapter 6) explores the consequences for people and neighborhoods uprooted by the dynamism of urban economies. Noting that the choice for urban development sites rarely affects the affluent or middle classes, Koenig establishes that, in high-density urban areas, even small projects can displace many people. Often, it is their very poverty that subjects the poor to the processes of displacement and resettlement. Particularly in the developing world, the poorest may lack formal title to the land they occupy, in both rural and urban areas, becoming subject to eviction when that land is found desirable for development purposes. Moreover, in urban resettlement, Koenig finds that an excessive attention to housing and services, congruent with World Bank guidelines on restoring standards of living, to the detriment of programs aimed at restoring livelihoods, has led to increased impoverishment for the displaced. Therefore, Koenig counsels that improved outcomes for urban resettlement projects must be based on better understanding of urban economies and the roles that displaced populations play in them.

Anthony Oliver-Smith (chapter 7) maintains that conservation, although not generally thought of as a form of development, becomes a development strategy when invoked in discourses of sustainable development and the valorizing of resources and environments. Noting the similarities between DFDR and conservation-forced displacement and resettlement (CFDR), Oliver-Smith adopts a political ecological approach to trace the evolution of conservationist thought and policy regarding both nature and the peoples residing "in nature" in the West, from the national park model to contemporary forms of integrated conservation and development models. Although indigenous and traditional peoples are generally not "natural ecologists," they are hardly to blame for the vast majority of environmental devastation that has taken place in the world. Many biodiversity "hot spots" are inhabited by indigenous peoples, but logging, mining, petroleum exploration, cattle ranching, and commercial agriculture are responsible for far more environmental destruction. In advocating the expulsion of indigenous and traditional peoples from protected areas, the conservation movement has chosen targets of least resistance, the marginalized and disparaged indigenous and traditional rural peoples, instead of confronting directly the powerful economic and political interests that have driven the devastation of nature.

William Fisher's chapter 8 focuses on the dynamic political character of the development processes within which DFDR policies are made and development decisions formulated, against which project-affected peoples must mount organized resistance or efforts at mitigation. Specifically, chapter 8 discusses the roles played by NGOs, social movements, and other civil society groups in the ongoing struggle to develop better policies and accountability mechanisms. Fisher highlights four key aspects of a larger story about transnational advocacy: the extent to which DFDR obliges local people to develop new alliances and political forms; the importance of changing the information environment to influence policy and alter power relationships; the effect of engaging in these new activities on project-affected groups; and the tension between democratic participation and the need for efficiency and effectiveness in altering policies. These issues make clear that addressing the complex problems of DFDR involves not only identifying best practices and penning new guidelines but also understanding and engaging these dynamic, transnational political processes.

Dana Clark, whose work as an environmental and human rights lawyer has focused on displacement and resettlement policy issues, examines in chapter 9 the policies developed within the World Bank, revealing their strengths and weaknesses regarding affected people. She analyzes two recent, in-depth multistakeholder reviews, the World Commission on Dams (WCD) and the Extractive Industries Review (EIR). Particularly significant are the adoption of a rights and risk approach to development planning by the WCD and the principle of free, prior, and informed consent (FPIC) in the EIR. These recommendations, however, have not been effectively translated into World Bank policy. She notes that recent developments in both World Bank and International Financial Corporation (IFC) policies do not bode well for the displaced. Landless people and people without legal title to land have been placed in jeopardy by policies that recognize compensation only for legal titleholders. The situation becomes even more worrisome in the IFC endorsement of the use of force by the state to benefit private sector investment.

Barbara Johnston's contribution to this volume, chapter 10, focuses on the legacy of poverty, misery, and intergenerational disaster that some development projects have bequeathed displaced communities. Johnston discusses the movement to secure reparations for development disaster, drawing from the case of the Chixoy Dam in Guatemala. She outlines the basic protections, conditions, and actions needed to achieve reparations for development-forced disaster. Ideally, these efforts inform responsible parties, encourage participation in a negotiation process, and help shape and structure meaningful remedy. In reality, as the Guatemalan case aptly illustrates, this world is a place where rights-protective arenas are increasingly under siege and legitimate human rights complaints are recast as threats against the state. Johnston poses the important question of how to support and facilitate struggles to secure meaningful remedies in today's context of the militarized state's resurgent supremacy and the related erosion of rights-based governance.

Ted Downing and Carmen Garcia-Downing (chapter 11) argue that insufficient attention has been paid to the psycho-socio-cultural (PSC) impoverishment inflicted by involuntary displacement. Mitigation of PSC damages has proven much more problematic. Few projects consider mitigating, or even attempting to mitigate, this risk. Five fallacies block discussions and actions, offering those who should bear responsibility an untenable rationale for not addressing the issue.

The first, the "compensation is enough" fallacy, asserts that compensation payments meet all the moral and economic obligations due displaced peoples. The second fallacy blocking action is the "strict compliance" fallacy, which holds that resettlement risks are addressed by adherence to project plans, policies, and laws. Assuming that the policies, politics, and economics have been addressed but PSC impoverishment still occurs, a third fallacy is to "blame the victims" themselves: they are incapable of understanding or taking advantage of economic opportunities offered them. A fourth, "the clock stops with construction" fallacy, asserts that responsibilities to displaced people end at the completion of the Resettlement Action Plan (RAP) or with completion of the construction phase. Fifth and finally, the "someone else should pay" fallacy holds that the project designers, governments, and financiers are not legally or economically liable for PSC changes.

Chapter 11 reframes the sociocultural dimension, arguing that, in the psycho-socio-cultural (PSC) realm, it is highly improbable that a pre-displacement routine culture may be recovered, let alone be restored. However, this does not mean that nothing can be done. The relative success of PSC recovery must be measured by different criteria from those for economic recovery or legal liability. Relative success is determined by how well the transformed routine culture answers the primary questions of the displaced, compared with the pre-displacement culture. Primary questions include, Who are we? Where are we? and How do we relate to one another? The applied question thus becomes, What can be done to facilitate the new routine culture so that it adequately addresses the primary cultural questions faced by the displaced peoples?

Gregory Button, leaving his field research with the survivors of Hurricane Katrina to attend our seminar, presented a field report on the conditions he was encountering with the displaced in Houston. His participation in the seminar proved to be invaluable in assessing the differences and similarities between disaster-caused displacement and DFDR. To conclude the volume, his primary aim in chapter 12 is to narrow the gap between the two seemingly different, but actually closely allied, literatures on disaster-caused displacement and DFDR. Noting certain disparities in cause, Button asserts that, after the impact stage is over, the challenges confronting displaced peoples in disasters and in development projects begin to resemble each other. Both involve a process of reconstruction. To explore these similarities, Button applies and tests concepts from DFDR research (many of which were developed by authors in this volume) against the challenges and problems that the displaced victims of Katrina suffered in the roughly eighteen months following that catastrophe. With Wittgenstein, he sees important "family resemblances" between disaster displacement and DFDR that offer insights into the total phenomenon of displacement and can lead to greater understanding and improved capabilities for mitigation. Indeed, given the recent massive displacements driven by disasters and environmental forces such as desertification, deforestation, pollution, and contamination, many of them closely related to development processes and climate change, the need for this mutual exchange between disaster-induced and development-forced displacement becomes even more acute.

As will become apparent to the reader of these chapters, there are diverse interpretations of fundamental questions that are philosophical, theoretical, or practical in nature. Should development that displaces individuals and communities be allowed? What are the development rights of the state and of private capital? Are there limits? Are the problems that result from displacement and resettlement simply the consequence of inadequate economic resources, or do other aspects inhibit success? Who represents the displaced, and in what forums and venues? Can reparation payments compensate for the losses experienced in displacement and resettlement, or should other forms of restitution be considered? These and many other questions became the focus of our discussions at the School for Advanced Research and are articulated here in this volume.

CONCLUSION

As the debates on development evolve in the twenty-first century, the concerns for continued infrastructural and economic growth will continue to be countered by concerns for more environmentally sustainable and more democratic forms of development, particularly at the local level. Because of the human rights issues of displacement and resettlement and the environmental concerns, development projects have increasingly become the sites in which these interests and issues are contested and played out through different models of development by individuals and groups from a variety of communities, local and nonlocal. As Fisher (1995:8) points out, to some extent, both sides of the discussion share similar rhetorics of social justice and material well-being, but they differ markedly on the deeper philosophical meaning of development as a social goal and the means by which that goal should be achieved.

Dominant development models, promoting large-scale infrastructural projects, transform social and physical environments and espouse the concept of "the greatest good for the greatest number" while attempting to safeguard local rights and well-being. Although their record hardly reflects it, they assume that the less powerful will benefit eventually through well-designed and implemented resettlement programs. For many, realism about the framework of current international and national economic structures and conditions obliges acceptance of this development ideology. However, many others prefer to focus on the rights of the less powerful and the significance of cultural and environmental diversity rather than on the pursuit of what they consider to be ecologically destructive and economically dubious projects. In this volume, anthropologists, employing their knowledge, analytical skills, and energies in good faith on both sides of the debate, disclose and analyze the complexity and urgency of the problem.

Note

1. The participants in the SAR seminar now submit that "development-forced displacement and resettlement" (DFDR) is more appropriate than the previous term, "development-induced displacement and resettlement" (DIDR). The reasoning behind this change is that *induced* is not an appropriate term for something that is determined by fiat, decided and planned in advance (Michael Cernea, personal communication, February 2007). *Induced* is inadequate also because it suggests that people may be convinced by arguments or rewards to be resettled. In such a case, involuntary resettlement becomes voluntary, not forced or imposed.

2

Resettlement Theory and the Kariba Case

An Anthropology of Resettlement

Thayer Scudder

In the early 1960s, David Brokensha (1963) emphasized the need for a "sociology of resettlement." Forty-three years later, there is no question that development-forced displacement and resettlement (DFDR) has become an important subfield of anthropology with an extensive literature. Guggenheim, for example, listed more than eight hundred references in his 1994 annotated bibliography on involuntary resettlement.

DFDR provides a rare, quasilaboratory setting of great potential for advancing significant, policy-relevant theory in the behavioral and social sciences. This setting enables us to complete pre-resettlement "benchmark" studies and then to compare how communities and households that are in different environmental and cultural settings around the world and are encompassed within differing political economies respond to involuntary resettlement. What evidence we have suggests that individuals and sociocultural systems are affected and respond in remarkably similar ways throughout the resettlement process.

We have not, however, gone about our research in a very scientific fashion in regard to testing what theory we have. Although community resettlement in connection with large dams has been more carefully researched than have other DFDR types, during a four-year study I found sufficient case material on dam resettlement for statistical analysis in only fifty cases (Scudder 2005a). In only one of those, the Kariba case analyzed in this chapter, had the resettlement process been adequately studied over at least a two-generation period, starting with a pre-removal benchmark study followed by frequent updating. In all the other cases, conclusions as to outcomes (defined for analytical purposes as living standard improvement, restoration, or impoverishment) were qualified with the caveat that data inadequacies made conclusions tentative.

This is a pretty sorry research record and is even worse in regard to other types of DFDR. Anthropology and the other social sciences are way behind the environmental sciences in carrying out the type of systematic and comparative long-term research needed for improving policy-relevant theory. A model could be the Long Term Ecological Research (LTER) Network, a series of long-term studies of ecosystems initiated with National Science Foundation (NSF) funding. Today there is a collaborative network of more than 1,800 "scientists and students investigating ecological processes over long-term temporal and broad spatial scales" (www.lter-net.edu, accessed June 2008). Currently, the US network includes twenty-six sites in the fifty states, one in Antarctica, and one in Puerto Rico. Two include cities (Baltimore and Phoenix), and several have social science components. LTER is also linked to long-term research programs in other countries (www.ilternet.edu).

Oddly, we have nothing equivalent in the social sciences to deal with human societies involved in major development interventions. It is not too late to initiate such a program, which would also include detailed follow-up studies of such important past examples as Aswan High Dam and Arenal Dam resettlement. But will it be done? And will the necessary comparative long-term research on other DFDR cases be carried out? These remain to be seen.

DFDR CHARACTERISTICS RELEVANT TO THEORY BUILDING

Emphasis in theory building is on the involuntary resettlement of communities instead of individual households. The focus on communities is necessary because it is more applicable to theory building in the social sciences. Community relocation also involves the large majority of resettlers. In the World Bank's review (1994) of resettlement Bank-wide, which Michael Cernea organized, dams were responsible for 63 percent of the people displaced by 146 ongoing, Bank-financed development projects. By 2000 an estimated forty to eighty million people had been relocated in connection with forty-five thousand large dams located around the world (World Commission on Dams 2000a). By this time, fewer dams were being built;

urban redevelopment dominated as the major source of displacement in a growing number of countries. But, like dam resettlement, urban development impacts mainly communities, in terms of numbers of resettlers (see Koenig, chapter 6, this volume).

Four DFDR characteristics are especially relevant for theory-building efforts: the faster rate of social change, the mostly involuntary nature of resettlement, resettlement as a by-product of a different development initiative, and the complexity associated with DFDR.

DFDR Accelerates Social Change

Regardless of outcome, DFDR accelerates social change in some behavior patterns, institutions, and belief systems, compressing change into a shorter time span. Consequently, a comparative analysis of DFDR (based on long-term research initiated before physical removal occurs) provides social scientists with a major opportunity for theory building.

DFDR Is Involuntary

I am aware of only one case of dam-induced resettlement in which a majority are said to have welcomed removal initially. This was under such unique circumstances that I consider it an exception that "proves the rule." The case involved the Aswan High Dam resettlement of fifty thousand Egyptian Nubians who already had been resettled one to three times because of the earlier construction of the smaller Aswan Dam in 1902 and its subsequent heightening in 1913 and 1933. On each occasion, the majority resettled on Sahara Desert sands and rocks on the reservoir margin. Labor migration rates increased because of flooding of most arable land, becoming the highest rates in Africa. Literally, no males over the age of thirteen lived in communities closest to the site where the High Dam was subsequently built. To reunite families, both men and women were ready to move in the 1960s to a major irrigation scheme that the High Dam authorities provided for the resettlers.

DFDR as a Development By-Product

When dealing with people and human societies, exceptions to the rule seem almost inevitable. One could argue that forcibly resettling people in the Southern Sudan to avoid sleeping sickness (human trypanosomiasis) involved resettlement as a development initiative. But such cases are rare. Generally, DFDR results from other development efforts, including such infrastructure as dams, pipelines and roads, urban redevelopment, extractive industries, and the establishment of parks and reserves. In such cases, those who must resettle are seen, at worst, as "people in the way" or as "a nuisance" and, at best, as regrettable but necessary victims of the state's use of its power of eminent domain.

Being a development by-product is largely responsible for the five statistically significant causes for failed resettlement in connection with the previously mentioned fifty-dam survey: lack of political will on the part of project authorities and governments, lack of finance for planning and implementing resettlement, lack of capacity in terms of numbers and expertise of resettlement staff, lack of development opportunities for improving livelihoods, and lack of community participation in the resettlement process. Countering those deficiencies was important but not necessarily sufficient for implementing a successful resettlement process.

The Complexity and Difficulty of Achieving an Equitable Process of DFDR

Chris de Wet, in a recent publication (2003), addressed the question of whether DFDR is too complex and difficult for achieving a higher living standard outcome, even where planners and project authorities want to achieve an equitable result. There is support for such a conclusion. DFDR has impoverished the majority in most cases. Other factors add to the complexity, in addition to planning weaknesses and lack of development opportunities and community participation. In the fifty-dam survey, I found that unexpected events had a significant (P <0.008) and adverse impact on outcomes. Inability of resettling communities to compete with more powerful, experienced, and capitalized immigrants (in 43 percent of 47 cases where data were adequate) and hosts (32 percent of 44 cases) was also a problem.

Comparing DFDR with large-scale, voluntary land-settlement schemes suggests, however, that complexity need not preclude a successful outcome. In the first edition of Cernea's *Putting People First* (1985), he refers to the agricultural settlement of new lands by volunteer households "as socially the most complex of all development interventions, both to design and implement."[1] Yet, favorable economic rates of return are not that uncommon among Bank-financed schemes. In an evaluation of twenty-seven projects, the World Bank reported that 62 percent of those that "had been audited had economic rates of return (ERRs) of 10 percent or better" (World Bank 1985:ii). Those that had been planned as land settlements (rather than being a component of another project) had a still higher ERR, and half of the successful projects in both categories "had major multiplier effects" (World Bank 1985:ii).

In a later World Bank publication, Eriksen (1999) states that a higher success rate with voluntary land-settlement schemes is primarily due to planning differences. In DFDR, planners "clearly treated the involuntary resettlement component as subordinate to construction processes and schedules...and as an economic externality with poorly identified costs and no defined 'benefits'" (Eriksen 1999:86).

EXISTING THEORETICAL FRAMEWORKS

There are two major theoretical frameworks dealing with the involuntary resettlement process that researchers and policy makers have found useful in explaining different DFDR outcomes. The first in time was my four-stage framework (Scudder 1981b with updatings), which deals with the first and second generations of resettlers.[2] The second was Cernea's impoverishment risks and reconstruction framework (Cernea 1990 with updatings). Emphasis is on eight characteristic impoverishment risks that have been associated with DFDR and on their avoidance through a well-planned and implemented reconstruction process. Synergistically interrelated rather than prioritized, the eight risks are landlessness, joblessness, homelessness, marginalization (involving downward mobility), increased morbidity and mortality, food insecurity, loss of access to common property, and social disarticulation.

The Four Stages Model

Emphasis in the four-stage framework (table 2.1) is on how a majority of resettlers can be expected to behave during the four stages, which must be completed through the second generation if resettlement outcomes are to be considered successful. If the majority reach only Stage 2 or slip back from Stage 3 or Stage 4, they will be unable even to restore, let alone improve, their pre-project livelihoods.

Even among colleagues, the four-stage framework requires more explanation than does Cernea's impoverishment risks and reconstruction framework. This is because the four-stage framework has usually been referred to as the Scudder (or Scudder/Colson) stress model. Involuntary resettlement is now generally accepted as stressful, especially during the first two stages of the resettlement process, during which physiological, psychological, and sociocultural stresses are synergistically interrelated. But the framework is much more than just a stress model, and failure of colleagues to deal with, and critique, its broader significance has puzzled me.

In dealing with the resettlement process over a two-generation period, the four-stage framework is primarily a behavioral one. It predicts how the

TABLE 2.1

The Four-Stage Process for Achieving Successful Resettlement

Stage 1:	Planning for resettlement before physical removal
Stage 2:	Coping with the initial drop in living standards that tends to follow removal
Stage 3:	Initiating economic development and community-formation activities necessary for improving the living standards of first-generation resettlers
Stage 4:	Handing over a sustainable resettlement process to the second generation of resettlers and to nonproject authority institutions

majority can be expected to behave in the last three stages, commencing with physical removal. It also explains in detail why, during the first two stages, living standards of the majority can be expected to decline, a predicted outcome that requires both compensation and development to restore or improve their living standards. The predicted behavioral response to physical removal is for the majority to be risk averse during Stage 2.

To me, the most fascinating aspect of the four-stage framework is the shift from a risk-averse stance during Stage 2 to a risk-taking one at the commencement of Stage 3, as well as the range of indicators that can be used to document a shift in emphasis from living standard restoration at the household level to community formation and economic development, followed by or overlapping with Stage 4. Yet, to the best of my knowledge, few colleagues have tested the applicability of this fundamental shift in behavior against their own data. Such testing is necessary because there are so few cases in which a majority of DFDR resettlers improved their living standards by the end of the resettlement process or at least enjoyed a number of years of improvement that was, unfortunately, not sustainable into the second generation. Currently, Stage 3 is based on only about 10 DFDR cases and 5 cases dealing with other large-scale settlement and resettlement schemes. The indicators I have used to pinpoint a transition from Stage 2 or Stage 3 initially were based on 3 DFDR cases, as well as on a large number of cases involving volunteer households in connection with large-scale land settlement projects. The three DFDR cases are Kariba, Aswan High Dam, and Parigi—the last involved the forced removal by Dutch colonialists of Balinese communities to Sulawesi for political reasons (Davis 1976).

In case after case, economic indicators illustrate a shift from attempts to achieve household food self-sufficiency to an emphasis on improving living standards by diversifying the activities of family members through a remarkably similar set of activities. Food crops also become cash crops, with specialized cash crops added, along with sale of livestock. Nonfarm activities receive increasing importance, including small family shops and crafts such as masonry and carpentry. Other businesses include rental of newly purchased farm equipment and use of one or more sewing machines to produce clothing and school uniforms for sale. Especially significant is growing emphasis on the education of children of both sexes, showing that the family is willing to forego their labor with the intention of receiving greater future returns.

In project after project, upgrades to housing and household furnishings follow a remarkably similar trend in resettlement/settlement. Construction is upgraded and rooms are added, including one or more rooms for rental. Remarkably similar furnishings are acquired. Petromax lamps or electricity are added for lighting; fuel and appliances for cooking and heating are upgraded. Ubiquitous is a stuffed couch-and-chair set, along with a glassed-in cabinet that displays family souvenirs, toys, and treasures that usually include a tea or coffee set. Walls have prominent clocks and also tend to be decorated with brightly painted calendars and pictures of weddings, graduations, and family members in uniform. Radios are joined by radio-cassette players and battery- or electricity-operated TVs.

Social and cultural indicators include formation of such community institutions as funeral and credit societies, various kinds of cooperatives, and, in the case of irrigation, water user associations. Especially important is the reestablishment of community ritual, which includes the building of earth shrines, churches, temples, or mosques. The resettlement experience itself, as well as the resettlers' cultural identity, may be incorporated in dance, drama, folktales, poetry, and song, along with a renaming of landscape features. In the three cases, I associated the full emergence of a number of such indicators with what I deemed, perhaps with some exaggeration, a cultural renaissance. Still, what happened is that the communities not only again knew who they were but also wanted surrounding communities to know that they were a force to be reckoned with.

Framework Similarities

Both the four-stage and the impoverishment risks and reconstruction frameworks are based on the hypothesis that, regardless of cultural or environmental setting, a majority of resettlers will take advantage of appropriate opportunities for improving their livelihood, provided that appropriate assistance is available to enable them to benefit from those opportunities.

TABLE 2.2

Resettler "Well-Being" in Relation to Outcome (P <0.000)

Nature of Outcome	Mean	N	Std. Deviation
Adverse well-being	6.6	31	2.4
Positive well-being	10.9	9	2.2
Total	7.6	40	2.9

Sociocultural shortcomings are not a major cause of DFDR-induced impoverishment. Testable hypotheses emphasize lack of political will and funding, insufficient staff capacity and expertise of the planning and implementing agencies, and inadequate opportunities for, and participation of, resettlers (Scudder 2005a).

Both frameworks also lend themselves to specific hypotheses that can be tested. For example, is the four-stage framework less applicable to urban resettlement? Do indicators such as diversification of household production systems through education of children and shifts into higher-value crops or nonfarm activities accurately predict a shift to the risk-taking stance associated with Stage 3's economic development and community formation? If Stage 2 tends to be characterized by an emphasis on household activities for adjusting to a new habitat and neighbors, then does a greater emphasis on community institutions, the renaming of rural and urban features in the new habitat, the celebration of ethnicity, and political activism sufficiently characterize the shift from Stage 2's risk-adverse behavior to a risk-taking stance in Stage 3?

As for Cernea's impoverishment risks and reconstruction requirements, to what extent can they be prioritized? John Gay and I found certain impoverishment risks to be significant for analyzing and therefore, in the future, for forecasting the nature and extent of the failed resettlement process that characterized 36 (82 percent) of the 44 cases of dam-induced resettlement for which sufficient data for statistical analysis existed (Scudder 2005a). We combined five of the seven risks into a "well-being" index that correlated nicely with outcome (table 2.2). The same was true for each of those risks (landlessness, joblessness, food security, marginality, and access to common property).

Each of the five risks also had a statistically significant relationship to outcome, with marginalization (table 2.3) having the highest association with an adverse outcome (P <0.000). Cernea defines marginalization as occurring "when families lose economic power and spiral downwards" (Cernea

TABLE 2.3

Marginalization in Relation to Outcome (Crosstabulation P <0.000)

	Outcome		
Marginalization	**Adverse**	**Positive**	**Total**
A problem for the majority	25	0	25
	100.0%	0.0%	100.0%
A problem for a minority	2	2	4
	50.0%	50.0%	100.0%
Not a problem	6	8	14
	42.9%	57.1%	100.0%
Total	33	10	43
	76.7%	23.3%	100.0%

1999:17). Moreover, "it is often accompanied by social and psychological marginalization, expressed in a drop in social status, oustees' loss of confidence in society, and in themselves" (Cernea 1999:17). In other words, marginalization involves a fundamental threat to "the socio-cultural system in which resettlers' livelihoods are imbedded—a major cause of impoverishment that planners seldom acknowledge" (Scudder 2005a:72). This conclusion has important policy implications because it emphasizes the inadequacy of donor safety-net policies that leave out so-called intangibles, including a wide range of cultural variables (Downing 1996a).

As for the other four impoverishment risks, in order of significance, landlessness was a problem in 38 (86 percent) of 44 cases, joblessness in 33 (80 percent) of 41 cases, food insecurity in 33 (79 percent) of 42 cases, and loss of access to common property resources in 27 (77 percent) of 35 cases. Least impoverishing of the other two risks was homelessness, with housing inadequate in 9 (19 percent) of 47 cases. Social disarticulation, defined as loss of social capital, was impoverishing in 15 (34 percent) of 44 cases, those being largely situations in which resettlers were not allowed to move in social units of their choice.

Both theoretical frameworks deal with processes over an extended period of time. Operating at a high level of generalization, they are, as Koenig pointed out during the SAR advanced seminar, "abstract" or, as I stated, "theoretical frameworks that simplify complex phenomena." Although it is possible to derive hypotheses for testing from each, we must be careful because of the complexity and variability involved. Take Cernea's eight impoverishment risks. Can they be prioritized for all types of DFDR? I doubt it, because the significance of each can be expected to vary not only from one situation to another and over time, but also within any particular community, between female and male and between different age, wealth, and positional categories. As for the relative importance of political will, staffing capacity, funding, opportunities, and participation, in aggregate they are necessary but not sufficient for achieving success. For example, unexpected events and other variables can alter outcomes.

Differences and Inadequacies

Aside from different approaches (mine dealing primarily with resettler behavior and Cernea's with risks) that explain why the two frameworks complement each other, there are some major differences between them in assumptions and hypotheses. Fundamental is whether the stress and downturn in living standards associated with the second stage in the four-stage framework can be reduced by the prompt implementation of livelihood improvement to the extent that the second stage is eliminated. Cernea believes this to be the case, as does Robert Goodland (2000), who believes not only that improved planning and plan implementation will enable a majority of resettlers to become project beneficiaries at the time of removal, but also that relocation, under such circumstances, can become a voluntary instead of an involuntary process.

The evidence is overwhelming that individual households can benefit immediately from involuntary resettlement. As the Aswan case shows, a majority may welcome it initially, as may some communities characterized by extreme poverty. Resettlement currently under way in connection with Laos's Nam Theun 2 Dam is one example. In this case, the villages of approximately six thousand people were impoverished during the Vietnam War because they happened to live along the Ho Chi Minh trail.

In spite of such exceptions and the increasing ability of both civic society and resettling communities to reduce the costs of contemporary DFDR (see Fisher, chapter 8, and Clark, chapter 9, this volume), evidence is lacking that improved plan implementation "can eliminate the drop in living standards, the multidimensional stress, and the initially conservative coping behavior that characterizes Stage 2" (Scudder 2005a:44) or that DFDR's involuntary characteristics can become voluntary. Making resettlement voluntary could be expected to be especially difficult when communities, as with the construction of major infrastructure and urban redevelopment, must cope before removal with a long period of planning during which living standards can be expected to drop, as well as with the uncertainty about what kind of future to expect.

Additional support for the hypothesis that Stage 2 behavior is a fundamental characteristic of DFDR is provided by Shi Guoqing (China's leading resettlement scholar) and Hu Weisong, who note "that the standard of living and production of most displaced persons declines" following physical resettlement in connection with dam construction (Shi Guoqing and Hu Weisong 1996:57). Downing and Garcia-Downing's research on dissonance intervals (chapter 11, this volume) before "a return to a new routine culture" is also relevant where they note that "the dissonance interval appears to take longer in development-induced displacement than in natural disasters."

Also, there are data inadequacies, which can be corrected through further research. Both frameworks emphasize rural resettlement at the expense of urban, which has been less intensively studied. More emphasis is also needed on gender impacts, and far more emphasis on impacts on children. Though not ignored by the two frameworks, more attention needs to be paid to the wider context in which DFDR occurs (Wali 1989), to organizational structures for managing resettlement (Rew 1996), and to cultural intangibles and human rights issues (Downing 1996a). And careful situational analysis is needed in each case, as illustrated by the Kariba case.

APPLICABILITY OF THE KARIBA CASE FOR THEORY TESTING

The construction of the Kariba Dam in the late 1950s required the involuntary relocation of fifty-seven thousand people, the large majority of whom were Gwembe Tonga. Thirty-four thousand people required removal on the north, or Northern Rhodesian, bank of the Zambezi, and twenty-three thousand from the Southern Rhodesian south bank. During our first two years of research, Colson and I worked primarily on the Northern Rhodesia side, where the Rhodes-Livingstone Institute (which sponsored our research) was based. After Rhodesia's Unilateral Declaration of Independence in 1965, we restricted our research entirely to the north bank in what had become Zambia in 1964. The analysis that follows applies primarily to the Zambian side.[3]

The relevance of the Kariba case for theory building and theory testing extends beyond its being the most detailed, long-term DFDR study we have.

Of most importance, both theoretical frameworks (Cernea's and mine) are applicable. After approximately seventeen years (1958–1974), a majority of the thirty-four thousand resettlers on the Zambian side of Lake Kariba had passed through the first three stages of the resettlement process (see table 2.1) and had commenced the fourth.

The situation was such that the World Bank's 1996 *Profiles of Large Dams* listed Kariba among its few success cases. Though noting various problems, the authors concluded that "there is evidence that there was an improvement in the standard of living" (World Bank 1996a:82). This was true in 1974, but this standard of living was not sustainable. Especially important was the resettlement-related environmental degradation of a reduced land base of less fertile land. Starting in the latter half of the 1970s, a major downturn occurred (which continues today), characterized by seven of Cernea's impoverishment risks. Also applicable are unexpected events and competition with hosts and immigrants.

Let me anticipate one criticism for using the Kariba case, namely, that it played a major role in the origins of my four-stage analytical framework and that I overgeneralized certain characteristic and situational features of the Kariba case to DFDR elsewhere (see Partridge, Brown, and Nugent 1982). This was definitely the case. One example was my emphasis on denial of forthcoming resettlement by those involved.

Kariba was the first major development-forced resettlement of which the Gwembe Tonga were aware, with their ignorance of what to expect influencing their behavior then. Times have changed. Not only have people threatened with DFDR become more aware of its implications through knowledge of other cases, but also, even if they are not so informed, people are apt to become informed by the growing number of NGOs concerned with human rights, resettlement, and environmental issues.

I, too, have learned, by reading the work of my colleagues. Since the late 1970s, I have applied and adapted the framework to more than 100 cases, of which more than 50 apply to DFDR (Scudder 1997, 2005a). Other scholars have also found the framework useful in dealing with DFDR (Bilharz 1998), government-sponsored land settlement (McMillan 1995), and colonial settlement (Kupperman 1993).

Wider Political Economy Issues of the Kariba Resettlement

In the late 1950s fifty-seven thousand people were involuntarily resettled because of wider regional and international economic and political events, illustrating the importance of reviewing the context in which DFDR occurs. At this time, Northern Rhodesia, as one of three members of the

Central African Federation, was becoming a major world producer of copper. A significant constraint on maintaining and increasing production was the unreliable supply of electricity. At the same time, electricity was needed for the expanding cities and mines in Southern Rhodesia. Northern Rhodesia favored dam construction on a Zambezi tributary located entirely within that country. Southern Rhodesia, whose white settlers dominated the Central African Federation, pushed successfully for Kariba, which not only would link the two Rhodesias by a larger dam across the Zambezi River but also would site the initial turbines and transmission facilities on their south bank. Kariba's construction also involved the World Bank, which contributed its largest loan to date for a single project.

Stage 1: Planning the Kariba Project and Resettlement

Kariba became the first mainstream dam on the Zambezi when the filling of a 3,000-sq-km reservoir began in late 1958. It was located within a rift valley inhabited by approximately eighty thousand people (fifty-seven thousand of whom required resettlement) and bordered by prominent escarpments. Aside from politically linking Northern to Southern Rhodesia, Kariba was a single-purpose facility for the generation of hydropower. Irrigation, which could have played a major role in raising resettler living standards, was ignored. Central planning was the responsibility of the federation's Power Board. Aside from stipulating a "restoration of living standards" policy and allocating funds for an undercounted population, the board paid no further attention to resettlement planning and implementation, both of which were handed over to district and provincial authorities in each country.

Local officials on the north bank had the political will to do a good job, but they had insufficient time for planning and implementing resettlement and lacked resettlement experience. At least initially, they also had inadequate funds, staff, and equipment. Nonetheless, especially for the times, they pioneered a number of "best practices." A major effort was made to resettle communities where they wanted to go and to shift them in social units of their choice. This involved finding land for neighborhoods of four to seven villages. The large majority of the displaced wanted not only to remain within the reservoir basin but also to move inland up the Zambezi tributaries closest to their current villages, so as to remain in a familiar territory with a host population of the same ethnicity.

All north bank residents belonged to a single district council, which was encouraged to participate actively in resettlement planning. The result was a list of ten concessions that received the approval of the governor of

Northern Rhodesia. Especially important were four: (1) people were to have a choice as to where they moved, whenever possible; (2) the government should not demand that people change their agricultural methods; (3) the government should attempt to remove the tsetse fly from proposed resettlement areas; and (4) the people should be allowed to reoccupy any land that was not flooded. For development purposes, the last two were especially important. Reduction of tsetse flies enabled the Gwembe Tonga to integrate cattle effectively into their farming system, providing a source of cash income. The option to reoccupy unflooded land sanctified the movement of hundreds of families back to the edge of the reservoir and the utilization of its drawdown area and inshore fisheries. Also important was a government decision that the inshore fisheries initially would be reserved for Gwembe residents.

The Northern Rhodesian government made a major attempt to implement all ten concessions. Its renegotiation with the Federal Power Board of compensation to be paid to the Gwembe Tonga Rural Council also provided additional funds for development, with a million pounds sterling paid into a Gwembe Special Fund over a five-year period. A development program was produced, focusing on small-scale irrigation and rain-fed agriculture, tsetse fly control and livestock development, production and marketing components of the Kariba reservoir fishery, feeder roads, and schools and public health clinics.

The first of a number of unexpected events that have plagued the resettlement process occurred toward the end of the first year. This was a decision by the Federal Power Board to heighten the dam by 6 m. Not only would that decision increase the number to be relocated on the north bank from twenty-nine thousand to thirty-four thousand, but also it would flood land that some villagers had already selected for new villages and, of major significance, reduce the amount of arable land available for resettlement.

Furthermore, land surveys had already shown that agricultural resources were inadequate. With the decision made to heighten the dam, government officials now had to consider areas where communities did not want to move. The major area selected involved arable land downstream from the dam. Although still within the Middle Zambezi Valley, this area, called the Lusitu after a Zambezi tributary, was inhabited by another ethnic group with a different language and different customs. They buried their dead in cemeteries, for example, whereas the Gwembe Tonga buried individuals outside the residence in which they had lived. Because of such differences, the six thousand people identified to move below the dam refused to go. Conflict ensued, and the police were called in. Gunfire erupted. At least eight villagers were killed and thirty-two wounded in what the resettlers subsequently called the "Chisamu War," after one of the villages involved. Immediately afterwards, a traumatized and defeated population was trucked to the Lusitu.

Stage 2: Physical Removal and Coping with the Initial Drop in Living Standards That Tends to Follow Removal

Stage 2 is the most stressful of the four stages. It is initiated during the process of physical removal and is likely to overlap Stage 1 planning to a certain extent. The focus is on attempts by household members to build or modify new housing, establish a consumption-oriented domestic mode of production that emphasizes food crops, and adapt to a new habitat, the host population, other immigrants, and what usually is a stronger and more intrusive government or project authority presence.

In the Kariba case, Colson and I believed that denial was occurring; even those who had visited the dam site tended to go about their lives as if nothing threatened them. But as development plans proceeded, concerns and stress built up. These were fueled not so much by construction at the dam site as by the belief that people were going to be removed so that white colonial farmers could steal their land—a belief fostered by the government's use of heavy equipment to clear thousands of acres of bush in preparation for a future gill net fishery.

Physical removal and its aftermath were stressful. Greater population densities and inadequate water supplies in the major resettlement areas led, we are convinced, to higher morbidity and mortality rates. Fried's "grieving for a lost home" syndrome and anxiety for the future were especially serious among married women. They lost access to familiar fields that had been passed down from one generation of women to the next. Aside from the few who had resources to hire labor, women also became more dependent on husbands, who now allocated them land that they, the husbands, had cleared.

Sociocultural stress was reflected by the loss of cultural inventory following removal and the loss of influence among household heads, who were unable to protect the rights of their families to live where and how they pleased. Political and religious leadership "at the neighborhood level was largely a victim of relocation, and was not clearly re-instituted even ten years later" (Colson 1971:206). Ritual leaders within neighborhoods, at least initially, were unable to rebuild shrines in host areas. Chiefs and headmen also lost influence, as did members of the district council, who had been required to support government orders to resettle.

In earlier versions of the four-stage framework, I oversimplified impacts on Gwembe Tonga leadership and generalized that oversimplification to other cases. I believe that it is true that leaders are placed in a catch-22 situation: if they agree to removal, they are apt to lose status (as was the case among district council officials); when their opposition fails to stop removal, they also lose status. But as Bilharz (1998) has shown in the case of the Allegany Senecas' move due to the construction of Pennsylvania's Kinzua Dam, resettlement creates new opportunities for leadership, especially among women and better educated, younger, up-and-coming leaders who replace their elders. In the Gwembe Tonga case, active but land-poor young men were able to gain greater prominence by clearing large fields in the resettlement areas. The opposition to the dam by the pro–Zambian-independence African National Congress also gave some Gwembe members a new leadership opportunity.

Cultural impacts were especially stressful because of removal. Less than two years after the project's completion, Colson made a brief return visit to the Gwembe Valley in 1960. Those interviewed told her how they saw being "removed from their homes and forced to live in hostile environments" (Colson 1971:71) as an attack on their humanity (*buntu*) and their vital force (*buumi*). Both of us heard similar comments during our 1962–1963 restudy, as did Father Cumanzula (2000:63) more than thirty years later, when he was told by Tonga in Zimbabwe how resettlement caused them to lose their "dignity and humanity." A few years later, Gwembe Tonga leaders from both sides of the reservoir made similar comments during the World Commission on Dams' Kariba Dam submission (Soils Incorporated [Pty] Ltd and Chalo Environmental and Sustainable Development Consultants 2000). Such comments involve the fundamental issues dealing with social and cultural well-being that Downing (1996a, 2002a) has written about and which continue to be ignored in World Bank and other resettlement safety-net policies.

Gwembe Tonga behavior was risk averse in responding to such stress. Behavior of kin was especially risk averse: "Spectacular reconciliations appear to have been the order of the day, soon to be given even more solid recognition in the form of new homestead alignments" (Colson 1971:72). Relatives who had lived apart before resettlement, because of witchcraft problems in some cases, not only rebuilt together immediately after physical removal but also did not reinitiate the usual process of village fission until almost ten years later.

Other examples of risk-averse behavior include building identical housing and other structures, in spite of attempts by the administration to "improve" village layout. One elder informed officials at the time of physical removal, "We shall live as we are accustomed to live following our own laws....Here a man builds as he wishes, and within his own homestead he follows his own law. We do not want your regulations. We do not want your assistance" (Colson 1971:173).

Stage 3: Initiation of Economic Development and Community Formation Activities That Are Necessary to Improve Living Standards of First-Generation Resettlers

The shift to a willingness to take risks is the most fascinating aspect of Stage 3. In the Kariba case, it took resettled communities eighteen to thirty months to clear enough land and grow enough food to regain food self-sufficiency at the household level. Four factors were especially important in helping a majority of villagers to raise their living standards during the next ten years. All involved resettlement planners, the district council, and the resettlers. One was control of the tsetse fly carrier of animal sleeping sickness. Before resettlement, villagers could keep cattle only in that minority of areas that was tsetse free. After resettlement, the government's major tsetse clearance program (District Council concession #9) left most areas tsetse free, enabling resettlers to shift from hoe cultivation to plowing with oxen. Cash compensation was the second, in that it provided funds that some household heads used for purchasing cattle and for education of children.

The third factor was a well-executed educational program whereby an increased primary school education was available in most resettlement areas at the time of physical removal, with the district's first secondary school opening in 1964. Important was the emphasis placed by the district council on the education of both boys and girls. The availability of a secondary school at this time was especially important, for it gave Gwembe youth the opportunity to compete for, and obtain, the new jobs that became available during the initial years of Zambian independence. A majority of such youth invested the income earned from such jobs in cattle, which they kept with elders in the valley, who could then use the cattle in their agricultural activities.

The fourth factor was a carefully planned, inshore gill net reservoir fishery that was restricted to resettlers and hosts until after Zambian independence in 1964. The importance of such a fishery in providing a new opportunity to local residents was emphasized early on by the district commissioner. Even before resettlement began, he distributed gill nets to various schools and individuals and arranged for government fishery personnel to teach students and villagers how to use these in Zambezi River backwaters.

Shortly after the reservoir began filling, the first villagers began to fish, with the number of fishers increasing from 407 to more than 2,000 during the first four years. The majority were resettlers; the pioneers were mainly younger men, whose nets and boats were capitalized by elders. These pioneers represented the minority that can be expected to take advantage of whatever initial DFDR opportunities exist at a time when most resettlers are involved in time-consuming Stage 2 activities to reestablish their households.

To facilitate fishery development, the government made equipment available through newly formed cooperatives, established boat builders, and built a fishery training center. A very successful credit program was set up for the purchase of nets and boats with a more than 90 percent repayment rate. By 1963, north bank fishers were dispersed along the length of the reservoir. Using more than five thousand gill nets, they caught four thousand tons of fish during 1963. Some were sold fresh at the markets provided by government planners. Others were smoke-dried and sold in Zambian towns, as well as in Southern Rhodesia until the border was closed in 1965.

Income from fishing was invested in marriages, consumer goods, education of relatives, purchase of cattle, and establishment of general stores, bars, and teahouses. The fishery also played an important role in bringing village women into a wider market economy. Even before resettlement, they had begun to commercialize the production of village beer. With the development of the fishery, some women brewed beer in the fish camps; others sold such village produce as eggs, fowl, and grain. By the time reservoir productivity began to drop in the mid-1960s,[4] the village agricultural economy had taken off. Using oxen to plow larger fields, villagers were selling surplus cereals. Some were also cultivating cotton, with the number of growers increasing from forty-three in 1963 to more than six hundred in the early 1970s. By that time, Gwembe District was the number one producer of smallholder cotton in Zambia. Cattle had also become a cash crop, with herd size increasing from twenty-four thousand in 1962 to more than fifty-two thousand by 1972.

During that ten-year period, it was a pleasure for Colson and me to return to the Gwembe Valley. Living standards were higher than at any time in the past, according to both our criteria and the people's. Diets had improved, with meat and fish regularly consumed. Improved housing was being built with sun-dried bricks rather than with wattle and daub construction. Rectangular instead of round, these houses now could accommodate such previously rare furnishings as spring beds with mattresses and sheets. Paraffin lanterns replaced candles, and bicycles and radios became common. All family members were better clothed, and wives increasingly had access to hammer mills for grinding grain.

In the Lusitu area, the shift to Stage 3 was still ongoing while I was resident there, during 1962–1963. That was the area below the dam where the six thousand traumatized resettlers had been resettled after the "Chisamu War." During the first year, death rates rose. One cause was dysentery due to a more closely packed population with inadequate water supplies. Then, toward the end of the first year, women and children began to die of a "mystery disease." Still undiagnosed, fifty-six deaths occurred over a four-month period. The resettlers' explanation for the cause of death was a particularly virulent form of witchcraft, though the probable cause was consumption of toxic plants that women and children had gathered toward the end of the dry season to supplement inadequate food supplies (Scudder 1975; Webster 1975:83).

The witchcraft explanation was due partially to the large number of host cemeteries in the area, along with a relatively sparse host population—perhaps caused by the 1918 influenza epidemic or an epidemic of human sleeping sickness. The stress accompanying the mystery deaths had been intensified by a warning from the host population that completion of the resettlers' full funeral ritual, and especially competitive village drumming, would only make the situation worse by alienating the resident spirits of the land. People were terrified. Residents of two villages fled the area; residents of others decamped to the protection of a nearby government subdistrict headquarters.

When I returned to the Lusitu area in September 1962, no further deaths from the "mystery disease" had occurred for several years, resettlers had become accustomed to living with the host population, and economic development was underway. Important as a coping mechanism was the modification of customary institutions to deal with new circumstances. Bond friendships between strangers involved in economic transactions had been expanded to include the host population. Combining customary cult features with Christian symbolism, resettler prophets had emerged and were able to convince villagers that it was not the land that was bad but rather evildoers, whose witchcraft they could counter.

For me, however, the most dramatic indicator of the end of Stage 2 was an event that occurred in the final month of that year. Sitting outside my tent one evening, I heard the recommencement of funeral drumming from one village. Then, as I listened, drumming began in surrounding villages. That event initiated what I called a "cultural renaissance." Thereafter, "neighborhood teams of drummers and singers not only eclipsed their performances in 1956–57, but were invited to the capital to greet political leaders on their return from trips abroad in the years immediately preceding and following independence" (Scudder 1993:143). In 1965, puberty rituals were reintroduced in Colson's Lusitu study village, and agricultural ritual, now involving both host and resettler shrines, recommenced during drought years.

Passage through Stage 3 was aborted in the mid-1970s when "things fell apart." Reasons included a downturn in the political economy of Zambia and the wider region, as well as resettlement inadequacies and unexpected events. Unrelated to the Kariba project were the Zambian government's impoverishing policies, the severity of which was exacerbated by the war for Zimbabwe's independence. Because of its location on the international border between the two countries, the Kariba Lake basin became a war zone during the 1970s. Rhodesian forces destroyed Zambian boats operating on the reservoir and caused the collapse of the gill net fishery, until Zimbabwe became independent in 1980. Rhodesian forces also carried out land operations in Gwembe District. Bridges were blown up. Fear of land mines effectively terminated government tsetse control activities and adversely affected agricultural services, schools, and health clinics. People were war casualties in each of our four study villages.

It was lack of arable land, however, as well as degradation of what land was available, that played the major role in curtailing the rise in living standards of a majority of resettlers and in contributing to a downward livelihood spiral. The second generation of newly married couples, no longer able to find new land to cultivate, became increasingly dependent on using a portion of the fields of first-generation relatives. Subdivided and cultivated year after year, those fields became increasingly degraded and bare of vegetation. Not only were soils bare, but also topsoil had been removed, with the area taking on a Sahelian-like appearance when the wind blew during the dry season. As more and more soil was removed, the subterranean roots of baobab trees were exposed until the trees fell over. Heavy grazing around villages also was associated with land degradation, with cattle dying of hunger toward the end of the dry season in the drier years. Located farther and farther from villages, roofing thatch took on a cash value, and scarcity also afflicted other common property resources.

Not seeing the relationship between their deteriorating living standards and government policies and resettlement, Gwembe District resettlers began to blame their misfortune on one another. Along with alcohol abuse, assault (including murder and wife and child abuse) increased dramatically within households and villages, as did theft of crops and livestock, with adult children, for example, stealing for sale the livestock of their elderly parents. A socially integrating belief system emphasizing the ancestors was replaced by a belief in witchcraft that attributes anyone's success to his or her own use of witchcraft and any misfortune to the witchcraft of others.

Although such beliefs remain dominant today, it would be wrong to give the impression that people are not seeking to improve their lives by other means. A significant minority of villagers, numbering in the thousands, has migrated to pioneer agricultural settlement in difficult, sparsely populated habitats on the Zambian plateau (Cliggett 2005; Scudder and Habarad 1991). The better educated, including hundreds who have attended the University of Zambia, have been able to merge into Zambia's small middle class or to emigrate to other countries, including the United States. Those remaining in villages are trying to adapt new institutions to improve village life. These include various committees that have their roots in national politics or are donor driven. Especially visible in recent years has been wholesale conversion to evangelical Christianity. Nonetheless, quality of life today within resettlement villages remains lower than what we found before resettlement in the mid-1950s. Cernea's impoverishment risks well explain what has happened.

The Applicability of Cernea's Impoverishment Risks to the Kariba Case

The Gwembe Tonga were unable to pass through Stage 3. Rather, the large majority backslid into an impoverished state of existence that continues today and has been characterized since the mid-1970s by all of Cernea's impoverishment risks except homelessness. Most severe is landlessness, followed by food insecurity, increased morbidity and mortality, marginalization, and social disarticulation. Assessing relative importance, however, is difficult because of, among other factors, increased impoverishment throughout Zambia due to the ongoing bankruptcy of the nation's political economy. I put landlessness first because this has been the major resettlement-related cause of impoverishment. It has also been a major cause of food insecurity, although drought has also been an important factor. Resettlement, I believe, is also partially responsible for increasing morbidity and mortality rates, especially in areas where population density was increased and inadequate water supplies provided. Such was the case in the two most populated areas, both of which have been adversely affected by cholera. Best documented is the situation in the Lusitu, where "provision of adequate good quality water…is the biggest social problem the people are currently facing" (Yambayamba et al. 2001:viii, 52). But two other factors are also of major importance: HIV/AIDS and the high level of national poverty.

Resettlement, I believe, also must bear major responsibility for greater marginalization and social disarticulation, as illustrated by the magnified role of witchcraft in explaining misfortune and by the social disorganization at household and community levels. Though common property resources have been reduced, Gwembe resettlers are better off than many other rural Zambians because they have Kariba project–related access to the reservoir fishery and the improved grazing in the reservoir drawdown area, cultivation of which also counters, to an extent, loss of access to arable land. Similarly, the commercial offshore reservoir fishery has provided a source of employment. Least problematical is lack of housing.

CONCLUSION

Development-forced displacement and resettlement (DFDR) has become a subfield in anthropology that presents the social sciences with a unique opportunity to formulate important, policy-relevant theories about the effects of complex development interventions on communities, as well as their responses to these interventions. This opportunity arises from the ability of researchers to identify—ahead of time, before resettlement commences—development situations that will cause DFDR. In effect, researchers can carry on long-term, comparative research in a quasilaboratory context, beginning with benchmark pre-resettlement studies, followed by further studies throughout the resettlement process.

Current research has been informed by two theoretical frameworks and a growing number of case studies. My four-stage framework derives from the hypothesis that most community members are affected by, and respond to, DFDR in the same way during the first two generations, irrespective of cultural, geographical, and political differences. Cernea's impoverishment risks and reconstruction framework identifies specific impoverishment risks associated with all sorts of displacement and specifies reconstruction policies for their avoidance.

Both theoretical frameworks need testing. The four-stage framework is based largely on case studies of dam-induced resettlement and large-scale land settlement projects. Its applicability to other types of DFDR, urban redevelopment in particular, has not been adequately tested. Moreover, further case studies are necessary to test the hypothetical transition between risk-adverse behavior in Stage 2 and the risk taking associated with Stage 3. As for Cernea's framework, research is needed as to whether the dynamics and length of the resettlement process allow risks to be prioritized to improve reconstruction efforts at different points in the resettlement process.

Notes

1. In the 1991 second edition, Cernea qualified this statement by noting that "agricultural land settlement is one of the most difficult of all development interventions. But difficult as voluntary resettlement on new lands may be, *involuntary* population resettlement has turned out to be a process even more complex and painful" (Cernea, ed., 1991:145).

2. My framework has also been applied to large-scale land settlement projects in which the large majority of settlers are volunteers.

3. What follows draws on my 2005 Caltech Kariba Working Paper (Scudder 2005b).

4. Productivity of reservoirs following inundation initially increases, for reasons including nutrient release from the flooded soil and vegetation. In the Kariba case, nutrient content (measured by total dissolved solids) increased from a pre-project 16 parts per million (ppm) to 65 ppm by 1963, dropping to 42 ppm after the mid-1960s (Balon 1974:139).

3

Financing for Development

Benefit-Sharing Mechanisms
in Population Resettlement

Michael M. Cernea

This chapter discusses a set of issues that are crucial for the success or failure of development-caused forced displacement and resettlement processes: these issues refer to the financing of reconstruction post-displacement. Nonetheless, the theme of financing and its corollaries is seldom examined frontally, despite its critical importance.

During the past decade, international research has generated an enormous body of findings relevant to the financing—or more accurately, the underfinancing—of development-caused forced displacement and resettlement (henceforth, DFDR). Many social scientists worldwide, employing the IRR methodology (the Impoverishment Risks and Reconstruction model), have explored deeper than ever before the causes and mechanisms of poverty generation intrinsic to forced displacement. To a large extent, the focus on the risks of impoverishment has shifted the center of gravity in the anthropological and sociological literature about DFDR toward a more refined causal deconstruction of poverty. This shift has produced both a vast mass of new empirical data and the conceptual premises necessary for revealing and understanding the economic and financial flows in how routine "Resettlement Action Plans" (RAPs) are planned and underfinanced.

Anthropologists and sociologists have traditionally left the research on the economics and financing of resettlement to economists. However, as a professional community, economists have overlooked this area, both in theory and in operational project analysis. Some eminent economists have openly recognized and criticized this oversight (Pearce 1999; Schuh 1993; for a similar critique of development economics by sociologists, see Cernea 1999, 2008a, and Mahapatra 1999, regarding economics in India).[1] In turn, this gap in economic research has negative effects on the practice of governmental agencies that plan the projects causing displacement, because they do so in the absence of sound economic theory, feasibility analyses, and financing norms for DFDR processes.[2] This persistent, chronic gap of knowledge and normative economic theory must be filled.

The shift of interest in anthropology towards the economic variables of displacement (for example, income drops, impoverishment dimensions, and compensation patterns) and towards the economics and financing of reconstruction beyond mere physical relocation is also a response to this perceived gap. It is not enough, of course, because the need for mainstream economic research remains acute.

This shift, however, has already produced results. First, it has accomplished an important change: the economic and financial dysfunctionalities in DFDR are more publicly visible and acknowledged now. The contradiction between the poverty reduction paradigm and forced displacement as a paradigm of impoverishment is documented and theorized. The considerably expanded research in the anthropology of resettlement has convergently concluded that the *dominant outcome* of displacement is not income restoration but impoverishment. The accumulated evidence is overwhelming, and it converges from many countries in Asia, Latin America, and Africa (Cernea 1996b, 2000b, 2005a, 2008a; Cernea and Mathur 2008; Downing 2002a; Gebre 2003; Mahapatra 1999; Mathur and Marsden 1998; Rew, Fisher, and Pandey 2006; Scudder 2005a).

COMPENSATION AND IMPOVERISHMENT

The main financial instrument employed for "restoring" the assets, income-generating systems, and livelihoods of those dispossessed and displaced is compensation. However, compensation alone has been proven to be financially insufficient, not up to the task of "income restoration." Although long observed and denounced, this inadequacy has remained uncorrected in both economic theory and project practice. Therefore, it is fully predictable that the outcome of projects offering those displaced only "compensation" will be, again, impoverishment. Repeating in new projects the same old pattern of financing DFDR by relying on compensation alone means financing for repeated failure, that is, generating further impoverishment. (It has been said that repeating the same mistake again and again, while expecting the result to be different, is one definition of the absurd.)

Yet, however important compensation is and will remain, this chapter focuses not primarily on the critique of compensation but rather on financial instruments that are additional to compensation and need to be incorporated in legislation and policies that govern forced displacement and resettlement. The critique of compensation is the central focus of a recent volume challengingly titled *Can Compensation Prevent Impoverishment?* The response is not just a simple no, but a reanalysis of the theoretical premises of the compensation principle—and of "compensation in principle" but not necessarily in practice—as the original compensation theory was formulated. The book's responses go further and analyze what can be called the "project context" in which compensation is planned and delivered and which aggravates the deleterious effects of inadequate compensation. The reader is invited to consult that volume and the analyses provided by its coauthors from the angles of several disciplines: sociology, economics, anthropology, geography, ecology, and even dam engineering (see Cernea and Mathur 2008; Daly 2008; Égré, Roquet, and Durocher 2008; Kanbur 2008; Pearce and Swanson 2008; Price 2008; Ramanathan 2008; Seymour 2008; Trembath 2008).

Therefore, this chapter addresses complementary financial instruments, such as investments (incremental to compensation), in the reconstruction and development of resettlers' livelihoods after the displacement phase and in benefit sharing with resettlers. Surely, money alone will not solve all resettlement problems either, but, by definition, as well as statistically, absence of adequate financing foreordains failure in resettlement. Financing is of such paramount importance for achieving economically sustainable resettlement that, when flawed, it can cause failure even when other necessary factors of success are present. This is why consideration on how to improve the financing of resettlement not only through correcting the distortions of compensation itself, but also through additional financial instruments, is indispensable.

The argument I advance in this chapter is that financing for success in resettlement requires radically reforming current compensation norms and practices, but not only this. It also requires making proactive financial investments in the reconstruction of resettlers' material income bases. Further, I argue that sharing project benefits is a necessary financial instrument to secure the resources for such investments in reconstruction after displacement. The rationale and mechanisms available for benefit sharing, and the logic and ethic of recognizing and legislating them as mandatory in DFDR, are the subject and argument of this chapter.

The socioanthropological literature tells the world at large much more about how displaced people become impoverished than about how they try, and succeed or fail, to reconstruct their dismantled economic base. Doing the latter is equally essential. In one of the few studies available on reconstruction post-displacement, Oliver-Smith emphasizes, in the same spirit as this chapter, that "some basic level of materiality is a necessary precondition for social reconstitution.... Conversely, social reconstitution in some form of cooperative action under-girds and enables material reconstruction" (Oliver-Smith 2005a:51). I propose to outline further several fundamental issues of financial capacity building for sound resettlement that are seldom treated yet crucial for positioning displaced people on a sustainable, economically productive basis.

FINANCIAL CAPACITY FOR SOUND RESETTLEMENT

Giving development projects the financial capacity needed for resettlement operations is a normal, elementary prerequisite for creating capacity to do the job. However, this fundamental premise is vastly underrecognized by governments. The projects that forcibly dispossess people of vital productive assets are seldom equipped by the project owners with sufficient financial resources to rebuild the livelihoods they dismantle.

Comparing governmental approaches to financing resettlement reveals significant differences among countries, but also a high correlation between financing levels and resettlement performance and quality. A 1996 World Bank analysis of "resource allocation for resettlement" in thirty-one projects (fifteen countries) compared the per capita resettlement allocation in each project with the respective country's GNP per capita, ranking the projects according to the ratio of resettler compensation to GNP. The study found that "none of the projects with a ratio of 3.5 or higher reported major resettlement difficulties" (World Bank 1996b:145–146). By country, the analysis found that China's projects, as a group, financed resettlement best: eight projects in China ranked among the ten with highest financing. In contrast, virtually all the projects with a ratio lower than 2.0 were experiencing serious implementation difficulties, reporting early failures or likely final failure. By country, six projects from India were among the ten ranked lowest and displayed significant resettlement problems; the other four were from Argentina, Brazil, Nigeria, and Madagascar (World Bank 1996b:145–146).

Our analysis of the compensation principle and practices has concluded that compensation is structurally inadequate to achieve full "restoration" and, obviously, even less capable of "improving livelihoods," leaving the goals of reintegration and reconstruction unachieved.[3] Moreover, research has found that the majority of RAPs contain no allocations for investment in development activities for the resettlers, as distinct from restorative activities, even though the resettlement policies of the World Bank, ADB (Asian Development Bank), and other development agencies do provide the room for investing in resettlers' development, over and above the payment of individual compensations. The insufficient financing not only chronically ruins resettlers' livelihoods but also undermines the overall economic performance of the projects.

Fortunately, new experiences in several countries reveal opposite emerging trends and seeds of alternative approaches. These are significant macro-societal measures, including the enactment of legislation to create financial capacity for resettlement.

"WHERE WOULD THE RESOURCES COME FROM?"

When the question of allocating more resources for RAP implementation is raised, the response heard most frequently is, "We pay compensation, and there are no other financial resources for the resettlers." Resource scarcity must indeed be recognized as a real constraint. But is it a constraint that cannot be overcome? Stringent expenditure analysis for each project would often find constructive solutions to resource scarcity. Shortage of funds for the resettlement component midstream in a project is often an artifact of erroneous pre-project cost undercalculations, not necessarily a proof of resource scarcity (Cernea 1999; Pearce 1999; Pearce and Swanson 2008). Incorrect valuation of losses and the underestimation of resettlers' reconstruction costs coalesce into underallocations of financing at the very start of the project. These are much harder to overcome during implementation, even if RAP implementers realize that resources are not up to their complex tasks.

Despite constraints and scarcity, there are ways to mobilize the necessary financial resources to do resettlement programs well and achieve resettlement with development. Economic theory points to significant resources generated by many of the very projects that impose displacement. These resources should be relied upon in financing post-displacement reconstruction.

The usual resource for financing RAPs and compensation payments has been and still is today an up-front budget allocation. As long as the mindset of decision makers and financial planners is entrenched in the belief that compensation is all that is due and necessary for resettlers' recovery, we can expect nothing more than a limited, up-front budget allocation, as well as constant attempts to keep this allocation at the lowest level possible. However, theoretically, this mindset is incorrect, and it conflicts with the policy objective stated formally in many national and international policies on resettlement.

For a policy to succeed, all available means for achieving the policy objectives need to be consistent and commensurate with these objectives. Financing is one of the critical means, and it must be allocated in the amounts necessary to render the objectives feasible.

Germane to this reasoning is also another principle of economic theory, namely, that project costs should not be externalized. Yet, such cost externalization on those displaced does occur whenever the financial means (including the compensation) fall short of covering all costs imposed on the displaced people. This means that those displaced are forced to subsidize the projects through incomplete restitution of what is taken from them. They give more than they get. Thus, they end up as losers, worse off and poorer than they were before the project. This aggravation of prior poverty is induced, by omission or by commission. The responsibility for such aggravation falls on the project's owners and sponsors.

Consequently, my argument is that resource allocation should be measurably keyed to the policy's objectives for resettlement, in each and every project with a resettlement "component." If the project's budget balance has its dial set only on the narrow task of *delivering* some compensation but not on what compensation can *achieve*, then the incentives will be to minimize the paid compensation and to set the compensation dial low from the outset. If, however, the dial of the budgeting balance is set on achieving the policy goal of livelihood restoration and improvement, then from the outset the reasons for mobilizing and allocating needed means would be strong, because achievement of the policy goal requires more than the delivery of limited compensation.

The outlays for resettlement are, in most projects, only a small fraction of the total budgets of large-scale projects. Exceptions do exist but are rare. Resettlers claim that if the public sector has enough resources to finance the physical infrastructure built by the project, then it should also allocate a sufficient amount for economically restoring and improving the livelihood of those whose existence is deeply disrupted and put at risk by the project.

This is a powerful argument, both economic and moral: it can be discounted only at the peril of growing political opposition and instability.

ECONOMIC RENT AS A POTENTIAL RESOURCE FOR FINANCING RESETTLEMENT

Returning to the question of where the resources would come from, I will refer to the experiences of several countries that decided to face the question head on and found novel solutions. Their solutions revolve around (a) the use of windfall economic rent generated by the exploitation of natural resources and (b) the use of a fraction of the projects' normal stream of benefits to reconstruct resettlers' livelihoods at higher-than-pre-displacement levels.

The projects in which such solutions are practiced are, so far, mostly in the hydropower sector, but the same rationale applies more widely to other sectors, particularly in the extractive industries.

The economic theory of rents supports the argument that certain categories of projects (many unfeasible without displacement) generate surplus (windfall) benefits. These benefits can be used for overcoming constraints to financing resettlement.

To examine the functions and utilization of economic rent, a 2000 World Bank study focused on the concept's definition and on "measuring and apportioning rents from hydroelectric power developments" (Rothman 2000:1–2). The study's author examines several rent-capture mechanisms and the reallocation of rent, drawing on a large body of economic literature. Though not written explicitly for analyzing financing of resettlement, the study is directly relevant to our argument in this chapter in favor of allocating a percentage of benefits to increase the financing of project-displaced populations.

Economic rent is defined in classic economic theory as a surplus return above the normal average return to the invested capital, materials, labor costs, and other factors of production. Projects that exploit natural resources (for example, mining industry projects, oil and gas extraction projects, and hydropower projects) require vast amounts of land and water, triggering displacement. Through expropriation (or purchase) of access to lands rich in natural resources, such projects gain the opportunity to harvest a substantial economic rent, above the average returns in other sectors. Economic theory shows that rent

> arises when exploiting a resource that Nature has endowed with a value that is independent of any labor, capital or entrepreneurial effort applied to the resource. Resource developers, therefore, do not "earn" rent as they do normal profits (i.e., return to capital and entrepreneurship). Rather, rent is a windfall created

by exploiting the bounty of Nature. The owner of the natural resource is the owner of the rent. Typically, the natural resource is an attribute of a particular piece of land that has minerals under it, or water falling over it, or some other attribute that produces rent. [Rothman 2000:5]

The amount of the rent depends on various factors, such as resource quality and scarcity. The higher the quality of a resource, compared with the same resource at a different location, the higher the rent that can be captured. The scarcity of certain natural resources and the inherent quality differentials in resources ensure the long continuity of economic rent accrual to the owners (or holders) of the resource. Such rent—and this is an important point directly relevant to the subject of compensation and benefit sharing—is defined in economics as a windfall, incremental to the normal rate of return to capital and resulting from exploiting the "bounty of nature." This is why ownership over the resource becomes most important: ownership gives entitlement over returns and determines how these are allocated and used.

When the public sector undertakes such resource exploration and exploitation projects, the economic rent captured is usually delivered back to the state, as representative of the public at large. Of course, there is great variety in the tenure regimes, and the rights to the rents are, in practice, regulated by local laws:

> In some cases, the owner of the land may also own outright all the rights to it. In many cases, governments own the land or the rights to its attributes that produce the rents. Governments, in the name of the public that owns the resources, then typically try to "capture" the rent through royalties, stumpage fees, competitive auctions, development license fees and other mechanisms. A very large body of literature examines the efficiency and effectiveness of rent-capture mechanisms. [Rothman 2000:5]

But after such rent is captured, how should this surplus be used? Is it appropriate to redistribute it evenly to the population at large? In the case of DFDR, should the adversely affected groups have priority in benefiting from its capture? Given the asset-dispossession and de-capitalization processes that occur when such projects are built, we assert that public sector policy makers should assign priority to populations that lose their livelihood and land.

PROJECT BENEFITS

Windfall profits are not the only financial resource. Regardless of the sector, each successful project has its expected stream of regular benefits, even if it does not capture a surplus economic rent from natural resources extraction. The avenue of benefit sharing can serve the objectives of the resettlement policies when sufficient up-front budgetary resources cannot be fully found and allocated. Financial investments for reconstruction can be increased also by directly and explicitly sharing part of future benefit streams from the new project. Van Wicklin (1999) outlines four powerful reasons—economic, financial, moral, and political—for allocating a distinct share of projects benefits to the project-displaced population.[4]

Would this approach face an intractable time discrepancy? True enough, the project's stream of benefits emerges after project completion, whereas the financial resources for resettlement with development investments are needed earlier. To resolve this apparent time conflict, credit arrangements can be made from project start, counting on employing resources that will emerge as benefits after (sometimes even before) the project's completion. A share of project benefits can start coming into the resettlement areas during the reconstruction period, as a continuous process. This will sustain the post-displacement reconstruction effort after the completion of the given project.

POLICY SUPPORT TO BENEFIT SHARING

Internationally adopted operational guidelines include, verbatim, the principle of "enabling resettlers to share in project benefits" (ADB 2003). The ADB states that projects should "treat involuntary resettlement as a development opportunity" and guides planners "to manage impoverishment risks and turn the people dispossessed and displaced into project beneficiaries" (ADB 2003). In practice, however, this supportive provision is far from being systematically implemented, even in projects that this very institution co-finances. This is one explanation for why numerous resettlement components are not endowed with sufficient resources to succeed. The non-use of benefit-sharing mechanisms results from inconsistent implementation of approved policies and an absence of political will to do so.

During the past ten to fifteen years, a number of countries have recognized the need—and the advantages—of channeling a fraction of benefits to the people and areas adversely affected. This recognition is embodied in adopted laws and regulations mandating benefit sharing as a general approach in one category of projects—hydropower dams. Being legally mandated, these benefits can be counted upon, starting from the project's design phase. Explicit measures for channeling a percentage of the project's financial benefits back to resettlers are now implemented legally and systematically in developing countries such as Brazil, China, and Colombia and sporadically in some other countries. These are what we call "advanced practices," innovative practices. But they are still far from being adopted as general practice in all developing countries.

The room for replication is therefore vast and wide open.

THE RATIONALE FOR BENEFIT SHARING

The rationale for project benefit sharing with those forcibly displaced rests on several solid grounds. Such approaches

- Go far toward reducing or preventing potential risks of impoverishment from becoming real poverty outcomes.

- Contribute to achieving the priority goal of poverty reduction.

- Are economically rational for the project itself, facilitating and speeding up the technical construction process by reducing delays resulting from resistance or protracted negotiations. Projects can be completed sooner rather than later, and the stream of project benefits begins earlier.

- Are equitable, meeting the moral rationale of development interventions by spreading development benefits wider.

- Are politically sound and necessary to increase satisfaction and prevent lingering adversity vis-à-vis the project among the surrounding area population.

Projects that build hydropower plants have introduced benefit-sharing mechanisms more often than have projects in any other sector. Such mechanisms are increasingly embraced as a legitimate source, additional to compensation on the family-by-family basis, for financial investments in the welfare of the displaced groups as large collectivities and in the development of the reservoir areas. Furthermore, the economic reasoning that applies to hydropower dam projects holds for other types of extractive industries projects.

A significant advantage of using project rent and project benefits is that the financing necessary to avoid displacees' pauperization becomes part of the economics of the displacing project itself. This type of financial capacity can be incorporated from the outset into the overall project's economic and financial architecture, easing the demands on budgetary resources.

Certainly, there can be—and usually are—competing demands on the rent and benefits that such projects generate. How these competing demands are prioritized and satisfied depends, again, on the ownership of the natural resources and on the entitlement to exploit them, as well as on the ownership of and direct responsibility for the project causing the displacement.

POLITICAL WILL: FINANCING IS NOT JUST A RESOURCE MATTER

Like all matters pertinent to resource allocation, the financing of resettlement is not only a matter of financial decisions. It depends on political will and political decision making by project owners, that is, by those who deliberately will the forced displacement when they decide to begin a project predicated on population relocation. In this respect, distinct consideration should be given to the two typical categories of projects in which these issues emerge and to how differences among them affect decision-making mechanisms: such projects are either public sector projects or privately owned for-profit projects in the business sector.

In public sector projects, the major decisions on benefit allocation are made at the political level, where priorities are ranked. This is why using a fraction of project benefits for sound resettlement is regarded as ultimately an issue of political will at the state and government levels. Compensation, in principle, is not in dispute; existing law secures it as a matter of property restitution, guaranteed in all constitutions. But the amount of compensation is subject to political decision.

Furthermore, compensation alone is not sufficient to achieve the objective of livelihood restoration. Allocating the increment of financing by using a fraction of economic rent returns and/or of normal benefits can make the critical difference.

The choice is stark. Given that the historical record of displacement is well known and a reliable predictor, the absence of policy decisions supporting benefit sharing in public sector projects causing displacement (but also making possible substantial financial returns) means not repaying in full the debt to those expropriated, in other words, condoning cost externalization and impoverishment.

The issue in public sector projects—and the political choices—is not about the principle of returning economic rent from resource development to the public as much as it is about the specific segments of the public to which resources are returned. The question is whether the displaced population is recognized as one of the parties directly cooperating in developing the hydropower resources and thus has higher-priority entitlement to the resulting project's stream of benefits. My argument is that it is necessary and moral to recognize displacees' entitlement *with priority* over the general population at large. In several key economic sectors, general mechanisms for the flow-back of benefits do exist for some time and are practiced. Indeed, "capturing economic rent from resource developers and delivering it back to the resource owners (the public) is common practice in the oil and gas, mining, forestry, and fishing sectors. It is rare, however, in the hydroelectric power sectors, where governments typically regulate tariffs such that the resulting rent flows to electricity consumer in the form of lower tariffs" (Rothman 2000:1). The hydropower sector is recently joining this path on an expanding scale, and the recognition of displacement's poverty risks is one reason behind this change.

The remarkable experiences described in the next section embody a new trend. The unique element in these cases is that the respective governments have adopted new procedures, enacted in law, for regularly allocating a percentage of benefits to resettlement areas, with mechanisms that distinguish the benefits to resettlement areas from benefits channeled to the general public (electricity consumers) in the form of lower tariffs. The examples show that these mechanisms chart a novel path. Such allocative procedures are replicable in other developing countries in various sectors, for example, in programs for coal mining and in other extractive industries (oil, gas, minerals). Although delivering the captured economic rent back to the public has already occurred at various times in many countries, it occurs most often without specially earmarking a certain percentage of benefits explicitly for the displacement-affected areas. Extending the mechanisms of targeted benefit sharing would go a long way towards enabling resettlement to avoid impoverishment.

In private sector resource-related projects, the same kind of economic rent is captured as a "windfall," in addition to average rates of return to investments. The argument for channeling a share of benefits to reconstruction post-relocation is therefore similar in essence. In fact, it is stronger in the for-profit private sector, where the rent and other benefits are not returned to the public at large but to the parties contributing to the project, investors and shareholders.

Shareholders in private power companies, as well as in mining enterprises, partake in the benefits and stream of dividends from these types of productive activities because they invest money through the stock market. The indispensability of displacees' lands should make them undisputed "stakeholders" as well. Their lands are "invested" in the new companies, albeit by being compulsorily "bought" through expropriation and compensation before project construction. The "price," under the name of compensation, may, at the very best, equal the replacement value of their land, but *this does not include the land's developmental potential.*[5] Without displacees' lands, house plots, and communal assets, the new projects would not exist. This is why the people who are giving their land to the projects could be reasonably regarded as "shareholders"; their contribution is their land. They can equitably claim a share of the opportunity, that is, of the development potential of their land.

The social contract embedded in the principle of land acquisition for development obliges the purchasers (or expropriators) not to worsen the condition of the land sellers but to help them recover and improve their livelihood. The displaced surrender not just any nonessential, indifferent good: they surrender the economic foundation of their very existence. It is this economic foundation that has to be reconstructed. If up-front compensation payments are not sufficient to ensure reconstruction of this foundation, as empirical evidence has irrefutably proven, then mechanisms for access to benefit sharing become essential.

GOOD NATIONAL PRACTICES FOR BENEFIT SHARING

As illustrations of new practices, benefit sharing in the several countries discussed below can set a trend and put in motion chains of replication. It is therefore worth examining carefully such cases and learning about their solutions for resource mobilization in projects entailing displacement.

Types of Mechanisms for Sharing and Conveying Benefits

Examination of international practices in both developed and developing countries distinguishes seven mechanisms for sharing benefits and reinvesting them in resettlers' development. These mechanisms also address the host populations, which suffer risks and impacts associated with "hosting": resources are channeled on an area basis to the geographic zone around the hydropower reservoir, where many resettlers are frequently relocated. The main mechanisms are

1. Direct transfer of a share of the revenue streams, fed into financing specific post-relocation development schemes.

2. Establishment of revolving development funds through fixed allocations. While the principal of those funds is being saved, the interests generated are used for post-resettlement development.

3. Equity sharing in the new project-created enterprise (and other productive potentials) through various forms of co-ownership.

4. Payment of special taxes to regional and local governments, additional to the general tax system, to supplement local development programs with added initiatives.

5. Allocations of electrical power on a regular and legally mandated basis.

6. Granting of preferential electricity cost rates or lower water fees, or other forms of in-kind benefits.

7. Sharing in the nonfinancial benefits and opportunities.

Obviously, each mechanism requires formal arrangements and legal enactment to ensure implementation over time and financial accountability. Through legal enforcement, the state recognizes responsibility in reestablishing resettlers and the area negatively affected. Resettlers' participation in negotiating for benefit sharing and in managing the redistribution of benefits is undoubtedly necessary for improving the effectiveness of such mechanisms and monitoring their implementation.

The search for effective methods of project benefit sharing with displaced populations has advanced considerably in different countries over the past ten to fifteen years (and even longer in some cases). The adopted regulations have gone through rounds of experimentation and repeated refinements in successive years to improve on prior rules. Each country has designated a somewhat different share of benefits to be invested in the development of the resettlement areas. Because these financial resources are additional to the resources provided as compensation, grants, and other resettlement expenses, the flows of shared benefits are apt to have a significant impact. In fact, compensation standards in some of the same countries have also been increased—see the case of China—in parallel with enacting benefit sharing. Together, they stimulate and support post-relocation development.

In all the cases described, the flows of shared benefits are not limited to a short period: they are deemed by law to continue for long periods, sometimes for the entire duration of the productive enterprises constructed by the project. The continuity of benefit flows becomes a corner-stone of long-term development for those who are uprooted and relocated.

A concise, country-by-country description of such effective approaches follows, after which I will distill some common characteristics of the mechanisms employed.

Colombia: Royalties Transfers

In 1993 Colombia began to enact a series of laws to effect benefit trans-fers to regions receiving populations displaced by hydropower develop-ment. National Law Nr. 99, "Decree 1993," and National Law Nr. 344 created an Environment Compensation Fund from 20 percent of the rev-enue from development projects. The Colombian legislation also desig-nated that 3.8 percent of the project revenue be transferred to the regions for water-saving and local irrigation projects, that 1.5 percent of revenues be transferred to municipal administrations bordering the reservoir, and that another 1.5 percent be allocated to upstream municipalities, beyond the reservoir proper.

These laws require that the transfers be reported publicly, be moni-tored, and be used for either social development activities or environmen-tal protection activities such as watershed protection and tree planting. This way, the benefits also help to maintain and lengthen the lifetime of the hydroelectric projects (for example, controlling siltation) while improving the general welfare of the populations in the affected area (Égré, Roquet, and Durocher 2008).

Brazil: Royalties Distribution

Over the past thirty years, Brazil's increase in hydropower dams and reservoirs has led to large displacements. Originally, Brazil had no national policy guidelines for displacement and resettlement, nor financial resources to address displacement-caused economic problems.[6] The affected people were severely impoverished, and many moved anarchically into slums around big towns.

To redress this somber situation, the country's constitution was revised explicitly to include the principle of transferring a percentage of royalties from hydropower generation to the resettlement areas (1988). Brazil then adopted laws to define entitlements and specific amounts of transferable royalties, together with procedures for ensuring a regular timetable for such allocations. Moreover, the laws were adopted at the federal level, to be binding for all of Brazil's states. Four federal laws were adopted between 1989 and 2000—Law 7990 (in 1989), Law 8001 (in 1990), Law 9433 (in

1997), and Law 9984 (in 2000)—to set balances between transfers to federal and state authorities (Gomide 2004; Trembath 2008).

From the outset, the policy decision was to direct roughly 90 percent of all the royalties from public hydropower plants to states and municipalities and only 10 percent to federal agencies (Gomide 2004). Royalties are to be paid throughout the power plants' lifetimes, to help provide for the long-term economic sustainability of affected communities (Égré, Roquet, and Durocher 2008; Gomide 2004).

Subsequent laws in 1997 and 2000 outlining national water resource policies and guidelines introduced a required payment for the use of reservoir waters and made a clear distinction between royalties and financial compensation, the latter to be paid specifically to the municipalities in which areas were inundated by the reservoir. Country-wise, the proportions and aggregate amounts of payments are very significant. Law 9984 (in 2000) created a national water regulatory agency to better implement those provisions. In 2004 the total amount of financial compensation and royalties was more than US$400 million (Gomide 2004).

Canada: Equity Investments

To exploit its large hydropower potential, Canada has embarked on a systematic program of building major dams, many severely impacting indigenous tribal populations, who have customary land rights recognized under Canadian law. In 1971, HydroQuebec, Canada's major power utility, announced plans for the James Bay Project, which would include as many as twenty dams (Scudder 2005a). The project would have negatively affected the entire homeland of the tribal Cree Indian population. The public protests and legal action against the dams by the Cree and later the Inuit, along with NGOs advocating for indigenous and environmental protection, significantly altered the position of the Canadian government and its public utilities.

Recognizing the contribution of this population in the form of land to the country's hydroelectric development, Canada's government and hydroelectric utilities adopted a strategy of partnering with the local indigenous communities. HydroQuebec established agreements with the affected indigenous groups for equity sharing in the envisaged hydropower capacities. Local indigenous communities would become investors directly in hydro projects by contributing their lands. In addition to an up-front compensation for the land and for assistance in adjusting the productive Inuit fishing economy, the option of sharing equity was made available. This equity enables the tribal Inuit communities to receive a share of project benefits as long-term partners, proportionate to their land share in the project. The power utility provides the full financing and constructs the dam power-plant system; the indigenous populations provide the lands, and then they proportionally share in the profits. This approach avoided the economic displacement of local communities and the risks of impoverishment from undercompensated displacement, by recognizing their financial entitlement to part of the project's benefits.

Norway: Taxation for Redistribution

A country in which electricity production and exportation is one of the main branches of the economy, Norway adopted a new law in 1997—the Power Taxation Act—intended to ensure new and higher tax payments from power companies, which could then be redistributed.

The law entitles counties and municipalities to receive three types of tax revenue from the power sector. First, all electricity companies must pay a 28 percent tax on all their profits. The proceeds from these taxes are distributed in virtually equal shares going to the central budget and to the county budget, with 4.75 percent going directly to local municipalities. Second, the companies must pay a 0.7 percent property tax to the municipalities in which they are located. Third and last, a tax on the use of natural resources, based on the average power generated over the preceding seven years, is levied and then redistributed to the municipal and county levels of government. The state also collects a tax for the use of natural resources, at a flat rate from the companies' net revenues (Égré, Roquet, and Durocher 2008). Norway also requires electrical companies to give 10 percent of the electricity they produce to the local municipality. And, of course, companies owned by the local governments are required to hand over all dividends to the local owners affected by hydropower development.

Japan: Land Lease and Adding Rent to Up-Front Compensation

In an attempt to minimize the tensions and conflicts inherent in land expropriation and population relocation, Japan has conducted land-leasing experiments and has voluntarily abstained from expropriating lands required for reservoirs. When the series of three Jintsu-Gawa small dams were built in the 1950s, the Japanese government, instead of applying the country's expropriation law, decided to lease the land required for the reservoirs from its owners (Nakayama and Furuyashiki 2008). Payment for the land lease was structured into two types of financial transfers, designed to keep revenue accruing to the affected people for a long period rather than to make only a one-time compensation payment and dislocate them.[7]

The twin financial transfers consisted of a payment up front as a substitute to immediate compensation, to enable these farmers to develop alternative livelihoods by investing the money they received into non-land-based, income-generating activities. Then, regular rent payments were made to the local small-holders for the life of the project.

This way, the leased land, although deep under the reservoir waters, remains a source of constant income for the affected farmers and their children. The regular payments of rent supplement the initial up-front compensation, ensuring livelihood sustainability for the former farmers even if their new, alternative economic activities do not succeed from the outset or do not produce enough.

This twin financing proved to be an effective risk-preempting mechanism. The test of time validated it fifty years after the construction of the three Jintsu-Gawa dams. The power companies are still paying the rents that accrue to the new generations in the families of the initial landowners (Nakayama and Furuyashiki 2008).

In designing Japan's large-scale Numata Dam, expected to displace some ten thousand rural people, the government made plans to convert 1,500 ha of dry land on the slopes of Mount Akagi into padi rice fields, introducing irrigation at the government's cost.[8] The objective was to achieve physical resettlement with improved livelihoods for the resettled people. Each resettler was to receive an area approximately twice as large as what he had previously owned. For people who lost only part of their land, the government planned to pay rent for the submerged portion, rather than merely pay a one-time compensation (Nakayama and Furuyashiki 2008). For other macro-economic reasons at the time, however, the building of Numata Dam was cancelled. Nonetheless, this original, creative approach is relevant for possible testing and replication.

China: Benefit Sharing for Financing Development through Developmental Resettlement

From the early history of China's unsuccessful resettlement operations in dams, its government has derived many important lessons, becoming one of the most innovative actors in making resettlement work. Some of the country's largest dams were built in the 1960s and 1970s, such as Xinanjiang, Sanmenxia, and Danjiangkou, each one displacing more than three hundred thousand people. At that time, inadequate financing and the lack of an equitable resettlement policy led to impoverishment, population resentment, and political instability.

Learning from failure, China radically changed its approach to resettlement and its financing levels. Heggelund's insightful analysis is correct in observing that "China's resettlement history itself urged the Chinese authorities to think about new alternatives in resettlement work" (Heggelund 2004:57).

Starting in the 1980s, China enacted regulations that directed each power plant to allocate RMB 0.001 per kWh to a development fund for investments in the reservoir area. In 1985 it created a country-wide Post-Resettlement Development Fund in which contributions from power companies would be deposited. This was the beginning of a long series of policy and financing decisions consisting of repeated increases in compensation levels and supplemental investment.

Based upon thirty years of experience, the government concluded that China must switch from a resettlement policy focused primarily on people's physical transfer, to a developmental resettlement policy. In terms of financing, the key change was to move from state subsidies for compensation only, to additional state investment support for new development activities, as well as new productive capacities to gainfully employ the masses of farmers separated from their lands. The formal acceptance of the new concept—"resettlement with development" or "developmental resettlement"—occurred in 1991 in the special policy guidelines for the Three Gorges Project.[9] To unify existing parallel laws and regulations, China adopted in 1986 a master land law—the Land Administration Law (LAL)—that placed explicit emphasis on limiting excessive land acquisition and forced displacement.[10] The revised 1998 land law contains explicit norms for people's sustainable resettlement, not just procedures for how to acquire their lands.

Furthermore, in 1987–2007, China steadily increased the financing for compensation channeled to the displaced populations and also initiated policy and financial efforts to add ex-post benefit sharing (figure 3.1). The steps along both lines enable the financing of resettlement, in a colorful Chinese metaphor, simultaneously to "advance on two legs." That these policies have financial substance and are not just flourishing metaphors is demonstrated by far-reaching political and economic decisions made during the 1980s and 1990s and intensified after 2000. Most persuasively, huge amounts of financing accompany the new policies.[11]

Four Distinct Sets of Financial Instruments

China's rapid industrialization, urban development, and agricultural changes continue to require massive DFDR processes, and the country's high population density and scarcity of arable land compound the difficulties of resettlement. The financial reforms for DFDR legislated in China

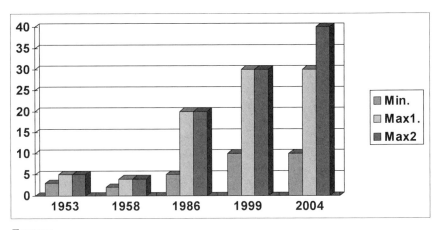

FIGURE 3.1

The evolution of land compensation in China, 1953–2004. Numbers on the Y axis represent compensation per unit of land.

during the past three to four years contain rich lessons of experience for other developing countries facing comparable DFDR issues. Some of these reforms are very recent (end of 2006), so there is little information about their unfolding.[12]

Four clusters of financial measures relevant to the theoretical and operational dilemmas discussed in this study can be distinguished in China's approaches: (1) Ex-ante financing measures increase the restitutionary ex-ante financing for lost land and assets for all families and communities uprooted by development projects. China has paid compensation for land losses since the early 1950s but, between 1953 and 1985, kept this compensation at very low levels and after 1958 decreased it from 3–5 times the annual output value (AOV) per unit of land to only 2–4 times the AOV (see Shi Guoqing, Zhou Jian, and Chen Shaojun 2006:graph 1).[13] The turnaround began in 1985, when the compensation range for land was more than doubled, from 2–4 times the AOV to 5–20 times the AOV; this, in turn, was increased later several times. In 1999 the compensation rates for the lowest level were doubled, with the option of paying as high as 30 times the AOV.

China's calculation of compensation is based on the actual output of land and produces a much more generous compensation than do conventional calculations based only on farmers' income returns per unit of land. The value of a farm's annual output is always much higher than the farmer's net annual income from the land, because it includes the cost of inputs and labor. Net income from the annual crop is, roughly, only about 50 percent of total output value. This means that compensation that is equal to 20 times the AOV is equal to a farmer's real income for a 40-year period (per unit of land).

In parallel, China has revised and tightened land-taking procedures, especially by local governments. In 2004 the maximum compensation level for land in urban and peri-urban areas was raised to 40 times the AOV, much above other land categories. Shortly thereafter, the State Council of the People's Republic of China (PRC) decided also to raise the minimum permissible compensation to 10–16 times the AOV for farmland acquired by water resource projects.[14] Other legislative measures converge: distinct from land acquisition acts in other countries, China's 1998 land law contains explicit support for sustainable resettlement.[15]

(2) Ex-post financing measures supplementing compensations consist of development investments in areas where resettlers reside. A percentage of the economic rent, or of regular project benefits, is earmarked for financing state programs that help create a more robust economic platform for income generation through nonagricultural enterprises. The vehicles for these programs are the development funds introduced first in the hydropower sector. The development funds add investments through ex-post benefit sharing, complementing the higher ex-ante compensation. The relevant regulations started in the 1980s with government decrees that required each power plant to allocate a tiny fraction per kWh to investments in the reservoir area for the life of the power plant.[16]

The relative downside of development funds targeted to an impacted area is that the additional financing is only partially managed by resettler families; a large part tends to be used in programs of area-based interventions managed by local authorities.[17] For self-investment activities that resettlers might initiate, other financial measures were adopted (see point 3).

(3) Measures feeding financially into the self-investing capacity of resettlers constitute a wholly new financing instrument. Introduced in China through legislation adopted by the State Council (2004, 2006), this consists of an annual allowance (grant) of RMB 600, equivalent to US$75 per year per capita, to be paid by the state to every individual involuntarily resettled by dam projects, for as long as twenty years after the date of physical relocation. Recipients can invest this new financial outlay for productive purposes or for consumption needs.

China's recent legislation introduces another new principle in this respect—a social innovation, compared with current international standards in resettlement policies. This legislation recognizes that displacement causes a sharp loss of security for older people who have been farmers most of their life and whom displacement may leave without any land. Retirement support and pensions for displaced old people are not provided usually. China's new decision introduces a "safety net" measure (Kanbur 2008): payments toward a Social Security Fund, comparable in its effects to a retirement pension (Shi Guoqing, Zhou Jian, and Chen Shaojun 2006; State Council of the PRC 2004, 2006). Empirical research about how this instrument works operationally will be necessary, beyond its legal description. Nevertheless, these measures (incremental to those described in points 1 and 2 above) place supplemental cash directly in the hands of resettled families, allowing them the choice of productive investments or consumption expenditures.

(4) Corrective financial measures for past undercompensation were adopted by China's State Council out of concern about the lingering effects of past failures in income restoration. Prior underfinancing errors are being rectified through retroactive payments to tens of millions of people displaced in the past five decades (State Council of the PRC 2006). Compared with international current standards, this is an extraordinary policy change, unprecedented in any other developing country. Specifically, from 2006 to 2026 the state is retroactively paying an annual sum of 600 yuan (US$75) per capita to all farmers displaced by dams between 1950 and 2006. This represents a massive and continuous investment in developing the capabilities and living standards of millions affected by forced displacement. For a peasant family of four persons, the payment represents a total of RMB 2,400 (US$300) per year, every year, as a "rent" for twenty years, a sizable addition to the current income of China's rural families. Its policy significance, as a governmental act of self-correction and reparation and as a forward-looking decision of development policy and social protection, is supported by its financial weight.

The financial outlays for these payments are indeed huge. Data received by the author from China's National Research Center of Resettlement (NRCR) put the number of dam-displaced people between 1949 and 2006 at about 18 million (Shi Guoqing, personal communication, 2007), which, over twenty years, will entail retroactive payments totaling US$27 billion.[18] But the corrective legislation also takes into account the natural growth rate of the formerly displaced populations and includes all current members of the displaced families who were born after displacement. This increases the number of beneficiaries from 18 million to about 22.88 million people (Shi Guoqing, personal communication, 2007). The total retroactive payments will amount to US$34.3 billion.

The way China secures the financial resources for such financing is by asking the society in its entirety to respond to resettlers' sacrifices, hardships, and needs. Just before enacting the September 2006 measures, China's government announced that additional financing for the people displaced by dams would be paid from a very small increase in the cost of a kilowatt hour (0.025 yuan, or less than one-third of one cent). Of this additional aggregate hydropower revenue, 40 percent would be returned to benefit the farmers displaced and resettled.[19]

The cumulative implementation of China's reforms will continuously inject large incremental financing, every year, into the economy of populations affected by past or future DFDR operations for hydropower projects. This financing improves incomes and livelihoods for tens of millions. Some of these reforms are unprecedented not just in China but internationally as well. Their diversity and magnitude express China's lucid recognition of the economic and political importance of sound resettlement, as well as the decision to preempt the risks and effects of failure. Some of these measures are not yet applied in all of China's economic sectors—the water resources sector is ahead of others—but preparation for further legislation appears to continue.

The grave social problems faced by China in DFDR are certainly not limited to China. The reform measures described here are China-specific, but the causes that led to them are not. Solutions need to be adjusted to the conditions of each country, but DFDR's fundamental challenges are virtually universal in the developing and developed worlds. This is why they require solutions not only in large countries such as China, India, and Brazil, but in all countries affected by DFDR.

SHARING THE NONFINANCIAL PROJECT BENEFITS AND OPPORTUNITIES

The mechanisms for accessing project benefits are *not* confined to financial transfers, however important these are. Other options are available, options that are not financial in form but produce convergent results. What matters is not the form, the mechanism of transfer, but the principle for which we are arguing: equipping evicted people with means additional to compensation for their socioeconomic reconstruction.

Alternative ways to access other benefits from the same projects must be employed. Among these, I can concisely list only two, because space limits prevent elaboration.[20] These are perhaps the most important: (a) in the case of hydropower and irrigation projects, enabling reservoir-displaced people to share in the newly irrigated land in the downstream command area through land redistribution or land swaps and (b) in other projects, giving displaced people priority entitlement to employment in the construction (civil works) and in the subsequent operation of the project that displaces them.

CONCLUSIONS

Populations displaced to make possible new projects are among the first entitled to share in these projects' benefits, both financial and nonfinancial. Compensation is not a share in project benefits, as some mistakenly interpret it: compensation is nothing more than simple restitution for "takings" and is usually incomplete "restitution," unequal to the losses. The compensation principle is distinct from, and not a substitute for, the principle of benefit sharing. Both need to be recognized equally, enacted legally, and applied consistently. Financing resettlers' development through ex-post benefit sharing should not become a perverse incentive to underpay the required up-front compensation (restitution) for losses, which is the first ex-ante payment (in kind or in cash, or both) towards recovery. This would undermine the purpose of both compensation and benefit sharing. The political hurdle is to get the principle of sharing in the benefits accepted. Once governments accept this, using its potential will become a key challenge for all project planners, sponsors, and owners.

In closing, I would draw attention to several key conclusions. First, compensation alone does not prevent impoverishment. The history of DFDR documents that impoverishment is recurrent in countless projects despite the payment of compensation. Inescapably, we must conclude that compensation alone does not fully restitute the values extracted through expropriation. Costs are substantially externalized. As long as resettlement processes remain chronically underfinanced, DFDR processes will chronically and predictably fail and further pauperize those affected. Compensation levels must be restructured and increased. Although compensation remains indispensable in DFDR, its criteria, calculation, and delivery must be radically improved.

Financing additional to compensation is indispensable for sound resettlement. The insufficiencies of financing cannot be corrected by heightening compensation levels, although such reform is essential and a priority. The very goals of sound resettlement require development-investment financing as well.

Resource allocation for DFDR processes is a matter of political will even before becoming a matter of finance availability. Allocation is a matter of distribution. Project benefit sharing cannot be enacted by project managers: it requires political decisions by governments or at high levels of private-sector corporate management and ownership. At the state level, rethinking the place of DFDR processes in a specific country's development and poverty reduction policy means not just tinkering with piecemeal, marginal measures. It means addressing the political economy issues of DFDR and legislation.

Financing resources can be mobilized. The actual practices of the several countries discussed above demonstrate beyond doubt that resources can become available when there is political will. That such mechanisms are being crafted and implemented, in industrialized countries and in developing countries, answers the question posed at the beginning of this chapter: Where would the money come from? From mobilizing part of the benefits derived from the project itself. If development projects that displace people "are as profitable as their promoters claim, (they)...should have little difficulty in offering displaced persons an irresistible resettlement package" (Drèze, Samson, and Singh 1994).[21]

Opposition to displacement and its impact is growing in many countries. In India, the clashes and losses of life at Kalinga Nagar, Singur, and Nandigram during 2006–2007 epitomize the resistance to displacement and dispossession. The strength of resettlers' demands and their militant opposition is increasingly influencing government decisions and resource allocation in public and private sector projects toward more recognition of resettlers' losses and impoverishment.

Tested mechanisms for investing in development-oriented resettlement are known. The several benefit-sharing mechanisms described above vary in details, but all have one common purpose: to invest in the redevelopment of those hurt by forced displacement. Different procedures reflect country particularities and suggest that there is not necessarily a "one prescription fits all" solution. A vast space for replication, adaptation, and creative innovations is open to many other countries.

Policies require *legislative* enactment; more than policy statements are necessary. To ensure consistency in implementation, transparency for the public, and legal accountability of managers, the policy decisions for better financing of DFDR need to be translated into law. Legislation specifies the proportions of sharing among various stakeholders, to prevent subjective decisions, and can prescribe specific uses of the financial allocations.[22] Laws also enable legal recourse in cases of transgression.

The current answer, compensation, to our starting question about the financial capacity for equitable resettlement is in need of substantial strengthening. Maintaining unchanged the current financing patterns based on compensation alone would only mean financing for a repetition of past failures in different forms. It would predictably cause further impoverishment. Financing is, in itself, a factor of such paramount importance for achieving economically sustainable resettlement that financing alone, when flawed, would cause failure, even with other necessary factors of success present. Other variables of DFDR policies must be changed as well. Money alone would not solve all resettlement's problems either. But absence of financially adequate compensation foreordains failure by definition. Reform is indispensable in the ways resettlement operations are legislated, planned, financed, and implemented. And political will can mobilize the means necessary for investing in resettlement with development. The people placed at grave risk to make way for development projects ought to be the first who are entitled to access the substantial benefits made possible by their loss and ordeal.

Notes

1. Notable exceptions to this widespread indifference are the valuable contributions made by Herman Daly (2008), Ravi Kanbur (2008), Vijay Paranjpye (1988, 1990), David Pearce (1999), and David Pearce and Timothy Swanson (2008).

2. L. K. Mahapatra (1999:17–18) wrote: "There is hardly any writing by Indian economists on the impoverishment caused by displacement or expropriation for development projects....As the economists occupy the highest positions in the government and corporate sectors, which determine the fate of millions in India, their awareness of, and sensitization to, the impoverishment of the project-affected persons and their proper rehabilitation as part of development planning are crucial."

3. For details, see Cernea 2008a, 2008b, regarding compensation theory and pitfalls; for a discussion of resettlers' income curve before and after forced displacement, see Cernea 1996b, 1999, 2000b.

4. See van Wicklin 1999 for a detailed presentation of some good, yet still isolated, practices, supporting the idea that "the stream of benefits created by the project should also be tapped to provide direct benefits and resources for the resettlers" (van Wicklin 1999:233).

5. In real practice, it is rarely equal. Usually, it is lower or much lower, and in the case of customary ownership of land, they are often not even recognized as legal owners.

6. As in India, where a national policy was nonexistent until 2004 and state policies existed only in a small minority of India's states.

7. About compensation, which was kept for many years at unacceptably ineffective, low levels, Heggelund (2004:65) writes: "The livelihood of compensation...was the 'lump sum' type compensation...with no thought of how the resettled people were to live....There was no focus on production...the resettled peasants lived in poverty after being resettled."

8. So far, international practice reports only sporadic uses of the new potential created by irrigation to benefit the farmers displaced from upstream. This is a missed opportunity. Such solutions have been considered in the past. India, for instance, has taken a pioneering position by adopting legislation, called the "ceiling laws," that makes land redistribution in the command areas legal and enforceable. Yet, the ceiling laws are seldom applied, so this important benefit-sharing option remains unused.

9. See Heggelund 2004 for a more detailed historical overview on the evolution of China's resettlement policies.

10. See China's Ninth National People's Congress, Land Administration Law of the People's Republic of China, Ministry of Land and Resources, Beijing, 90 pages. Protecting cultivated land from unlawful or excessive acquisitions is one of the law's basic thrusts. The revised law considerably restricted the authority of China's provincial and county governments to requisition land on behalf of the state, established higher thresholds for compensation, and enacted additional subsidies.

11. Noteworthy from a social science viewpoint, these policy reform and financial measures are informed by systematic research. China has established the world's first national research center on development-caused resettlement (NRCR) at Hohai University, specializing in resettlement policies, research, planning, implementation, and monitoring, as well as a large network of other resettlement institutions decentralized in all provinces.

12. Of these, some are decisions covering resettlements in all sectors; others are for selected sectors (hydropower and water resources) and are not yet generalized at the national level.

13. China's policy makers are now critically reassessing this period as one of erroneous approaches to DFDR, during which China lacked a sound resettlement policy. The affected people were severely impoverished by displacements, with little legal recourse to defending their entitlements and rights.

14. The mandated higher-minimum floor makes it illegal in China to pay farmers less than this minimum. The aim of raising the floor is to prevent local attempts to keep compensation close to the lower level of the range (previously, ten times the AOV). The increased levels of mandatory compensation act also as a disincentive and restraint to excessive land acquisition and displacement.

15. See analyses of land law in India: Guha 2007; Jayewardene 2008; Ramanathan 2008.

16. Issued by the Ministry of Finance and the Ministry of Electric Power.

17. The regulations for these funds provide that proceeds can be either handed over as cash allocations at a set rate per family or used as lump-sum group allocations to resettled communities, to be invested in collectively owned assets.

18. Equal to some 210 billion yuan (US$1 = 7.76 yuan).

19. Personal accounts are set up for the beneficiaries, into which the 600 yuan payments are transferred directly.

20. We may lump such measures under the "capability development" concept proposed by Amartya Sen, on which I do not elaborate in this chapter but which is germane to the effort to improve resettlers' livelihoods.

21. The example given by Drèze is forceful. Referring to a study concluding that the rate of return on the Narmada Sardar Sarovar Dam is about 20 percent, he pointed out its general economic implication, which is directly relevant to the argument of this chapter. Namely, the financing necessary to support sound resettlement under this project (and other comparable projects) "could be expanded to the extent of doubling the total cost of the entire project and still leave the project with a very respectable rate of return of 10%" (Drèze, Samson, and Singh 1994).

22. Notably, some uses refer to investing a part of the benefits in social development activities, and others, in better environmental protection in the project area, which also have positive effects on the populations' welfare. In all situations, benefit sharing becomes an added mechanism, diversifying the instruments used to counteract impoverishment risks.

4

Does Development Displace Ethics?

The Challenge of Forced Resettlement

Chris de Wet

The best-laid schemes o' mice an' men gang aft agley.

—*Robert Burns*

Massive technological development hurts.—*Elizabeth Colson*

Development projects, which are supposed to enhance overall access to resources and quality of life, displace up to fifteen million people worldwide per year (Cernea, personal communication, 2005). Such projects include the construction of dams, irrigation schemes, conservation areas, urban renewal and housing schemes, water and transport supply systems, energy generation projects, and mining projects. With few exceptions, this displacement has been forced, in the sense that the people have had to move; they have been seen as "people in the way of development" (Blaser, Feit, and McRae 2004). Only recently has this logic begun to be questioned.

Resettlement in this chapter refers to situations in which provision is made for people who have to move. They are usually compensated for resources left behind (although usually not adequately to reestablish themselves economically) and either are moved to new settlements or have to find a new place for themselves with compensation money. This contrasts with *displacement*, in which people are compelled to move without any effective provision being made for them. In India, the majority of people moved by development projects have been displaced; they have never been rehabilitated (Fernandes 2004:40). This chapter concerns itself with situations of forced resettlement, that is, forced removal but with provision.

Development is riddled with tensions and contradictions, particularly around issues of power and inequality (Power 2003:9; Simon 1999:29). This has perhaps been nowhere more apparent than in the field of development-forced displacement and resettlement (DFDR), because forced community displacement effectively takes place only where a disparity of power exists. These tensions are reflected particularly in the state's ability to "exercise its right to appropriate private property for public use (that is, exercising its right of *eminent domain* within its sovereign territory) against a relatively impoverished and powerless group of its own citizens" (Turton 2002:50)—and also in the state's ability to define what constitutes the "public good," in the name of which it justifies forced removals.

Those subjected to forced resettlement have overwhelmingly experienced serious, and often permanent, socioeconomic and cultural suffering and impoverishment as a direct result. In many cases, the natural environment has also suffered, as a result of the imposition of the project and the altered population densities arising from resettlement (for example, with dams or villagization schemes, see de Wet 1995:chap. 2; World Commission on Dams 2000a:chap. 3). DFDR projects have provoked ongoing controversy and widespread resistance (Oliver-Smith 1996, 2006), with calls for the abolition of any development projects that necessitate population displacement and create "victims of development" (see Raina, Chowdhury, and Chowdhury 1997).

This raises questions of how to approach DFDR projects in ethical terms and what to make of the ethical tensions arising out of such projects. By *ethics*, I understand a systematic concern with the principles by which we seek to distinguish between right and wrong in our behavior towards other people and towards nature.

Many real-life situations do not allow for a coherent ethical approach. We may be confronted by situations in which we have to choose between equally compelling, but competing, moral values within our ethical framework (for example, equality and liberty). Or it may not be clear how we should apply a particular value or principle in a specific situation (for example, making free or subsidized medicine or education available to the poor). At times, treating some people as ends in themselves seems possible only if we treat other people as a means to achieve that first goal—as may well be the case with DFDR. To the extent that situations confront us with apparently intractable challenges, seemingly making it impossible for us to apply our ethical principles in a consistent fashion, such situations could be said to "displace ethics" and thus challenge our ethical frameworks. I suggest that development projects that give rise to forced resettlement constitute one such situation, particularly when we try to establish a coherent basis for deciding whether and on what basis to go ahead with such projects.

THE ETHICAL TENSION INHERENT IN DFDR

Development projects that give rise to forced resettlement have a contradictory aspect that makes for inherent ethical tension: they simultaneously promote and undermine human well-being.[1] Development projects that fulfill their mandate will promote human well-being to the degree that they provide potentially more ordered and efficient access to, for example, water, food, shelter, services, and employment. In so doing, they help people meet their basic or "vital needs," creating the conditions to sustain life and ongoing, minimal human functioning and potentially meeting related needs and achieving fuller human functioning (Hamilton 2003:chap. 2). Most of the rights literature and declarations (for example, see Messer 2004; UN 1948, 1986) hold that human beings have the right to be able to fulfill their basic or vital needs.[2] Development projects thus contribute to the "greater good" (here defined minimally as meeting the needs of large numbers of people, particularly the poorer sections of society, in the manner defined above) and thereby promote human well-being and human rights. (See Penz 1995 for a discussion of public interest in DFDR projects.)

However, such development projects also undermine human well-being. The forced resettlement of those people who have to make way for development projects constitutes a significant human rights violation. No matter how well the resettlement process is planned and funded and no matter how participatory the exercise is, the complexities involved are such that it simply cannot be guaranteed that people subjected to forced resettlement will emerge from the process any better off than before. The contradiction inherent in DFDR projects cannot be overcome.

This raises the ethical problem of whether to go ahead with projects that produce such simultaneously contradictory outcomes. One way of dealing with this problem is to adopt a broadly utilitarian ethical approach and to ask what will bring about the greatest overall benefit/utility and human well-being: to reap the benefits of the development project together with the costs of forced resettlement (even trying to lessen those costs through generous compensation or benefit-sharing policies) or to forego the development project and therefore the costs of resettlement. In planning terms, the decision would be made through a cost benefit approach (CBA).

Our problem is that we need a way to make decisions about resettlement, but these decisions do not make the problem of resettlement go away. Serious questions remain as to the political and cultural assumptions behind ideas such as "general welfare" and "cost benefit analysis." Who gets to define general welfare, how are costs and benefits to be identified and priced, and what assumptions are made about the commensurability of values across cultures to monetary terms? Moreover, no matter how carefully one goes about matters—planning, participation, and compensation notwithstanding—at the end of the day, "some people enjoy the gains of development, while others bear its pains" (Cernea 2000a:12). The cost benefit calculus may generate an overall "profit" in the gains column, but the actual pain in the pains column remains. Cost benefit analysis implies treating people as a means for the purposes of making decisions and achieving collective outcomes, but those who have to move are never happy with being on the receiving end. Although this may be "necessary for the greater good," we know that subjecting people to forced resettlement will involve subjecting them to certain suffering in the short term, with no promise of anything better in the longer term. Forced resettlement, seemingly inescapably, involves not being able to treat resettled people as ends in themselves, as full beneficiaries of development. However, if the project is necessary to serve the greater good and there is no way to avoid resettlement, then refusal to undertake the project in order to prevent the negative effects of forced resettlement would mean not treating the majority of people, who are not to be resettled and who stand to benefit, as ends in themselves.

Decision makers around DFDR projects directed towards the greater good (as defined above) seem to be caught up in situations in which they have to trade off competing notions of good because these do not seem reconcilable on the ground: the greater good, as embodied in the idea of overall welfare, versus the good embodied in the idea of treating everybody involved as full beneficiaries of development. Similarly, decision makers are often unable to reconcile the just (as in the procedurally fair or equitable) and the good (as in treating people as valuable).[3] Development confronts us with what Goulet (1985) describes as "cruel choices." The substance of this chapter supports arguments for, and explores various aspects of, these ethical tensions in relation to DFDR.

WHAT ARE THE SOCIOECONOMIC CONSEQUENCES OF FORCED RESETTLEMENT?

Scudder and others have argued that forced relocation gives rise to stress and trauma because of the physical, economic, and sociocultural uprooting involved and the subsequent demands of adjustment and recovery. Stress is particularly acute during Stage 2 (Adjustment and Coping), with results such as increased morbidity and mortality (because of food insecurity, lack of potable water, social disruption, anxiety, and so on) occurring almost as a matter of course among forcibly resettled populations. This has led Scudder to argue (personal communication, 2005) that, even in a resettlement project that turns out to be successful in terms of making it through the four stages of his model (Scudder 2005a:32–41; see also chapter 2, this volume), the negative results experienced during the stage of Adjustment and Coping will be such that one can speak of human rights violations in most forced resettlement projects.

Forced resettlement effects a change in people's sociospatial setting that is imposed from outside, within a time frame that is also imposed from outside. Such imposed change also challenges people's value systems, because of the way in which planners and bureaucrats conceptualize the process of compensation. In order for them to justify the land alienation required for proposed development projects, they place people in a situation in which these people experience agonizing conflicts around whether to accept money for land or water that they regard as sacred or in other ways constitutes incommensurable values (Espelund 1998:chap. 5; Oliver-Smith 2005a). Forced resettlement not only disrupts people's lives and values but also casts them into wider sets of structures and relationships and into a process of accelerated socioeconomic change. This serves to loosen their cultural anchors, lessen their material well-being, limit their choices and control over their circumstances, and increase conflict within settlements. Dissonance seems directly related to the forced nature of resettlement.

These stresses and disruptions result in Cernea's well-established interrelated impoverishment risks (Cernea 2000a:20–55; 2005a:203–204). These have increasingly been confirmed across different kinds of development projects throughout the world (for example, see Schmidt-Soltau 2005 for conservation-induced displacement). Downing has expanded on Cernea's concept of social disarticulation, with his analysis of the way forced displacement disrupts what he calls the "social geometry" of peoples. Routine culture, which "is defined by *roughly* the same people, or groups, repeatedly reoccupying the same places at the same times" (Downing and Garcia-Downing, chapter 11, this volume; Downing, 1996a), is fundamentally disrupted by displacement and has to be reconstituted.

Such impoverishment risks do not strike in a uniform fashion: forced resettlement hits people differently, according to their gender, age, health, status, and economic position (Cernea 2000a:31; Kedia, chapter 5, this volume; Koenig 2006:115–121; Scudder 2005a:42). Inasmuch as forced resettlement has usually served to impoverish those whom it has moved, it has all too often created inequality and polarization between those who "enjoy the gains of development" and those who "bear its pains" (Cernea 2000a:12).

If forced resettlement had resulted only in socioeconomic impoverishment and disaster for those who have had to move, it would be very difficult to justify projects involving forced resettlement. Success stories might change our "ethical calculus." What evidence do we have of successful resettlement? Scudder claims that "good practice" cases show that "it is possible for a majority of resettlers to become project beneficiaries whose improved living standards can contribute to a project's stream of benefits" (Scudder 2005a:73).

However, such good-news cases seem to be fairly thin on the ground. In a survey of large dams across the world, Scudder found 50 cases for which there was sufficient evidence to code a range of relevant variables. Of these, "opportunities were sufficient in 3 of 44 cases…to raise the standards of living of the majority, and to restore them [that is, to their pre-resettlement level, which does not properly measure up to his definition of success] in another 5 cases" (Scudder 2005a:56). We are actually looking at a very small percentage of positive cases, with questions about the sustainability of those raised living standards: "In the remaining 36 cases (82 percent), the impact was to worsen the living standards of the majority" (Scudder 2005a:62).

Although these few positive cases do demonstrate that success can be achieved, most of them (for example, Aswan on the Egyptian side, Pimburetwa in Sri Lanka, and Shuikou in China) would appear to be special cases enjoying favorable circumstances not readily replicable on a regular basis elsewhere. Arenal in Costa Rica achieved Scudder's Stage 3 in both economic and socioinstitutional terms. It was characterized by potentially more replicable factors, such as thorough preliminary research, timely planning, and meaningful participation by those to be resettled, which made proposals more viable (Partridge 1993). However, no study of Arenal takes us beyond six years after resettlement, so we do not know whether the successes have been sustainable (Scudder, chapter 2, this volume).

Together with material from other types of DFDR, such as that relating to mining (for example, Ahmad 2003), Scudder's survey shows that the vast majority remain impoverished by the experience of forced resettlement and do not achieve positive economic and social development and autonomy. The forced resettlement record is overwhelmingly negative, despite increasing efforts to turn the tide. We therefore need to ask why this should continue to be the case.

WHY IS IT SO DIFFICULT TO REVERSE THE NEGATIVE EFFECTS OF FORCED RESETTLEMENT?

Most commentators agree that development projects requiring forced resettlement involve an exceptional degree of complexity (for example, in the kinds of sociospatial changes they effect and in the nature of the resettlement project as an institutional process). This makes a successful outcome much more difficult to achieve, and opinion is divided on whether this complexity can, in fact, be mastered to good effect.

Cernea shows optimism when he argues that "the general risk pattern in displacement *can be controlled through a policy response* that mandates and finances integrated problem resolution" (Cernea 2000a:34). Scudder (2005a:50) is cautiously optimistic. Oliver-Smith (2005a:55) is pessimistic because of the difficulties in reconstituting the social geometry or in achieving the social reconstruction of resettled communities.

Whether or not one believes that the complexities of the resettlement process can, in principle, be mastered and the risks effectively dealt with is of some ethical consequence. If the complexities can be mastered, then we can, in principle, guarantee satisfactory outcomes for those undergoing resettlement. If we cannot master the complexities, then not only can we not guarantee any satisfactory outcomes, but also the very nature of the "resettlement beast" may tend towards unsatisfactory outcomes. This would go at least part of the way to explain the disastrous track record thus far. The latter view of complexity would make it increasingly hard to find a justification for forced resettlement.

I incline towards the view that a complexity inherent in the process of DFDR projects works against successful outcomes. There clearly are cases (see above) in which forcibly moved groups have been economically better off. And we need to sharpen our understanding of the circumstances around their success and to separate out the situation-specific factors from the replicable factors at work. But these are also a very small minority of the cases of forcibly resettled communities. And we need to sharpen our understanding of why they remain a minority and why, in spite of international policy developments in the past two decades, the suffering and the impoverishment continue on such a large scale. We also need to keep in mind Oliver-Smith's reminder that economic recovery does not necessarily equal social reconstruction (Oliver-Smith 2005a:51).

I now briefly consider some of the complexities involved in the DFDR process (see de Wet 2006 for a more detailed discussion). Resettlement imposes sociospatial transformation and accelerates socioeconomic changes. The resettlement project itself is a problematic institutional process, with a number of its aspects tending to combine in such a manner that the development goals of the resettlement component are not achieved and the resettlers are left impoverished. Projects usually have to adapt themselves to larger political agendas and take place within the context of mutually reinforcing critical shortages, of money, staff, skills, and time. Competing visions of development and of the project, different time frames, happenstance, resistance, all feed into the way a project unfolds. Therefore, it cannot be effectively planned for.

This has resulted in many resettlement projects lacking any significant consultation or participation. The complexities of people's situations are overlooked, and resettlement, as a complex process over time, tends to be reduced to relocation, a simplified one-off event. The predictable outcome has been the realization of Cernea's impoverishment risks.

This analysis essentially sees the forced resettlement process as one that is too complex to manage, with too many variables and "unpredictables," and that takes on a life of its own—with largely uncontrollable, mostly negative outcomes. However, several key factors have the potential to render the complexity of the resettlement process more manageable. Foremost amongst these would be *the development of resettlement policy over the past twenty-five years*, with that of the World Bank widely recognized as the pioneer and the most influential. Clark, a legal activist, argues that "the [resettlement] policies and laws, even if imperfect, are important safeguards of local people's most fundamental rights" (Clark, chapter 9, this volume). However, resettlement policy, in terms of both content and implementability, is increasingly beginning to look like a two-edged sword.

Recently, it has been argued (for example, Downing 2002b; Scudder 2005a:281–283) that the latest (2001) version of World Bank policy is actually a step backward. It does not adequately address the need for resettlement with development, thereby potentially legitimizing a process of forced resettlement that leads to impoverishment. The latest version of the proposed revision of the International Finance Corporation's policy on involuntary resettlement is likewise seen as retrogressive in terms of the protection of the rights and development needs of affected people.[4] Cernea (chapter 3, this volume) argues that resettlement policy's narrow focus on compensation has been fundamentally flawed and is therefore insufficient to put the resettled people on a development path, condemning them to impoverishment instead.

At country level, there are also serious questions about the degree to which policy is being implemented in practice. Chinese resettlement policy, highly respected in the resettlement world, gives local-level officials considerable discretion over the allocation of resettlement funds, leaving room for corruption, which is evidently becoming a serious problem in the Three Gorges Project (Tanner 2005). Rew and his colleagues (Rew 2003; Rew, Fisher, and Pandey 2006) have showed us how policy is negotiated and transformed in the process of implementation as it interacts with political and logistical realities along the way.

Benefit sharing is another key factor challenging the argument that the resettlement process is too complex to control or to achieve predictable and satisfactory outcomes. Benefit sharing involves "the stream of benefits created by the project [being] tapped to provide direct benefits and resources for resettlers" (van Wicklin 1999:233). Those people whose forced displacement makes the project possible become direct project beneficiaries, so resettlement with development becomes possible. Benefit sharing, in principle, promotes development equity by spreading the benefits of development, as well as sustainable development for the resettlers (Égré, Roquet, and Durocher 2002:7–10).

In practice, does benefit sharing fulfill these promises? A number of benefit-sharing schemes are in operation around the world; however, most of them seem to have been initiated fairly recently (see cases in Égré, Roquet, and Durocher 2002 and van Wicklin 1999). We need to wait in order to see what consistent trends emerge: What exactly is done with income from the sale of electricity? How fairly are jobs spread? Are attractive incomes from aquaculture wrested from resettlers by outsiders, as happened in Indonesia (van Wicklin 1999:244)?

Development equity in benefit sharing takes us directly to the issue of capacity. Many local authorities are ill equipped to handle large sums of money; there are problems around administrative capacity and accountability (Milewski, Égré, and Roquet 1999:pars. 6.1, 6.2), as well as corruption, as in the case of the Three Gorges Project (Tanner 2005). The benefits may not make it through to the resettlers.

Paradoxically, benefit sharing may create inequity for the affected people; benefits from projects are not always channelled directly to them, but instead, as in the case of the Hubei hydroelectric project and the Lesotho Highlands Water Project, to the region or the nation as a whole (Égré, Roquet, and Durocher 2002:52–53, 61). Administrative incompetence and corruption easily dissipate resources that are not specifically earmarked; one cannot assume that general distributive mechanisms will necessarily ensure specific distributive justice.

There is a further potential for inequity, not only within the implementation of benefit sharing but also in securing its implementation in the first place. Van Wicklin observed that "of great concern should be the consistent evidence that benefit-sharing is seldom used in projects financed domestically without assistance from international donors" (van Wicklin 1999:250). Countries that can do without loans with conditions attached do not have to bother themselves with setting up benefit-sharing provisions.

We are continually brought back to the same problem: although the chances of a deliverable outcome must seem better with benefit sharing on the drawing board than without it, *we cannot guarantee outcomes.* We know only after the people have been forcibly moved, *that is, when it is too late,* whether the benefit-sharing mechanisms are working in an efficient and sustainable manner.

A third key factor that may help to deal with the complexity inherent in forced resettlement relates to *capacity,* of the officials and the people being moved. I now briefly discuss two examples to show that capacity provides the moral space that is essential in bringing about the meaningfully negotiated outcome and effectively implemented process necessary to achieve a successful resettlement outcome.

In Mexico, local peasants negotiated their resettlement conditions with the Comisión Federal de Electricidad (CFE) around the construction of the Zimapan Dam (Aronnson 2002). Guggenheim argues that "difficulties within CFE in institutionalizing participation processes continue[d] to inhibit local participation" (quoted in Aronnson 2002:134). A lack of capacity on the part of the implementing agency meant that it did not have the know-how to create the enabling conditions, that is, the moral space, for effective participation. This interacted with a similar lack of negotiating capacity on the part of the peasants, serving to disempower both parties. The peasants and the implementing agency were unable to express their opinions and choices and to negotiate in an open and unthreatening context. Because of their lack of experience and capacity, the two main parties came to form what I would term a "community of mistrust." They felt themselves locked into the negotiating process and, because they saw no way out of it, came to identify with the process, even though they mistrusted each other. Lacking the capacity to be either constructive or flexible, as well as the option to break off negotiations completely, both sides adopted confrontational tactics.

By way of contrast, the Cree of northern Quebec provide a rare illustration of a response by an indigenous grouping to a large-scale development project, in large measure because of capacity that they had built up over time to influence the course of events. With the assistance of local Canadian funding and expertise, the Cree organized themselves into a unit cutting across their original nine bands and, over time, built up the capacity, networks, and resource base to pressure and negotiate successfully with the Quebec authorities and with the hydroelectric parastatal Hydro-Quebec. They succeeded in getting the Grande Baleine Project suspended and the James Bay and Northern Quebec Agreement renegotiated, which went together with a significant benefit-sharing agreement in 2002. This involved revenue sharing and the establishment of a Cree development fund. This also gave the Cree an active say in the management of natural resources in their territory and in the implementation of a key hydroelectric project. From the implementation side, the progressive and flexible approach of HydroQuebec to benefit sharing and to negotiations enabled positive developments to take place (Craik 2004; Scudder 2005a:204–210).

The effect of its absence in the Zimapan case and of its presence in the Cree case shows that capacity on both sides of the negotiating table is critical to the creation of the moral space necessary to generate and realize options that may, in cases of rare good fortune, help us avoid forced resettlement and, when this is not possible, to soften its contradictions. To a limited extent, one can develop capacity through training, but training by itself cannot guarantee the kind of capacity needed in DFDR situations, those rare attributes such as the ability to work with other people and to play the system without destroying it, inventiveness, trustworthiness, staying power. Capacity is a pearl of great price because it purchases options, sometimes also outcomes, for people undergoing resettlement. There is no telling beforehand whether, or in what ways, capacity will manifest its riches in particular resettlement situations. We cannot guarantee a basic ingredient, so, again, we cannot guarantee the outcome.

I suggest that the arguments in this section indicate that the complexities inherent in the process of forced resettlement make it impossible to control the outcomes and therefore to reverse the negative effects. As a result, we cannot guarantee success in making resettled people socioeconomically better off. The argument raised in some quarters, that all projects involving forced resettlement should simply be abolished, might become more attractive. Yet, our cruel choices seem to be sharpened for us; the evidence suggests that the incidence of forced resettlement is actually rising across the world.

WHY, DESPITE OUR BEST EFFORTS, IS FORCED RESETTLEMENT ON THE INCREASE?

The World Bank Involuntary Resettlement Policy states explicitly that

> involuntary resettlement should be avoided where feasible, or minimised, exploring all viable alternative project designs....

> Where it is not feasible to avoid resettlement, resettlement activities should be conceived and executed as sustainable development programs, providing sufficient investment resources to enable the persons displaced by the project to share in project benefits. [World Bank 2001:2 (a), (b)]

Yet, such policies notwithstanding, the number of people involuntarily displaced by development projects has increased, with Cernea revising his estimate upwards from ten million to fifteen million per year (personal communication, 2005).

Options assessment argues that potentially affected people, via their representatives, should be involved from the outset of a development project in the identification of the development need that the project is to serve and in the "open and systematic assessment of options and alternatives in planning exercises—ranging from policy formation to project planning" (World Bank 2003:2). One of the key priorities in assessing the range of options available to meet that need should be to avoid or minimize displacement.

A place at the table does not, however, guarantee effective participation in negotiations about a project's outcome. Although steps should be taken to counteract this possibility, through training programs and the use of professional facilitators (World Bank 2003:51–52, 81), there is a danger that "participatory approaches may mask different levels of power and influence, exaggerate the level of agreement reached, and expose disadvantaged groups to manipulation and control by more powerful stakeholders" (World Bank 2003:81).

A major concern is that options assessment may well not be implemented in a majority of development projects. It is a time-consuming process and involves initial expenses, which tends to put many governments off implementing it (World Bank 2003:17). This is particularly the case if governments are not under pressure to do so from foreign funders and, as Ainslie (personal communication, 2005) suggests, if they lack a strong human rights culture in the first place.

The range of options may, in practice, not always be that extensive. Thus, water harvesting alternatives such as watershed development and smaller reservoirs are frequently put forward as alternatives to large dams, which have such damaging social and environmental consequences. Anything that lessens the number of large dams and the amount of forced resettlement is to be welcomed, but water harvesting alternatives will not provide any kind of magic bullet in this regard.

Large dams still seem necessary in some sectors, for two reasons. First, the world's environmental and political problems notwithstanding, we increasingly depend on irrigation to feed ourselves (Scudder 2005a:94, 297; World Commission on Dams 2000a:137). With 46 percent of the world's population living in cities (World Commission on Dams 2000a:4) and with the urban population growing, large dams as a source of water and energy remain unavoidable. Second, although large dams have a number of environmentally negative consequences (McCully 2001:chap. 3; World Commission on Dams 2000a:chap. 3), they have an important environmental plus factor: "Power generation [currently] directly accounts for up to 30 per cent of human-generated greenhouse gas emissions, mostly from thermal power plants" (World Bank 2003:4). Hydroelectricity represents a much cleaner source of energy.

In some cases, it may be possible to negotiate where the site of a particular dam should be to minimize displacement, but large dams and the forced resettlement they bring with them are here to stay. Witness the plans to build sets of new dams in India and China (for example, Menon et al. 2003:4).

Increasingly, the cities of the world are becoming the major sites of forced resettlement as city fathers try to keep providing housing, roads and rail links, and water and other infrastructure-based services to constantly growing populations. Coupled with this "public good" source of forced resettlement is the pressure from private developers seeking to drive poor people out of areas with development potential (Koenig 2006).

Development alternatives that increase the chances of more local-level development and that lessen the amount and the impact of forced resettlement are to be welcomed. Depending on the development need to be met, the terrain, and other factors, there are, however, limits to which such alternative options can be generated. Forced resettlement is actually on the increase worldwide, and unless something meaningful can be done to reverse its seemingly inherent negative impacts, the ethical problems with which it confronts us are here to stay.

ON WHAT GROUNDS SHOULD WE DECIDE WHETHER TO PROCEED WITH SPECIFIC PROJECTS INVOLVING FORCED RESETTLEMENT?

Social decision makers often resort to a kind of utilitarianism when making decisions between different development options or potential "social states," the preferable social state being that which is "consistent with the maximization of the *sum* of the utilities of all individuals" in the society (Sugden 1992:267). Which valuables are reckoned (and by whom) as "utilities" and how the "sum" is arrived at are, of course, central to the process. Planners usually employ a cost benefit approach (CBA): various costs and benefits are ascribed to each development option, and monetary or numerical values are ascribed to the various costs and benefits seen as attached to each option (Heap 1992:240). The option that emerges with the greatest overall social benefit or utility is then chosen. If a development option involving resettlement emerges with greater overall social benefit than costs, compared with an option providing different development benefits but not requiring resettlement, then, in terms of the CBA way of making decisions, the development option requiring resettlement should go ahead.

Serious concerns have been raised about the assumptions behind this method of making decisions and therefore its ethical plausibility. "CBA is utterly insufficient because it is only a macroeconomic tool that does not explore *the distribution* of either costs or benefits *among project stakeholders*" (Cernea 2000a:47). CBA lends itself to the inclusion of costs and benefits that can be expressed in numerical terms (Heap 1992:241), which raises problems for the inclusion and commensurability of culturally conceptualized items such as space, water, and sacred sites. People may find the reduction of their culture to monetary terms deeply alienating and insulting (Espelund 1998:chap. 1). One of the central ways to make a CBA approach ethically acceptable is to have those who stand to gain compensate those who stand to lose. However, compensation is often either not paid or grossly inadequate. Cernea (chapter 3, this volume) argues that it is, in principle, structured in such a way that it effectively makes resettlement with development impossible. As argued above, we do not have the wherewithal to secure resettlement with development. This means that we cannot guarantee development outcomes (certainly not for resettled people) and therefore cannot guarantee overall utility, thereby rendering the overall CBA logic problematic. If we cannot deliver effective compensation or development to those upon whom we impose the costs of development, then the intellectual and ethical foundations of this approach seem too shaky to justify use as a basis for making decisions about projects involving forced resettlement.

The Approach in Terms of Development Equity

Drydyk approaches the issue of making the decision in terms of the value of development equity, arguing for development welfare to be extended to everybody on an equitable basis. (He uses the term *displacement*, although much of the time effectively dealing with resettlement.)

Drydyk sees us as having to deal with the claims of those who stand to be displaced by a project and thereby are at risk for impoverishment, as well as the claims of the "even more people [who] may be left in poverty elsewhere if the project does not go ahead" (Drydyk 2001:2). We can develop a "consistent rationale" (Drydyk 2001:3) for deciding when "displacement-inducing development" (DID) projects are justified and when they are not, in terms of the concept of the human right to development, "especially insofar as it requires equity in development" (2001:3), "the benefits of which are shared throughout the communities in which it occurs" (2001:16). Indeed, "benefit-sharing in the larger development project is a necessary condition for permitting any displacement effects at all" (2001:17). Drydyk utilizes Sen's concept of "capability gains" as the touchstone for the justification of resettlement. "If a particular process of DID cannot be shown to generate capability gains for social groups including the worst-off (and shown to be the most effective at generating capability gains for the latter), then it fails the test of equity in development and should not proceed" (Drydyk 2001:21).

However, if considerations of development equity can be used to veto a project because of inadequate benefit sharing, then they can equally be used to justify—indeed, to require—resettlement. "If the only alternative to displacement-inducing development is that a region or community foregoes development benefits that have become normal for others elsewhere...then the principle of benefit-sharing *requires* this development, displacement effects included" (Drydyk 2001:17).

A significant reason that forced resettlement involves the stress and impoverishment that it does relates to the fact that it is *forced*. Human rights documents are clear that it involves a prima facie human rights violation (for example, UN 1993). However, Drydyk (2002:9) argues that, though "forced evictions are inconsistent" with the UN Declaration on the Right to Development, to allow full veto power to people faced with displacement when such veto would place development on hold would "not [be] consistent with equity" (2002:9).

We thus seem to have a problem reconciling the value of equity with the values of consent and voluntariness. Drydyk privileges equity over voluntariness. Displacement, qua displacement, can never be fully voluntary (Drydyk 2002:9). However, the ethical obligation must be to "harmonize the requirements for voluntariness" (2001:17) with those of equity and to make displacement and resettlement "as voluntary as can be" (2002:9), *through a set of deliberative procedures.* "Involuntariness is removed to the extent that the individuals or community negotiate or participate in the planning and execution of the project" (Drydyk 2001:4), as well as by arbitration when agreement cannot be reached. As important as participatory and arbitration procedures are, reservations must remain about the extent to which they can ultimately render the involuntary voluntary. Forced resettlement involves some people having the power to make other people move.

Development equity is a way of seeking to treat the affected people as ends in themselves, but its gains may come at significant trade-off costs. And, crucially, the argument that development equity brings the gains that it does—and therefore serves as a justification for forced resettlement in specific situations—assumes successful resettlement, that is, resettlement that is efficiently planned and implemented, with development and effective benefit sharing actually take place. As Kanbur (2002) and Cernea (chapter 3, this volume) argue in relation to compensation and as has been argued in relation to the complexities of the resettlement process, this is a problematic assumption that might undermine the foundation of the equity-based justification for forced resettlement.

The Approach in Terms of Minimum Standards

Another approach to deciding whether individual projects should go ahead is to evaluate whether they conform to a set of minimum standards below which displacement or resettlement *should not take place*—period—in order to protect the rights of potentially affected people. Resettlement guidelines stipulate such minimum conditions (see also Drydyk 2002:3–17). Such a set of standards would have teeth only in the following situations:

- When pressure can be brought to bear on the implementing governments and agencies to respect these standards (for example, through foreign funding bodies, governments, or transnational movements, or possibly through litigation). Increasingly, DFDR projects are not funded through bodies such as the World Bank and are therefore not bound by responsible resettlement policies or subject to their pressures.

- When, in the case of a proposed project that does not conform to the set of standards, alternative sites or options can be found that can attain the desired development goals while conforming to the set of minimum standards.

If alternative sites or options are not entertained or are not feasible and if pressure to comply is not effective, such standards will have limited practical value. Indeed, the same standards can also serve as the minimum conditions under which such projects *are* held to be acceptable. Minimum standards intended to protect the interests of potentially affected people may, paradoxically, have the opposite effect. Drydyk warns us, "Promises to meet ethical commitments can (like other promises) function to lure stakeholders into supporting a development and resettlement project, only to discover, when it is too late, that the promises were empty.... Harm can result from the very fact that ethical norms have been put forward" (Drydyk 2002:16).

Scudder (2005a:278–281) and Downing (2002b) argue that the World Bank's 2001 resettlement guidelines, by settling for the minimum standard for restoring previous living standards, rather than for actively improving resettlers' living standards, have actually contributed to their impoverishment. In a trenchant demonstration of the way in which inadequate (minimum standards) policy standards cause suffering, Cernea (chapter 3, this volume) argues that the very concept of compensation—which is at the heart of resettlement policy—as well as the way it is formulated, calculated, and financed, is inadequate to allow for resettlement with development and therefore, in effect, guarantees the impoverishment of resettlers.

Clearly, it is better to have development equity as a guiding principle in a project than not to have it and better to have a set of minimum standards acting as a safeguard than not to have them. However, the arguments advanced in this section suggest that both remain sufficiently problematic. Although they can help us decide when not to proceed with projects involving forced resettlement, they are of only limited value in helping us to decide when we should proceed.

CONCLUSION

In many instances, forced resettlement seems unavoidable in the context of "public good" development projects. In spite of some cases of successful (or relatively more successful) resettlement outcomes, the complexities of the resettlement situation are such that we cannot guarantee successful outcomes. Negative outcomes are still overwhelmingly the order of the day, and, as suggested here, there are good arguments as to why this should continue to be the majority outcome. A strong argument can be made that people undergoing forced resettlement suffer human rights violations.

DFDR projects that do address meeting human needs and the public interest work to promote *and* to undermine human well-being, and there seem only limited prospects of softening this contradiction. One is unable to apply an ethical approach consistently when seeking to decide whether to proceed with a project involving resettlement. One cannot apply utilitarianism consistently because the methodology through which one applies it in the world of planning and resettlement (cost benefit analysis) is riven with all sorts of problematic assumptions and inefficiencies. If our ethical concern is with human rights and treating all involved parties equally and as ends in themselves, both as a value and to promote human well-being, we will, again, be unable to apply our ethical approach consistently. Tragically, inefficiency does seem to impact ethics. We do not appear to have the wherewithal to square the circle, to create the moral space, so that "everybody can win."[5] Development requiring resettlement does indeed seem to "displace ethics" because it renders one unable to apply consistent criteria for justifying a project.

One therefore seems driven to a less satisfactory position, of sometimes having to condone forced resettlement in the interests of that problematic construct, the greater good. Even if one qualifies that condonation with all sorts of policies, provisions, protections, and procedures, it remains an essentially risky business, with no guarantee that people's lives may not be significantly worsened in the process.

This chapter discusses development projects that promote human well-being in that they are designed to serve the public good. Development projects that serve sectional interests, with only limited public good spin-offs (such as only a few jobs or transfers into state coffers via company taxes) cannot be held to promote well-being in a strong sense. Yet, they often call for forced resettlement. Unless projects much more clearly promote (or potentially promote) the public good, one cannot justify going ahead with them. Such sectional-interest projects should therefore not take place.

If forced resettlement is sometimes unavoidable in public good projects, then "doing resettlement as properly as possible" becomes the only acceptable course of action on the part of those implementing forced resettlement. Resettlement theory, development equity, minimum standards, and best practice procedures (including Kanbur's [2002:15] plea for "specific compensation mechanisms and generalised safety nets") are valuable but limited tools; these cannot guarantee resettlers protection from the risks of suffering and impoverishment. But these are all we have, so we need to use these with respect for both the people and the science involved, as well as with empathic imagination and humility.

In the words of the anthropologist Kirsten Hastrup, "if there is anything common to humanity, it is that we are imaginable to one another.... To perceive and understand different worlds of whatever scale, we must extend our imaginative powers as far as possible, and make more events of understanding happen" (Hastrup 1995:76). Forced resettlement, as a concept and in the way it has been applied, has been a massive failure of the imagination. If the capacity to imagine the other and to make space for the other is at the heart of the capacity to be moral, then forced resettlement has also been a moral failure—perhaps because one does not have to entertain a "co-imaginability" towards those over whom one has power. Unless this sympathetic and moral imagination leads us into conversations that cause us to rethink the very relationship between development and resettlement, and particularly what has been taken as self-evident in this relationship, we are not likely to make any headway. We need a more creative way of conceptualizing how to create the moral and institutional space to overcome the deadlock and the problems in which we are currently mired. It was Einstein who reminded us that imagination is better than knowledge. Imagination—that peculiar combination of the moral and the intellectual—opens up new possibilities for us all, including, perhaps, even a non-contradictory form of development.

Acknowledgments

My special thanks go to Tony Oliver-Smith, Peter Penz, Ted Scudder, and David Turton, who so generously gave of their time and expertise in 2005, provided me with access to material, and helped me prepare this chapter. I am very grateful to the Ernest Oppenheimer Memorial Trust in South Africa for providing the funding that enabled me to travel to spend time with these four specialists in the field. The Trust should not be regarded as associated in any way with any opinions expressed in this chapter. My thanks go to the participants of the SAR advanced seminar and particularly Michael Cernea, whose comments have been of great assistance in preparing the final version. Thanks, also, to Andrew Ainslie, Andre du Toit, Detlev Krige, Peter Vale, Marius Vermaak, and Francis Williamson for their valuable comments on earlier versions of this chapter. My wife, Elizabeth, has been the constant and enabling source of confidence behind this and all my research and writing.

Notes

1. *Well-being* here refers to the healthy state resulting from people's ability to position and maintain themselves in the world, that is, to function effectively in biological, economic, sociocultural, and psychological terms.

2. This chapter is not the place to start an extended discussion on the concept of human rights. Some political scientists would regard rights declaration–type language as very loose language. Hamilton (2003) sees contemporary rights discourses as internally inconsistent and leading to unworkable rights proliferation. He argues that

political philosophy (and, by implication, development theory) should be based on a theory of needs, not rights. However, every country and ethical system enshrines the right to life. Infant and child mortality indicators in countries where citizens do not have regular access to clean water or regular nutrition (UNDP 2006) paint a grim and unmistakable picture. This shows us that, sophisticated analyses aside, basic needs remain basic. If they are not met, the "right to life" becomes increasingly meaningless: more children die. Messy as this may be theoretically and practically, we need to keep open the question of access to the means to satisfy basic needs, which prevents the death of the young and the weak, as a possible rights/policy issue.

3. Sugden (1992:262) makes the distinction between what is good and what is just in a different context, and I borrow the distinction from him.

4. Letter to Mr. P. D. Wolfowitz, President, World Bank Group, and Mr. L. Thunell, Incoming Executive Vice President, The International Finance Corporation (IFC), 12 December 2005, from the International Accountability Project, Berkeley, expressing concerns about the IFC's revisions to its environmental and social policy framework.

5. I thank Marius Vermaak for the distinction between issues of efficiency and of ethics. He suggested to me that I might, in fact, be conflating the two ideas. In this case, issues of efficiency/capacity/wherewithal do seem to impinge directly upon our capacity to act ethically.

5

Health Consequences of Dam Construction and Involuntary Resettlement

Satish Kedia

The World Commission on Dams (2000c) reports that dam construction alone has displaced between forty and eighty million people since 1950. It is projected that this number will rise even higher because dams currently under construction or in the planning stages are larger than those already in existence (Gardener and Perry 1995). Although dam projects have enormous potential to provide electricity, increase agricultural productivity, and control flooding, they bring many adversities for people living in the areas affected by such development. These include land and livelihood losses, increased poverty, food insecurity, social disarticulation, psychological stress, and higher morbidity and mortality rates.

The resettlement policies of international development agencies and local governments primarily focus on land and housing compensation and, to some extent, basic amenities for project-affected people; actual delivery of these resources, however, has often been deficient (Cernea and Guggenheim 1993; Downing and McDowell 1996; Hansen and Oliver-Smith 1982). Significantly, development policies have largely ignored the critical issue of health impacts on such populations (Hughes and Hunter 1970; Partridge, Brown, and Nugent 1982; Waldram 1985). Published research and anecdotal accounts have identified the serious health risks associated with development projects both during and after displacement (resulting from overcrowded conditions, unhygienic environments, increased pollution, unsafe drinking water, and inadequate food). Compounding these problems is a lack of healthcare provisions. Although there are guidelines for conducting health impact assessments (HIAs) (ADB 1992; ECHP 1999; Health Canada 2004; PHAC 2005; WHO 2000; WHO and CEMP 1992), including a cursory reference to adverse effects on health in the World Bank Operational Policy on Involuntary Resettlement (World Bank 2001), systematic implementation of such assessments has not been adopted in development practices. In fact, the majority of the World Health Organization's (WHO) HIAs are designed to be performed only during the initial policy-making phases of a project. These HIAs cannot possibly address the many unforeseen, dramatic health problems that gradually and consistently occur and escalate across the decades that a massive development undertaking usually requires for completion. Many populations suffer for generations. With no tools in place to gauge the health effects of development projects on these populations, their development-inflicted health problems go largely unrecognized and unaddressed.

This chapter presents the health consequences of hydroelectric dam projects for communities in proximity to dam sites and for displaced populations in order to show the severe, wide-ranging burdens inflicted by development projects. The data are derived from long-term ethnographic fieldwork conducted during the past fourteen years among the Garhwali peasants affected by the Tehri Dam Project in northern India. This research argues for the importance of integrating health impact assessments and healthcare provisions in all economic development projects that involve forced displacement and resettlement. The Tehri Dam case study demonstrates how implementation of appropriate policies and provisions could have prevented or largely alleviated the suffering of those affected.

THE HEALTH IMPACTS OF DAM CONSTRUCTION

Although any number of development problems or circumstances can lead to the displacement of populations, the data for this study focus on displacement due to dam construction. Therefore, a general understanding of the health problems associated with dam construction is necessary in order to appreciate fully the evidence presented for this case study.

Hydroelectric dam construction impacts the health of two project-affected populations: people who inhabit the area surrounding the dam site and people who are displaced and resettled to clear the way for the dam, catchments, and associated infrastructure. Although the initiation and implementation of development policies should address the needs of both groups, the literature on the health impacts of dam projects is limited primarily to diseases contracted by the first group, caused by the alarming increase of parasitic agents and vectors emanating from water impoundments and canals. There are few comprehensive studies on the health problems experienced by the dam-displaced communities in adapting to their new environment and living conditions. As the health of displaced individuals worldwide continues to be negatively impacted, this deficiency demands immediate attention.

The Population around the Dam Site

The most frequently reported diseases in the literature include those caused by the proliferation of vectors and parasites resulting from dam construction activities. Malaria, yellow fever, schistosomiasis (bilharzia), lymphatic filariasis (elephantiasis), Japanese encephalitis, dengue or dengue hemorrhagic fever (DHF), onchocerciasis (river blindness), gastroenteritis, trypanosomiasis (African sleeping sickness), and visceral leishmaniasis (*kala azar*, or black sickness) have been widely associated with communities near dam impoundments (Bradley 1993; Brown and Deom 1973; Cernea 2000a; Heyneman 1979; Hughes and Hunter 1970; Jobin 1999; Kedia 1992; Kloos, DeSole, and Lemma 1981; Meakins 1981; Partridge, Brown, and Nugent 1982; Rew and Driver 1986; Scudder 1973b; Waddy 1973). These illnesses have serious and debilitating short- and long-term effects: fever, weakness, fatigue, itching, swelling, skin sores, scarring, disfigurement, nausea, vomiting, diarrhea, aches, stiffness, extreme pain, tremors, stupor, disorientation, blindness, liver/spleen/bladder or brain damage, coma, and even death.

The stagnant waters of artificially created lakes and blocked irrigation systems become fertile ground for the proliferation of insect and snail vectors (Jobin 1999). Reservoir weeds also support mosquito larvae that have been associated with dramatic increases of filarial parasites (Meakins 1981). In the still water, aquatic snails serve as intermediate hosts or vectors for schistosomiasis, particularly if the sides of the reservoir are gently sloped (Bradley 1993). Naturally occurring bodies of water undergo frequent periods of drying or partial drying that render these vectors harmless, but dams ensure a year-round water supply that undermines this balancing feature (Meakins 1981). The spill-off water from dams also has health consequences, especially onchocerciasis, which is carried by the tsetse fly breeding in the aerated water and rocks around waterfalls (Meakins 1981; Waddy 1973). For example, researchers studying communities around the Owen Falls Dam in Uganda found a high prevalence of onchocerciasis (Meakins 1981).

Other common diseases associated with dams and water projects include gastroenteritis, as reported in populations surrounding the Victoria Dam reservoir in Sri Lanka (Rew and Driver 1986), and endemic chagas (trypanosomiasis), as observed in persons living near reservoirs of the Brazilian Amazon (Coura et al. 1994). Most mosquito-borne diseases related to dam projects are reported in Africa. In fact, the spread of schistosomiasis has been observed among inhabitants living near most of the major dam systems in Africa, such as those located at Lake Kariba, Kainji Lake, Lake Nasser, and Volta Lake (Brown and Deom 1973). The proportion of persons infected with schistosomiasis in the Akosombo Dam region in Ghana increased from an estimated 1.8 percent before development to 75 percent of all adults and 100 percent of all children after dam construction; in Mauritania, 75 percent of all schoolchildren in the area became infected following the completion of the Forum Gleita Dam (Cernea 2000a:18). In Egypt, 85 percent of the population living next to the irrigation system of the Nile was infected with schistosomiasis, but only 20 to 25 percent in communities located away from the canal (Heyneman 1979).

Dams and water impoundment can also impact people's health as a result of food insecurity and malnutrition. The dam projects usually involve the loss of productive fields along riverbeds, where soil tends to be more fertile from greater sedimentation. Reservoirs, which are not conducive to topsoil buildup, increase water salinity, which reduces agricultural productivity (Jobin 1999). As the population becomes concentrated upon available farmland, the demands of higher population density, combined with erosion and silt, cause formerly rich soil to degrade. The ensuing decline in productivity leads to nutrition problems soon after construction is completed. The development of fisheries, claimed to be a corollary benefit of dam construction, often does not offset the reductions in migratory fish populations (Scudder 1973b). The physical barriers and dangers posed by the mechanisms of many dams alter the ecology of native fish and thus reduce availability of protein for the local people (Jobin 1999). Resultant malnutrition causes increases in prenatal mortality and developmental deficiencies in children, as well as general weakness and heightened susceptibility to pathogens among the entire population.

Beyond creating disease-inducing environments and food insecurity, dams and catchments can pose a health hazard resulting from lack of construction and mechanical safety practices. Occupational hazards are not typically assessed for construction personnel. During the construction of the Hoover Dam (1922–1942), more than 114 workers and visitors accidentally drowned or were killed by rock slides, explosions, heat, falls, electrocution, falling materials, and dislodged equipment, among other causes (USDI 2006). In 2000 three men were accidentally killed and many more injured while working on the Yangtze Three Gorges Project in China when a conveyor belt fell, prompting the manager to require a review of all equipment and safety measures (Guo Xiaohong and Li Jingrong 2000). Just one year later, failure to follow proper safety features killed nine workers on the San Roque Dam in the Philippines when too many workers were forced on the platform in order to maintain production rates (PESC-KSP 2001).

In addition to safety hazards, flooding poses a threat. The World Commission on Dams (WCD) has found evidence that flooding potential actually increases with the construction of dams (rather than decreases, as proponents would have local populations believe) (PESC-KSP 2001). In the Philippines, the Ambuklao Dam was rendered nonfunctional when siltation and erosion buildups in the reservoir caused flooding downstream; the same result is anticipated from many dams currently under construction (Imhoff 1999). In Indonesia, more than 110 people drowned in the first fourteen months following the water impoundments of the Saguling-Cirata Reservoir Project (Cernea 2000a:19).

The Displaced Population

If earlier development projects had conducted appropriate HIAs, developers now would better understand the effects on displaced populations. The Tehri Dam research, paired with other studies, reveals that factors such as exposure to new diseases, increased mental health problems, and sociocultural variables all contribute to an environment that challenges the health and well-being of displaced communities.

There are multiple etiologies for the infectious diseases found at resettlement sites, several of which mimic those found around dam developments. Displaced people may bring diseases with them or become exposed to unfamiliar diseases of the host population. Development activities, unsanitary conditions, and lack of clean water create favorable conditions for the proliferation of disease vectors and agents. Overcrowding facilitates the transmission of communicable diseases such as malaria, schistosomiasis, onchocerciasis, ancylostomiasis (hookworm or tunnel disease), ascariasis (large intestinal roundworm), and pneumonia and other respiratory diseases (Kloos 1990:643). The intrusion of humans into sparsely populated areas can bring communities into more intimate contact with animal species with zoonoses (diseases caused by agents transmitted between or shared by animals and humans) such as trypanosomiasis, leishmaniasis, and yellow fever.

There are multiple documented examples of resettlers' suffering from disease. In Sri Lanka, in the Mahaweli's System C Resettlement, displaced people experienced an increase of malaria from 8.9 to 15.6 percent (Jayewardene 1995). In the Victoria Dam Reservoir, widespread gastroenteritis was found among displaced communities (Rew and Driver 1986). The Tadavi resettlers of the Sardar Sarovar Dam in western India complained of a number of symptoms related to waterborne diseases such as malaria, dengue, hookworm, cholera, and gastroenteritis (Kedia 1992). Cernea (2000a) noted that diseases such as diarrhea and dysentery arising from poor hygiene and from unsafe and insufficient water supplies are commonplace in resettlement sites.

Like those around the construction project, resettlement communities also face food insecurity and malnutrition (Cernea 2005a). Nutritional habits are altered because foods must be produced and processed differently and traditional herbs or foods are often unavailable. Frequently, agricultural production declines (Kloos 1990; Sapkota 2001; Singh 1992), as does livestock production (Ben-Achour 2000). Resettled farmers are often forced to shift their agricultural methods, changing from diverse crop productivity and self-sufficiency to cash crops in order to generate income for purchasing food and other basic goods they are no longer able to produce (Hong 1987; Kedia 2004; Waldram 1985). Incorporation of a cash economy means that resettlers often sell the milk and eggs produced by their animals, thus foregoing sufficient protein in their own diet and further increasing market dependencies. Activities associated with gathering alternative protein sources, such as hunting and fishing, may be limited in the new location, as seen with the Garhwali resettlers, whose hunting and fishing is restricted in the conservation forestry area adjacent to the resettlement site (Kedia 2004). Consequently, resettlers' nutritional intake is generally high in carbohydrates and lacking in sufficient or diverse proteins (plant/animal) and adequate fruits and vegetables (Waldram 1985). The resulting malnutrition can lead to stunted growth or marasmus (a serious form of protein energy malnutrition, or PEM), particularly among weaned children at resettlement sites (Cernea 2000a, 2005a; Kloos 1990). PEM increases morbidity, mortality, and suboptimal physiological maturation.

In addition to physiological complications, a host of mental health concerns accompany displacement. The challenges associated with rapid adaptation to new environments, together with new economic and cultural systems, can be stressful for resettlers and frequently result in increased mental illness, along with higher morbidity and mortality rates (Beiser 1982; Corruccini and Kaul 1983). Scudder (2005a) emphasizes that stress is deeply embedded not only physiologically in the lives of displaced persons but also psychologically and socioculturally. Psychological stress stems from grieving for what is lost and from anxiety about the future; sociocultural stress results from the loss of former cultural practices and livelihoods. According to Werner (1985), displaced people experience more stress than do those who are not displaced. Using a thirteen-item scale developed to measure social stress, Werner found significantly higher levels of stress among Barra Dollman farmers displaced by the Upper Itajai Dam in Brazil than among those who had not been resettled. Cernea (2000a) has documented the increasing incidence of chronic illnesses caused by high levels of psychological stress accompanying resettlement. Other researchers have found diabetes and cardiovascular problems such as high blood pressure (Ward and Prior 1980), as well as behaviors associated with psychosocial problems, including alcoholism, drug abuse, and suicide (Hanna and Fitzgerald 1993:1169; Kirby 1989).

Despite resettlers' significant physical, psychological, and sociocultural ties to the land, large hydroelectric dam projects are being justified in the name of national economic benefits (Oliver-Smith 2005b), with no effective policies in place to enable healthy resettlement.

THE GARHWALI CULTURE

Many of the health problems imposed upon the Garhwali people by the Tehri Dam construction are consistent with problems associated with dam construction in general. The health implications of dam construction have been well documented, so it is of great concern that more has not been done to provide health care for those displaced. The project should have anticipated and addressed the health problems typically accompanying displacement due to dam construction. However, this case study reveals that appropriate measures were not taken to facilitate a healthy transition for the Garhwali people. In the absence of such provisions, people have suffered physically, mentally, emotionally, and spiritually. The debilitating effects of displacement on the Garhwali people illuminate the need for improved health assessment and care (HAC) policies, which should be implemented as soon as development projects are undertaken. The Garhwali people represent only one example of the unnecessary suffering endured by displaced persons worldwide as the result of poor planning, suffering that could have been prevented by appropriate healthcare measures.

At a height of 261 m (about 856 ft), Tehri is the highest dam in India and the seventh highest in the world, along with the Manuel M. Torres Dam in Grijalva, Mexico (ICOLD 2003). It is located in the central Garhwal Himalayas in the state of Uttaranchal in northern India on the Bhagirathi River, the main tributary of the Ganges. Construction work on the Tehri Dam began in 1978. After multiple delays, Phase 1 of the main dam was completed in 2004 and was expected to produce about 1,000 megawatts (MW) of power by the middle of 2006. When all phases are completed, the dam will have the capacity to generate 2,400 MW of electricity and to provide enough water to irrigate a quarter million hectares of land. The Tehri Dam is also expected to help fill the supply–demand gap of an estimated 289 million gallons daily (MGD) for potable water in the state of Delhi by providing 140 MGD of raw water (GNCTND 2000). The Tehri Dam's water impoundments displaced approximately one hundred thousand Garhwalis from more than 125 villages and one major town, populations that were subsequently resettled in one of thirty-six sites in the foothills of the Himalayas. Another fifty thousand people, living near the impoundments and canal systems, have been adversely affected by the resulting changes in their environment and livelihoods but have not been relocated.

Garhwalis are predominantly Hindu peasants whose lifestyle reflects the traditional caste system; individuals are born into various occupational categories.[1] Garhwalis follow patrilineal practices and cohabitate in joint families; the parents head a household consisting of their unmarried children and married sons with their own wives and children. Compared with women in many other parts of India, Garhwali women are afforded a relatively high status and participate more widely in public activities. Until dam construction began, the majority of Garhwalis had little or no exposure to the outside world.

Nearly 85 percent of Garhwali peasants engage in intensive agriculture; however, only about 10 percent of the land in the mountain region they inhabit is suitable for cultivation. Garhwali agricultural practice largely comprises terrace cultivation, in which crops are planted on hilly slopes in narrow strips. To supplement the food grains and vegetables cultivated in the mountains, most households raise livestock for milk, eggs, and meat. Goats and sheep are the main herding animals and are used for milk, meat, and wool. Economic activities include horticulture, forestry, and cottage industries such as weaving and other handicrafts.

The Garhwalis believe in both natural and supernatural causes of illness. Natural causes comprise the weather, hygiene, nutritional sources, pathogens, and physical and emotional imbalances. Supernatural causes include spirit and ghost intrusion, ancestral neglect, the wrath of deities, the evil eye, witchcraft, and sorcery. According to Garhwali beliefs, any combination or any one of these factors can trigger illness. Accordingly, Garhwali healing practices are very eclectic, combining biomedicine, local herbs, Ayurveda (a cohesive set of traditional beliefs and practices that involve healing the body with natural elements), and rituals designed to rid afflicted persons of sorcery or to appease angry gods. These healing traditions are employed by a variety of practitioners, including medical doctors, nurses, Ayurvedic vaidhyas, herbalists, priests, and shamans and other magicoreligious healers.

THE TEHRI DAM COMPENSATION POLICIES

The compensation policies for land losses of those affected were inadequate and were implemented on an ad hoc basis, often depending upon the priorities of certain officials and the political party in power. Existing policies were frequently modified without retroactive provisions to close the gap between earlier compensation and the current arrangement. Fully affected families, defined by resettlement authorities as having more than 50 percent of their land acquired for project purposes, were offered land and monetary compensation. Partially affected families, those with less than half of their land acquired, were offered only monetary compensation deemed equivalent to the amount of land taken. Fully affected families were compensated with 2 acres of land in the resettlement site. In addition, they were given 12,000 rupees (about US$274) for each acre of irrigated land acquired by the government or 6,000 rupees (about US$137) for each acre of uncultivated land acquired, a compensation that was strongly opposed and considered grossly insufficient by those displaced.

THE TEHRI DAM HEALTH IMPACTS

The environment in the Garhwal Himalayas has drastically altered in the thirty years since the Tehri Dam construction began, particularly with regard to deforestation, pollution, and population density. All of these changes have increased the health risks among people who continue to live near the dam, reservoirs, and irrigation canals. Large portions of forest have been cut down to accommodate construction activities, inadvertently causing greater soil erosion and land depletion. In addition, grassy vegetation has spread because the Tehri-expanded water systems generate more moisture, facilitating the proliferation of disease-bearing vectors and parasitic agents. The blasting of rock for dam building and other construction activities has created air and noise pollution. Thick layers of fine dust cover the area and the vegetation, even fresh plantings. According to the local people, dust allergies and respiratory infections have plagued the three generations that have been forced to suffer these circumstances.

Dam construction added about eight thousand transitory workers to the area at any given time, which necessitated temporary housing and significantly increased the region's population density. This compounded the unsanitary conditions faced by permanent residents and facilitated the spread of infectious diseases. The workers introduced new pathogens to which the local populace had little immunity; in turn, the workers often became sick from the local microbes that were foreign to them. Sexually transmitted diseases increased with the presence of transient workers, which was not unexpected, given the separation from their families. Further (as seen in the construction of the Hoover Dam, the Three Gorges Project, and the San Roque Dam), the workers were highly susceptible to occupational hazards at the construction site. Many major and minor accidents occurred during tunneling and blasting for the dam channel. For example, in 2004 a tunnel collapsed and crushed twenty-two workers.

Residents in close proximity to construction sites reported high levels of stress and anxiety due to uncertainties about the future when the reservoir would become completely filled with water. They were especially concerned that the additional impounded water would intensify the local soil's tendency to absorb moisture and then erode, further depleting the land available for cultivation. Some feared that they would lose their land completely.

Higher Morbidity among Tehri Dam Resettlers

At the resettlement site, authorities cleared a segment of the Rajaji National Forest to accommodate the displaced because the plains at the base of the mountains were already densely populated. The resettlers were moved from their mountain village to an uninhabited site in the foothills of the Himalayas, an area situated between rich forest and arid plains.

The resettlers' dietary intake changed from a locally produced, diversified, high-protein diet to a market-bought, nutrient-poor, high-carbohydrate diet, negatively affecting the resettlers' health. They sold the milk and eggs produced by their animals, instead of consuming the products. In addition, the replacement of self-sustaining crops with cash crops made the community more dependent on income and market consumables. Further, resettlers could not hunt game in the forest or fish because of strict prohibitions in the nearby conservation area. Before displacement, they had access to game, fish, wild plants, fruits, root crops, and herbs.

The uninhabited resettlement site was already contaminated with various disease-causing microorganisms. With the influx of humans, the unchecked vector and parasitic agent population expanded dramatically, resulting in a greater number of communicable diseases. Moreover, the resettlers had no immunity to certain parasites among the neighboring community. Upon arrival at the resettlement site, many contracted serious illnesses and have remained in poor health ever since. The self-reported, six-month health history of the resettlers indicates that they suffered more incidences of fever, malaria, typhoid, measles, gastrointestinal ailments, asthma, and tuberculosis compared with the community remaining in the mountains. During interviews, many of those displaced shared their concerns about the community's declining health. One woman said, "This is a forest area, and there are a lot of mosquitoes. Here, there is a lot of malaria and fever. There is no one in the village who did not have to go to the doctor continually for several months."

The new climate in the plains caused a number of ailments. Garhwali humoral theory attributes sickness to changes in cold, heat, rain, and wind that disturb the balance of body fluids and make it vulnerable to disease. An appropriate HAC would require healthcare personnel to be trained in local medicine so that both traditional healing practices and biomedicine could be incorporated to establish sustainable health care for the local people. Many resettlers believed that body aches (headache, backaches, stomachaches, and joint pain) and diarrhea resulted from the plains climate. They frequently complained that there was bad *hawa-pani* in the resettlement site compared with their former mountain habitat. Garhwalis use the term *hawa-pani* not only to refer to the air (*hawa*) and water (*pani*), as literally translated, but also to symbolize holistically the natural, cultural, and moral ambience of a location. Typical of the views held by most resettlers, one villager expressed his discontent with the new habitat:

> We are sick here. Bad air and bad water. We just don't feel good here. We are helpless. Illnesses in this place are plentiful and kind of strange. And our cures don't work here either. There is a lot of difference between the water in the mountains and the water here. You think electricity-driven water is any good? It is the natural water that is good. We are old traditional people, and our bodies do not agree with this new, artificial water.

Most resettlers identified bad *hawa-pani* as the critical cause of a majority of illnesses in their community. In the mountains, they had obtained drinking water directly from the earth, but after resettlement, people mostly accessed water through a tap, canal, or tube well. The resettlers believed that water derived from these sources was polluted and that people in the community were falling ill because of it. In fact, they considered the water to be the cause of an outbreak of gastroenteritis and other communicable diseases in the village. Another respondent noted:

> Everyone is suffering, especially older people. There is so much pollution here. There, I had pure water and fresh open air. If I get the chance, I will go back to the mountains. There, I feel free. Here, the problem is water. That is the biggest problem, and so are the wild animals. There was water there. When there is no water here, how do you expect good diet?

In addition to laboring hard during the day, farmers maintained watch throughout the night to protect crops from wild animals in the outlying forest, a schedule that took its toll on resettlers' general health. One informant related, "Here, you see your standing crop in the evening, and next morning it disappears. Wild elephants come in the night from the jungle and ruin the whole field." Another one said, "I have to be awake and watch my crops in the night. If I don't do that, I will die out of hunger. I can't sleep here. There, I used to sleep in peace."

The resettlement site was not well suited to the Garhwalis' traditional hygiene practices. Had a thorough HIA been conducted before displacement, this problem would have been exposed. Traditionally, children urinate and defecate outside (in fields, around nearby bushes, even in the streets), and residents throw garbage outside houses or at the village periphery. Because the resettlement site was more densely populated and much warmer, such hygiene practices created very unsanitary conditions. Further, because there were few bushes and the children tended to avoid the nearby forest, the amount of feces and garbage in the streets increased, and the heat and humidity only worsened the potential for disease. In addition, no sewage system had been built, nor garbage collection organized. Through an adequate HAC policy, the Garhwalis would have received basic health education and would have been offered healthier solutions for waste management.

In addition to concerns about their own health, the resettlers expressed fears about their children's health and growth with poor and frequently insufficient nutrition.

Mental Health Consequences for Tehri Resettlers

To discern how displacement and its consequences had affected the Garhwali people, I conducted a brief survey comparing the rates of depres-

TABLE 5.1

Symptoms of Depression Disorder among Mountain Villagers and Resettlers:
A Comparison Using the Nonparametric Mann-Whitney U Test

Items for Depression Scale	Mountain Villagers (N = 108) Mean Rank	Resettlers (N = 108) Mean Rank	Level of Significance 2-Tailed P
1. You feel regret for past events. ±	121.82	87.35	0.0000*
2. You fear impending disaster. ±	119.68	89.34	0.0000*
3. You feel insecure. ±	115.52	94.10	0.0002*
4. You avoid confiding in others. ±	117.42	94.69	0.0015*
5. You have trouble sleeping. ±	111.14	91.07	0.0057*
6. You feel you have committed a sin. ±	112.12	99.93	0.0071*
7. You are tired all the time. ±	113.55	94.38	0.0075*
8. Your sleep is disturbed by worry.±	112.93	98.35	0.0338*
9. You feel guilt for anything unpleasant. ±	113.12	98.16	0.0448*
10. You feel your problems will not end. ±	112.07	99.18	0.0683
11. You fear going anywhere at night.	112.69	101.36	0.0981
12. You get into arguments easily.	112.12	99.93	0.1021
13. You worry even during leisure time.	107.70	101.42	0.3726
14. You are sad most of the time.	97.93	110.70	0.0329
15. You are nostalgic for preresettlement days.	101.26	106.61	0.4755

The Mann-Whitney U is also referred to as the Wilcoxon Rank Sum W Test, a nonparametric test that, when applied here, shows a lower mean rank score, indicating poorer mental health status on an individual item.

± Items derived from the DSM-IV (APA 1994).

* Statistically poorer mental health status for resettlers on individual item at p = <0.05

(Probability = .0000; reliability coefficient alpha = .7434; standardized item alpha = .7503)

sion among resettlers with those of mountain villagers who had not been displaced.[2] Both resettlers and mountain villagers were asked fifteen questions designed to assess mental health. A comparison of the two populations' responses clearly demonstrated that the resettlers were displaying higher levels of depression (table 5.1).

Mental health problems manifested in various ways, as reflected in the survey items. Sleep was a major problem area for resettlers. Their levels of depression were significantly higher than those of the mountain villagers when asked whether they had trouble sleeping, felt tired all the time, and experienced sleep disturbed by worry. Guilt was also a major concern. Resettlers indicated that they felt regret for past events, felt guilt for abandoning their ancestral spirits and for "anything unpleasant," and felt as if they had committed a sin, at much higher rates than the mountain villagers. They reported much more alarming levels of depression than mountain villagers in their fear of impending disaster, avoidance of confiding in others, and feelings of insecurity. Although not as statistically significant, the resettlers also reflected higher rates of depression by reporting that they felt that their problems would not end, got into arguments easily, worried even during leisure time, and feared going anywhere at night. An HIA would have readily made the mental health struggles of the Garhwali evident, and appropriate mental health services could have been provided. With no such policies implemented, mental health continued to be a problem area, and the Garhwali resettlers saw no end in sight.

In response to open-ended questions, resettlers frequently expressed a repressive mood of passive compromise: "Ye to aise hi chalega [This is how it's going to be]." From what the resettlers shared in interviews, it appears that this attitude had persisted since they relocated almost fourteen years earlier. Their responses further suggest that most Garhwali resettlers had accepted this mood as a way of life. Typical resettler sentiments were well demonstrated by the following response: "I feel lost here. I am here not by choice. They [project authorities] have thrown us here forcefully. What can I do? Persons of my age are sad because they have spent most of their lives in the mountains." Many complex factors contributed to their poor mental health. Several had skills that were rendered obsolete in the new economy and ecology, a problem not easily remedied, given the few opportunities or funds for retraining. One elderly resettler expressed concerns about uncertain financial circumstances:

> There was always something to do in the mountains. There is not much work here for me to do. I lose my sleep over thinking the worst. Earlier, the older men used to sit together to chat and share *hukka* [a kind of tobacco pipe shared by more than one person at a time]. Now, no one does that. I sit alone in my house, and so do most of the retired persons.

For many Garhwalis, depression was compounded by disruption of their magicoreligious system. Ancestral spirits and important deities are linked to native villages; as a punishment for moving away and abandoning these spirits, the Garhwali believe that the spirits inflicted illnesses upon them. In the new location, there were fewer traditional healers for appeasing these mystical powers. Many of the priests and shamans from their original or neighboring villages stayed back in the mountains, and the cost of bringing folk healers to the village each time their services were deemed necessary was extremely prohibitive. Additionally, the traditional herbal pharmacopoeia, which grew naturally in the area from which the resettlers had been displaced, was nonexistent in their new surroundings. Culturally appropriate healthcare services, which a responsible HAC policy would have encompassed, were not available, and despair ensued. One of the older female resettlers detailed her feelings concerning the lack of spiritual support in her new habitat:

> I don't like it here. I have bad luck. I think everyone has to die one day. Today or tomorrow, how does it matter? But this life is pathetic....Earlier, I used to treat minor illnesses with the herbs. There are neither herbs here nor people who know how to use them. There, on the mountains, I used to sacrifice goats. I used to worship. I used to beat drums. I used to do all these things a lot in the mountains. I don't do it here.

Resettlers' health problems, mental and physical, were exacerbated by economic barriers to accessing biomedical healthcare systems, their common alternative when folk healing methods were unavailable. For the Garhwali people, as with any displaced population, health and health care are linked to social and economic factors. When displaced people are thrust into a new environment in which the social and economic structure inhibits their access to health care, it is only to be expected that they will not benefit from whatever healthcare system is in place. Instead, because they lack the economic means to get help, their health worsens. One villager stated, "Here, you have to have money to go to the doctor. That's the way it is in the plains. There, I had access to herbs in the forest and used to treat myself. I used to go to the doctor only when it was a very serious condition."

Not only did the resettled Garhwalis experience more physical ailments, but they were also under pressure to find economic resources for health care. The inability to access treatment and the frustration of being largely left alone without help also increased stress and thus the incidence of mental health problems.

Compounding the resettlers' depression from lack of meaningful work and fulfilling recreation were their negative coping strategies, such as alcohol abuse, which created even more problems in the long run. As a primary means for managing stress, alcoholism soon became a social evil for the resettlement village and was particularly destructive in households with limited resources, a situation that generated its own set of public health issues. A frail man lamented:

I am very restless here. The big problem is alcohol. People spent their food money on the alcohol. The country liquor shop draws not only elderly but also most adults in the evening. People have destroyed their lives over alcohol here. I, an old man, will somehow spend the rest of my time, but what will happen to these children? How are they going to manage? On top of this, gambling is becoming widespread. Now, people spend whatever little they have got on daily lottery draws. They are addicted to it now.

Many resettlers shared the insurmountable chaos of their new life as they gathered in a little thatch-roofed liquor bar that opened for business soon after this resettlement site was established. They flocked there every evening to seek respite. The main topics of conversation in the bar ranged from frustrations with life's hardships at the new site to politics and gossip about neighbors. The villagers reported that a majority of the male adults soon took to drinking in order to cope with stress. For some, alcoholism depleted what little cash they had received as compensation from dam authorities. For others, family resources of any cash value, along with significant amounts generated from cash crops, were spent on this indulgence. Female resettlers consistently complained that alcohol wreaked havoc on their families and that cash needed for buying healthful food at the market had been wasted on alcohol consumption. Consequently, alcoholism adversely affected the health of everyone in the family—men, women, and children alike.

DISCUSSION

The rapid social changes caused by big development projects generate numerous health risks for displaced people, an aspect of resettlement that demands the immediate attention of organizations and governmental agencies involved in development projects. At present, policies that might address the physical and mental health impacts of displacement lack a definitive research base. This study clarifies the relation between economic development and health in terms of the human cost. In addition, this research provides preliminary but substantive data documenting the serious health consequences not only for the people remaining in communities around the water impoundments of large hydroelectric dam projects, but also for those forced to resettle, especially when relocation requires them to face an unfamiliar ecology. For many developing countries in which the national government is responsible for providing basic healthcare services, this research indicates the need for modification and implementation of health programs and policies, as well as training of health professionals who work with resettlers.

Traditional communities interact closely with their immediate physical and social environment. When powerful outside sources bring about sudden environmental alterations and cultural intrusions, as is the case with development projects, displaced people face serious challenges in coping with these changes. During my fieldwork experiences among the Tehri Dam resettlers, seven themes emerged in resettlers' narratives: land, water, food, health care, housing, amenities, and employment. Most resettlement plans are confined to land and housing compensation. Only minimally do they address basic amenities and infrastructure needs, leading to woefully inadequate remediation strategies with regard to health and nutrition. The provision of sanitation facilities, potable water, adequate and balanced nutrition, and primary health care is often completely overlooked. In most areas, water for irrigation or drinking is still nature's responsibility. Food and nutrition are largely left to resettlers' ingenuity. Health care, though recognized as a need, has not yet been addressed. In light of this, Wirsing's (1985) characterization of the displaced and involuntarily resettled as victims of the "disease of substitution" is apt; their illnesses are not self-inflicted but instead have been brought about by external forces beyond their control. Indeed, as the results of the Tehri Dam study indicate, development projects have adversely impacted resettled populations most severely.

Before the Garhwalis' resettlement, primary medical care facilities were available in the neighboring town, and basic healthcare needs were met through a nexus of family, friends, neighbors, local experts, and traditional magicoreligious healers. At the resettlement site, the Garhwalis' therapeutic network disintegrated, resulting in poor health. During my last visit, in 2004, I found that a disproportionately higher number of the resettled population (compared with the mountain villagers) had died because of accidents or chronic illnesses. The resettlers had more difficulties adjusting to the climate of the new site, suffered more infectious diseases and parasitic base infections, and were compelled to accommodate a diet with less nutritional value that frequently led to malnutrition. Some of these illnesses may have been attributable to adapting to a new ecology, but contaminated water and poor sanitation facilities also contributed to the prevalence of physical maladies.

Further, the resettlers experienced more mental health disorders and psychosomatic illnesses than did those remaining in the mountain village, mainly because of their feeling disconnected from sociocultural roots. The high levels of reported depression were attributed to the loss of traditional lifestyle and the inability to establish a viable and sustainable livelihood since their former skills had been rendered useless in the new, market-driven economy. Resettlers responded with maladaptive coping measures (for example, consuming alcohol and gambling) that siphoned already scarce resources from their impoverished families and increased the probability of depression. The displaced Garhwalis' poor mental state was compounded by their belief that they had abandoned their sacred ancestors, gods, and spirits and that illness and tribulation were the consequences. Traditional redemptive spiritual measures were lost when the Garhwalis' connection to their native land was severed.

It is apparent that a great need exists for public policy measures to assess the health impacts of development projects on involuntarily displaced and resettled populations. Development policies—and resettlement policies, in particular—have made minimal reference to the magnified health risks in affected communities. Therefore, compensation packages generally do not address the health problems. The rhetoric of most development literature focuses on rehabilitating displaced populations and helping them restore their livelihoods to the greatest extent possible, but attention to public health would strengthen these rebuilding efforts. Although research in this area is limited, Cernea (2000a) has emphasized that better project planning can prevent diseases resulting from poor, unsafe, and insufficient water supplies. Inadequate policy provision to protect health and preserve food production systems invariably results in long-term health problems for resettlers. Policy makers should explicitly commit to addressing the health needs and care of affected people by incorporating HIAs and an adequate public healthcare plan before, during, and after implementation of a development project.

I propose that development agencies, whether government- or organization-based, adopt a three-phase HAC policy solution to this problem. *Phase I, Initial Assessment*, would involve conducting an HIA at the village and regional levels as part of the overall environmental and social impact assessment that is already a standard practice in development projects. *Phase II, Continual Assessment*, would entail ongoing health monitoring of permanently resettled populations to gauge their progress toward healthy adaptation, determining whether their physical and psychological health needs are being met. *Phase III: Sustainable Health Care*, would focus on the restoration of physical and mental health via the provision of basic amenities and culturally appropriate health services that would integrate traditional healing and biomedical practices for the long-term sustainability of the affected communities.

Health monitoring and sustainable care require that program officers draw upon traditional therapeutic resources, as well as modern healthcare facilities. Contrary to the belief that economic development results in greater use of biomedicine and concomitant changes in the use of an ethnomedical system by resettled communities, my research indicated that the Garhwalis did not completely accept biomedicine. Rather, there was an ongoing and possibly greater reliance on traditional magicoreligious and other folk healing practices. Indeed, only a small percentage of the resettlement community had the resources to take advantage of available biomedical practitioners and treatment. The provision of basic health education and preventive health measures will help people adapt to their new environment. But it is crucial that program personnel have a comprehensive understanding of local health practices and the extent to which culturally constructed ideas about "health" (or the lack of it) are embedded in ethnomedical systems. Sustainable health care can be achieved only through the protection or re-creation of local communities' ethnomedical systems, drawing on indigenous knowledge and cultural sensitivities to address socially constructed pathologies.

No economic development or resettlement plan can be truly effective unless health concerns become an integral part of related policy. Certainly, individuals are entitled to both health care and a healthful environment. Indeed, international conventions guarantee these rights, and it is the responsibility of development agencies to ensure that these rights are protected. Development initiatives should include health policy measures such as the HAC plan presented here, with financial support guaranteed by project allocations. Funding agencies should demonstrate greater commitment to the rights of displaced indigenous populations and should strive to provide these communities with the resources and support systems they need in order to adapt and thrive. The results of this study extend beyond hydroelectric dam projects. They should inform and guide policy, programs, and plans for all people involuntarily displaced, whether by other types of development projects, by war or conflict, or by forces of nature. If development agencies, public and private, would take heed, many lives could be saved and made productive, for the common good of all.

Acknowledgments

This research was funded by a National Science Foundation grant (SBR-9321818). An earlier draft of this chapter benefited from the discussion at the SAR advanced seminar and from the valuable comments by Margaret Kedia, Heidi Kenaga, Hannah Johnson, and Nathan Tipton.

Notes

1. Study populations: I collected qualitative interviews with 30 individuals and quantitative data from 108 individuals in each village. In the mountain village, the quantitative data were collected on 74 men and 34 women with a mean age of 42.7 and 48.1 years, respectively. The mountain village comprised roughly 1,250 persons at the time of the study. Approximately 20 percent belonged to the Brahmin (priest) caste, 70 percent were Rajputs (warriors and landlords), and 10 percent were Harijans (in low occupational categories), a group consisting mostly of *luhars* (blacksmiths), *badais* (carpenters), *sunars* (goldsmiths), and *bajgi* (Harijans who perform various functions such as drum playing, basket weaving, and tailoring). A majority of the households maintained a joint family structure. Situated near the Tehri Dam at about 700 m elevation along the river valley, inhabitants of this village farmed the relatively flat land rich with alluvial soil along the Ganges River and used the natural resources of the neighboring forests and communal animal grazing grounds. These villagers practiced subsistence agriculture, mostly self-contained and confined to family members sharing the same hearth. Economic inequalities existed within the mountain village, as evident in the unequal ownership of land: almost half of the families owned less than one acre, barely enough to produce adequate food; several families owned large tracts of land between 4 and 17 acres; and one household had 52 acres.

In the resettled village, I gathered data on depression from 108 villagers, 76 men and 32 women with a mean age of 44.4 and 43.8 years, respectively. The population was approximately 1,350 persons at the time of the study. Approximately 10 percent were Brahmins, 88 percent Rajputs, and 2 percent Harijans. Nestled between the plains and the foothills of the Himalayan mountains, this village of Garhwali peasants was founded as a result of the resettlement in 1981, approximately fourteen years before my first data collection.

2. Data collection: I collected the empirical data during long-term fieldwork conducted between 1993 and 1995 and during three brief summer trips, the last one in the summer of 2004. I selected the two locations for data collection (a mountain village close to the Tehri Dam in the Garhwal Himalayas and a resettlement site close to the Himalayan foothills) because they represented the two types of populations of interest to this study and were similar in terms of cultural background and economic status. Also, the people in the resettlement site had been involuntarily displaced and relocated from a neighboring village close to the mountain village under study in the early 1980s, which made it possible to examine the long-term impacts of dam development.

Following Bernard's Two-Group Posttest Only Design (1995), I conducted interviews with inhabitants of both villages on their health experiences. I used a triangulated methodology incorporating participant observation, in-depth interviews, case studies, and a structured questionnaire to collect data on morbidity and mental health status. To ensure that culturally appropriate measures were used in the study of the resettlers, I developed and tested the reliability of a fifteen-item scale, using items from the existing psychometric scales and DSM-IV (APA 1994) criteria to measure depression in the two study communities. Ten of the items reflect the criteria or associated factors for depression as listed in the DSM-IV. The other items address concerns typically expressed to me by the Garhwalis in conversation. All respondents were asked to rate each of the items on an ordinal scale of "strongly agree," "somewhat agree," or "disagree," based on their perceptions of the presence or absence of a particular condition or situation.

6

Urban Relocation and Resettlement

Distinctive Problems,
Distinctive Opportunities

Dolores Koenig

Urban DFDR (development-forced displacement and resettlement) often promises direct benefits highly desired by the inhabitants of poor urban neighborhoods: better housing, clean water, sanitation, and transport. Because of high density, providing these improvements usually involves some displacement, depriving residents of another valued good, the ability to remain in their homes. Moreover, promises are not always kept. If, in theory, urban DFDR offers better lives in improved neighborhoods, in practice, urban residents do not always benefit.

As in other DFDR, the poor suffer disproportionately. Middle-class and wealthy neighborhoods are sometimes relocated, but poor neighborhoods more commonly feel the impact of urban infrastructure initiatives. These neighborhoods are, by definition, the explicit target of urban renewal and slum upgrading.

This chapter first addresses the causes of urban DFDR and its effects on the human rights of residents, specifically, rights to housing, improved living conditions, and livelihoods. Data show that the unsatisfactory results of urban DFDR derive from the emphasis on housing and services over livelihoods. The conclusion offers recommendations for better urban DFDR, including improved understanding of urban economic systems and efforts to build on urban diversity and activism.

URBAN DISLOCATION AND RELOCATION IN THE EARLY TWENTY-FIRST CENTURY

Many developing countries have experienced extremely rapid urban growth; in 1996 the world's population became 50 percent urban (Byrne 2001:6). By 1989 China had sixty-two cities with more than 1 million inhabitants (D. Byrne 2001:64), and Bangkok grew from about 2 million to almost 6 million from the 1960s through 1999 (Wilson 2003:208). Mexico City grew from 3.14 million in 1950 to 17.3 million in 2000 (Ward 2004:166), and the Johannesburg region, from about 2 million to more than 7 million in the same period (Crankshaw and Parnell 2004:354). Cities also grew spatially to accommodate more people; the area of metropolitan Delhi quadrupled between 1951 and 2000 (Dupont 2003). The number of mega-cities is projected to increase through 2025 (Cernea 1993:7), although growth has slowed in some major cities, such as São Paulo, Mexico City, and Cairo (Gugler 2004:4–5).

New arrivals look for jobs and inexpensive housing, creating the spontaneous, unzoned, or unregulated settlements commonly called slums, generally near to employment or opportunities for entrepreneurship. Inhabitants and entrepreneurs often build housing on public land and environmentally hazardous areas, such as riverbanks and steep slopes. A significant proportion of the population may live in these settlements; many would like, but cannot get, legal title (Agrawal 2003:168). "Squatters" make up an estimated half of urban Manila's population (Meikle and Walker 1998:36). In Delhi, some 20–25 percent of residents live in unregulated settlements, despite ongoing slum clearance (Dupont 2003). About 50 percent of Mumbai's 10 million residents live in uncontrolled settlements (Agrawal 2000:21), and about 30 percent of Calcutta's population of more than 10 million live in "slums" (Agrawal 2000:22). Kinshasa has approximately ten illegally developed parcels for each legal one (Simone 2004:196). Although irregular occupation is more widespread in the developing world, people in poor neighborhoods in the developed countries also face substandard housing and insufficient services (Humphrey 2003; Skifter Andersen 2003).

For many years, social scientists and urban planners have studied poor neighborhoods in developing and developed countries, emphasizing similar issues (Gans 1962; Perlman 1982; Suttles 1968). On the one hand, analysts decry poor conditions such as overcrowding, inadequate housing, and lack of transport and communications infrastructure, as well as their links to poor health, violence and crime, illegal economic activities, a culture of dependency, and devaluation of human life (Lomnitz 2003; Morgen and

Maskovsky 2003; Simone 2004; Smart and Smart 2003; Vigil 2003). On the other hand, urban neighborhoods are seen as arenas of positive individual, community, and intercommunity action as people pursue multiple strategies of betterment, including the creation of new social relationships and networks, secular and religious associations, and political and social movements (Lomnitz 2003; Mullings 2003; Simone 2004). Although urban quality of life should be neither romanticized nor demonized, some urban DFDR projects address the rights-violating features (see chapter 4 by deWet and chapter 10 by Johnston, this volume) of urban neighborhoods, including poor housing, sanitation, education, and transport.

New infrastructure may be focused on poor urban neighborhoods but often is aimed at entire metropolitan areas. Initiatives address transport (construction or improvement of railways and roads, bridges, airports, rail terminals, port areas, and facilities), water and sanitation systems (pipelines and purification, sewage treatment), and environmental problems (monitoring and flood control). Some projects displace only a few people. In Brazil, the Pecem Industrial and Port Complex was expected to displace approximately 200 families (Tankha, Burtner, and Schmandt 1998); the Qunli Dyke Project, to control flooding in Harbin, China, was to displace 229 households (HPPO 2001:16–18). More commonly, high urban-population density means that even small projects displace many. A new light-rail terminal in Manila displaced some 4,050 families, and the creation of a business park, some 5,000 (Meikle and Walker 1998:35–36). The numbers can become very large. The Pasig River Rehabilitation Project in the Philippines was expected to affect about 60,000 (Agrawal 2000), and the Mumbai Urban Transport Project displaced approximately 19,000 households (MMRDA 2008).

Other projects target the comprehensive improvement of poor urban neighborhoods. By definition, these "urban renewal" projects displace whole neighborhoods; they range from upgrading slums to conform to sanitation and density regulations, to the wholesale removal of people from existing neighborhoods to permit more remunerative industrial, commercial, or residential development. One neighborhood renewal initiative in Karachi affected some 100,000 people (Lari 1982:57); an estimated 700,000 Delhi residents were forcibly displaced from the central city to resettlement colonies on the outskirts in the 1970s (Dupont 2003).

The displacement and relocation of urban residents are frequently carried out through rights-violating initiatives. Governments may evict thousands of people under the pretext that they do not have legal title or do not respect zoning and building regulations. In the 1980s and early 1990s, the

Dominican Republic evicted some 30,000 Santo Domingo families, and Myanmar (Burma), some 500,000 Rangoon residents (Robinson 2003). Between 1973 and 1995, twenty-four forced displacements were carried out in Lagos, Nigeria (Simone 2004:195). Although World Bank guidelines require project assistance regardless of legal title (World Bank 2001:par. 16), many countries have hesitated to give these benefits. In the Philippines, squatting was criminalized under the Marcos regime (Meikle and Walker 1998:36). An Indian high court ruled that encroachers on the right-of-way of national highways should not receive compensation (Reddy 2000:179). Many Latin American countries will not compensate those without legal title (Mejía 1999:156). In China, those without urban residency permits generally have not been compensated (Meikle and Walker 1998). The number of mass evictions has decreased under pressure from human rights organizations and donor agencies, but they still continue. In the late 1990s, India evicted an estimated 167,000 people in Mumbai; the Philippines, an estimated 165,000 families nationwide; and Bangladesh, an estimated 100,000 in urban areas (Robinson 2003). In the summer of 2005, the government of Zimbabwe forcibly removed up to 700,000 urban residents and vendors (Wines 2005).[1]

Urban renewal projects often are carried out to prepare areas for private development for wealthier residents, who can pay higher taxes and portray a more prosperous urban image. As central cities are restructured, offices, hotels, luxury housing, and restaurants displace poorer residents (Gugler 2004:16). In many Latin American countries, governments consider slum dwellers third-class citizens (Mejía 1999:154). Yasmeen Lari, a Pakistani architect who developed innovative housing to enable poor Karachi residents to remain in the central city, was continually criticized by those who believed that the land should have high-rise apartments and prestigious buildings (Lari 1982:64). She said, "I believed that planners wanted to clear the central city of the poor" (Lari 1982:60). This attitude is not unique to the developing world. Walter Fauntroy, a Washington DC activist and minister, said that he saw 1960s freeway plans as part of an ongoing effort to push low- and moderate-income African Americans out of the city, an effort that began with the voluntary gentrification by whites of the Georgetown neighborhood and continued with urban renewal in the city's southwest (Levey and Levey 2000:25).

Government desires for a higher tax base are complemented by the interest of private sector developers in new income opportunities. In both developed and developing countries, public–private partnerships frequently facilitate the development of prime urban areas. For example, the government of the Philippines sold land in Manila and on the coast to private developers as part of its privatization program (Meikle and Walker 1998:34). In the United States, an estimated 3,722 government condemnations were carried out on behalf of private enterprises from 1998 to 2002 (Downey 2005). State and municipal governments have used relocation to facilitate private development since a 1954 US Supreme Court decision affirming the District of Columbia Redevelopment Act, which ushered in urban renewal programs. In June 2005, the US Supreme Court argued that the promotion of economic development was a normal government function, and it upheld the right of states to require property owners to sell when officials decide that private development would provide public benefits (*Kelo v. City of New London*) (Lane 2005). This decision provoked much discussion about the relationship of private sector development to the public good and raised the consciousness of the American public about forced displacement.

Alongside public–private partnerships, completely private urban development, called gentrification, occurs piecemeal as individuals and developers buy houses, apartment buildings, and commercial establishments. For example, in Washington DC, young professionals move into neighborhoods radiating out from the central city, pushing out poorer residents, typically minorities (Mabeus 2005). Gentrification also occurs in developing countries; in Bamako, Mali, building owners tore down older structures as they renovated the central business district. Because much gentrification occurs incrementally, through individual action, it falls below the radar of policies. Laws may regulate sales, but the displaced rarely benefit from formal resettlement programs.

Much urban displacement takes place without international assistance, through the private sector, and in piecemeal fashion. When it pays little attention to effects on the displaced, it is usually rights violating. Nevertheless, some urban displacement does take into account the effects on the displaced; project planners attempt to design initiatives in light of DFDR policy guidelines. However, even these "best practice" efforts usually ignore major problems of the displaced. The rest of this chapter focuses on these efforts and the extent to which they address basic human rights and the reconstitution of livelihoods. Although a minority of urban resettlement initiatives, they illustrate the poor consequences of even the best urban DFDR.

DFDR POLICIES AND HUMAN RIGHTS

Urban DFDR is rights violating when it deprives people of the communities in which they have created livelihoods, social structures, and meaningful lives. At the same time, it has the potential to be rights affirming insofar as it assists people to move toward improved living conditions, including better food, shelter, and livelihoods (see chapter 4 by de Wet, this volume). Of particular relevance to urban DFDR are the rights based on Article 11(1) of the 1966 UN International Covenant on Economic, Social, and Cultural Rights, which recognizes the right to an adequate standard of living, including food, clothing, housing, and the continual improvement of living conditions (Barutciski 2006). In addition, the rights to life (Article 3) and to work (Article 23) in the Universal Declaration of Human Rights protect the right to livelihoods (Robinson 2003). To make infrastructure more compatible with human rights and sustainable development, Rajagopal (2000) has argued for an expanded interpretation of the right to development that includes self-determination and participation by local communities.

Urban DFDR can improve living conditions by offering services such as water, sanitation, transport, education, and public facilities; it can improve rights to livelihoods by increasing access to jobs, economic assets, and property. This thinking is congruent with World Bank policy, which mandates that the displaced "should be assisted in their efforts to improve their livelihoods and standards of living or at least to restore them" (World Bank 2001:par. 2[c]). These issues are also reflected in Cernea's risks and reconstruction model (2000a), which emphasizes action to address the risks of loss of land, jobs, and common property, as well as homes. W. Courtland Robinson (2003:13) added the loss of community services, essential to adequate living conditions.

Organizations and countries such as China and the Philippines have adopted guidelines to provide benefits to the displaced and to ensure rights-affirming rather than rights-violating resettlement (Meikle and Walker 1998). The 1995 policy of the Asian Development Bank was also instrumental in encouraging borrowers to develop resettlement plans that stressed livelihood restoration and the mitigation of social impacts (Agrawal 2000). For example, the draft guidelines of the Lao People's Democratic Republic stress the importance of improving or at least restoring livelihoods and income-earning opportunities for all whose living standards have been negatively impacted, whether or not they are physically displaced (Agrawal 2003:9, 25). Participation is emphasized, with special attention to vulnerable groups (Agrawal 2003:9). A separate section discusses the challenges of doing urban DFDR fairly and well.

Alongside policy changes, the activism and pressure of the displaced and potentially displaced have motivated governments to improve urban resettlement (Lomnitz 2003; Reddy 2000). With pressure coming from below and above, urban DFDR strategies have changed substantially, in many ways for the better, over the past ten or twenty years. Nevertheless, significant problems remain. This is largely because some rights (to housing and services) have been privileged over others (to livelihoods).

PRIORITIZING RIGHTS

Urban DFDR projects involve three categories of rights and reconstruction. First is adequate shelter: projects improve the substandard housing common in poor neighborhoods. Second, projects augment city services: electricity, water, sanitation, education, and health services usually are inadequate, even nonexistent, in spontaneous neighborhoods. Finally, projects address livelihood issues.

Urban DFDR: An Emphasis on Housing and Services

Urban DFDR is habitually defined simply as improved housing and is then given to a housing organization to implement. The Philippine National Housing Authority carried out DFDR throughout the country (Meikle and Walker 1998); Latin American urban resettlement often became subject to the standards of public housing programs (Mejía 1999:154). New housing must comply with legal requirements for titles, space, and infrastructure.

Rather than look for ways to reuse the land on which people already live, many projects look for inexpensive new parcels, generally in peripheral areas. Even if people already live in city centers, government agencies are usually reluctant to buy land there when cheaper land is available in larger parcels on the periphery. Other projects attempt to decrease costs by using "donated" government land for resettlement. In either case, the availability of inexpensive land, rather than an analysis of the needs of the displaced, dictates resettlement sites. Agencies also may use social concerns to justify peripheral locations, arguing that they can resettle entire communities together, conserving social groups to combat social disarticulation.

In-place urban renovation and extensive central-city resettlement usually require the reconfiguration of communities and changes in housing styles. Many slums are horizontally dense, with small substandard houses built on narrow streets lacking easements for sanitation and other services. Rebuilding according to regulations means that some people must move elsewhere or that horizontal density must be replaced by vertical density, usually multistory apartments. People sometimes resist these changes. When Lari (1982) worked with Karachi residents to create culturally appropriate, in-site resettlement, she argued against high-rises and created dense, small-scale housing. Nevertheless, many people who understand the trade-offs and options are willing to change housing styles. In the Pasig River Project in the Philippines, an apartment building was the first of five alternative sites to be occupied, because it allowed people to remain in metro-Manila (Agrawal 2000:5, 19). In the Mumbai Urban Transport Project, people also moved into multistory buildings; despite significant problems with resettlement, many people saw the opportunity to get even a small apartment as a way to improve social status (World Bank Inspection Panel 2005:226).

Once housing plans are decided, the issue of payment arises. Although some have argued that the resettled should not be required to pay for improved housing that they did not choose, others maintain that paying some housing costs increases the sense of ownership and capacity for self-management (Mejía 1999:157–158). However, decisions are often based on criteria other than what is best for the displaced. Many DFDR initiatives, aided by national governments, have tried to avoid giving what they consider "too many benefits" to the displaced and to avoid precedents for dealing with other "squatters" or "encroachers."

Although many resettled do get improved housing, it may come with a mortgage, based, at minimum, on the difference in value between old and new housing. In response, the involuntarily displaced have repeatedly rejected being forced to assume these new costs, primarily by not making monthly payments. In a Rio project, 70 percent of families resettled for more than one year were not making these payments (Mejía 1999:158). In the Philippines as well, many people were behind in their payments (Meikle and Walker 1998).

People are attracted to resettlement areas by the promise of highly desired new services, including clean water, electricity, sewage systems, and upgraded transport. Sometimes the proposed services arrive very late or not at all, and people find themselves no better off (Menon 2001; World Bank Inspection Panel 2005). Moreover, these new services must be paid for, creating new costs (Bartolomé 1993:127; Perlman 1982).

New living situations often mean that people must pay for services, such as child care, that they previously accessed as members of kin or friendship networks. Some also have new concerns about security when groups from different areas come together or when new developments are only partly finished. Those who keep old jobs in the city center have to spend more time and money to get to work. When residents of Rio's favelas (slums) were obliged to relocate in the 1960s, 65 percent had to commute more than an hour each day to get to old jobs (Perlman 1982:234).

More recently, relocatees to distant sites in the Philippines found themselves spending 10–30 percent of household income on commuting. Some decided to stay in the city during the week and come home on weekends, which increased housing costs and sometimes strained family relationships. To meet additional commuting expenses, some scrimped on education or food (Agrawal 2000:17–18).

The new expenditures faced by people in peripheral sites would be acceptable if their incomes went up as well, but instead, incomes generally decline. Many urban poor depend on informal sector employment and economic networks with people outside their communities. Moving usually ruptures those networks, leading to loss of jobs and clientele. Most particularly, informal sector jobs for women, essential for survival of poor families, decrease. Relocated people face declining real incomes at the same time as their expenses mount.

These deficiencies are linked to the definition of urban DFDR as housing and have been known at least since Perlman's (1982:233) classic work on favela removal in 1960s Rio de Janeiro, which demonstrated the impoverishing impact on those displaced. These consequences are now quite predictable, yet projects continue to move people to new housing developments in peripheral locations, citing lack of affordable land in more central areas as the reason. Although better housing can be seen as rights affirming, urban DFDR projects need to remember that urban resettlement is "more than just replacement housing" (Mejía 1999:182). Projects need to look at other rights as well, especially the right to livelihoods.

Livelihoods

The major issue in urban resettlement projects is that livelihood restoration has been ignored in practice, even though its importance has been recognized in theory. In part, this is because "restoring the livelihoods of people displaced in urban areas is one of the most complex tasks in resettlement" (Agrawal 2003:172). Urban populations have high population densities, with concentrated demands for goods, services, and land. People have diverse income levels, standards of living, and ethnic and regional affiliations. Using industrial and natural raw materials, they carry out formal and informal economic activities on sites with mixed land uses (Agrawal 2003:166). They face serious problems of pollution and waste disposal (Lusambili 2007). Faced with these complex systems, many urban projects focus on housing and either avoid economic reconstruction or pay lip service to it.

Livelihood restoration needs to start with an understanding of the existing economic systems of urban communities, especially those of the urban poor. The characteristics of urban economic systems have not been sufficiently recognized by planners who try to move whole neighborhoods to single new settlements; planners often use the model of the village, a residential community that may also be linked by kinship or common property ownership. To be sure, many urban neighborhoods, even slums, do have horizontal ties and a residential sense of community. Their daily routine culture includes socially constructed space and time in their neighborhoods (Downing 1996a; Downing and Garcia-Downing, chapter 11, this volume; Fried 1963). However, urban communities normally extend beyond residential areas and vertically integrate multiple classes.

Many urban residents who rely on informal sector activities depend upon links with other neighborhoods to earn adequate incomes. Some goods and services may be produced for neighbors, but many are targeted at classes with greater resources, as Perlman (1982) found in Rio in the late 1960s. More recently, in the Philippines, poorer residents did the laundry and collected garbage for people in more affluent neighborhoods; they also sold them food and other goods (Meikle and Walker 1998:50). In Latin America, the displaced sold tortillas in downtown offices and were tailors for government workers (Mejía 1999:177). In India, networks among women of different classes gave poorer women income-earning opportunities and complementary resources (Menon 2001). The interclass and interresidential networks upon which the poor depend are compromised when they move to urban peripheries.

Urban communities also have multiple forms of households. There are often substantial numbers of female-headed households, although the numbers can vary widely. In one Latin American project, 15 percent of households were female headed; in another, 66 percent of households were headed by women (Mejía 1999:163). If livelihoods analysis is rare, analysis of women's specific occupational needs, whether heads or members of households, appears to be even rarer. Women in one Brazilian project noted that they were not consulted on post-move income restoration (Tankha, Burtner, and Schmandt 1998). Menon (2001) noted the minimal role of gender in OD 4.30, the World Bank guidelines in force when she wrote her review; OP/BP 4.12 continues to identify women as a vulnerable group but no longer mentions women-headed households. There is no requirement for gender-disaggregated data, except indirectly through reference to household organization (World Bank 2001:Annex A, par. 6[a]ii). Nevertheless, income restoration strategies should consider all income earners.

Urban neighborhoods include people with different levels of human capital and assets; some are renters or boarders, and others own property or businesses (Dupont 2003; World Bank Inspection Panel 2005). Business owners, theoretically more advantaged, are typically ignored by resettlement planners. They suffer multiple costs but often receive minimal benefits. Infrastructure development affects their access to clients or supplies. Some vendors and shopkeepers have to move; merchants may lose customers. In some cases, businesses are technically illegal because they operate without appropriate licenses (Agrawal 2003:169; Meikle and Zhu 2000). Governments may offer the same rationale for not compensating them as they do those without regularized housing. Even when projects are willing to compensate businesses, owners may find it difficult to estimate potential losses (Agrawal 2003:62), and business owners may not be compensated for a move from a prime location to a more peripheral one (Meikle and Walker 1998:29). Proximity to other businesses; accessibility to clients, raw materials, and supplies; and location are all important for business survival (Agrawal 2003:169), so business owners who are not required to move may still find that their means of earning are seriously compromised. Policies may explicitly take them into account (for example, Agrawal 2003), but in the projects reviewed, there was little evidence of planning to reconstitute their livelihoods.

Sometimes businesses are promised improvements from infrastructure development. They are told that the problems they are facing are temporary, that after construction is over, they will have access to better facilities or more clientele. But small businesses typically operate on tight margins. US newspapers carry stories of merchants negatively impacted by infrastructure construction that blocks access to them. These stories raise the question of whether businesses will survive to benefit from planned improvements. Even if businesses are offered alternative locations, owners may face higher rent or other overhead charges. Improvements that lead to property appreciation may negatively affect them through higher taxes or rents (Agrawal 2003).

Local customers, whether or not displaced, also suffer from problems when businesses are affected by DFDR. To forestall future losses, business owners may close enterprises when they hear of potential resettlement (Tankha, Burtner, and Schmandt 1998). Bartolomé (1984:189) noted that the very announcement of potential resettlement led store owners to deny credit to customers because they feared default. Residents employed by local businesses may lose jobs.

Even if the first and best option for reconstituting the livelihoods of the urban displaced is to look for housing options that enable them to conserve employment, economic resources, and social support networks, projects still need to analyze economic issues directly and formulate plans for income restoration. The issue of jobs and entrepreneurship opportunities for relocated residents needs to be explicitly addressed. Although many policy documents recognize the problems, urban projects that directly address economic issues seem to be rare. In addition, recent guidelines decrease attention to specifically urban issues, even as urban DFDR is increasing. For example, the neoliberal strategy of reliance on market mechanisms has meant less attention to jobs in the most recent World Bank policy. The previous policy, OD 4.30, noted the importance of culturally acceptable income-earning strategies and incentives for firms to locate in resettlement areas, but there is little attention to employment and income earning in OP/BP 4.12 (World Bank 1990, 2001). OD 4.30 states:

> The resettlement plan should, where feasible, exploit new economic activities made possible by the main investment requiring the displacement. Vocational training, employment counseling, transportation to jobs, employment in the main investment project or in resettlement activities, establishment of industries, incentives for firms to locate in the area, credit and extension for small businesses or reservoir aquaculture, and preference in public sector employment should all be considered where appropriate. [World Bank 1990:par. 18]

This has decreased substantially in OP/BP 4.12, which only perfunctorily mentions training and job opportunities (World Bank 2001:par. 6[c]ii).

Other policies show the same trends. The 1994 revised Orissa (India) water resources policy dropped provisions for mandatory or preferential employment, which Pandey (1998a:20) considered to be "completely out of tune" with its otherwise progressive changes. In China, when the state was the universal employer, state-owned enterprises would take on the displaced when rural residents were resettled to urban areas (Meikle and Zhu 2000:134). Now, jobs for the displaced must be found through the private job market because even state-owned enterprises strive for economic efficiency (Meikle and Zhu 2000).

To be sure, strategies for preferential employment for the displaced were not always successful. For example, policies that offered jobs to those displaced by mines were criticized on a variety of grounds. Not all resettlers benefited; the policy tended to favor men; many of the jobs offered little social mobility (Menon 2001; Pandey 1998a; Robinson 1986). In the

Philippines, when one project trained resettlers for work in new factories, most remained unemployed because employers had very strict selection criteria (Meikle and Walker 1998:50).

For people to take advantage of new opportunities, they usually need skills upgrading, entrepreneurship development, and leadership training (Agrawal 2003:85). Those who want to start businesses also need access to credit. Because training does not automatically lead to gainful employment or enhancement of household incomes, programs also need to build people's capacity for technology transfer and to enhance their management skills (Agrawal 2003:87).

Overall, there is still insufficient attention to the reconstitution of livelihoods in urban DFDR projects. Even though analysts have known that the urban displaced typically become impoverished because their economic and social support systems are demolished, little has been done to improve outcomes. Urban DFDR projects need to address more directly the problems of economic reconstruction and to do so in the context of comprehensive urban planning. They need to pay as much attention to the right to livelihood as they do to the rights to housing and improved living conditions. They need to pay as much attention to the risk of joblessness and loss of access to economic resources as they do to the loss of housing and to social disintegration.

TOWARD BETTER URBAN DFDR

The first step to improving urban DFDR is to take seriously basic issues already learned from rural DFDR. Reconstruction is not possible without paying attention to the economy; the risks of economic loss, especially joblessness, need to be targeted. People who lose jobs or businesses and those affected without being displaced merit more attention. Planning needs to embrace all three categories of rights—to livelihoods, to housing, and to improved living conditions.

Understanding Urban Economies

The first step in better urban DFDR is to develop a more comprehensive understanding of urban economic systems. Just as rural resettlement gained from links to regional rural development, so, too, urban initiatives need to be planned in light of regional urban planning and development efforts. Without a doubt, urban DFDR should include resettlement specialists, but projects also need urban planners and social analysts.

The frame of reference should include the entire metropolitan area to facilitate coupling DFDR with plans for job creation and economic development. Urban resettlement planners should be familiar with the extensive literature on urban development, planning, and gentrification. For example, some literature suggests that planned urban-development areas can be magnets for spontaneous migration. In outer Delhi, the new industrial center of Noida (an acronym for New Oklha Industrial Development Authority), created in 1976, grew rapidly through the 1980s and 1990s as people flocked to its residential neighborhoods. About half the inhabitants in the housing developments worked in Noida; the rest continued to commute to Delhi proper. At the same time, jobs in Noida attracted new immigrants, who created new neighborhoods close to their jobs (Dupont 2003). DFDR may be linked to planned industrial development. For example, the Pecem Industrial and Port Complex near Fortaleza, Brazil, included an export processing zone and factories. In this case, the complex displaced a primarily rural population. The coordination of industrial or commercial development with the infrastructure displacing urban residents appears to be relatively rare, and policies do not encourage planners to think in this direction.

The idea that comprehensive regional development will enhance DFDR outcomes is not new. In the 1980s Scudder (1981a) emphasized the importance of regional economic growth in resettlement zones; planners need to understand how the zone is likely to grow and to look for ways of deliberately integrating relocatees into new sustainable opportunities. More recently, Agrawal (2003:169) has emphasized the importance of looking at urban DFDR in the context of urban development and land use planning, including zoning, markets, roads, transport, and services. New settlements need areas for commerce, artisanal production, and industry, as well as residential areas (Agrawal 2003:173).

Planners need to realize that residents with increased incomes and thriving businesses provide a better tax base than do impoverished inhabitants. In fact, some urban development specialists have argued that providing both jobs and housing for poorer urban residents is precisely what is needed to reinvigorate cities and enhance urban life. In an online discussion of the *Kelo v. City of New London* decision, J. Peter Byrne (2005) noted that job creation can help the urban poor and municipal governments by increasing the tax revenues that support urban schools and other essential public services. In this sense, planned urban development should be seen as an investment in the displaced and relocated, rather than as a transfer payment to them.

Planning for urban development needs to be participatory, a lesson learned from rural DFDR. In Brazil, at the Castanhão Dam, a new city

(Nova Jaguaribara) was planned consultatively with displaced urban residents, but this kind of urban planning has been uncommon. Lack of participation leads to results that planners usually try to avoid, especially resistance through demonstrations, protests, and court action, which usually lead to higher costs. Mejía (1999:170, 171) noted that actual costs were frequently 300 to 400 percent higher than the initial estimates in a sample of Latin American projects because projects that paid inadequate attention to social context had to spend time and money to respond to unanticipated events and consequences. Even in Chinese projects, some of the best planned in a technical sense, local officials often had to change programs to address new problems (Meikle and Walker 1998). Like rural projects, urban initiatives need to adopt more participatory and incremental planning and strategies of benefit sharing to help address unanticipated outcomes and costs.

Although urban DFDR can learn from rural experiences, it faces the particular challenges of working in high-density urban situations, where people and information are highly mobile. To meet these challenges, urban DFDR should build on urban heterogeneity and activism.

Building on Heterogeneity

Displaced urban neighborhoods can be economically and socially heterogeneous, even when they appear poor. Incomes of the displaced are highly varied in both amount and structure; houses range in quality of construction and size; family sizes are diverse. However, the complexity of viable urban economic systems is usually poorly reflected in resettlement policies and plans (Mejía 1999:163), except when resettlement organizations use divergent interests to fragment resistance and facilitate their own goals. Commonly, urban rehabilitation projects target only the very poor and recognized vulnerable groups. Those with more assets may receive compensation but are not eligible for additional project benefits. Sometimes this has led wealthier individuals simply to leave (Tankha, Burtner, and Schmandt 1998), compromising the organic structure of urban neighborhoods and leaving a population with more limited resources and skills. As noted, the settlement of the poor in homogeneous, peripheral neighborhoods compromises beneficial social networks with more affluent urban residents.

Instead of ignoring community heterogeneity and the potential conflicts of interest among groups, urban DFDR projects should embrace and build upon the diversity of urban populations to create more economically and socially sustainable forms of urban reconstruction. For example, it may be worth offering incentives to affected business owners to encourage them to relocate in resettlement areas. The present focus on micro-enterprises should be complemented by strategies to assist medium-scale businesses, which are better able to take advantage of economies of scale and resist economic cycles. These employers may also offer more employee benefits, such as pensions and health insurance. In some cases, medium-scale businesses have provided significant opportunities. In China, for example, medium-scale town and village enterprises have provided employment for the displaced (Meikle and Walker 1998).

Planning for housing should be linked to economic planning; carrying these out together may help solve some of the problems associated with high land costs. Multi-use sites have been suggested as a way to gain acceptance of in-place resettlement by governments and private developers. A Karachi urban development scheme planned to auction off some of the more valuable land on the site to private developers to generate funds to pay for new housing (Lari 1982). Yet, this strategy may meet resistance. When a substandard rental complex in Washington DC tried to get funding to create a tenant-owned cooperative, it first proposed selling one of the three buildings at market rate to generate funds to renovate the others for low-income housing. The city would not support this approach. Residents were ultimately able to create affordable housing in all three buildings but faced greater financial challenges than if they had been able to sell one (Wilgoren 2005).

Even with innovative housing strategies, it is usually difficult to settle entire neighborhoods in one urban area. At the same time, some may not want to make the changes required to live at high density and would prefer to move to less densely populated neighborhoods. In the Karachi scheme, people were offered a second option of moving to a new development with more spacious housing (Lari 1982:61). Multiple options, instead of a single choice, better reflect urban residents' attitudes toward place. Some urban residents may echo the place attachment found in many rural communities, especially when several generations have lived in a neighborhood (Fried 1963). In developing countries where recent urban growth has been the norm, however, the "fondly remembered childhood places" (Downing 1996a:40) that orient people's identities are usually elsewhere. Moreover, urban residents often move spontaneously with the hope of bettering their lives. Place attachment can be quite variable in urban situations, with some strongly attached and others less so (Fried 1963).

Another aspect of urban heterogeneity and density is the wide array of public and private organizations. For example, one Brazilian initiative involved fourteen state agencies (Tankha, Burtner, and Schmandt 1998:10). Chinese resettlement documents also present long lists of involved agencies (for example, HPPO 2001). Judged by the documents reviewed for this chapter, even impoverished urban areas may have access to many existing programs. Clearly, urban projects need to confront the many coordinating and organizational issues discussed by Rew, Fisher, and Pandey (2000), including weak institutions and lack of interagency coordination. Local governments responsible for providing services to resettlers may not have the budget or the training to cope with their new responsibilities in a timely manner (Meikle and Walker 1998). Comprehensive urban planning is needed not only to address the needs of heterogeneous displaced populations but also to coordinate and take advantage of the many organizations present.

Building on Activism

Critics are likely to argue that a more comprehensive approach to urban resettlement will be dauntingly expensive. Yet, as noted, the costs of urban DFDR are already problematic, in part because of the high level of activism to resist urban displacement. When DFDR organizations try to keep information from reaching the public because they fear public reaction, the public responds instead to rumors, which arise quickly in the dense urban context. Whether in response to inaccurate rumors or actual intentions, resistance is common because people do not want to be forced to move.

Urban resistance groups may organize quickly because they build on the organizations that urban communities already use to manage their lives (Mejía 1999:152). Community-based organizations (CBOs), often with prior experience, have worked with NGOs and community organizers to resist urban DFDR in both developed and developing countries. This activism can stop, delay, or change planned infrastructure development.

Sometimes urban activism completely halts projects interpreted as rights violating. For example, activists in Washington DC waged a twenty-two-year battle to stop freeway construction (Levey and Levey 2000). Resistance began in African American neighborhoods with protests organized by people experienced in the civil rights movement and union organizing. At the same time, groups from white neighborhoods took other parts of the plan to the courts. Over time, the different groups created an effective alliance, combining street protests with court actions and emphasizing the disproportionate effect on African American neighborhoods, arguing against "White Men's Roads through Black Men's Homes." Most of the planned freeways were eventually dropped, and funds were put into public transport after the US District Court ruled that proper planning procedures had not been followed and "local voices had not been adequately heard" (Levey and Levey 2000:24).

Smaller organizations rarely stop projects, but they can improve benefits for particular groups. In the Philippines, one people's organization negotiated with the Public Estates Authority to get rights to in-place lots; in other cases, resistance to demands improved compensation packages, sometimes substantially (Meikle and Walker 1998:52, 72). In Kenya, a local NGO working with Oxfam was able to procure a settlement for residents impacted by a road (Oxfam 1996:29).

Local activists have built on widely varying forms of organization and traditions. In communities affected by Brazil's Castanhão Dam, resistance galvanized a group that had previously worked with a Catholic nun to increase the wages of local teachers and to implement a cadastre of the city and its surrounding communities (Tankha, Burtner, and Schmandt 1998). When the group heard about the dam, it procured an audience with the governor, during which residents stressed their opposition. They also sought assistance from MAB, a pan-Brazilian anti-dam movement. The group ultimately negotiated 300 sq km for a new city with better infrastructure; members participated in its design and in a general stakeholders' group that consulted on resettlement issues.

As these examples show, strategic local activism, combined with coalitions and alliances, has the potential to stop projects or bring about substantial design changes. The alliances are sometimes unexpected when disparate groups focus on common goals. For example, opponents to New London, Connecticut's urban plans included libertarian property-rights activists and advocates for elderly and low-income residents who feared dispossession (Lane 2005). The ability of resisting groups to combine popular action such as demonstrations with the use of official channels such as the courts or public hearings increases the likelihood of making an impact. Although resettlement organizations are tempted to avoid participation because it can be time-intensive, expensive, and logistically cumbersome (Agrawal 2003:105), these examples show that the lack of transparency, consultation, and participation hinders urban resettlement by pushing resistance to the streets and the courts, leading to delays, cost overruns, and even cancellation.

In contrast, when resettlement agencies involve activists from the beginning, their organizations can facilitate approaches to reconstruction that better serve the needs of the displaced. For example, post-apartheid South Africa faced a challenge to improve housing and amenities for those, especially black South Africans, in informal and squatter housing in urban townships. Among other strategies, the government offered subsidies to construct housing in or near existing neighborhoods. When the subsidies proved insufficient, the government, building on new South African ideals of participation and citizen representation, encouraged NGOs to work with local groups to enhance available funding. Local NGOs in metropolitan Capetown created community-based housing projects in which local groups used peer lending to create savings funds to build houses. Self-selected small groups, with approximately ten participants each, had access, in turn, to funds they saved; group members also provided sweat equity on one another's houses. Groups hired local builders instead of large-scale developers, increasing local employment (Greene 2002). This strategy, which took the time needed to build trust among group members, maximized participation. It may not work when infrastructure displaces many at a single time, but it could be adapted to some urban situations.

Participation can also involve multiple stakeholders. Brazil has experimented with what it calls Multiparticipatory Groups (Tankha, Burtner, and Schmandt 1998). These organizations, created by the administration, bring together all major stakeholders, from government agencies to community members. Although these groups did not resolve all the issues between the community and the government, they were important players when problems were resolved (Tankha, Burtner, and Schmandt 1998:15). The organizations sometimes evolved into forums for treating issues beyond resettlement and rehabilitation.

Participation in local organizations to resist DFDR repeatedly brings progressive changes to communities even when the communities do not substantially change DFDR plans. Interracial cooperation grew among Washington DC freeway activists and among participants in the Harrison–Halsted Community Group, a neighborhood coalition that unsuccessfully fought urban renewal on Chicago's Near West Side (Suttles 1968). Women have also increased their skills. The Harrison–Halsted Community Group was led by Florence Scala, who served as a model for other women to take community leadership roles (Squires et al. 1987). As noted, the major community organizer at Castanhão was a nun. Women came to the Multiparticipatory Group meetings and raised issues important to them, such as dependent care and public safety (Tankha, Burtner, and Schmandt 1998). Women in Capetown's community housing projects increased their knowledge of building materials and technologies and gained construction skills. They also learned how to enhance their legal rights to housing by regularizing relationships with male partners (Greene 2002). Within urban resettlement, women often act and are perceived as competent political actors, even if their economic roles receive insufficient attention.

When planning is not participatory and implementing agencies do not take into account the interests and desires of those who will be displaced, urban resettlement becomes rights violating, even if there are rights-affirming aspects to it. Urban resettlement needs to respect the policy emphasis on transparency, the publication of accurate information, and the involvement of NGOs and CBOs as partners in participatory resettlement (World Bank 2001:pars. 14, 19, 22).[2] Participatory resettlement must be allowed to mature organically; it cannot be entirely structured, thoroughly planned, or politically stage-managed (Agrawal 2003:105). An initial investment in time and resources for shared decision making has the potential to create more acceptable projects that run smoothly over the long term. To become rights affirming rather than rights violating, urban resettlement needs to build on local activism rather than try to sidestep it.

CONCLUSION

The first step in improving urban DFDR involves taking the existing guidelines seriously, especially the need to avoid resettlement where possible, and understanding the importance of economic reconstruction, respect for the rights of those without formal tenure, and the consequences for those affected but not physically displaced. Many existing urban-resettlement projects have not done this. People are displaced without any consideration for in-place resettlement; many of those defined as squatters or illegals are summarily evicted; businesses whose owners do not move are typically ignored; and urban resettlement is defined as housing instead of economic reconstruction.

Although existing guidelines are useful, they are insufficient because of implicit biases toward rural resettlement. They do not pay attention to significant aspects of urban living. Some urban residents do make their living from land or common property resources, but many more depend on jobs or their own entrepreneurial skills. Existing guidelines inadequately address job-based reconstruction. Displaced urban populations tend to be more economically, socially, and culturally diverse than resettled rural groups. Urban populations are dense and well organized, and communication flow is relatively easy. Activist organizations quickly recruit participants, politicizing urban resettlement more quickly and more completely. Although many resettlement projects recognize this diversity and activism, they do little to harness it for reconstruction. It is seen as a problem rather than as a chance for sustainable development based on complementary resources.

Urban resettlement offers the opportunity to move beyond development-bank framing of DFDR toward a more systematic understanding of urban growth and change through comparison of worldwide initiatives, from completely private, household-by-household gentrification, to formal urban-reconstruction projects, to political eviction of shantytowns. Action for enhancing urban DFDR needs to go beyond formal project frameworks and involve citizens of both developed and developing countries. Because many aspects of urban resettlement have the potential to be rights affirming by offering the displaced improved living conditions and better livelihoods, transparency and true participation have the potential to lead toward more equitable development. Involuntary resettlement will always have the potential to be rights violating, but a more focused approach to understanding urban DFDR should enable us to find ways to increase its rights-affirming aspects, moving toward better lives for the poor.

Acknowledgments

I would like to thank Jacqualine Reid, Ana Yu Ching Hsu, and Rebecca Frischkorn, research assistants for this project.

Notes

1. Many governments realistically fear new squatter invasions when existing residents are moved as part of upgrading plans; in India, attempts to regularize illegal squatter colonies encouraged the establishment of new ones (Dupont 2003). Others move into zones specifically to get project entitlements (Mejía 1999), one factor in government reluctance to assist those without legal tenure. Even progressive approaches to urban resettlement stress the importance of doing an early census of residents and establishing a clear cut-off date for project entitlements (Agrawal 2003).

2. It is important to involve NGOs and CBOs, but their involvement does not ensure the necessary skills or the desired participation. In the Mumbai Urban Transport Project, several NGOs were contracted to carry out feasibility studies and major implementation activities. They had experience working with local slum dwellers, but neither sufficient staff nor technical skills to do the required tasks. Some praised the earlier organizing work done by these NGOs, but others accused them of collaborating with municipal authorities when they should have been protesting (D'Monte 2005; Panchal 2005; World Bank Inspection Panel 2005).

7

Evicted from Eden

Conservation and the Displacement of Indigenous and Traditional Peoples

Anthony Oliver-Smith

When a new national park or wildlife reserve is established, the press releases tend to evoke images of the rescue of pristine nature and the protection of imposing and noble species like the sequoia or the jaguar from the ravages of human greed and growth. Human beings have been frequently portrayed as destructive interlopers in a purely "natural" environment in which they have no place. This tension between human beings and nature has deep cultural roots in the West, often manifesting in the displacement of indigenous and other traditional peoples from their homelands by large-scale conservation projects, especially national parks, wildlife preserves, biosphere reserves, and other protected areas. Dubbed "Fortress Conservation," such efforts are posited on an alleged incompatibility between human use and sustainable biodiversity (Brockington 2002). As more and more land is given protected status, traditional and indigenous communities join the millions of people displaced by development projects.

It could be contended that conservation is not a form of development, because it seeks to conserve rather than change. But conservation becomes a development strategy when it is invoked in discourses of sustainable development and the valorizing of resources and environments for their contribution to natural cycles of renewability, as well as their economic value as natural resources and ecotourism attractions. It could also be contended that such "protected" environments are immune from exploitation. But this has not always been the case (Osun 1999).

Conservation-forced displacement and resettlement (CFDR) shares some important commonalities with development-forced displacement and resettlement (DFDR). First, the record of success in DFDR is poor, and in CFDR, poorly documented. The few CFDR cases for which we have information, however, tell us that the situation mirrors that of DFDR (Agrawal and Redford 2007:8). The projects in both instances have not always achieved their goals or the successful resettlement of the affected populations. For example, dams have not always generated the electricity or the irrigation water for which they were designed. Conservation projects, though successfully limiting deforestation in protected areas (Naughton-Treves, Holland, and Brandon 2005), have undermined biodiversity in zones surrounding protected areas or in the areas where people are resettled (Colchester 1994:15). Fabricius and de Wet (2002:145) maintain that forced eviction in South Africa actually undermined conservation efforts, contributing to unsustainable resource use outside protected areas, local hostility toward conservation efforts, and more poaching, vandalism, and land invasions. Also, the limitations imposed on local people by conservation projects and the state's withdrawal of human services (in establishing a national park) may force locals to abandon their territory, a form of "soft eviction" (Adamson 2003). Most recently, Hayes (2006:2066) contended that there is little evidence to support the claim that parks are necessary to conserve biodiversity. Similarly, Agrawal and Redford (2007:9) found it difficult to establish the extent to which protected areas involving displacement have advanced biodiversity conservation.

Project implementers often consider CFDR and DFDR burdensome tasks, part of the "cost of doing business" in the more important development and conservation projects. Therefore, projects tend to be poorly conceptualized, planned, and implemented, resulting in the impoverishment of the affected peoples. The poor planning and implementation in both CFDR and DFDR are often due to a lack of rigorous research and accurate quantitative and qualitative information about the affected population. CFDR does not even require social impact assessments or cost-benefit analyses, integral elements in assessing the viability of DFDR projects, however dubious their application or utility may be (Agrawal and Redford 2007:10). DFDR and CFDR projects may also include a variety of covert and not-so-covert agendas beyond their stated goals of energy generation or conservation, such as population control, land acquisition, or resource access (Bridgeland 2005). Finally, DFDR and CFDR projects have, in some cases, been developed and carried out with blatantly racist agendas, often expressed in assimilationist goals to enhance control over people considered outside the mainstream (Hitchcock 2001). Like many development projects, conservation projects often express national, local, class, and ethnic power inequalities.

Conservation-forced displacement involves fundamental questions that have long concerned anthropology, as well as society in general: Is humanity truly distinct from nature? In other words, are human beings part of nature, or are they separate, occupying an external position as observers and actors upon nature? Is there now, or has there ever been, a "pristine" nature, totally unaffected by humanity? Do the cultural differences among various peoples produce qualitatively different relationships with nature? Are some people (and cultures) better suited than others to serve as custodians of nature? What is the nature of rights (property) over nature? What is the value of nature? What is the role of land (nature) in the construction of cultural identity, particularly indigenous identity? These and other questions are interwoven in both the description and the analysis of conservation-forced displacement and resettlement.

As noted, many values that have inspired conservation and CFDR are deeply rooted in Western society. In their most recent expression, the need for the conservation of nature has acquired a scientific basis. Often referred to as the biodiversity crisis, the need for conservation is based on two fundamental axioms of ecological and evolutionary biology, and the foundations of all modern ecology and evolutionary biology rest, in part, on the consequences of these. The first axiom is that organisms are exuberantly overproductive. The second axiom is that space, time, and energy inevitably set limits. In other words, populations have the inherent propensity to grow exponentially, inevitably reaching or exceeding the limits of their external environment (Holling 1994).

As Holling pointedly asks, then why has the world not fallen apart? The answer lies in a third axiom, concerning the processes that generate variability and novelty, salvaging the position from a crude Malthusianism. The continual propagation of variation in species attributes provides the source for continual experimentation in an environment that, itself, is constantly changing. Through variability, nature achieves the resilience and capacity to adapt to internally and externally induced change. However, this variability is now being impacted by human-induced environmental destruction, triggering what has become known as the biodiversity crisis and endangering the renewability cycles of local and global ecosystems (Holling

1994). Survival of natural ecosystems (and therefore life itself) depends on the continuity of variability in floral and faunal species and the ecological systems that support them. Diversity is the foundation of the adaptation that enables life to evolve in changing circumstances. The loss of biodiversity profoundly threatens the sustainability of global ecological systems.

Habitat destruction by many forces and groups, mostly originating from the industrialized world, is proceeding at a frightening pace. Traditional and indigenous people—a source of cultural diversity in themselves because of their residence in areas rich in biodiversity—are frequently blamed for this loss. Indeed, the process of indigenous removal from desired lands and their resources has been underway for at least five centuries. Today, many indigenous and traditional peoples face either eviction from or severely curtailed use of the natural environments in which they have lived for generations. They have been judged a threat to the continued repro-duction of their environments. The policies of declaring and implement-ing national parks and the failure (of those who impose these policies) to take the appropriate steps to compensate losses and restore communities impose enormous risks of impoverishment upon these indigenous and tra-ditional peoples (Cernea and Schmidt-Soltau 2006). Displacement for any group can be a crushing blow. For indigenous peoples, it can prove mor-tal. Land tenure is essential to the survival of indigenous societies and their distinctive cultural identities. According to the International Covenant on the Rights of Indigenous Nations, the terms "*land, territory,* and *place* mean the total environment of land space, soil, water, sea, sea-ice, sky, flora and fauna, and other resources which indigenous people use historically and on which they continue to depend to sustain and evolve their culture" (CWIS 1994; Bolaños 2008).

A POLITICAL ECOLOGY OF CONSERVATION

Although the need to conserve biodiversity is scientifically justified, the various forms of intervention it has taken are as deeply embedded in the history and ideology of Western cultural constructs of nature and society as they are in science. Conservation involves the human relationship to an environment and its resources, as well as human rights to these—in other words, how we use an environment. Therefore, exploring the displacement of people by protected areas falls under the rubric of political ecology. As a field, political ecology emerged partly in reaction to cultural ecology and its emphasis on the internal, homeostatic processes of local systems. Political ecologists asserted that far more than local dynamics are key to understanding human–environment relations. Conversely, in spatially defining protected areas, conservation implicitly concerns itself with local dynamics (Mulder and Coppolillo 2005).

Therefore, equally subject to analysis are indigenous peoples and peasants in the local context and national governments and international conservation and development organizations in global capitals. In particular, class, ethnicity, race, and gender play key roles in the disposition of resource access (Wilshusen 2003). Political ecology largely focuses on conflicts over rights of access to resources and environments, as well as ownership and disposition of these, among groups widely differing in sociocultural identity and economic adaptation. These conflicts produce a "fractal" politics in which the different participants (as allies, opponents, and mediators) interact across various scales of space and time (Little 1999). This interaction encompasses the transnationally allied activities of GROs (grassroots organizations), NGOs (nongovernmental organizations), social movements, lawyers, courts, corporations, and multilateral organizations. It affects and is also affected by global and national politics dealing with normative issues of human rights and the environment (Oliver-Smith 1996, 2006; see Fisher, chapter 8, this volume).

In conservation, although the stakes may be expressed in terms of biodiversity or sustainability, the fundamental issue is the political contestation over rights to a place or to its resources. The conservationist perspective, however, is far from monolithic. The ethic of conservation is interpreted and applied in different ways by many types of interests, some transparent and others much less so. Biocentric or ecocentric philosophies claiming an intrinsic value of nature, including Deep Ecology, Bioregionalism, Biophilia, the Gaia hypothesis, and spiritual ecology, vie with more utilitarian, anthropocentric approaches emphasizing the goods and services provided by nature. Several authors employ the larger rubric of environmentalism and then break it down into conservationists and preservationists, the former protecting nature as a resource *for* human use and the latter protecting nature *from* human use (Meffe and Carroll 1997:179; Milton 1996:74). The conservationist approach is perceived as more dynamic and evolutionary because it permits human influences on environments to be conserved. The preservationist approach emphasizes stability and excludes normal evolutionary processes (Meffe and Carroll 1997:179). This distinction is only the first of many among the broad array of perspectives and strategies concerning the protection of nature: from national parks, national monuments, wilderness areas, strict nature reserves, habitat/species management areas, protected landscape/seascape, and managed resource protected areas (Mulder and Coppolillo 2005:31), to the proliferation of private sector conservation forms such as formal parks, ecotourism reserves, biological stations, NGO reserves, hunting reserves, and corporate reserves (Langholz 2003:120–121).

Many of these categories reveal deeply rooted cultural values regarding the relationship between humans and nature, which might not be universally shared by resident populations. The areas to be protected under these mechanisms exist in environments that are also very diverse. The World Wildlife Fund (WWF) in 2000 developed an approach to conservation based on the idea of the ecoregion, which was to become the basic unit for conservation. The WWF mapped approximately nine hundred ecoregions around the world, designating 238 to be of great importance for biological diversity. In collaboration with the international NGO Terralingua, these high-biodiversity ecoregions were cross-mapped with indigenous, tribal, and traditional peoples, revealing a strong correlation between biodiversity and cultural diversity (WWF and Terralingua 2000:1).

The significance of this correlation is debated. Some argue that the correlation points to the sustainability of traditional ecological practice (Oviedo, Maffi, and Larsen 2000:11), positing a kind of "double diversity" based on the mutual reinforcement between cultural and biological variation. Many argue that, over the years, indigenous peoples have developed ways of life that are sustainable within their environments, making them the best custodians of nature. The fact that many environments occupied by indigenous peoples are far less degraded than nearby contexts exploited by non-indigenous groups is frequently noted to substantiate their capabilities to care for nature (Colchester 1994:25). Traditional ecological knowledge (TEK) is often underscored as an important resource for the implementation of conservation projects (Chapin 1990:3). Interestingly, recent archeological research in the Amazon reveals that pre-Columbian population densities, settlement patterns, and landscape transformations were much more extensive than has been portrayed. Far from being a "pristine" natural environment, the Amazon was evidently a deeply affected cultural landscape in the pre-Columbian era that, nevertheless, did not endanger biodiversity (Heckenberger et al. 2003). Moreover, the subsequent forest recovery from such large-scale transformations conforms to Holling's understanding of resilient nature rather than to nature in a delicate balance, unable to rebound from human impacts (Stokstad 2003: 1646). The key issue would seem to be that pre-Columbian Amazonian populations, dense as they appear to have been, did not impair the basic variability and diversity necessary for adaptation.

Other researchers are less sure, noting that traditional peoples historically have been responsible for habitat degradation and species extinction in certain circumstances (Redford 1992). Interpreting an ethic of conservation and sustainability in indigenous religion and economic practice is also a very subjective undertaking (Colchester 1994:27). It is clear that indigenous peoples and conservationists view the environment differently and have very different agendas regarding its use. Most indigenous and traditional peoples do not view the environment as wilderness, nor do they have an explicit conservationist ethic. Instead, there is often a view of the environment as giving, engaged in a reciprocity with people that they must recognize and to which they must respond (Bird-David 1990). Instead of being purposefully conservationist, their systems achieve a balance with nature through the functioning of political systems, settlement patterns, and social segmentation that reduce population pressure and keep local populations from endangering carrying capacity (Colchester 1994:27).

Indigenous societies around the world, however, are experiencing significant and rapid change. Greater population densities and loss of traditional territories are upsetting their customary relationship with nature (Colchester 1994:26). Many indigenous and traditional peoples find their lands invaded by other marginalized populations, who may have experienced displacement, thus increasing population densities (Lohmann 1999). New technologies coupled with new demands occasioned by increased contact with and integration into regional, national, and international markets have intensified the impact of local populations on their environments. Increased contact with dominant societies has created new perceptions, values, and needs that endanger both traditional environmental knowledge and the sustainability of local populations' interaction with the environment. The debate continues currently and remains far from resolved. Nonetheless, the correlation between high biodiversity and high cultural diversity brings many indigenous and traditional peoples into a relationship with the interests and organizations concerned with conservation, a relationship that involves potentially conflicting understandings of the rights that human beings have over an environment and its resources.

THE SOCIAL AND IDEOLOGICAL FOUNDATIONS OF CONSERVATION

The evolution of the conservation movement is too detailed to discuss adequately here, but a few broad trends are useful to note for understanding the movement's complex relationship with indigenous and traditional peoples. Although the idea of a nature preserve is traced to royal hunting preserves and the English enclosure movement (Igoe 2004), the eigh-teenth-century construction of two particular categories, wilderness and tropicality, played a particularly significant role in the application of this model of human–environment relations.[1] Despite eighteenth-century con-cepts of wilderness as barren, savage, and desolate, by the end of the nine-teenth century, wilderness had become viewed as sublime and sacred, an opportunity to glimpse the hand of God. Following closely on the Indian wars, demands for the protection of wilderness sites resulted in a move-ment to create national parks and wilderness areas from which all people, particularly native people, had been removed (Cronon 1995).

A similar process drove the idea of "tropicality." Commencing with images of fertility and exuberance, the notion of tropicality attracted painters and writers to represent these regions also as Eden but, again, remarkably free of people. In the nineteenth century, the actual experi-ences of Europeans in tropical zones shifted these representations away from the idyllic to the dangerous and corrupt. The climate now became physically and morally unhealthy for Europeans. Natives were seen as sloth-ful and incapable of civilized behavior. These characterizations came to embody constructions of the tropics and tropical people as disordered, wasteful, unhealthy (Arnold 1996).

Contemporary imagery and attitudes toward nature—whether glossed as wilderness or tropicality, underexploited or uninhabited—owe much to these nineteenth-century ideas. They are refracted into development poli-cies that aim to order nature for human use and also to assimilate the peo-ple of these regions into national logics. As Colchester and Gray note, the logic of contemporary development regarding nature produces an inter-esting duality. On the one hand, nature must be protected from the rapac-ity of human beings; on the other, it must be sacrificed for the goals of development (Colchester and Gray 1999:301).

Confronting these images and accompanying norms for action toward nature are innumerable alternative constructions of nature held by the enormous variety of peoples around the world (Surrallés and García Hierro 2005). Despite difficulty in generalizing, it is usually accepted that many indigenous and traditional cultures do not hold with the dichotomy between nature and society that has undergirded Western economic posi-tions regarding nature. Moreover, local models do not separate strictly the biophysical, human, and supernatural worlds but rather pose a continuity among the three, which is established through ritual and symbol and is embedded in social relations. In general, local models of nature are com-plexes of meanings and usages that cannot be rendered intelligible through modern constructions, nor understood without reference to local culture and place (Escobar 2001:151).

The construction of the category "wilderness," in particular, was key in the emergence of a conservation policy and the development of the national park model in the United States. A national park was considered to be a large area generally unaltered by human exploitation and occupation, and its flora, fauna, and geomorphology, of great scientific, educational, and aesthetic value. To conserve all of this was the responsibility of the highest national authority. In the creation of Yellowstone and other national parks, the claims of Indian residents were simply erased, and their "local, informal set of rules and customs relating to the natural world [was replaced] with a formal code of law, created and administered by the bureaucratic state" (Jacoby 2001:195). Ultimately, the indigenous peoples were expelled from this particular cultural construction of Eden. Ironically, most of the "pristine" environments that parks and other protected areas were (and are) meant to conserve were (and still are) inhabited by people (Colchester 1994:12).

Inspired by the aesthetic, sporting, and spiritual urges of urban European Americans, the model of the national park was quickly adopted by other nations for their own territories and colonial possessions. The post–World War II era of independence of those colonies coincided with a surge in environmental consciousness and the growth of the environmental movement, resulting in an increase in national parks and other protected areas in the new nations, particularly in Africa, Asia, and the Pacific.

The post–World War II era also saw a relatively continuous spread and institutionalization of global norms and principles in three domains in particular: human rights, the environment, and the rights of indigenous peoples. Internationally, human rights norms were among the formative principles behind the organization of the United Nations (Khagram 1999:27). Similarly, national normative principles and organizations have taken shape around the issue of the environment, along with the growth of private, nongovernmental organizations (Khagram 1999:25). Ironically, much national environmental legislation, particularly pertaining to the establishment of national parks, requires the relocation of residents. Environmental legislation is directly pitted against national human rights legislation and international human rights conventions and covenants.

The worldwide expansion of an indigenous movement began to establish itself only in the 1960s. The enormous challenges and problems faced by indigenous peoples around the world, including discrimination, confiscation of territory, violation of treaties, and exploitation and extraction of resources, have given rise to literally thousands of organizations, particularly in the post-war period of decolonization. The rise of civil rights issues to prominence and the resources to promote them in many of the industrialized nations contributed to the emergence of a global indigenous movement, spreading from Europe and North America in the late 1960s to Latin America in the 1970s, Asia and the Pacific in the 1980s, and in the 1990s to Africa and the former Soviet Union. Internationally, institutions such as the United Nations Permanent Forum on Indigenous Affairs, the Organization of American States, the African Union, and the International Labour Organization provide venues for indigenous peoples to express their concerns about rights to land and territories, to social and cultural freedom of expression, to be represented by their own institutions, and to consent and control over development (Gray 1996:113). Increasingly, legislation safeguarding the rights of indigenous peoples is being added to national constitutions around the world. Consequently, it is in this broader context of an emerging transnational civil society—more specifically, in a transnational political economy of development addressing such issues as general human rights, the environment, and the rights of indigenous peoples—that conservation-forced displacement of indigenous and traditional peoples must be understood.

THE SOCIAL STRUCTURE AND SOCIAL RELATIONS OF CONTEMPORARY CONSERVATION

For much of the modern era, the integrationist or conservationist perspective toward nature occupied a distinctly inferior position to the "command and control" model. The late twentieth century saw the resurgence of environmentally sensitive positions regarding the society–nature relationship, partly because of the extraordinary destruction and transformation of many natural features (air, water, soil, wetlands, forests) and entire environments. In the United States and Western Europe, the environmental destruction resulting from the post–World War II development boom spurred the passing of protective legislation. In 1982 the World Commission on Environment and Development published *Our Common Future*, more widely known as the Brundtland Report, establishing sustainability as the model and discourse to mediate between economic and ecological concerns. Discourses focusing on the importance of biodiversity for resilience and adaptation at the species and ecosystemic levels fueled efforts to set aside ever more parcels of land to protect animals and plants.

The interactions and discourses among national and state government agencies, NGOs, and local people about conservation projects and their goals and methods are patterned by nested local, national, and global social systems' hegemonic and contesting value orientations regarding bio-diversity. Policies and actions are outcomes of power relations within and among the various local, national, and international systems that produce the aforementioned "fractal" politics (Little 1999). The interactions among the GROs, NGOs, social movements, lawyers, courts, corporations, and multilateral organizations—each with its own agenda, which may shift over time—take place in the context of both global and national politics deal-ing with normative issues of human rights and the environment (Oliver-Smith 1996:96).

In the dynamic context of 1980s research, questions were raised about traditional models of conservation based largely on the national park and the removal of resident peoples. Conventional models of ecosystems as purely the outcome of current operating mechanisms and forces came under close scrutiny, as did the assumption that human beings inevitably bring about the depletion of biological diversity (Chatty and Colchester 2002:8). Research on land use history has demonstrated that, in certain cases, human activity actually enhances biodiversity (Brosius 2007:109). For example, Brown (1985:49) found in his research on biological taxonomies among foragers and farmers that subsistence farming changes the local environment in ways that increase biological diversity. More recently, Anderson (n.d.) found that landscape heterogeneity associated with cur-rent patterns of shifting cultivation in the Rio Platano Biosphere reserve in Honduras appears to increase raptor diversity. This research conforms to the perspective that ecosystems are better understood as dynamic and changing and that the role of people in their development and function-ing can be important in positive ways (Chatty and Colchester 2002).

A fundamental shift in ecological thinking has been taking place, from viewing ecosystems as static entities in equilibrium, to the perception that they are dynamic and non-equilibratory. Indeed, the current view is that ecosystems are in a constant state of flux in which disturbances, whether of natural or human origin, are inherent. Many now consider humans an integral component in ecological, evolutionary, and environmental processes. According to Wallington, Hobbs, and Moore (2005), these shifts in perspective, however, are not reflected in contemporary conservation policies and programs, which continue to be informed by equilibratory assumptions about static species assemblages, purchase and protection of conservation areas, isolation from surrounding altered landscapes, and prevention of human disturbance.

In 1980, however, just before the Bruntland Report, the International

Union for the Conservation of Nature (IUCN) published the World Conservation Strategy, which proposed an alternative to the national park model: it advocated incorporating local people into the conservation process. Attention to more local participation and the sustainable use of resources characterized the approaches to conservation favored at the Third World Congress on Parks and Protected Areas, held in Bali in 1982 (Fortwangler 2003:27). The World Bank followed this initiative with a program called Integrated Conservation and Development Projects (ICDP), intended to integrate local people into projects to enable them to benefit economically. This process has also been referred to as co-management or community-based natural resource management (CBNRM).

The 1980s and 1990s saw a multitude of nongovernmental organizations, such as the World Rainforest Movement, the Forest Peoples' Alliance, the International Working Group on Indigenous Affairs, Cultural Survival, and Survival International, directly addressing the issue of conservation and the rights of indigenous and traditional peoples. By the same token, many international conservation NGOs, such as the World Wildlife Fund, The Nature Conservancy, Conservation International, and the World Conservation Union, integrated participatory frameworks into their projects, an effort that generally has come to characterize the conservation movement today, but with very uneven application and results (Naughton-Treves, Holland, and Brandon 2005:239). International covenants and conventions regarding indigenous rights to participate in environmental management also came into existence. The 1982 Third World Congress on Parks and Protected Areas called for greater participation from resident populations in conservation projects. The UN Declaration on the Right to Development, adopted in 1986, included the right to sovereignty over natural resources. The International Labour Organization established the Convention on Indigenous and Tribal Peoples (no. 169), affirming the rights of use, ownership, management, and control of traditional lands and territories (Fortwangler 2003:27). The 1992 Convention on Biological Diversity, the first global agreement on conservation and sustainable use of biodiversity, called upon its 183 parties to

> respect, preserve and maintain knowledge, innovations and
> practices of indigenous and local communities embodying tradi-
> tional lifestyles relevant for the conservation and sustainable use
> of biological diversity and promote their wider application with
> the approval and involvement of the holders of such knowledge,
> innovations and practices and encourage the equitable sharing

of the benefits arising from the utilization of such knowledge, innovations and practices. [CBD 1992]

These and other conventions and covenants stimulated and supported a variety of methodologies through which indigenous and other traditional peoples were to become full participants in conservation and sustainable use projects. However, as Cleaver (1999) and Chatty and Colchester (2002) note, "participation" and "participatory methods" come in many guises, some more empowering than others. Some methods adopted included employing local people in project staff positions, direct payments or "conservation concessions, strengthening tenure rights through participatory mapping of community lands, market-oriented approaches based on developing ecotourism, shade tree coffee or community logging, and capacity building and organizational training" (Bray and Anderson 2005:13). These methods notwithstanding, many of the strategies and methods adopted by conservation NGOs fell far short of engaging local people in full-fledged participatory planning and implementation roles, limiting them largely to receiving information regarding project intentions under the guise of "consultation." In the past several decades, the majority of conservationists have worked with a model that includes participation of the people living within parks and other protected areas, but actual practice has fluctuated between generally uneven local participation and conservation by administrative fiat backed by force. Colchester (1994:49) noted that the operation of projects was characterized by top-down strategies that strengthened the power of states and intergovernmental institutions at the expense of indigenous peoples.

In the 1990s, dissatisfaction with the outcomes of CBNRM projects generated a more exclusionary strain within the conservation movement, dubbed "the new protectionist paradigm." Redford reactivated debate with an article titled "The Ecologically Noble Savage" (1991), in which he attacked the idea that indigenous peoples were good custodians of the environment. Considering indigenous and traditional peoples more opportunistic than conservationist in their relationship to nature, he accused anthropologists especially of romanticism in their assessments of traditional indigenous cultures.

Based, in part, on a model of nature that repudiates integrationist perspectives, the new protectionist paradigm returns to the old oppositional perspective regarding humans and nature (Brechin et al. 2003). In the 1990s the uneven results of CBNRM strategies convinced the authors of several influential publications to militate explicitly for top-down forms of conservation (Oates 1999; Terborgh 1999). Notwithstanding the well-documented fact that human beings have been integral parts and active shapers of "nature" throughout time, some conservationists resumed their calls for the removal of long-resident populations from environments in which the floral and faunal species were considered endangered (Redford and Sanderson 2000). This strategy is sometimes referred to as "greenlining" or "ecological expropriation" and produces yet another kind of "environmental refugee" (Geisler and de Sousa 2001). People are forced from their homelands, often without notice or consultation. Even though conservationists recognize that low-impact rural dwellers inflict much less damage on environments than do large-scale agents such as logging and mining enterprises, plantations, and extensive cattle ranches, some are insisting that fully protected, people-free areas are now necessary for adequate conservation. Basically, this position within tropical biology holds that human residence in tropical forests is incompatible with the conservation of biological diversity (Schwartzman, Moreira, and Nepstad 2000).

Although criticized for misunderstanding the dynamics of local systems, the protectionist position also advocates radically restricting resource use practices employed by people who remain resident in reserves and parks (Dove 1983; Guha 1997; Peluso 1993). Such restrictions constitute a form of structural displacement. Altering the institutionalized ways in which people have engaged the environment in the process of social reproduction effectively forces them to develop new norms and practices if social reproduction is to continue (Oliver-Smith 2001). At least in regard to agriculture, recent research indicates that, in most cases, "adequate planning can enable the coexistence of agriculture and biodiversity without compromising either" (Gorenflo and Brandon 2005:199).

The World Bank, taking a more economically based resource-access approach, has recently defined the restriction of access to indigenous and other people in parks and protected areas as a form of involuntary displacement, even when spatial displacement does not occur (Cernea 2005b). Cernea noted that there is abundant data to show that, for the affected people, resource access restrictions "end up being virtually the same as if they were physically forcibly displaced" (Cernea 2005b:48). Both the Asian Development Bank and the African Development Bank have adopted similar definitions in the recent past.

To be fair, many protectionists acknowledge the rights of people residing in areas that are to be protected, seeing them as allies in the struggle against the larger forces embedded in state and private interests that are destroying fragile areas. However, they also mark a clear distinction between their own interests and those of affected peoples: "They [forest peoples] may speak for their version of the forest, but they do not speak for the forest that we want to conserve" (Redford and Sanderson 2000:1364). In a sense, a conflict of knowledges exists here. On the one hand, the discourse of conservationists finds its source of truth in the scientific knowledge of biology based on what they consider to be tangible and measurable proof. On the other hand, lay or local knowledge is narrative and historical in character, dealing with human experience of the world as lived. Local knowledge is eclectic, deriving its truth from the biographical, from that which is learned from various sources of teaching and experience (Kroll-Smith and Floyd 1997). Today, indigenous peoples are engaging the issue of nature conservation and elaborating their own concepts and approaches to it (Alfalit International 1993; CONAIE 2004). At stake in this tension between global and local knowledge are the credibility and legitimacy of those who espouse science in order to displace those whose knowledge base is local and experiential. But, as Brosius (2007:111) cogently observed, "all the expert knowledge in the world will not make rights claims disappear."

As Milton (1996) suggested, the strain of conservationists who seek to maintain people- and use-free areas is more appropriately designated as "preservationist." Others are concerned with conservation for purposes of "wise use," however that may be defined. Some argue that conservation is the exact opposite of development; its goal is to conserve, not change. Others equally argue that conservation is an enlightened form of sustainable development; it valorizes resources and environments as contributing to the sustainability of natural cycles of renewability and promises economic reward. Many ardent developers have joined the ranks of environmentalists, realizing that unlimited exploitation of natural environments undermines the material source of value, basically destroying its own conditions of production and reproduction, referred to by O'Connor (1998) as the second contradiction of capitalism. By the same token, both the real and the potential use values of plant and animal species now lie in their being a source for new drugs, genetic banks for agricultural crops, and environmental services such as flood control; they also have non-use values of an aesthetic and recreational sort (Brechin et al. 2002). Sustainable development is a discourse intended to resolve the contradiction between nature and capital, by moving capitalism into an ecological phase in which nature is valorized and therefore must be protected. According to Escobar (1999), however, sustainable development (and preservationist) discourses frequently lay the blame for environmental destruction not on capitalist development, but on its victims—the urban poor, the rural swidden agriculturalists, the few remaining hunter/foragers, often marginalized by development into fragile areas where they struggle to survive.

In 2004 Chapin asserted that the major conservation NGOs—the World Wildlife Fund, Conservation International, and The Nature Conservancy ("The Big Three")—are employing increasingly top-down strategies in their projects, excluding indigenous and traditional peoples from participation (Chapin 2004). He attributed the failure of most of the ICDP projects to conservationist incompetence: "On the ground, ICDPs were generally paternalistic, lacking in expertise and one-sided-driven largely by the agendas of the conservationists, with little indigenous input" (Chapin 2004:20). Moreover, he criticized the science behind large-scale approaches to conservation, stating that such concepts as "eco-regions," "hotspots," and "conservation landscapes" are as much marketing tools for the vast funds now available for conservation as they are valid scientific concepts. Chapin claimed that conservationist priorities start with the need to establish people-free, protected areas. Projects have been reluctant to engage with the agendas of local peoples, withholding support for indigenous efforts to secure land title and tenure or resist the incursions of oil, mining, tourism, and logging companies, which account for enormous environmental destruction around the world (Goodall 2006; McElwee 2006; Rangarajan and Shahabuddin 2006). Moreover, Chapin (2004:21, 18) accused The Big Three, in particular, of partnering with multinational corporations (gas, oil, mining, and pharmaceuticals) that are deeply implicated in forest destruction. In fact, a group of twenty-one environmental scientists presenting "A View from the South" largely sustained Chapin's position and backed his call for greater reliance on local leadership and investment in local capacity (Rodriguez et al. 2007:755).

Needless to say, the response to Chapin's article, especially from the leadership of The Big Three, was a denial of the majority of his accusations, strongly asserting their commitment to working with indigenous and traditional peoples to conserve biodiversity. Clearly, Chapin's article had touched a nerve in the community of conservation NGOs and among conservationists in general. Indeed, the article (among others) ignited a major effort on the part of conservationists to address the issue of displacement and resettlement (Redford and Fearn 2007; Redford and Painter 2006). Notwithstanding their declared commitment to integrated conservation and development projects, biodiversity conservation organizations must recognize that their methods need to be altered and their approaches to local communities improved in order to avoid future displacement and major human rights violations.

Both conservation biologists and anthropologists have recently intensified their efforts in this direction (Redford and Sanderson 2006). For example, Redford, a conservation biologist, and Painter, an anthropologist, have posited that the survival of both indigenous peoples and nature depends on finding common ground for mutual assistance (Redford and Painter 2006). Citing the collaboration between the Wildlife Conservation Society and the Capitania de Alto y Bajo Izozog, an organization of roughly ten thousand Guarani-speaking peoples in eastern Bolivia, they contend that the Gran Chaco National Park's Integrated Management Area constitutes an important example of successful cooperation between indigenous people and conservationists. They further assert that if conservationists and indigenous peoples and their allies continue to fight each other, the crucial decisions regarding nature and indigenous culture will be made by those with only personal, economic, and national power interests in mind. Chicchon (2007) and Bodmer and Puertas (2007) adopt similar positions, citing specific cases in which partnerships between conservation and indigenous peoples have produced positive outcomes.

Most recently, Agrawal and Redford have asserted that, in conservation projects, there is no ethically satisfactory way to handle the problems of the displaced without consulting them. Agrawal and Redford (2007:12) have called for "a positive-historical" program of action that would address their needs more comprehensively, including reparations for past conservation-forced displacements. Such a position bodes well for future productive collaborations. However, productive steps in theory and in action will be rapidly challenged as the destruction of natural and cultural diversity proceeds at alarming rates around the world. Also, economies will become stressed by the many competing demands for added resources that such collaborations will require.

PROTECTED AREAS AND CONSERVATION-FORCED DISPLACEMENT AND RESETTLEMENT (CFDR)

In the period between 1900 and 1950, roughly six hundred protected areas were established around the world to conserve treasured environments (Ghimire 1994). By 1995 there were almost ten thousand protected areas, encompassing roughly 5 percent of the earth's surface, and conservationists hoped to double that amount quickly (Stevens 1997). Indeed, by 1997, a scant two years later, there were more than thirty thousand. By 2003 the number of protected areas had increased by more than ten times over the 1995 total, to more than one hundred thousand, comprising 17.1

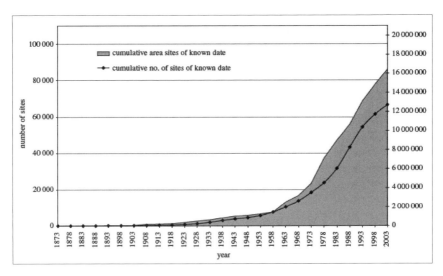

Figure 7.1

The increase in number and size of protected areas worldwide. (Chape et al. 2005:450)

million sq k or 11.5 percent of the globe's land surface (IUCN/WCPA 2004). The United Nations List of Protected Areas established that by 2003 the number stood at 102,567, covering 19,216,175 sq k. Recently, drawing on data from the World Commission on Protected Areas (WCPA) World Database on Protected Areas, West, Igoe, and Brockington (2006:254) put the total number of protected areas at 105,005, covering 21,520,853 sq k or 11.34 percent of the earth's total surface. This trend is illustrated in figure 7.1. If this trend continues, the potential for more displacement is high.

Data on the growth in number of protected areas show some disparities, for example, between WCPA/IUCN data and the United Nations List of Protected Areas data (UNEP/WCMC/WCPA/IUCN 2003). Some differences can be attributed to variations in how a protected area is defined for analytical purposes. Chape and others (2005), for example, found substantial underestimation in the total size of protected areas. The United Nations used a much more flexible definition than did the WCPA/IUCN, but by either standard, the trend of increasing numbers of protected areas is clear. Since 1981, when the WCPA-WDPA began collecting data, its database has become the standard source for information on protected areas, but its gaps and omissions make it problematical. For example, only state-declared protected areas are included in the WCPA-WDPA database, which draws on information supplied by nations and collaborating nongovernmental organizations. Private individual and collective preserves are not included. West, Igoe, and Brockington have pointed out that in South Africa, for example, private game farms comprise more than 13 percent of the national territory and only 6 percent are state- or province-protected areas. Furthermore, 35 percent of the WCPA-WDPA database entries do not have dates of establishment, and 12 percent of the entries have no information on size (West, Igoe, and Brockington 2006:255). In fact, the WCPA-WDPA database is now undergoing a major rebuilding effort in partnership with the Proteus Partnership (http://proteus.unep.wcmc.org), a consortium composed largely of oil companies (nine of eleven partners) that support the effort to make biodiversity information more accessible.

Unfortunately, good data on the number of conservation projects that displace communities and on the number of people displaced are not readily available. Clearly, because indigenous, traditional, and immigrant populations occupy the majority of protected areas, an enormous potential exists for displacement, resettlement, and the conflicts and human rights violations these generate. The truth of the matter is that, at present, we have a very incomplete picture of the general impact of protected areas on resident populations and even less clarity on the quantitative and qualitative aspects of displacement and resettlement beyond specific case studies. Indeed, we have to ask whether one reason we lack good data on the numbers of people displaced by conservation projects is that the displaced are largely indigenous. Not only are indigenous people frequently outside the information-collecting powers of the state, but also they are, as Arundhati Roy has said, "non-people" in many states (Roy and Barsamian 2004:4). That is, they do not count; in some cases, their indigenous identity is denied or erased. Traditional, non-indigenous peasants are also considered redundant in schemes of national development (Bryceson, Kay, and Mooij 2000). In this day and age, many states view indigenous and traditional peoples as a drag on development ambitions, an obstacle to be eliminated, usually by neglect or the cruel logic of a system built on various forms of "structural violence," rather than by actual genocidal strategies (Farmer 2004). Thus, despite recent efforts, the research community has not been able to document in any comprehensive way the numbers of people displaced spatially or structurally by conservation projects (Agrawal and Redford 2007; Brockington and Igoe 2006; West, Igoe, and Brockington 2006). Several regional attempts have produced highly disputed numbers (Cernea and Schmidt-Soltau 2006; Maisels et al. 2007).

Nonetheless, in September 2003 the World Parks Congress in Durban, South Africa, demanded that efforts be made to "improve the knowledge and understanding of the impact of protected areas on the livelihoods of the rural poor, negative and positive" (WPC 2003:R29, quoted in Schmidt-Soltau 2005:283). Apart from any ideological challenges the task may present to state functionaries, the lack of baseline data on the economic and social utilization of land in most developing countries presents a major obstacle (Schmidt-Soltau 2005:287). We need further research on the impacts of CFDR to assess their scope, particularly in the regions of high biodiversity and maximum effect. To that end, the World Bank in 2005 initiated a review of the roughly one hundred conservation projects it had funded that displaced people or restricted their access to resources (Cernea 2005b:49). The case studies suggest that the impacts are severe and constitute very real human-rights violations at both the specific and the broader levels.

Although indigenous and traditional peoples all over the world face the challenges presented by conservation projects, the most intense pressure is being exerted in those areas characterized as biodiversity hotspots, which are concentrated generally in tropical regions, particularly forested areas. Not entirely coincidentally, these ecosystems are also among the most culturally diverse areas, sustaining at least 1,400 indigenous and traditional peoples in existing forests and 2,500 if the original expanse of tropical moist forests is included (Oviedo, Maffi, and Larsen 2000:9). Some groups have sought the assistance of the national courts to halt resettlement efforts, but few have had success (Hitchcock, Biesele, and Lee 2003). Despite their profound economic, social, and cultural losses, indigenous and traditional peoples thus far have not sought reparations for resettlement or for loss of access to resources from conservation projects (see Johnston, chapter 10, this volume). Indeed, where we do have good research on CFDR impacts, projects have left the displaced destitute and with little opportunity for redress (Brockington and Igoe 2006; McClean and Straede 2003).

The current debates on CFDR revolve around discontinuing displacement as the mainstream strategy for park creation (Cernea and Schmidt-Soltau 2006). This becomes particularly important in that many protected areas simply expel people with no provision for relocation, however devastating any resettlement project may turn out to be for the evicted peoples. At the levels of policy, strategy, and implementation, complete recognition of the double diversities mentioned earlier in the chapter necessarily eliminates displacement as a strategic option. Biodiversity and cultural diversity can be mutually reinforcing in protected-area creation. Both the biosphere and people's livelihoods can and must be sustained. Finally, there is currently considerable pressure on the big three NGOs (Conservation International, The Nature Conservancy, and the World Wildlife Fund) to repudiate publicly the policy of displacement and resettlement. It is more than a little surprising that these organizations actually lag far behind the international financial institutions and the aid agencies of the OECD, a situation criticized in a recent conservationist perspective on displacement (Agrawal and Redford 2007:5).

CONCLUSION

There is no question that the appalling decimation of habitats around the world must be halted to protect the sustainability of local and global ecosystems. The importance of conserving biological diversity for global ecosystem health ensures that the conservation movement and the number and area of protected regions will continue to expand. However, the presence of indigenous and traditional peoples in these areas challenges the conservation movement's values and methods. Ecological protection should not be obtained at the expense of those most vulnerable and least culpable for environmental devastation. The history of the conservation movement, from its earliest roots in royal hunting preserves, has been generally characterized by an elitist, authoritarian ideology and practice. The establishment of national parks, first in the United States and then elsewhere, generally resulted in the expulsion of indigenous and traditional peoples from these supposed Edens.

More recently, new approaches, based on more nuanced understandings of the human–environment relationship, emphasize co-management of conservation projects with local populations. Despite sincere avowals by many conservationists that the rights of local peoples to their traditional lands must be respected, most conservation projects, even those organized under the rubric of co-management, have been relatively top-down, with participation limited to a passive reception of information or occasional employment for individuals by projects. Some analysts attribute the poor performance of many of these projects to their nonparticipatory, authoritarian nature. Conservation projects lacking local support and participation have a poor prognosis for success. The authoritarian style of most conservation projects has been buttressed by the fact that, generally speaking, national governments have honored indigenous rights only when these have already been breached. Moreover, discontent among conservationists over the poor performance of co-management projects has led to the reemergence of more draconian approaches displacing local peoples from protected areas and further threatening the basic human rights of indigenous and traditional peoples. Indeed, if the conservation legislation that is currently on the books is actually applied, the rate and level of displacement will increase dramatically (West, Igoe, and Brockington 2006:259).

Although indigenous and traditional peoples are generally not "natural ecologists," they are hardly to blame for the vast environmental devastation that has taken place in the world's biodiverse "hotspots." Logging, mining, petroleum exploration, cattle ranching, and commercial agriculture are far more responsible. In advocating the expulsion of indigenous and traditional peoples from protected areas, the conservation movement wants to evict the relatively powerless, marginalized, and disparaged indigenous and traditional rural peoples rather than confront directly the powerful economic and political interests that drive the devastation of nature.

Until more equitable forms of land distribution are developed, many protected areas will also be seen as the solution to survival for people marginalized by the incursion of powerful economic and political interests. In turn, there will be attempts at forcibly relocating such communities because of their impact on the environment. In the case of recent migrants and colonists, usually marginalized in their place of origin, the response should not compound that marginalization, as CFDR does; it should confront the forces behind environmental destruction. In the final analysis, doing this means addressing forces at work in the dominant society that create both environmental havoc and displacement. For recent migrants and long-term residents of protected areas, inclusion in the conservation process with authentic participation and decisive power is the only acceptable alternative to CFDR. The conservation movement began to move in that direction in the 1980s. It is imperative that the effort toward inclusion and equity not be abandoned because of flaws in implementation. The alternative is the perpetuation of systems of oppression and exploitation of both nature and people. In the end, these conversations about the conservation of nature are fundamentally conversations about society.

Note

1. I am grateful to my colleague Laura Ogden of Florida International University for alerting me to the importance of the concepts of wilderness and tropicality in this context and for introducing me to the work of Cronon (1995) and Arnold (1996).

8

Local Displacement, Global Activism

DFDR and Transnational Advocacy

William F. Fisher

This chapter addresses the dynamic political character of the development processes within which development decisions are made and DFDR policies formulated. Within this complex political context, project-affected peoples must mount resistance to DFDR (development-forced displacement and resettlement) or launch efforts to mitigate its impact. Specifically, the chapter discusses the roles played by NGOs, social movements, and other civil society groups in their ongoing struggle to influence development policies and accountability mechanisms. It examines the contexts within which these groups operate as brokers between locally affected populations and international development institutions. This different and still evolving form of transnational politics offers benefits and poses dangers for local people and their interests. It also presents challenges to scholars and activists seeking to comprehend and influence these structures and forces in the larger world and the way they impinge upon the local people with whom we work.

This chapter is part of a larger project that examines in detail the emergence and evolution of new transnational political structures, processes, and strategies over the past two decades, specifically, the movement against large dams and the forced displacement and resettlement required by dam projects. The larger project traces these processes over time and argues that contemporary studies, while focusing on the local impacts of displacement, also need to follow and analyze the flows of information, advocacy, and people through expanded and changing, translocal, civil society networks.

The question this chapter asks is how local populations adversely affected by development-forced displacement and resettlement can influence the global conditions and forces shaping their situation. To address this, it highlights four key aspects of the larger story: (1) the extent to which the challenges of DFDR oblige local people, in most cases, to engage in new forms of transnational alliance building and networking if they are to have any hope of resisting displacement or mitigating the negative impacts of resettlement; (2) the transformation of the information environment—accessibility, content, dissemination, and creation—through the efforts of advocacy alliances in their attempts to influence policy and alter power relationships; (3) the extent to which transnational collaborations can be difficult to sustain and have unintended impacts on the project-affected groups; and (4) the tension between advocates' desires to cultivate democratic participation in the process and, at the same time, to be effective and efficient in improving policies and outcomes. These issues make clear that addressing the complex problems of DFDR entails not just identifying best practices and penning new resettlement guidelines but also understanding and engaging the opportunities and hazards that arise with these evolving, transnational political processes.

The goal of this chapter is neither to praise nor to criticize transnational advocacy efforts in the case of DFDR, but simply to understand what happens in the processes of resistance to infrastructural development projects and in the processes of transnational advocacy. Large-scale development efforts that result in displacement and resettlement can be, and usually have been, wielded as political instruments. They are potent symbols for regional and national pride and have been revered as temples of modernity—tangible evidence of progress, the state's commitment to modernization, and the human ability to tame and reshape nature through technical ingenuity. Alternatively, they are viewed as tombstones for lost ecosystems, peoples, and societies.

This chapter looks at DFDR as a product of wider processes of social, economic, and political change, viewing not only DFDR's technical requirements but also its political and moral implications. The chapter highlights how DFDR both emanates from and contributes to growing divides in standards of living, access to security and justice, and protection of rights. It addresses what the SAR advanced seminar noted as the central issue in DFDR—the political nature of the development process.

TRANSNATIONAL NETWORKS AND ADVOCATES

Transnational advocacy has evolved as local struggles such as those over large dams or displacement and resettlement have become increasingly globalized. Today, social movement alliances frequently extend translocally, linking local communities to more influential domestic and international groups of activists, NGOs, media, and academics.[1] Over the past two decades, transnational alliances and movements have challenged the dominant model of development as environmentally and socially unsustainable and damaging to the livelihoods of marginal populations. Their struggles have helped to shape a transnational political field within which governments, local grassroots organizations, and international organizations and NGOs (INGOs) adapt innovative strategies. Their challenges have prompted governments to take seriously any external threats to the completion of politically important, domestic development projects.

The transnational alliances of NGOs operate on many levels, organizing and supporting local affected people and lobbying multilateral development banks, international organizations, governments, and international dam-building consortia. Focusing on them helps us to unpack and understand the potential of, and risks to, some of the new and expanding lines of communication and political influence. Of central interest are the advantages and disadvantages involved when locally based groups of project-affected peoples reach beyond the boundaries of the state to join transnationally with individuals, other groups, and movements to influence the actions and policies of international organizations, private companies, and their home states.

Certain contemporary social-movement networks work in support of, or on behalf of, those displaced by development projects. Some seek to improve the conditions of displacement and resettlement, others oppose projects that entail displacement, and still others object to the decision-making processes that enable these projects. In the 1980s, groups resistant to the construction of large dams and the negative impacts of displacement and resettlement did not initially seek to extend their activism outside the boundaries of their own states. They were compelled to do so as they came to understand that the decision-making processes included international funders and organizations. Anil Patel of ARCH-Vahini in India, for example, has described how his small group of activists—working with those to be ousted from their homes by the construction of the Sardar Sarovar

Project along the Narmada River in the Indian state of Gujarat—slowly came to realize that it was up against a much more complex and widespread set of actors than anticipated:

> Needless to say, we knew nothing about the maze of land laws, about the Forest Act, about the Tribunal's decisions on resettlement and rehabilitation. We did not even know of the World Bank Guidelines: and even if we knew, of what good could that be to us? The World Bank, even to us, was distant, remote, and powerful—a mere abstraction. If we had known of these intricacies and the legal tangles, we would have been repelled by the sheer immensity of the task. [Patel 1997:183]

Medha Patkar of the Narmada Bachao Andolan (a national coalition of Narmada valley residents and Indian activists) has similarly described the changing strategies of her activist group as it realized the complexity of what it was up against. The account of the connection of the India-based Narmada Bachao Andolan with the transnational Narmada Action Committee is a classic and central story about innovative and effective transnational advocacy in the later part of the twentieth century. The case continues to exemplify how the globalization of resistance to domestic development projects can arise from and, in turn, affect global flows of people, technology, money, influence, and ideas.[2]

Opposition to the Sardar Sarovar Dam grew steadily from the mid-1980s; valley residents swore that they would rather drown than move. Representatives of rural communities along the Narmada and independent nongovernmental organizations and social action groups lobbied prime ministers of India, chief ministers of the states of Gujarat, Maharashtra, and Madhya Pradesh, state and national bureaucrats, the Japanese government, the World Bank, and governments funding the Bank. By welding the Narmada Bachao Andolan to a loose network of INGOs, advocacy groups, and individuals through the Narmada Action Committee, the international Narmada campaign was remarkably effective. It played a critical role in convincing the government of Japan to withdraw its commitment to provide a loan for the project,[3] forced the governments of India and the Indian state of Gujarat to mount counter–public relations campaigns in international settings, influenced the 1991 decision of the World Bank president to commission an unprecedented independent review of a World Bank project, and ultimately encouraged reforms within the Bank, including the establishment of a new internal review panel in 1993.[4]

Similar national and transnational coalitions formed to support the local opponents of other dams.[5] Both international and local actors played important roles in all of these efforts: INGOs, for instance, dispersed information quickly and widely, and local groups added moral legitimacy to the coalitions' efforts. The activities of these coalitions took on a broader focus when they linked directly with the anti–World Bank campaign "Fifty Years Is Enough."

During the past two decades, the resistance of affected communities to involuntary displacement has benefited from more effective coordination at the local level and also from strengthened transnational alliances that contribute information, resources, and political leverage. These struggles illustrate the (sometimes) symbiotic relationship between Northern-based INGOs and Southern grassroots movements and organizations, the increasing importance of transnational alliances of NGOs to local social movements, the ability of such alliances to bring change within international institutions such as the World Bank, and the effect of these alliances locally.

Many analysts have commented on the associational revolution that has swept the world since the late 1980s. This period has seen a dramatic increase in the number of NGOs working on issues as diverse as poverty alleviation, the environment, inequality, human rights, democratization, indigenous rights, women's rights, and global health. Indeed, the 1990s have been called "the decade of civil society." The beginning of the twenty-first century saw these movements joining together in the vibrant, innovative, and potentially groundbreaking process of the World Social Forum. So far, this is the most promising effort to create a space within which global social and political action groups can "become better educated about one another, learn more about the processes of neoliberal globalization, plan collective actions, and develop alternatives" (Fisher and Ponniah 2003:4).

There has been much speculation about the transformational potential of the associational revolution, as well as a recasting of academic and activist discourse in terms of "civil society." Over the past decade, scholars have widely discussed the role of civil society in development, ways to build vibrant civil societies, the relationship between civil society and the state, the role of civil society groups in transnational connections, the emergence of a global civil society, and the ability of civil society to empower people and contribute to processes of democratization. But, despite the enthusiastic way in which the term *civil society* has been embraced, we still have great difficulty in making useful connections between the abstraction and the hard realities of our research experiences. There is good reason to express considerable skepticism about the analytic utility of terms, such as

NGO and *civil society*, that mean whatever anyone seems to want them to mean. Too frequently, these terms are used "as if" they carry some analytic meaning; in fact, they carry very little.

Most significant about the evolving transnational civil society field is the increasing cooperation within it and with governments, local and international organizations, private sector organizations, and academics. Civil society groups serve as critical intermediaries and, in that role, as gate-keepers and political brokers between sets of people with differing political goals and values. But the politics of these relationships are not always transparent. Furthermore, although the role of civil society groups is significant, accountability is questionable, and powerful forces work to delimit their role and contribution and to undermine their credibility.

The diverse civil society field is simultaneously dangerous and opportune. It threatens danger insofar as civil society is a means by which citizens are disciplined or brought under control, a process Foucault referred to as governmentality. It offers opportunity insofar as civil society can be protected as a space where counter-hegemonic discourses become possible. The civil society field is most certainly imperfect and is fast becoming a terrain for which various groups are competing. Some prominent civil society groups are cooperative, accommodating, and assimilationist, seeking to sit at the table with other major political decision makers. But other groups remain defiantly noncooperative, struggling to stay independent of dominant power structures. Might we more usefully conceive of the field not as dichotomized but as richly diverse with groups, including prominent anti-dam activist networks, that present an innovative if risky alternative by taking a middle path of cautious, occasional, and conditional cooperation. According to specific circumstances, these groups alternately engage with and resist governments, the private sector, and international institutions to achieve limited ends that can then be built upon in future struggles. Activists themselves acknowledge and debate the dangers of this approach, valuing engagement as a necessary strategy but concerned about the risks of cooptation, assimilation, and accommodation.

CHANGING THE INFORMATION ENVIRONMENT

The struggle over large dams and DFDR demonstrates how advocacy alliances attempt to influence policy and alter power relationships by changing the information environment: through a variety of means and with multiple audiences in mind, they provide information to parties who previously lacked access to it; they interpret and challenge existing sets of "facts"; and they present alternative "facts." To do this, the participants in anti-dam coalitions rely upon mastery and dispersal of a vast amount of knowledge and information, both local and scientific, about climate change, construction codes, human rights and environmental conventions, local cultures, global politics, and much more.

Efforts to ensure a wider flow of information took an unprecedented step forward with the first meetings of dam-affected peoples, in Curitiba, Brazil, in March 1997 and in Thailand in December 2003. The initial effort to bring together affected groups from diverse countries in the global South laid the groundwork for a wide transnational network and advocacy campaign. After affected peoples shared their experiences of the losses and threats they faced because of large dams, they jointly declared, "Though our experiences reflect our diverse cultural, social, political, and environmental realities, our struggles are one" (Declaration of Curitiba, March 14, 1997). The participants demonstrated awareness that (1) each local struggle was part of a larger, single process; (2) their transnational solidarity wielded influence; (3) they needed to address governments, international agencies, and investors; and (4) privatization and the role of export finance agencies in the global rise of private finance pose dangers to them. Their declaration states:

> Over the years, we have shown our growing power....Nationally and internationally, we have worked in solidarity with others fighting against destructive development projects and together with those fighting for human rights, social justice, and an end to environmental destruction. We are strong, diverse, and united, and our cause is just. We have stopped destructive dams and have forced dam builders to respect our rights....From the villages of India, Brazil, and Lesotho, to the boardrooms of Washington, Tokyo, and London, we will force dam builders to accept our demands. [Declaration of Curitiba, March 14, 2007]

The 2nd International Meeting of Dam-Affected Peoples and Their Allies endorsed twenty resolutions that included demands for compensation of displaced people and fair resettlement, participation of local communities in dam planning, local ownership and control of agricultural land and forest, freedom from repressive state and international politics, preservation of livelihoods and land, decommissioning of existing dams, promotion of family agriculture, rural electrification and investment in renewable energy alternatives, distribution of land title, creation of areas of environmental conservation and extractive reserves, and improved education in rural areas (available at http://www.irn.org/riversforlife/pdf/RFL_resolutions.pdf, accessed August 2006).

These networking efforts, though significant steps forward, are logistically difficult, expensive, and hard to sustain or repeat without support from Northern-based NGOs. Following the initial meeting of dam-affected peoples was an important period of sustained advocacy organized informally through a network that came to be known as the International Committee on Dams, Rivers, and People (ICDRP). This loose network helped bring about the multiyear study of the World Commission on Dams (WCD) from 1998 to 2000.

The ICDRP evolved informally from a network of NGOs and from peoples movements against large dams for the purpose of influencing the form of the WCD reports and as a means to use the two-year term of the commission to establish more extensive, transnational networks against dams. The name emerged in May 1998 at a meeting of civil society groups involved in the establishment of the WCD, but many core members had already been involved in the global struggle against dams. Most had long been active in transnational coalitions against specific local dams, and the key members had cooperated in organizing the first meeting of dam-affected peoples in Curitiba in 1997. The ICDRP never established a formal membership; it relied on a core group of individuals to organize meetings, prepare reports, and relay information.[6] Among the participating groups were affected-peoples groups (MAB, NBA, the Cordillera Peoples Alliance, Sobrevivencia, Sungi), regional support organizations (PNDRP, SANDRP), Northern-based support organizations (the International Rivers Network; the Berne Declaration; the Swedish Society for Nature Conservation; the Reform the Bank Campaign; World Economy, Ecology and Development; the Bretton Woods Project; the Environmental Monitoring Group), and research institutes (The Corner House, Focus on the Global South). All of the affected peoples groups affiliated with the WCD Forum were active in the ICDRP, as were some (but by no means all) of the NGOs and research institutes affiliated with the forum.

Most ICDRP interactions occurred through electronic means or a series of face-to-face gatherings around the globe: there were meetings immediately before and after each of the four WCD regional public hearings, the three WCD Forum meetings, and the nine WCD commissioners' meetings. Meetings before and after the regional hearings were more numerous and larger because the ICDRP took advantage of location to encourage the establishment of regional civil society networks or to strengthen existing ones. As many as five of the commissioners, as well as some members of the WCD secretariat, occasionally attended open ICDRP meetings to pass on information or listen to the concerns of participants. ICDRP participants effectively networked with a wide range of affected-peoples groups, NGOs, and research institutes that were not formally represented on the WCD Forum. Thanks to the efforts of the ICDRP, these groups participated in the anti-dams network and actively lobbied the WCD. Deliberately excluded from ICDRP activities were many of the more well-known INGOs commonly visible in the ad hoc conferences and other symbolic global arenas.

For two years, the ICDRP participants actively coordinated a key component of the civil society input into the WCD. They solicited experts willing to provide submissions to the WCD, informally organized the submissions of experts and the testimony of dam-affected peoples for WCD public hearings and forum meetings, reviewed and responded to the substance and language of the many interim WCD drafts and reports, disseminated information, and gave practical advice and assistance to emerging regional NGO and social movement networks. By simultaneously highlighting the local and linking the local to global concerns and values, the ICDRP ensured that some attention was given to the voices of the affected peoples. In this, the ICDRP provided a key element of legitimacy to the WCD's work. The most dramatic of its vocalizations occurred during the WCD South American hearings in Sao Paulo in August 1999. Largely through the efforts of the Movement of People Affected by Dams, hundreds of Brazil's dam-affected people descended on the site of the hearing, filling the auditorium and spilling out of the building. The most effective effort, however, was the persistent presentation by experts of every possible case study and thematic topic. Indeed, the ICDRP spent enormous time and energy collecting, shaping, and presenting knowledge.

Transnational advocates have played a role in creating a number of significant instruments to put forward the issues of people displaced by development. These include the statements of the international meetings of dam-affected peoples, the WCD report, and the UN Guiding Principles on Internal Displacement (UN 1999). DFDR "best practice" is now informed by the findings and recommendations of the WCD, which reviewed the development effectiveness of large dams and formulated international standards and guidelines for large dam projects, including those concerning resettlement. The WCD recommendations call for a socially and environmentally comprehensive and transparent decision-making process.

After the publication of the WCD report, the United Nations Environmental Programme (UNEP) sponsored the Dams and Development Project

(DDP, established in November 2001) with the general goals of finding common ground on controversial issues and monitoring follow-up activities to the WCD. The DDP's specific mission was to facilitate communication between members about dams and development initiatives, provide a neutral platform for multistakeholder communication and discussion, and coordinate meetings of a Dams and Development Forum (modeled on the previous WCD Forum meetings). Significant efforts were made to expand the representation of governmental stakeholders in the Dams and Development Forum. Between July 2002 and November 2006, five meetings of the DDP forum took place (UNEP 2006). Despite the DDP's work, as of 2007, institutions dealing with resettlement had done little to turn the WCD's recommendations into binding policies.

Successful transnational advocacy by the ICDRP reflected mastery of what Peters (1997) has called a bifocal perspective—the ability to see and comprehend (and, one might add, the ability to communicate and explain across borders) both the near and the far, the local and the global, the familiar and the unfamiliar. This skill often requires the knowledge of multiple languages, discourses, and styles of speaking. In fact, the arenas within which activists operate are so varied that the term *bifocal* fails to capture this complexity, unfortunately implying a continuing simplistic dichotomy between the local and the global.[7] The term *multifocal* better describes the critical ability of some alliance actors to understand and operate within more than one social or political "locale."

Like other advocacy alliances, the ICDRP actively sought to transform the information environment. It dispersed information to "publicize" secretive deliberations and the noncompliance of states and international organizations with publicly stated goals and norms. The principle of public access to state decisions and the legitimating idea of democracy can be extended to describe the process by which transnational advocacy organizations strive to hold international organizations accountable to emerging global human rights and environmental norms.

Advocates not only publicize "facts" (be they technical, scientific, or procedural) but also employ testimony (stories told by people whose lives have been affected by DFDR). Activists select and frame this testimony with several objectives in mind: effective testimony demonstrates the "authenticity" of the affected people, the degree of their suffering, and the flaws of the policies involved. It also demonstrates the advocates' connections to "real" people in "real" places. A multifocal perspective is essential to the success of this strategy, whereby activists mediate the interaction of local communities with international institutions and package issues for target audiences.

The ICDRP's use of testimony and the effectiveness of this testimony depended on the forum in which it was employed. To some degree, testimony trumps facts in some forums: that is, to some influential constituencies, immediate personal accounts of those who suffer are more compelling than the impersonal institutional recitation of costs and benefits. At the same time, these accounts often serve to legitimate the intervention of affected-peoples groups in the policy-making and implementation processes of international institutions.[8]

Actors' varying abilities to see and communicate bi- or multifocally or to frame "facts" and testimony for target audiences help to explain the relative positions of groups and individuals within the ICDRP alliance, as well as how, through participation in the alliance, local-based groups affected by dams can gain an audience for their story or lose their control over it.

THE DIFFICULTY OF SUSTAINED ADVOCACY AND ITS UNINTENDED IMPACTS

As noted earlier, transnational advocacy has produced important outcomes, but it is difficult to sustain and has some significant, unintended negative impacts. To achieve any success, local groups typically need to have strong international support and to oppose a government that is willing to listen to protestors. Protests against multilateral banks and international organizations usually require an influential sector within those institutions to be critical of the project or of the government's plans. But even under these circumstances, success is never easy and is rarely certain. The Sardar Sarovar Project is a case in point. Opposition helped to establish an independent review that offered a damning critique of the project and the World Bank's involvement in it. Despite this critique, the governments of Gujarat and India stepped up their efforts to complete the project. Since then, the Indian government and the World Bank have underscored their commitment to investing in large dams.

The kinds of efforts exemplified by the Narmada campaign, the ICDRP, and similar transnational efforts are enlightening for a number of reasons. For one, they reveal that the different agendas and interests within complex local conflicts do not all originate there, nor are they all played out there. It is important, then, to analyze the capability of locally based groups and activists to reach beyond local boundaries (and often beyond the boundaries of the state) and to join translocally with individuals, groups, and movements in order to influence the actions and policies of other groups, international organizations, and their home states.

This leads us to reflect upon how what we might call the "globalization" of activism both emerges from and impacts global flows of people, technology, money, influence, and ideas. By focusing on subsets of these flows, we can examine how ethnographies of local activism can take into account transnational activism and the advocacy networks along which communication and values move freely across national borders. At stake is an accurate perception of the relationships among local lives, local social movements, and global processes: how do studies of activists and their transnational connections, flows, and alliances contribute to contemporary understandings of interrelatedness between globalization processes and lives lived locally?

The very visible and well-organized advocacy associated with the Narmada project and the World Commission on Dams demonstrate how enormously difficult it is to achieve lasting success through these transnational efforts. The Narmada activists managed to bring about an unprecedented independent review of a World Bank project, the Bank's withdrawal from the project, and the creation of a new review panel within the Bank. Nevertheless, the Gujarat government remained as determined as ever to complete the project. Despite remarkable efforts by activists in India and transnationally, the lives of the project-affected people along the Narmada have not improved.

The multiyear studies of the World Commission on Dams and the activists associated with the International Committee on Dam, Rivers, and People were no less heroic. The guidelines established by the WCD report set a new standard for dam projects: "Impoverishment and disempowerment have been the rule rather than the exception with respect to resettled people around the world" (WCD 2000b:11). But these guidelines remain without any means to enforce them.

The WCD and ICDRP processes raise questions about the engagement of transnational alliances with the disparate voices of a widely varied civil society. Inevitably, some local voices came to be amplified, and others failed to find an effective outlet through the practices of NGO advocacy alliances. There are intentional and unintentional constraints on this process of selection, and interactions among activists and possibilities for effectively participating vary, depending on two factors. One is the nature of the domestic political context within which local groups operate: some institutions and states are more open to leverage, and activist groups from democratic states are more easily integrated into transnational alliances. Second, among these local groups, those whose values and principled ideas fit or can be made consistent with INGO campaign goals and those whose members have demonstrated highly developed "multifocal" framing skills are more prominent and influential in the transnational alliances.

TENSIONS BETWEEN PARTICIPATION AND EFFECTIVENESS

The difficulty of making transnational advocacy effective and the unintended adverse impacts of transnational organizing converge to create tension between the democratic values of civil society groups and their desire to be efficient, effective advocates. There are lessons for academics and activists to learn about building bridges, expanding dialogue, and contextualizing our understandings of what happens in a specific time and place.

Many transnational actors clearly believe that much is at stake in claiming to be a legitimate voice of civil society. Effectiveness may rest, in part, on access to arenas of decision making; legitimacy derives from a plausible claim to represent the interests of a genuine local constituency. In ICDRP participants' discussions, they highlighted distinctions among civil society groups and placed high value on those who could claim a close connection to and familiarity with the interests and views of project-affected peoples. At the same time, they recognized the dangers of cooptation, which can result from excessive cooperation, and of marginalization, which can stem from complete noncooperation. Desire to be part of the governance structure was regarded very suspiciously by many participants; they recognized the fine line between their own strategies and those of "conference goers."

From the beginning of the WCD process, some activists were divided over the wisdom of cooperating with international organizations, the private sector, and governments. Activists differed in their assessments of the potential short- and long-term political gains and risks to themselves and to the project-displaced peoples whose interests they represented. Throughout the WCD process, many participants were troubled by compromise, worried that the process was sapping the energy and resources of activist organizations, and concerned that facts and principles were being ignored for the sake of consensus. Some activists continually urged the ICDRP participants to withdraw from the WCD process before their credibility was compromised. When the WCD final report was issued in November 2000, many of these activists were disappointed that it stopped short of holding dam promoters accountable for what they saw as forty years of ecological and social destruction.[9]

Despite extensive efforts to ensure widespread participation by Southern groups of affected peoples, key organizers of the ICDRP have acknowledged that the alliance often had an elitist character. The fast-paced exchange of information in English meant that individuals proficient in that language and with access to high-speed Internet had a distinct advantage in making substantive contributions to the process.

Inadvertently, this meant that the agenda for ICDRP was more influenced by a limited set of organizations and individuals.

By focusing on the global arena as an uneven and fragmented space within which battles from society at large are internalized and on the ever-changing local, regional, national, and international processes and connections that potentially support and also suppress "an insurrection of subjugated knowledges" (Fisher 1997), studies can avoid simple generalizations and reveal the rich ideological and functional diversity of civil society processes. Examining a fluid web of relationships reveals the connections of actions to numerous levels and fields and draws our attention to the flows of funding, knowledge, ideas, and people through these levels, sites, and associations. These multiple relationships include those among intermediaries; governments; constituencies; communities; leaders; elites; municipalities; state institutions; local, national, and international NGOs; social movements; and NGO coalitions. For civil society groups, this fragmented global civil society presents opportunities and considerable risks. Negotiating its shoals requires skill and luck, assets with an unequal availability that still favors Northern groups over Southern.

BEYOND BEST PRACTICES

As already noted, it is enormously difficult for local populations adversely affected by DFDR to influence their own situation. Even reaching beyond local and national boundaries to join in transnational alliances with networks of civil society groups offers no certainty of success—these interconnections often entail unanticipated changes that are not yet well understood. Inevitably, groups, intellectuals, and activists from the global North have the most influence in determining "best practices" and shaping DFDR policies. These are important efforts. But it is clear that addressing the complex problems of DFDR requires us not only to identify best practices and insist on more comprehensive and enlightened resettlement guidelines but also to understand and engage the opportunities and dangers that arise with changing transnational political-economic processes.

Social scientists in general and anthropologists in particular have just begun to consider how the actions of transnational civil society alliances are changing the way state agencies and citizens relate to each other and how each relates to the international political arena.[10] The transience of these alliances, their "location" in both local and translocal spaces, and the fluidity of their boundaries present some peculiar problems and require research that incorporates multiple sites and differently situated sets of actors in order to get at the political and social space these networks create.

The complexity of uneven power relationships and the multiplicity of translocal and transnational linkages make it difficult to map these relationships without oversimplifying or misrepresenting them. Like other contemporary transnational struggles, the controversy over large dams involves institutions and individuals who interact within and across local, national, and transnational arenas of action. In light of this increased "blurring of the boundaries between international and domestic arenas" (Keck and Sikkink 1998:199), models that separate and differentiate these arenas fail to capture the integral connections between them and to explicate the complexity of each arena, including the unequal relations of power existing within and between them. Complex linkages and conflicts among institutions and individuals occur within and between arenas. Within a single arena, linkages and conflicts occur within and among national and international development institutions and nongovernmental organizations.

Transnational connections are by no means limited to those forged by civil society groups in opposition to development efforts. Networks of power relations likewise extend transnationally. It is in response to domestic networks of power relations, as well as to transnational networks, that advocacy alliances arise. In the case of DFDR, local opposition groups reached out transnationally as they came to recognize the need to do so to counter the transnational reach of the development apparatus supporting projects that displace populations. Thus, these struggles are not simple stories of monolithic development regimes pitched against an overwhelmed local populace, nor of domestic development efforts derailed by a heroic transnational alliance. These stories involve complicated, fluid, and parallel networks engaged in struggle not only over the construction of dams but also over the meaning and purpose of development efforts themselves.

Understanding complex, transnational development interactions requires a broad enough perspective on transnational linkages to include those networks that operate in support of development projects and those in opposition, as well as the ideologies underlying them. These linkages crosscut other national, regional, and local allegiances and build upon unequal relationships of power at local and global levels. The aim of such an analysis is to understand how planned development influences local people and how global political processes determine the role local people may play in contesting global development processes.

Acknowledgments

I gratefully acknowledge the contribution of Anne Hendrixson, who assisted with the research and editing of this chapter.

Notes

1. See, for example, discussion of this in Fisher 1997; Jordan and van Tuijl 2000; Keck and Sikkink 1998; Smith, Chatfield, and Pagnucco 1997.

2. This account has been recorded by numerous authors, for example, McCully (1998) and Udall (1997). No precise number of institutions or individuals was affiliated with the international Narmada campaign. A November 1993 letter published in support of the Narmada Bachao Andolan carried the names of seventy-eight non-governmental organizations from fourteen countries. A September 21, 1992, letter printed in the *Financial Times* stating that the World Bank must withdraw from Sardar Sarovar "immediately" was signed by 250 organizations, coalitions, and movements from thirty-seven countries.

The NGOs affiliated with the Narmada Action Committee include the US-based Bank Information Center, the Environmental Defense Fund, Friends of the Earth, the International Rivers Network, and the Natural Resource Defense Council, along with European and Japanese NGOs, including Action for World Solidarity, the Committee on Environment and Development, Friends of the Earth (Japan), Probe International (Canada), the Rainforest Information Center (Australia), Survival International (England), and the Swallows (Sweden).

3. The government of Japan had already lent US$20 million through the Overseas Economic Cooperation Fund and was considering lending more. In 1990, one month after the first International Narmada Symposium, hosted by Japanese non-governmental organizations, the Japanese Ministry of Foreign Affairs announced that it would not further finance the Sardar Sarovar Project because of local opposition, the lack of resettlement planning, and the absence of a comprehensive environmental assessment.

4. The first project reviewed by this office, the Arun III hydroelectric project proposing construction along the Arun River in eastern Nepal, was eventually dropped by the World Bank. The international coalition supporting the protest included many who worked with the Narmada Action Committee.

5. Other prominent national organizations include the Movimento dos Atingidos por Barragens in Brazil (The Movement of People Affected by Dams [MAB]), the Cordillera Peoples Alliance in the Philippines, Sobrevivencia in Paraguay, and the Southeast Asia Rivers Network in Thailand (SEARIN).

6. The November 2000 ICDRP press release commenting on the final report of the WCD (Dams and Development: A New Framework for Decision-Making) listed the following organizations: The Association for International Water and Forest Studies (Norway), the Berne Declaration (Switzerland), the Campaign to Reform the World Bank (Italy), the Coalition of People Affected by Large Dams and Aqueducts (Spain),

the Cordillera People's Alliance (Philippines), The Corner House (England), the Environmental Monitoring Group (South Africa), Friends of the Earth (Slovakia), the International Rivers Network (USA), the Movement of People Affected by Large Dams (Brazil), the Save the Narmada Movement (India), Sobrevivencia (Paraguay), the Southeast Asia Rivers Network (Thailand), the Swedish Society for Nature Conservation, and World Economy, Ecology, and Development (Germany). In the preceding two and a half years, some of these groups had interacted largely through the Internet; other groups and individuals not listed participated in the face-to-face meetings. Over the course of almost three years, beginning in May 1998, ICDRP meetings were held in Washington DC, Colombo, Prague, Sao Paulo, Cairo, Hanoi, Capetown, London, and Bratislava. Usually, representatives of other Southern groups not in the list above were in attendance at these meetings.

7. The term *bifocal* oversimplifies the problems of communication facing transnational activists and lends itself too easily to replicating an old dualism (tradition/modernity) with a new one (local/global).

8. This legitimacy is by no means assured, and the intervention of NGOs comes under severe attack by states that question the right of NGOs to "represent" the interests of their citizens.

9. See Imhoff, Wong, and Bosshard 2002.

10. Lopez, Smith, and Pagnucco 1995:36. A few studies of transnational advocacy networks have been undertaken by political scientists interested in the effects of these networks on international and state politics (see, for instance, Keck and Sikkink 1998; Lipschultz 1992; Smith, Chatfield, and Pagnucco 1997). The global activities of human rights, peace, feminist, and environmental activists, which occur mainly through NGO global networks, have attracted some scholarly attention, but the effects of linkages among subnational and cross-national interest groups, international organizations, and other actors, as well as the pressure they place upon national governments and international organizations, have yet to be fully explored.

9

Power to the People

*Moving towards a Rights-Respecting
Resettlement Framework*

Dana Clark

As an environmental and human rights lawyer, I have worked with
communities that have been resisting, or dealing with the consequences of,
development-forced displacement, often in the context of projects
financed by international financial institutions such as the World Bank. As
part of the process of seeking accountability for the wrongs suffered by people displaced by development projects, I spent more than a decade focusing on World Bank resettlement policy. In my experience, the key problem
with the existing World Bank resettlement policy framework is not that
there is a blindness to the problems and risks inherent in forcibly uprooting people from their traditional lands and means of livelihood. In fact, as
discussed in other chapters, Michael Cernea, the former World Bank chief
sociologist, who worked internally for the development of the Bank's first
involuntary resettlement policy, has established a well-known impoverishment risk matrix associated with forced evictions (Cernea 1991:195–196).

It is well understood that people who are involuntarily displaced by
development projects often suffer from severe alteration of their physical
and social landscapes. Their homelands, crops, production systems, social
support networks, and economic relationships are lost. Sustainable ways
of life depending, for example, on rivers or farmland can be seriously

impaired when rivers are turned into stagnant reservoirs or fertile land is submerged or converted to industrial uses. Loss of livelihood, as well as difficulty establishing viable alternatives, has been particularly problematic.

RESETTLEMENT AND HUMAN RIGHTS

Improperly implemented development-forced displacement can violate a multiplicity of human rights, leading in the worst cases to death, in the majority of cases to impoverishment, and in most cases to the negation of rights to adequate housing, security of tenure, food security, freedom of movement, and choice of residence. The UN Committee on Economic, Social and Cultural Rights, in General Comment No. 4 on the right to adequate housing, made clear that "the Committee considers that instances of forced evictions are *prima facie* incompatible with the requirements of the Covenant and can only be justified in the most exceptional circumstances, and in accordance with the relevant principles of international law" (UN 1991:par. 18).

Along these lines, the World Bank has recognized that the "heightened risk of impoverishment as a consequence of displacement runs contrary to the Bank's goal of alleviating poverty through developing the productive potential of the poor" (Shihata 1993:46) and that the "potential for violating individual and group rights under domestic and international law makes compulsory resettlement unlike any other project activity" (World Bank 1996b).

The World Bank took leadership in addressing development-forced displacement when it issued a policy on involuntary resettlement in 1980. This policy, as well as its subsequent variations, provides basic development protections to people facing displacement: inter alia, a share in the benefits from the project; an improved standard of living; restoration of livelihoods, with land-based resettlement options for people with land-based livelihoods; inclusion in the design and implementation of the project; and special provisions for vulnerable people, including those who lack title to land.

It is the implementation of policy objectives that has proven to be a vexing problem. In the more than twenty-five years since the World Bank has had a policy on involuntary resettlement, the most fundamental policy objectives and premises—that people adversely affected by development projects should benefit from the projects and have their standard of living improved or at least restored—have proven elusive. International financial institutions (IFIs) such as the World Bank have come up with innovative policies recognizing the hardships facing forced migrants and have vowed to make them beneficiaries of development projects. But these institutions are failing to hold up their end of the deal. This chapter discusses some of the recent trends and policy debates at the World Bank Group regarding involuntary resettlement and then makes recommendations for policy changes to strengthen implementation and address impunity.

As it stands, the World Bank policy framework provides a veneer of protection for local people, a statement of rights, a set of duties and obligations. But the terms of this policy on involuntary resettlement are rarely enforced, and the objectives are even more rarely accomplished.

Why is this? The reasons are many, ranging from lack of proper planning (including consistent underestimation and undervaluation of costs and losses) to institutional weaknesses (including lack of capacity and lack of enforcement) and the lack of political will to rehabilitate affected people fully. The latter problem is compounded by the fact that projects are often sited in areas where people are politically and economically marginalized. The political sensitivity and legal complexity are enhanced by the fact that these projects invoke national power against local communities for the benefit of powerful international players such as the World Bank Group and/or multinational corporations. In this local/national/international context, a great imbalance in power exists between the various parties. This is not to say that local people are powerless—they can and do resist. However, as Tony Oliver-Smith has noted, to be displaced is the ultimate expression of powerlessness (Oliver-Smith 1996:78; Rodman 1992:650).

In such situations, it is insufficient to rely on the legal fiction that the nation-state speaks for and represents the interests of its citizens. In fact, in this context, the national government has decided that certain people must make sacrifices in the name of development, that these people are in the way of national progress, and that it is willing to invoke its police powers to move them out of the way. Furthermore, large infrastructure projects often coincide with geopolitical ambitions for control over or access to territory, resources, and markets. Classic examples of this are the Chixoy Dam in Guatemala (described by Johnston, chapter 10, this volume) and the Yadana gas pipeline in Burma (EarthRights International 1996). This tension between local and national interests is one reason why international standards, including international human rights and international policies, are so important and why there must be independent monitoring of these types of projects.

However, the fact that people are usually internally displaced by development-forced displacement makes it more challenging for international monitors to gain access to the development-displaced persons and to provide a meaningful response to their plight. "People who are displaced by development projects undergo hardships and human rights violations similar to those suffered by other kinds of forced migrants, but the areas of international law that specifically address the situation of forced migrants (international refugee law and international humanitarian law) do not protect them" (Barutciski 2002:7). Similarly, while there are often national and international outpourings of aid in response to refugees or natural disasters, development-forced displacement takes place largely under the radar screen.

"What distinguishes DIDR [development-induced displacement and resettlement] from other types of internal displacement is that it occurs in the name of an ostensibly greater economic good and that the government which is responsible for the displacement is also responsible for ensuring the protection of the affected population" (Barutciski 2002:7). The national government has a conflict of interest in these two roles. There can also be a conflict between national laws and customary laws, as well as a clash of interests between national authorities and subnational entities such as indigenous peoples and ethnic minorities. In many cases, institutionalized discrimination and/or discriminatory attitudes and laws affecting women and indigenous peoples are in play, particularly when it comes to issues of land ownership, participation, consultation, and decision making, which are all critically important in situations of resettlement and displacement.

In the context of World Bank–financed projects, one could argue that the World Bank should play a sheltering role, using its relationship with the borrower to promote the development objectives of people who are threatened with displacement or have been displaced as a result of the projects it finances. However, decisions at the Bank are ultimately made by its Board of Executive Directors, which represents member governments. Many governments assert that displacement situations are part of the "internal affairs" of a country and criticism of or challenges to the way these projects are unfolding are viewed as unwelcome meddling. And because member governments are content to exercise the power of eminent domain in their own countries, they are less likely to champion the rights of people affected by its exercise abroad.

This hands-off approach is also apparent in the crippling weaknesses in the supervision and accountability systems at the World Bank, including the Bank's minimal attention to compliance with environmental and social policy requirements after the disbursement of funds. Although the Bank has acknowledged that it has the legal right to demand compliance with loan agreements until the loan is repaid, in practice, it tends not to supervise implementation—or exercise its available remedies—beyond the point at which the funds have been disbursed (World Bank 1999:18). Even when supervision is more intensive, achieving results and improvements has proven difficult, particularly if the borrowing government is unwilling to make modifications to ensure compliance.

Furthermore, affected citizens cannot seek accountability for policy violations for most of the project's lifetime. Although the World Bank took the lead in establishing an accountability mechanism to enable affected citizens to lodge complaints about harm suffered or threatened as a result of policy violations in projects, its Inspection Panel suffers from an important constraint in responding to requests for an investigation. It is barred from investigating complaints about projects for which the World Bank has disbursed more than 95 percent of the funds to the borrower. Therefore, even though the loan agreement and World Bank policies are supposed to apply until the loan has been repaid, neither Bank supervision nor Inspection Panel oversight serves as any guarantee of project compliance beyond the point of disbursement. For most of the project's life, there is simply no meaningful institutional accountability, and, concomitantly, compliance and implementation are weak.

This combination of power imbalances and institutional impunity all too often results in broken loan covenants, including breaches of promises of mitigation and improvement that have been made as justification for the project. A pattern occurring under existing policies is that promises are made, loan covenants are agreed to, money is given, a project is built, and people are displaced. Once the money is disbursed, implementation of the loan agreement terms and accomplishment of the (supposedly) binding policies are often ineffective or incomplete with regards to resettlement and rehabilitation. In these situations, the loose social contract reflected in the loan agreement and the Bank's environmental and social policy framework —to receive public funds for public benefit and, in exchange, to promise mitigation and avoidance of harm—is violated. Rehabilitation becomes illusory, and resettlement sites become dead-end places that lack meaningful livelihood opportunities and, in many cases, basic functioning infrastructure.

Time and again, social and environmental loan covenants are broken, often with the full knowledge—and, one might argue, the knowing complicity—of the lending institutions. A recent example from Brazil involved a private-sector borrower, Tractebel, which initially borrowed money from the Inter-American Development Bank (IDB) and a Brazilian bank to construct the Cana Brava hydroelectric project. The project led to displacement of thousands of people, but compensation arrangements excluded hundreds of families. Agitation by the local people, supported by the national anti-dam group Movimento dos Atingidos por Barragens (MAB) and including occupation of the Tractebel headquarters in Rio in 2001 and occupation of the IDB headquarters in 2005, resulted in an agreement to create a compensation fund. Although a claim was filed with the IDB's inspection mechanism in 2002, it was not acknowledged for more than two years, and the IDB inspection panel did not start investigating the project until March 2005. The panel's final report, completed in July 2005, was not publicly released; the IDB claimed confidentiality and released only an abstract summary of the findings.[1] Meanwhile, in May 2006, Tractebel's subsidiary, Companhia Enegética Meridional, took out loans from private-sector banks to prepay the IDB loan. After the pre-payment, both the dam-building company and the IDB claimed that the IDB therefore lacked any ability to enforce the terms of its resettlement policy (see note 1; Rede Brasil 2005).

Logic dictates that this type of behavior will intensify in the future. The borrower can get the start-up cash, get the project going, and then prepay the loan and shirk the hard part—fixing the harm. With the loan repaid, the bank can claim that it no longer has any legitimate role in overseeing the project. This behavior is a sign that the system has a fundamental design flaw.

Given these well-documented problems, one could conclude that it is unethical to continue promoting a model that emphasizes and permits "involuntary" resettlement. The old system—involuntary resettlement even through force and often for projects with dubious development benefits if the true costs are properly accounted for—is not working. Development benefits that come at the expense of other people's human rights are antithetical to sustainable development. Rather, they represent exploitative and inequitable development.

CURRENT TRENDS

In June 2005 *The New York Times* observed the significance of a recent World Bank loan by stating that "to bank watchers, environmentalists and multinational corporations, the announcement of $270 million in grants and guarantees for the Nam Theun 2 dam was a landmark event. It represented the bank's return to big dam projects" (*New York Times* 2005:3). This article was picking up on a renewed momentum within the World Bank to support what it terms "high-risk, high-reward" infrastructure, such as large dams and power plants.

The problem, of course, is that these "high-risk, high-reward" projects have tended to externalize the risks and costs to local people and the global environment while allowing the rewards to be misallocated and increasing inequality and impoverishment. This is exactly what the environmental and social policies were designed to prevent. Although some systemic improvements in approach to such projects have been made, disturbing gaps in avoiding and mitigating harm and properly allocating benefits still remain.

There have been two relatively recent, in-depth multistakeholder reviews of the World Bank's portfolio involving some of the highest-risk projects. These reviews evaluated two of the Bank's most contentious sectors—dams and extractive industries—both of which have significant displacement impacts. This section of the chapter briefly, but not exhaustively, covers some of the recommendations of these two processes—the World Commission on Dams and the Extractive Industries Review—that have important implications for displacement policy.

Despite having played a role in establishing these two in-depth reviews of its portfolio, the World Bank has sought to distance itself from the findings and recommendations, so these recommendations have not yet been effectively translated into World Bank policy. To the contrary, they have triggered a backlash inside the Bank. Certain people who are wedded to these industries have sought to sabotage the recommendations and push forward with more Bank lending for these sectors.

The final part of this section on trends looks at the resettlement policy revision process at the International Finance Corporation (IFC), a private-sector arm of the World Bank. The IFC completely revamped its approach to the environmental and social safeguard policies. Unfortunately, the IFC also distanced itself from the lessons of past experience and the recommendations of these two independent reviews.

The World Commission on Dams

The World Commission on Dams (WCD) carried out a review of large dams around the world with commissioners from across the spectrum of experience—representatives of dam-affected people, representatives of the hydro industry, and other expert participants, including fellow contributing author Thayer Scudder (chapter 2, this volume). The WCD published its final report, Dams and Development, in November 2000 (available at http://www.dams.org, along with a wealth of background research and information). The report contained detailed recommendations for how to make dams and development projects more equitable and sustainable (WCD 2000a). Because of space constraints, this chapter does not provide an exhaustive overview of this process or its final recommendations, but the following highlights a few salient points.

One of the most basic is the emphasis on a rights- and risks-based approach to development planning. In addressing the power imbalances discussed earlier, the WCD recommended a comprehensive stakeholder analysis (WCD 2000a:Guideline 1) that would include identifying and addressing "constraints to establishing a level playing field for stakeholder involvement," would recognize existing rights, and would perform a vulnerability or risk analysis to ensure that those facing vulnerability would be represented as core stakeholders. In addition, the WCD called for recognition of the right of indigenous peoples to give their free, prior, informed consent (known as FPIC) at all stages of project planning and development (WCD 2000a: Guideline 3). The WCD also recommended benefit-sharing mechanisms (Guideline 20) (see Cernea, chapter 3, this volume) and enforceable negotiated settlements (Guideline 2). Despite repeated calls for the WCD findings and recommendations to inform and shape the Bank's then-evolving policy on involuntary resettlement, the Resettlement Thematic Group of the World Bank effectively ignored the WCD recommendations during the conversion of the policy from Operational Directive 4.30 to Operational Policy 4.12.[2]

The Extractive Industries Review

In July 2001 the World Bank commissioned an independent review of its role in the extractive industries. The review was designed to be a multi-stakeholder consultation that would result in recommendations to guide the Bank's involvement in the sector. Its particular task was to evaluate the compatibility of the Bank's involvement in the sector with sustainable development and poverty alleviation. The Extractive Industries Review (EIR) was commissioned by then-president James Wolfensohn in response to repeated external critiques of the Bank's role in supporting oil, mining, and gas projects. The EIR followed an "eminent person" model and was headed by Emil Salim, a former environment minister from Indonesia. In 2003 the EIR issued a report and recommendations.

One of the EIR's more significant recommendations was that the principle of free, prior, informed consent (FPIC)—which the WCD recognized as a matter of international law for indigenous peoples—should also be extended to other local communities. The EIR defined FPIC as "a process by which indigenous people, local communities, government and companies may come to mutual agreements in a forum that gives affected people enough leverage to negotiate conditions under which they may proceed and an outcome leaving the community clearly better off" (EIR 2003b:50). One goal of the EIR recommendations was "to lift up civil society so [that] it is balanced in the triangle of partnership between governments, business, and civil society" (EIR 2003b:7).

With respect to the World Bank's policy on involuntary resettlement, the Executive Summary of the EIR noted that the

> IFC and MIGA [the Multilateral Investment Guarantee Agency, a private-sector arm of the World Bank Group that provides political risk insurance to private investors] should engage in consent processes leading to free prior and informed consent before resettlement takes place. This means [that] projects would only result in voluntary resettlements, not forced ones. Compensation and project-derived benefits should lead to genuine improvement, assessed by independent reputable third parties, when traditional subsistence patterns are being rapidly transformed by development. [EIR 2003b:4]

The EIR also addressed benefit sharing, noting that the World Bank Group should support only those projects it can show will benefit all affected groups, including the most vulnerable. Also, the Bank should decline to invest in projects if such equitable benefit sharing cannot be ensured or should "redesign them so that the standards of living for local groups clearly improve" (EIR 2003b:2). It further recommended that the Bank require revenue sharing with local communities, mandate the use of poverty indicators that are monitored systematically, encourage the incorporation of public health components, urge NGOs to build the capacities of affected communities, and help set up independent grievance mechanisms (EIR 2003b:2–3).

Significantly, the EIR also called for the Bank to "make a strong commitment to helping governments tackle the legacy of extractive industry projects" (EIR 2003b:5):

> Compensation funds should be established for people affected by past developments. In cooperation with other funding agencies and in partnership with all the stakeholders, the World Bank Group should establish a targeted program aimed at restoring degraded lands, improving the life of the poor who are affected by previous project closures, and generating new employment and skills training. [EIR 2003b:5]

The International Finance Corporation Policy Revision

Another significant recent development is the International Finance Corporation's revision of its environmental and social policy framework.

The IFC is an arm of the World Bank Group that provides financial support to private-sector investors for projects in developing countries. In literature on the World Bank, the term *World Bank* is often used to describe the public-sector arms of the Bank (the International Development Association, or IDA, and the International Bank for Reconstruction and Development, or IBRD), whereas the term *World Bank Group* denotes those two entities and also the private-sector arms of the Bank (the International Finance Corporation and the Multilateral Investment Guarantee Agency).

When I first drafted this essay for the advanced seminar at the School of American Research in 2005, the public was anticipating the release of a second draft of the IFC's completely revised policy and "performance standards." The initial consultation draft had provoked widespread concern about a variety of procedural concerns and substantive issues. Many of these concerns, particularly with the new IFC approach to involuntary resettlement, were unfortunately borne out in the final outcome of the IFC's policy revision.

The IFC created what it called a Sustainability Policy, which was supplemented by a series of performance standards (PSs) covering issues such as labor standards, biodiversity, environmental assessment, and displacement (IFC 2006a). Performance Standard 5 covers involuntary resettlement. The most significant problem with the IFC's new performance standard is that it reversed the approach taken under the World Bank policy with respect to recognizing the vulnerability of landless people. The public-sector arms of the World Bank Group (the International Development Association and the International Bank for Reconstruction and Development) are governed by a separate policy framework from the one that has since been developed by the IFC to cover its private-sector operations. The World Bank policy covering IDA and IBRD projects involving resettlement is now known as OP/BP (Operational Policy/Bank Procedure) 4.12. This OP/BP 4.12 replaced a previous version of that involuntary resettlement policy, known as OD (Operational Directive) 4.30. Even though the OP/BP had replaced the OD for the rest of the Bank, the IFC claimed to be following OD 4.30 on involuntary resettlement prior to adopting its own Sustainability Policy and Performance Standard 5.

Both OP/BP 4.12 and OD 4.30 emphasize an "improvement" in the standard of living of all adversely affected people. Both explicitly forbid discrimination against landless people and require respect for the vulnerability of the many people—women, indigenous people, the landless and semi-landless—who, though displaced, may not be protected under national land-compensation legislation. In contrast, the IFC's PS 5 and nonbinding "guidance notes" include confusing language that, when read carefully, constitutes overt discrimination against landless people and a privileging of those with nationally recognized title to land.

The IFC's PS 5 reverses the World Bank's policy with respect to landless people. The World Bank's resettlement policy (OP 4.12) and the IFC's preceding safeguard policy (OD 4.30) explicitly allow for compensation for loss of land (in addition to land-related assets), even for those people without nationally recognized or recognizable claims to the land. For example, OD 4.30 par. 3(e) states: "Land, housing, infrastructure, and other compensation should be provided to the adversely affected population, indigenous groups, ethnic minorities, and pastoralists who may have usufruct or customary rights to the land or other resources taken for the project. The absence of legal title to land by such groups should not be a bar to compensation." In contrast, "PS 5 only requires compensation for loss of land for people with nationally recognized or recognizable title to land, but not necessarily for those tenants, sharecroppers, family members and others who are physically or economically displaced from that land but have no 'recognizable' claim to title" (Clark 2006:17).

The IFC also sought to define a much narrower scope for the resettlement policy. In earlier drafts, the IFC had stated that the involuntary resettlement performance standard would cover only land takings that involve the transfer of title or granting of an easement or right of way. If, for example, people's lands are flooded (temporarily or permanently) but title is not transferred, or if pollution emissions from a factory make it impossible for people to remain in their homes in the vicinity of an industrial project, or if an industrial facility drains down the water table, thereby driving people from their lands or depriving them of livelihood resources, but they do not grant an easement, nor does the government seek to condemn their land, the IFC intended that these people would not be protected by its policy. The ethical and economic flaws within this idea are clear: it sends a signal to private-sector clients that it is acceptable development practice to externalize the negative impacts of their projects onto the surrounding communities and the local and global environment. Advocacy and analysis denouncing this language resulted in interventions by concerned staff of the Board of Executive Directors, which required the IFC to include the following language in PS 5:

> In the event of adverse economic, social, or environmental
> impacts from project activities other than land acquisition (e.g.,
> loss of access to assets or resources or restrictions on land use),

such impacts will be avoided, minimized, mitigated or compensated for through the process of Social and Environmental
Assessment under Performance Standard 1. If these impacts
become significantly adverse at any stage of the project, the
client should consider applying the requirements of Performance Standard 5, even where no initial land acquisition was
involved. [IFC 2006a:Performance Standard 5, par. 6]

Finally, one other very disturbing trend reflected in the IFC's policy is
the endorsement of the state's use of force to benefit private-sector investment. The performance standard and accompanying (nonbinding) guidance notes make clear that the performance standard would apply *only* to
situations in which the private sector either is relying upon the government
to exercise its power of expropriation and eminent domain or can fall back
on government invocation of eminent domain if negotiations with affected
communities fail to lead to their acceptance of the project. It will therefore
not apply in situations that are truly voluntary (and no guidance is provided for truly voluntary resettlement). The IFC fails to recognize the complex policy issues involved in the use of state power to forcibly evict people
from their lands, not for a public use or purpose but rather for private
profit (see de Wet, chapter 4, this volume).

Kelo v. New London

The issue of the private sector benefiting from the exercise of eminent
domain was debated at the US Supreme Court in *Kelo v. New London*. In
that case, landowners challenging an urban redevelopment project that
was taking their homes argued that because the development was being
conducted by and for the benefit of private-sector actors, it could not be
viewed as a "public purpose" or "public use" as required under the Fifth
Amendment to the US Constitution. The Fifth Amendment states, "Nor
shall private property be taken for public use without just compensation."
The case focused on the public use/private benefit issue. Just compensation was not at issue in the case; one amicus brief indicated that the displaced persons were being offered about $100,000 above fair market value
(Community Rights Counsel 2005:fn. 12).

In what has been described as the most controversial decision of the
2005 term, the Supreme Court upheld the constitutionality of the condemnations, ruling that "there was no basis for exempting economic development from the broad definition of 'public purpose'" and that "although
the City would no doubt be forbidden from taking petitioners' land for the

purpose of conferring a private benefit on a particular private party...the takings issue before us...would be executed pursuant to a 'carefully considered' development plan," which was "not adopted 'to benefit a particular class of identifiable individuals'" (US Supreme Court 2005:2670–2671). The Court also noted that, "quite simply, the government's pursuit of a public purpose will often benefit individual private parties" (US Supreme Court 2005:2684).

MOVING FORWARD FROM HERE

In this section, I suggest policy reform that could help inform the development of a less contentious and more successful IFI policy relating to development-forced displacement. Among other things, as recognized in both the EIR and the WCD reviews, it is important that the development planning process acknowledge and address differentials in bargaining power between the project sponsors and those they are threatening with eviction. The recommendations regarding free prior and informed consent, though highly controversial within the World Bank because they are portrayed as "veto" rights, constitute a crucial element in elevating the bargaining power and negotiating strength of affected communities.

In addition, power differentials in access to information and in participation in decision making must be addressed upstream during the process of evaluating potential development projects. Detailed policy prescriptions should ensure a fair process for situations involving negotiated settlements, including reliable mechanisms to ensure that all terms agreed to as a result of such negotiations are fully implemented, that all applicable laws and policies are complied with, that the process results in equitable benefit sharing that tangibly improves the quality of life of affected people, including full restoration of lost livelihoods, and that the end result reflects the development priorities of the affected communities.

Changing the Sequencing of Displacement and Disbursement

A fundamental flaw in current policy approaches and project design is that they put the cart before the horse: the project is funded and moves forward without first rehabilitating the people and ecosystems that will be irrevocably altered by project impacts. My primary recommendation is, therefore, that policy frameworks and project planning ensure a substantive/procedural connection so that development projects cannot move forward unless and until the required mitigation and rehabilitation are undertaken. A resettlement plan on paper is not enough. You cannot build your dam, for example, until you first compensate the affected people, rehabilitate them, resettle them, and improve their quality of life, as well as take the necessary actions to mitigate other environmental and social impacts. You must create and legally designate any proposed compensatory wildlife reserves, protect sacred groves and other locally significant cultural and ecological resources, and develop the institutional capacity for environmental mitigation and for ongoing resettlement and rehabilitation management.

This would help address the risk of externalization. Project proponents should be required to pay for the mitigation up front. Then, project costs will fully absorb the true cost of acquiring suitable replacement land and providing security of tenure to those displaced, restoring community infrastructure and homes and livelihoods, compensating for all the costs incurred as a result of the move, and so on. In other words, rehabilitate up front, not in the face of impending disaster. Waiting until the floodwater rises behind the dam wall, for example, further increases the power of the dam authorities, who can bring in state police power to "save" the stubborn "holdout" villagers from death.

Requiring that mitigation precede the action that causes the harm is a procedural guarantee of a substantive right. That is, the project proponent must provide acceptable rehabilitation before displacement and before project final clearance. The argument for a fundamental shift in the procedural approach to World Bank projects involving resettlement is not radical. Existing laws in both developing and developed countries already recognize this.

In August 2005 the Madhya Pradesh High Court enjoined any further increase in the height of the Indira Sagar Dam on the Narmada River because it found that the government officials had not rehabilitated people in advance, as required by Indian law. In the *Kelo v. New London* decision mentioned above, the US Supreme Court's decision included a commentary that, in a case involving urban economic redevelopment and relocation, "orderly implementation of a comprehensive plan requires all interested parties' legal rights to be established before new construction can commence" (US Supreme Court 2005:2660). And the United Nations has recognized that "appropriate procedural protection and due process are essential aspects of all human rights but are especially pertinent in relation to a matter such as forced evictions which directly invokes a large number of rights recognized in both the International Covenants on human rights" (UN 1997:par. 15).

The "gap between rhetoric and reality" is a worn-out phrase used to describe World Bank policies and actual practice. The gap exists not just between policy and practice, but also between resettlement plans and resettlement implementation. Things often change in unanticipated ways. The need for a reality check supports the argument in favor of doing the mitigation up front; the reality when displacement is taking place often deviates from that anticipated by the plan. When gaps appear between planning and reality, the plan must adjust to the reality. The policy needs to make clear that when a problem arises, the project authorities must undertake intensive efforts to resolve the problem and that World Bank staff should work with them in a supportive capacity to help improve project outcomes, promote compliance with Bank policies, and accomplish the policy objectives. For example, in the Madhya Pradesh case mentioned above, the court ordered the grievance redressal authorities to be present in the affected villages on a weekly basis to resolve problems in the project.

Providing rehabilitation and mitigation before the project proceeds might slow down project implementation. But this, in and of itself, will help correct historical imbalances in project implementation whereby, in many cases, the civil works are built on time or ahead of schedule but the social and environmental mitigation falls behind schedule. This will make the projects inherently more sustainable. In addition, it will benefit project proponents by reducing uncertainty and helping to soften local resistance —which can be very costly and lead to significant project delays.

Additional Recommendations

One fundamental problem with monitoring and understanding the impacts of the World Bank's resettlement policy and practices is that the Bank is not keeping accurate data or monitoring the rehabilitation status of displaced people over time. It has been well over a decade since the Bank undertook a comprehensive review of its portfolio with respect to resettlement. It is high time for the World Bank to undertake another review to cover the period since 1994. Other international financial institutions should also implement regular reviews of their portfolios to examine the resettlement implications thoroughly. In addition, all IFIs should be required to include in their annual report the number of people displaced by projects they financed that year and then, in subsequent annual reports, the rehabilitation status of the displaced over time.

In addition, a glaring gap in the policy architecture of the World Bank and other IFIs is the lack of policy guidance on voluntary resettlement. As recommended by the EIR, the Bank needs to start promoting voluntary, not involuntary, resettlement. In either a voluntary or an involuntary resettlement situation, the process must ensure that affected people have the opportunity to identify their development priorities and the benefits and results they want to achieve. Project sponsors should not be dictating benefits.

Where involuntary resettlement is being invoked, project proponents must bear the burden of showing that evictions are necessary to serve the public interest and that the impacts on affected communities are proportionate to the reason articulated for displacement. An "eviction impact assessment" should thoroughly evaluate all alternatives that would avoid involuntary resettlement. This should include a cumulative impact assessment that plans for the long term: that is, where will everyone go when the maximum area is affected? There must be a time period for review and comment on the proposed plan. Then, public hearings should provide a forum for people to discuss and challenge the proposal, present alternatives, and articulate their development priorities.

In addition, any projects that are claiming to evict people in the name of the greater public good must satisfy these minimum conditions: (a) incorporation of gender analysis into all processes, including socioeconomic surveys, benefit sharing, decision making, implementation, monitoring, and evaluation; (b) baseline socioeconomic studies before displacement; (c) respect for the rights of all vulnerable people, including women, children, and indigenous people; (d) suitable alternative housing and infrastructure that meet all the needs of the affected people, reflect their development priorities, and improve upon their original situation; (e) provision of documentation to the displaced people for replacement lands or homes, with a guarantee of secure tenure at the new site; (f) legal and social counseling to help people prepare and adapt; (g) fair administration, including checks on corruption, involvement of affected people in monitoring and evaluation, and reasonable response to and corrections of problems in implementation; (h) transparency with respect to plans, rights, rules, and reporting; (i) benefit sharing throughout the life of the project, with the project benefit stream feeding into ongoing mitigation and compensation funds—that is, for schools and scholarships, vocational training, environmental restoration, and revenue for displaced persons as partners in the investment; (j) reliable and accessible systems of enforcement; and (k) access to recourse and impartial judicial review by the affected people if problems are not resolved to their satisfaction.

CONCLUSION

The key problems with the existing policy framework lie in implementation lapses and impunity. Current power imbalances work in favor of project proponents, who benefit at the expense of others. This is inequitable and contrary to broader societal interests. As currently practiced, involuntary resettlement all too often leads to involuntary impoverishment, which is contrary to the right to development (see UN 1986:Art. 2, par. 3). Furthermore, economists have never properly factored in the costs of lost productive potential of communities that are cut off from traditional livelihoods without adequate replacement opportunities.

How to move forward from this legacy of failed resettlement and unsustainable development is still an issue very much in play. On the one hand, the International Finance Corporation recently revised its policy framework, with changes privileging those who have nationally recognized title to their lands and discriminating against those who do not.

On the other hand, the terminology of "gaining public acceptance" (WCD) and a "social license to operate" (EIR) reflect a heightened recognition of corporate and institutional obligations to operate in a socially conscionable manner and to move away from unsustainable practices. Civil society advocates are also expanding their toolkits for holding international financial institutions and multinational corporations accountable or liable for human rights violations and environmentally destructive practices. Accountability systems are becoming an expectation for public international financial institutions, and corporations and private-sector lenders are increasingly recognizing the need to integrate social and environmental concerns into their operations. For example, at the time of this writing, forty-one private banks had signed up to abide by the voluntary Equator Principles, which commit the banks to complying with environmental and human rights norms. Unfortunately, the Equator Principles are closely linked to IFC policies.

Nonetheless, one could argue that for both public-sector and private-sector project proponents, the smart thing to do in the twenty-first century—in terms of business sense and from the "social license to operate" perspective—is to shift towards developing projects with negotiated settlements that reflect the development priorities of affected people; respect ecological, cultural, and social values; and offer a solid economic rationale that has factored in all costs and risks. These costs will entail greater payments to and benefits for local people, but the payoff could be community support, more cooperation, less strife, reduced reputational risk (and enhanced good will), and better-planned development that meets global and local needs and priorities.

This will be a difficult shift for those who are used to externalizing costs with impunity. Corporations such as Chevron and Exxon/Mobil will no longer be able to ignore the people living in the forests and deltas and dismiss their concerns. However, the legal landscape has already shifted for companies with a history of negative environmental and social impacts. Many of them are currently being sued for human rights violations committed in their operations. Unocal recently settled the first of these lawsuits, brought under the Alien Tort Claims Act; although the settlement amount is secret, it was reported on ABC's *20/20* as $30 million. These multinational corporations—and international financial institutions—are far better placed to absorb the full costs of their operations than are those communities that have, for too long, been forced to bear the brunt of unsustainable practices.

Benefit sharing can lead to a better project in the end (see Cernea, chapter 3, this volume). It will also introduce a complicated dynamic into current development debates, because some communities may choose to "sell out" their lands on terms they can live with, which may be distressing to the environmental community. If this is done through a fair process that is enforceable and in compliance with local, national, and international standards, there will be less basis for challenging these projects. The downside, from the corporate perspective, will be that sometimes corporations will have to walk away from a project they want to do. This can happen for other reasons too (that is, technical feasibility, financial issues). In some cases, it will happen because of the exercise of FPIC. But if that is the local population's choice, then respecting that choice will save project sponsors many headaches down the road. Project proponents will also have to respect and accept that there are "no go" zones of extreme environmental and social significance, for instance, territories where uncontacted people have withdrawn and are asking to be left in peace (La Torre López 1999). Thus, each side of the spectrum has to recognize that it is not always going to be happy with the outcome.

Much work must still be done to design policies that can incorporate these principles, improve systems of accountability to ensure that projects are carried out in an environmentally and socially sustainable manner, and enforce the terms of these negotiated agreements and existing policies and laws. Negotiated consent agreements will also require effective enforcement mechanisms in order to be credible and meaningful.

> Progress in such Panel-type legal mechanisms of enforcement would thus seem to depend on the willingness of development banks and international funders to jeopardise projects for the sake of the human rights of development displacees. This in turn will depend on public pressure, and the resultant realisa-

tion by institutions that concern with human rights makes good economic as well as moral sense. This is because it allows development and allows funders to continue with projects—unlike cases such as Sardar Sarovar and Arun III, where the World Bank withdrew from the projects after they had begun. [Barutciski 2002:7]

The victory in the Indira Sagar case mentioned above illustrates that the policies and laws, even if imperfect, are important safeguards of local peoples' most fundamental rights. The system needs to be fundamentally strengthened, but the core objectives continue to be valuable. There are opportunities for moving forward on the policy front; revising social and environmental policies seems to be a trend across institutions, as is the development of—and making improvements to—accountability mechanisms for international financial institutions. For example, the Asian Development Bank (ADB) recently strengthened its inspection process, based on the recognition that its old model was flawed and not functional for either affected people or the institution. Now the ADB is also preparing to revise its safeguard policy framework, which consists of its policies on involuntary resettlement, indigenous peoples, and environmental impact assessment. Also, as mentioned above, the private-sector lending institutions are gaining momentum in incorporating environmental and social considerations into their lending operations. We must now move towards progressive policy development that fully learns from the mistakes of the past and creates a new, rights-respecting framework leading to broad social empowerment and equitable and sustainable development.

Notes

1. Independent Investigation Mechanism: Cana Brava Hydroelectric Power Project: Abstract of Panel Report and IDB Management Response. Inter-American Development Bank (IDB) undated document (probably 2005). http://idbdocs.iadb.org/wsdocs/getdocument.aspx?docnum=671013, accessed September 2007.

2. For an in-depth analysis of the conversion of OD 4.30 to OP 4.12, see Dana Clark 2009.

10

Development Disaster, Reparations, and the Right to Remedy

The Case of the Chixoy Dam, Guatemala

Barbara Rose Johnston

On Hokkaido, the northern island of Japan, Ainu farmland along the Saru River was seized in the 1960s for the Nibutani Dam. This state-sponsored project was built without public input and without social or environmental impact assessment. The Ainu are an ethnic minority, with a customary livelihood and religion based on the river and wetlands. In 1997 the Sapporo District Court found that the Ainu people were indigenous people whose rights to the protection of their distinct culture, as stipulated in the UN International Convention on Civil and Political Rights and the Convention Concerning Indigenous and Tribal Peoples in Independent Countries (ILO no. 169), were violated: expropriation of Ainu land and approval of the dam had been illegal. The dam still stands, but reparations agreements have produced a number of significant actions. Floodgates are opened at times to create wetland areas that are held as sacred and used in cultural ceremonies and to allow replenishment of the local fish population and seasonal agricultural production. As a result of the court findings, in 1997 Japan passed the act Promoting of Ainu Culture and the Dissemination and Education of Knowledge Concerning Ainu Traditions, the first action taken by the Japanese government to recognize the rights of indigenous minorities. Implementation of the act provides ongoing redress for the social and cultural damages resulting from construction of the dam (Sonohara 1997).

***

In China, in May 1999 Wang Sumei, an official from the migration bureau in Wanzhou district, was sentenced to life imprisonment for embezzling Three Gorges Project resettlement money from the bureau. Subsequent investigations of some fourteen officials involved in dam corruption found that embezzled money was used to construct buildings, set up companies, and buy shares on the stock market. China's auditor general reported in January 2000 that around 600 million dollars earmarked for the resettlement of those made homeless by the project had been embezzled, 12 percent of the entire relocation budget. A subsequent press conference brought the embezzled figure down to 7.4 percent of the relocation budget. On February 25, 2000, the former director of the district construction bureau in Fengdu, China, received the death sentence for stealing 12 million yuan (1.44 million dollars) from the Three Gorges Project accounts (Agence France Presse 2000).

***

In Brazil, in October 2003 the Panará tribe announced a settlement with the Brazilian government after a ten-year court battle over damages associated with involuntary resettlement (forced airlift to a reservation), loss of land without compensation, and highway construction through traditional land. In 1973, construction of a highway allowed miners, squatters, and timber harvesters into the area. By 1975, with most of the tribe ill or dead from disease, the National Indian Foundation (FUNAI) arranged for the remaining seventy-five people to be airlifted from their traditional lands. In 1996 the Brazilian court found that the Panará have customary rights to their land and the right to return. The case was appealed and finally settled, restoring rights to 1.2 million acres of land and providing a $420,000 reparations payment for "moral and material damage" in the form of a community development trust. Interest from the trust will provide for community development needs over the life of the trust (Environmental Defense 2003).

***

In South Africa, in 1927 the Nama people were forcibly evicted from their lands in the Richtersveld area of northern Cape Province to allow the development and operation of a government-run diamond mine. In October 2003 the South African Constitutional Court ruled that the Nama people are the true and actual owners of Richtersveld land and mineral rights, that the laws dispossessing them in 1927 amount to racial discrimination, and that the Richtersveld community has the right to secure restitution and compensation from the South African government. The community filed claims seeking title to the Alexkor diamond mine, as well as compensation for land, lost resources, and environmental damages associated with eighty years of intensive mining. This claim was settled in October 2006 with an agreement to provide the community an initial 190 million rand, mining rights, and other benefits to restore the environment and livelihood of the Nama people (Merten 2005; Mines and Communities 2006).

***

These stories illustrate, to some modest degree, the concept of reparations as it applies to development disasters—those cases in which governments condemn and seize land and related resources in the name of economic development yet fail to provide due process, including meaningful compensation for losses and related injury. Host community response to development disasters often involves lengthy struggles to document rights abuses, consequences, and culpability. These are part of the broader effort to secure some form of reparative justice. Ideally, their documentary efforts will result in national or international court review (thus, public discussion and recognition that injustice occurred), with findings that order the state to take actions to restore the dignity and status of injured parties, with monetary awards providing a measure of restitution and indemnity and, in some cases, with the implementation of legal means to punish or ensure "never again."

The term *reparation* generally refers to compensation or remuneration required from a defeated nation as indemnity for damage or injury during a war.[1] This particular usage emerged from customary law established by The Hague IV Convention in 1907. The Hague IV Convention distinguished between combatant and noncombatant populations and property and forbade states to "destroy or seize the enemy's property, unless such destruction or seizure be imperatively demanded by the necessities of war" (Article 23g). Until Hague IV, violations of the customary rules of warfare did not require compensation unless explicitly stipulated in the peace treaty ending the conflict. The Hague IV Convention, however, provided that a "belligerent party which violates the provisions of the said regulations shall...be liable to pay compensation" (Convention, Laws and Customs of Wars on Land, Article 3, October 18, 1907).

After The Hague Convention, most states recognized the principle that private property, with certain exceptions, must be respected in the course of war on land and that confiscating such property without military necessity is prohibited. Through negotiated reparations, states are able to make peace by acknowledging and "repairing" the injuries caused by war. The 1948 adoption of the Universal Declaration on Human Rights and its Article 8, which stipulates that all individuals have the right to remedy when their fundamental human rights are violated, expanded categories of violation and obligations for remedial actions. In the years since, reparations have been secured for violations committed in the name of colonial expansion, economic development, and national security, especially cases involving crimes against humanity and other gross violations of fundamental human rights: genocide, slave labor, human subject experimentation, and the seizure of lands and property without due process or compensation.

The process to claim reparations is varied. Many states will make reparation on their own, without outside intervention, especially when facing the political consequences of breaching international obligations. For other breaches, injured parties may find it necessary to make a claim for reparations before a national or international tribunal. Which tribunal will hear a case depends on the law or treaty setting up the tribunal, any discretion that the tribunals may have in turning away cases, and whether the parties have agreed to adjudication before the tribunal. To make a claim, an injured party must have standing: is the party making the claim owed an obligation, and did the party, in fact, suffer injury? Most international agreements and court procedures seem to require negotiation as a prerequisite to filing claims in an international tribunal. Customary international law also requires claimants to exhaust local remedies before bringing certain types of claims.

In April 2005 the concept of reparation and meaningful remedy was further refined by the United Nations in its adoption of the Basic Principles and Guidelines on the Right to a Remedy and Reparation for Victims of Violations of International Human Rights and Humanitarian Law. In its most current meaning, *reparation* refers to remedy in the following forms: restitution, compensation or indemnity, rehabilitation, satisfaction, and guarantees of nonrepetition (UN 2005 [UN E/CN.4/2005/L.48]).

Restitution refers to actions that seek to restore the victim to the original situation before the gross violations of international human rights law or of international humanitarian law occurred. Restitution includes restoration of liberty; enjoyment of human rights, identity, family life, and citizenship; return to one's place of residence; restoration of employment; and return of property.

Compensation refers to economic payment for any assessable damage resulting from violations of human rights and humanitarian law. This includes physical and mental harm and the related material and moral damages. Rehabilitation includes providing legal, medical, psychological, and social services and care.

Satisfaction includes almost every other form of reparation, including measures that halt continuing violations, verification of facts and full and public disclosure of the truth in rights-protective ways, search for the missing, identification of bodies, and assistance in recovery, identification, and reburial in culturally appropriate ways. Satisfaction also includes official declarations and judicial decisions that restore the dignity, reputation, and legal rights of the victim and the persons connected with the victim, public apology and acceptance of responsibility, judicial sanctions against responsible parties, commemorations, and tributes to the victims.

Guarantees of nonrepetition include measures that contribute to prevention; ensure effective control over the military and security forces; guarantee that proceedings occur with due process, fairness, and impartiality; strengthen the independent judiciary; protect human rights defenders; promote the observance of codes of conduct and ethical norms by public servants; support mechanisms for preventing social conflicts or monitoring social conflicts and their resolution; and review and reform laws contributing to or allowing the gross violation of human rights.

Given the nature of damages resulting from human rights abuses accompanying economic development (most typically, loss of land and a way of life), reparations for development disasters imply remedies that acknowledge injustice, make amends and compensate for past failures, address urgent human environmental needs, reflect a commitment to restore human and environmental integrity, involve equitable decision-making processes, and create or strengthen rights-protective mechanisms.

Achieving reparations is, by no means, an easy feat, given victims' relative lack of power and the burden of proof required from them. Also, reparations mechanisms established by states through international treaties are largely geared towards resolving complaints among states. In the case of internationally financed development disasters—in which economic development occurs at the cost of lives, land, and ways of life and in which projects are subsidized, in whole or part, by non-state actors—effective, rights-protective mechanisms that receive complaints and generate enforceable remedies are largely nonexistent. The international organizations that finance development are party to foreign investment agreements and have obligations to uphold the rights and duties specified in the United Nations Charter, Declarations, and Instruments. Therefore, development-financing institutions such as the World Bank Group have created complaint mechanisms (the World Bank Inspection Panel and the Compliance Advisor Ombudsman). These are, however, internalized processes that limit investigations to current investments and lack significant means to enforce any recommendations or findings (Clark, Fox, and Treakle 2003). The lack of viable reparations mechanisms has caused many to appeal to the court of public opinion in the hope that media coverage, activist campaigns, and other forms of advocacy will draw public attention and generate the political will to attend to ulcerating conditions and demands for justice.

With reference to the displacement caused by development, because rights can be abused at every stage of the project (planning, construction, and operation), moral and legal culpability often involves multiple parties: individuals, national and transnational corporations, international financial institutions, states, and various international agencies. As illustrated so many times elsewhere in this book, despite the legal requirements of host nations and development project financiers to establish and implement social safeguards, actions to mitigate or minimize the adverse impacts of economic development often fail to meet even minimal requirements of just compensation (see chapters 2 and 3 by Scudder and Cernea, respectively, this volume).

The development-forced uprooting of families, communities, and entire cultural nations has created extreme conditions that are, in fact, *development disasters*: people lacking social and economic resources and disproportionately vulnerable to the many geophysical, climatic, biological, technological, and social hazards of modern life. For too many communities, economic development has occurred at the cost of land and livelihood, with devastating effect on the sociocultural and biophysical fabric of life. Consider, for example, the case of the first World Bank–funded development project. Some 57,000 Tongan people in the British colony of Northern Rhodesia (now Zambia and Zimbabwe) were forcibly evicted from their homeland in the late 1950s to build the Kariba Dam. The Tongan nation received no compensation, no replacement lands. Today, three generations later, an estimated 600,000 lack land, livelihood, and the means to sustain a viable way of life (Colchester—Forest Peoples Programme 2000; Colson 1971; Scudder 2005a and chapter 2, this volume).

The World Commission on Dams (WCD) review of fifty large dams found that the social impact of large dams, especially the experience of indigenous peoples and ethnic minorities, has typically involved cultural alienation; loss of land, resources, and the means to sustain a self-sufficient way of life; lack of consultation and meaningful participation in decision-making processes; inadequate compensation or none; human rights abuses; no substantial enjoyment of the benefits of development; and lowered living standards. In the public consultations held by the WCD, testimony demonstrated the overwhelming need for remedial action. The WCD's final recommendations noted that development had involved significant incidents of noncompliance to contractual obligations and national and international laws, resulting in the involuntary displacement of millions of people whose losses have never been justly compensated (Scudder 2005a; WCD 2000b). Many support the WCD's conclusion that reparations for development-affected communities are warranted under existing national and international law, arguing that moral and legal culpability belongs to those parties who planned and authorized projects, as well as those who benefit from dam development projects—including states, funding institutions, contracting and construction companies, and energy and water system management companies (see Bartolomé et al. 2000; Clark 2002b; Colchester—Forest Peoples Programme 2000; Johnston 2000, 2005; Lansing, Lansing, and Erazo 1998; MacKay 2002; Sonohara 1997).

Reparations may be warranted, but the question is, how can they be achieved?

Displaced and other development-affected communities live in extreme poverty yet bear all the cost and burden of documenting and proving their victimization. Constraints include language barriers, minimal levels of literacy, limited or no access to information (especially the full record of contracts, reports, and agreements relevant to compensation and resettlement rights and entitlements), limited or no access to technical assistance, and lack of time and funds to support organizing, participation, communications, technical assistance, assessing findings, attending meetings, and publishing and otherwise producing a defensible and evidence-based claim that substantiates anecdotal testimony. Furthermore, development-affected communities are often marginal members of society, living in countries that lack a rights-protective, independent legal forum where complaints against all potentially responsible parties can be lodged, judgments made, and findings enforced.

Demands for reparation necessarily involve analyzing the chain of events and uncovering evidence that violations have occurred in ways that demonstrate corporate, institutional, and governmental agency culpability. There are very real difficulties in initiating such investigations—especially when complaints involve the recent and sometimes bloody histories of people and institutions, the use and misuse of huge sums of money, and actors who have profited and are now well situated in positions of power.

Developing an evidence-based assessment of project history threatens those individuals and institutions that profited and those who participated in events that are now seen as illegal and prosecutable. Asking questions about who did and did not receive compensatory funds provokes and inflames tensions at all levels of society. Community collaboration in collecting narratives and developing testimony occurs in the face of extreme tension and the continual threat of violence.

In addition to societal constraints are the "nitty-gritty" problematic issues of building a case: how to identify the injured parties (who are the "affected" people?), how to determine whether allegations are legitimate, how to clarify the record of compensatory and remedial actions and identify remaining (contracted) obligations. Also, what flaws and failures are evident in the planning, participatory process, valuation, compensatory strategies, and social impact mitigation efforts? What are the consequential damages of development project failures, and what are the varied values of these damages? Who are the culpable parties, and what are their proportionate responsibilities? What constitutes an appropriate (culturally appropriate, locally defined) plan for remedy? In developing appropriate responses, is it better to provide remedy reflecting the sum total of lost and damaged property or to provide remedy that values not only the material basis of an individual's life but also the economic, social, cultural, and biophysical parameters that sustain the community's way of life? What is the best way to develop the political will and mechanisms to acknowledge project failures and their consequential damages and to implement a meaningful remedy that ensures "never again"? Can we challenge and transform the compensation principle, from direct assets compensation to provision of the means to sustain a healthful way of life?

These questions and constraints shaped and tempered my efforts to help bring about reparations for dam development disaster in Guatemala and are briefly discussed below.

SEEKING REPARATIONS FOR DEVELOPMENT DISASTER IN GUATEMALA

The Chixoy Dam in Guatemala was built in the 1970s and early 1980s to power a hydroelectric generation facility that now provides 80 percent of that nation's electricity (figure 10.1).[2] It was planned and developed by INDE (National Institute for Electrification) at a time when Guatemala was torn by civil war, and its financing (primarily from the Inter-American Development Bank and the World Bank) represented the major source of international funding for Guatemala's military dictatorships. Designs were

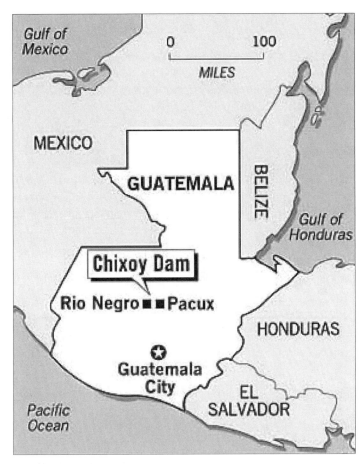

FIGURE 10.1

The location of the Chixoy Dam in Guatemala. San Francisco Chronicle
graphic. Public domain.

approved and construction begun without notifying the local population,
without conducting a comprehensive survey of affected peoples, without
addressing compensation and resettlement for the 3,400 mostly Maya residents. With dam construction well underway, title to land yet to be
acquired, and a new World Bank loan demanding a resettlement plan, the
military dictatorship of Lucas Garcia declared the Chixoy Dam site and the
surrounding region a militarized zone in 1978.

Some villagers in the soon-to-be-flooded river valley accepted resettlement offers but found poorer-quality housing, smaller acreage, and infer-
tile land. Others, most notably the residents of Río Negro, refused to move

and attempted to negotiate more equitable terms. Tensions escalated as the remaining residents were declared subversive, community records of resettlement promises and land documents were seized, and community leaders killed. Following the March 1982 military coup, in which General Rios Montt took over as military dictator, the Guatemalan government initiated a "scorched earth" policy against the Mayan civilian population, and massacres took place in small hamlets and villages throughout the Guatemalan countryside. It was at this time, under this policy of state-sponsored violence against Mayan civilians, that construction on the dam was completed and floodwaters began to rise. Villages in the river valleys were emptied at gunpoint, and homes and fields burned. A series of massacres took place, and when survivors fled to nearby villages, residents of those villages were also massacred. By September 1982, in one village alone, 487 people—half the population of Río Negro—had been murdered (EAFG 1997).

Following the 1994 Oslo Peace Accords ending Guatemala's civil war, a series of investigations broke the silence over the massacres. In 1999 a United Nations–sponsored commission concluded that more than 200,000 Mayan civilians had been killed, that acts of genocide were committed against specific Mayan communities, and that the government of Guatemala was responsible for 93 percent of the human rights violations and acts of violence against civilians. The Río Negro massacres were singled out as an exemplary case of state-sponsored violence and genocide (CEH 1999; REMHI 1999).

Today, while the completed dam provides power for much of the country, host communities continue to suffer. The failure to provide an equivalent size and quality of farmland and household land for the resettled has produced severe poverty, widespread hunger, and high malnutrition rates. Communities that were excluded from the resettlement program also struggle with an array of problems. Dam releases occur with no warning, and resulting flash floods destroy crops, drown livestock, and sometimes kill people. Most inhabitants of former fishing villages, their livelihoods ruined, have turned to migrant labor. Upstream communities saw part of their agricultural land flooded and access to land, roads, and regional markets cut off.

Community representatives presented their case of involuntary displacement and related human rights abuse in numerous national and international arenas, including formal presentations to the Organization of American States Human Rights Commission and the United Nations–sponsored truth commission investigating genocide in Guatemala. They argued that inadequate resettlement planning and implementation failures contributed to an array of actions and conditions leading to violence (threats, assassinations, and massacre) and producing serious harm to life, community, culture, and livelihood.

Staff of the World Bank, acknowledging that project planning and implementation were hindered by significant failures in the resettlement program, conducted a social program evaluation in 1996; it concluded that the Bank's obligations had been met. In the ensuing years, continued complaints, coupled with the gravity of social program failures, prompted occasional World Bank–funded assistance to resettled communities.

In 1998, INDE's distribution grid was privatized. The privatization allowed the World Bank and Inter-American Development Bank loans to be repaid, with interest, in full. It also resulted in the closure of INDE's resettlement office and the loss of a local complaint mechanism.

Dam-affected communities took their cause to national and international public forums, demanding compensation and assistance as defined by the World Bank policy on involuntary resettlement and as promised by INDE so many years before. They also demanded compensation and assistance for those excluded from prior compensatory efforts, noting that in several villages, negotiations were aborted or halted and agreements never reached. Even when tentatively reached, agreements were achieved under great duress—with the very real threat of violence and massacre. In essence, the communities demanded a new negotiation process.

In response to increased media attention to the plight of dam-affected communities, INDE asserted that its obligations had been met and that, since privatization in 1998, it no longer had the institutional mechanism, financial ability, or legal responsibility to respond to community complaints. Similar sentiments were expressed by the project financiers.

Given these complex conditions and varied perspectives, by 2003 the push to resolve the very real problems of Río Negro survivors and other dam-affected communities appeared to be at an impasse. It was at this juncture I was asked to advise communities and their advocates (Rights Action Guatemala, International Rivers Network, and Reform the World Bank Italy). In July 2003 I attended a meeting of representatives from dam-affected communities in the resettlement village of Pacux and presented a conceptual plan for achieving clarity in ways that might jump-start the political process. After much discussion, it was agreed that members of the dam-affected communities would collaborate with an independent scientific research team to document their histories and the consequences of these histories.

It is important to define here what is meant by "independent assessment." Typically, post-project assessment of the performance of social programs occurs in one of three ways: by in-house staff review, by consultants contracted by the financiers to conduct an external review, or by staff of the nongovernmental organizations that make up the activist community. In each of these situations, findings can be muted by controversy over the independent status of the review: one party or the other claims that an interest or agenda contaminates the objectivity of researchers and therefore the independent findings. In this case, conscious effort was made to ensure that the evidentiary record would be reviewed in ways that were transparent, thorough, and truly independent of the various parties. The assessment would occur with a peer-reviewed process facilitated by scientific organizations, without financial support of and contractual obligations to potentially culpable parties (project financiers or governments).

The resulting Chixoy Dam Legacy Issues Study generated evidence that confirmed, contextualized, or discounted the allegations and claims contained in the published and documentary record; assessed this evidence in comparative fashion (examining how Chixoy river basin community experiences and conditions differed from those of other rural Mayan communities); and identified specific consequential damages that could be directly or indirectly attributed to the failures and flaws in dam construction, planning, and social program implementation. The study involved holistic, evidence-based, historical analysis, with collaborative and participatory components that examined process and consequence. The overall goal was to encourage political will to address the issues and to do so in ways that would shape and advise a problem-solving process.

Key questions structured this work. Over the course of hydroelectric development planning in Guatemala and the planning, construction, and management of this hydroelectric project, what were the obligations of the Guatemalan government, INDE, project financiers, and project contractors with regard to dam-affected communities? What was the record of resettlement and compensation promises or agreements as reflected in testimonial accounts, project plans, contracts, and related documents? What methods and indicators were used to determine the affected population, their rights, and the value of goods, lands, and livelihoods adversely affected by the development? In what ways and at what times were resettlement, compensation, and related social problems reported? When reported, what were the responses? When specific promises and plans were made to remedy reported problems, what actions were implemented, and to what effect? Were the financial institutions and lender countries aware of the violence being perpetrated upon project-affected communities? Was there evidence in published and public records, forensic reports, news reports, witness testimony, and project consultant files that contextualized, confirmed, or clarified the testimony of members of dam-affected communities or, conversely, the views and conclusions of project financiers?

To address these questions, I reviewed the documentary record: reports, memos, and formal publications located in public and financial institution archives and the personal files of project consultants in Guatemala, France, and the United States. Assisting in this review were many volunteers (including former project consultants) who helped locate documents and translate materials. Findings from prior archaeological research demonstrated connections between existing villages and ancestral populations. Findings from earlier exhumations of Río Negro and other massacre sites helped substantiate informant testimony—people had been massacred. They had not simply fled the area, as claimed by the government.

In addition to evidence compiled from earlier research, a number of new evidence-generating projects were initiated to identify and measure the *consequential damages* associated with dam development, forced displacement, and related loss of the means to sustain a healthful way of life. We hired a land title specialist to examine the record of deeds and address the question of how access and control over land title changed before, during, and after the project. We hired research and support staff to train community representatives and help develop local histories and needs assessments. With the aid of a linguist/ethnographer team and the trained community representatives, we conducted 176 household surveys to establish the material well-being of pre-dam households (circa 1975) and the relative status and current access to critical resources for a representative sample of the affected population.

Because the household survey strategy might be of use in other contexts, additional detail was warranted. The affected population was defined as the households physically displaced by the construction of the dam and its reservoir, as well as the upstream and downstream residents who suffered the loss of land and property and decreased access to and use of critical resources as a result of the project construction and operation of the hydroelectric facility. Participatory ethnographic methods and documentary resources were used to identify traditional patterns of resource value, access, use, and control; to identify key events and conditions that adversely impacted these resource relations and thus altered or destroyed people's ability to be self-sufficient; to document the sociocultural and biophysical damages associated with these events and conditions; and to assess the socioeconomic consequences of these changes. Key indicators included household demographics, housing conditions, household resources, patterns of access and use of river and forest resources, access to land and agricultural productivity, ability to produce surplus and to participate in the market, other income-generating strategies, and access to potable water, electricity, sanitation, and telephone. To substantiate informant accounts of pre-dam socioeconomic conditions and to measure change over time, household survey findings were cross-checked with the land title record, the census, and ethnographic documents from the periods before and during dam construction. A significant portion of the 2004 household survey sample (75 percent) participated in a census conducted by Gustavo Adolfo Gaítan (1979) in four visits to the Río Negro and Chixoy river basins. That census reports family names, household size, number of structures in the household compound, size of farmland, number and kinds of domesticated animals, agricultural products, and market participation for fourteen communities living on the riverbanks upstream of the dam site.

In addition to household surveys, previously published informant testimony detailing massacre events was reviewed, and ethnographers conducted a series of follow-up interviews with key informants. To verify testimony and substantiate accounts of the major violations of human rights, accounts were cross-checked with at least three independent sources, per standard human-rights reporting protocol.

All materials were developed, peer-reviewed, revised, and then published in Spanish and English. Community needs assessments, household surveys, and key informant interviews produced data supporting consequential damage findings. The research plan, findings, and recommendations for reparation were discussed with the affected communities, their advocates, and representatives from the Guatemalan government, World Bank, and Inter-American Development Bank. All findings were supported by substantiated documentary evidence.

MAJOR FINDINGS

Before the dam, land rights were secure, and communal rights in many cases dated back to the 1800s. Fertile river basin lands provided a biannual harvest, fish were plentiful, and communities held title to large tracts of grazing and wooded lands. The majority of people had access and use rights to resources that sustained household and community needs.

In 1975, Chixoy Dam designs were approved, the project financed, and construction begun. Affected communities received no notification, no census was conducted, and no land acquisition occurred to support construction works, the dam, hydroelectric generation, and the reservoir or host resettled communities.

Throughout the development project history and contrary to contractual agreements, the Inter-American Development Bank and the World Bank released loan funds with no evidence that INDE held legal title to the development site and with the knowledge that the project lacked resettlement and compensation plans and agreements.

The Guatemalan constitution allows condemnation of lands for hydroelectric development and requires just compensation. However, the constitution prohibits the taking of private and communal land when title predates 1956. Review of land title in 2004 found that twenty-six fincas on the margins of the Río Negro and the Chixoy and around the dam were properly registered titles with dates first inscribed between 1883 and 1910. The dam is located on lots 15 and 18. The intake building is on lot 15. Only lot 18 is in the name of INDE. Thus, the lands that support a portion of the dam, the hydroelectric facility, and the majority of land beneath the reservoir are, to this day, owned by individuals and communities.

The Inter-American Development Bank and the World Bank in their loan agreements obligated INDE to develop and implement a viable resettlement and compensation plan. Efforts to shape a last-minute resettlement and compensation plan were grossly inadequate, excluding communities upstream, downstream, and adjacent to the dam. Last-minute plans were written and submitted to the banks without the meaningful input of affected people.

The dam-affected population is significantly larger than presently or historically recognized by INDE and the project financiers. Downstream and upstream communities were visited by resettlement officers on a number of occasions and were promised compensatory actions for damages relating to the dam's construction. Massacres and related violence halted resettlement officer visits, however, and no compensation documents were prepared as promised. When reservoir waters rose and dam operation problems began, communities lost land and property. But threats of violence, including threat of massacre like Río Negro, discouraged them from submitting claims. Thus, the dam-affected population includes not only some 3,500 mostly Mayan residents who were recognized by INDE as displaced, but also more than 6,000 households in more than 480 surrounding communities. These communities petitioned the Guatemalan government in 1983 for formal recognition as dam-affected communities experiencing flooding of land and other property, loss of sacred sites, loss of access to land, and disruption of transportation routes. The socioeconomic ties among these communities and access to their traditional markets had been severed.

The failure to implement a viable plan for resettlement and socioeconomic development at the time of dam construction contributed to the violence in the area. Communications with the affected population about the development project, impending impacts, and possible compensatory options typically occurred in the presence of armed soldiers. Communities that voiced concern over the plans and compensatory options and attempted to negotiate more equitable terms were declared guerilla-supporting communities. Military and civil patrols were used to remove people forcibly from the reservoir site. In two villages, community leaders were required to bring negotiation documents and land titles to INDE offices. En route, they were kidnapped, tortured, and killed, and the land title documents disappeared. Similar actions in a third village resulted in the community leader's detainment and the disappearance of land title and the community record of compensation negotiations.

When reservoir waters rose in January 1983, the river valley population had been taken away at gunpoint by military and civil patrols or murdered in four massacres (figure 10.2). Many survivors were forced to live in militarized "model villages." Model villages like Pacux were later built in other areas of Guatemala to concentrate and control the Maya civilian population, but most were demilitarized by the mid-1990s and residents were free to return to their former homes and lands. At the time of its decommissioning, on December 21, 2003, Pacux was the only militarized village remaining in Guatemala.

The failure to provide the full extent of compensation promises (fertile lands, adequate housing, compensation for property losses, electricity and water, support for community health and education workers, and effective economic development) had a degenerative effect on the culture, economy, and health of both displaced and still resident communities. Before the dam, household production provided for all food needs in 79 percent of the total survey population. At the time of the field study (2004), household production sustained all food needs for 28 percent of the survey population. In resettlement communities, deterioration of household production was even greater; 93 percent of the 119 surveyed households in the resettlement communities reported the ability to provide all household food needs before the dam, and only 26 percent reported this ability in 2004. The declining ability to produce food related directly to the loss of productive agricultural land, pastureland, and access to viable river and forest resources. For the many people forced to

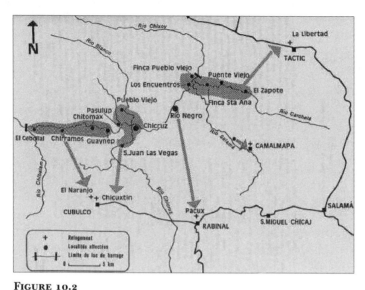

FIGURE 10.2

Chixoy resettlement communities and villages of origin.

abandon their traditional lands and settle in an urbanized "resettlement" village, productive lands were scarce and, when provided, were located at great distances from the home.

Not surprisingly, these changes produced a measurable decline in dietary protein. Households reporting regular consumption of fish several times each week dropped from 74 percent before the dam to 23 percent in 2004. The consumption of meat several times each week dropped from 30 percent to 21 percent. Some 82 percent of the population raised pigs before the dam; in 2004, only 26 percent had the household space to raise pigs. Before the dam, 96 percent of the survey population reported keeping an average of 34 poultry per household. In 2004, only 69 percent reported the ability to keep poultry, with the average dropping to 14 per household. Access to milk and other dairy products also significantly declined, as evidenced by the reduced ability to keep and feed dairy cows. Before the dam, 70 percent of the households reported ownership of 1,115 cows; in 2004, 21 percent reported ownership of 121 cows. These changes were a contributing factor to the region's extraordinarily high rates of malnutrition and infant mortality.

The loss of access to fertile lands, pasture, and river and forest resources also produced measurable change in household ability to generate monetary income. Surplus production and sale of garden products, eggs, chickens, and livestock dropped from 44 percent to 12 percent. The number of households catching and selling fish dropped from 49 percent to 3 percent. The number of households producing surplus crops to sell in the marketplace diminished from 37 percent to 7 percent. Also, the number of households involved in the harvest and sale of forest products changed: collection and sale of palm leaves dropped from 81 percent to 32 percent; ocote torches, from 56 percent to 2 percent; firewood, from 29 percent to 11 percent; and construction timber, from 25 percent to 1 percent.

In 2004, people in the resettlement villages were living in extreme poverty, with homes crumbling and few economic opportunities. For those who remained in the Chixoy river basin, periodic flooding had seriously affected the length of the agricultural season and the number of harvests per year. Downstream, land was periodically flooded, so erosion was severe. Varied river flow in the summer and winter had created stagnant pools and breeding grounds for mosquitos, which transmit malaria. Many fishing villages had seen the complete loss of local fisheries. When dam repairs were made in the mid-1990s, no social impact assessment occurred, and no program was created to protect downstream communities from the hazards of dam operations. Those communities had experienced water shortages, crop failures, and loss of fisheries as a result of inadequate or interrupted stream flow in dry seasons. Flash floods from unannounced dam releases had caused at least three documented fatalities in downstream communities.

The Chixoy Dam Legacy Issues Study concluded that hydroelectric energy development occurred at the cost of land, lives, and livelihood in violation of national and international laws. At the same time, World Bank and Inter-American Development Bank loans were repaid, with interest, in full.

The study also generated a plan for reparations urging the government of Guatemala, with the financial and technical support of the Inter-American Development Bank and the World Bank, to

1. Provide for needs such as water, electricity, and housing; assess the health, education, and economic needs of the affected communities; and identify resources and strategies to address them.

2. Develop the economic, social, cultural, education, health, and physical infrastructure of the dam-affected communities and the broader regions where they live.

3. Restore, repair, and improve conditions of life in those communities most seriously affected by Chixoy.

4. Support reconciliation and reparation efforts addressing the violence that occurred, and create and implement political actions to acknowledge the wrongs and ensure that these never again occur.

The overriding compensation principle structuring this reparations framework is the notion that meaningful remedy involves the broad array of efforts that restore the dignity of affected people and their ability to enjoy a healthful way of life.

THE IMPACT OF THE REPARATIONS STUDY

Many of the indigenous representatives of dam-affected communities are also massacre survivors and key witnesses in cases of crimes against humanity and genocide: the UN-sponsored truth commission cited the Río Negro massacre as an example of state-sponsored genocide. Hence, the political climate in which we worked was difficult, at best. When the reparations study was begun in 2003, there was no rights-protective forum in which to present the case. Our primary goal was to develop the evidence and summarize findings in ways that would encourage such a mechanism to come into being.

As we proceeded, various individuals, participants as well as investigators, received threats. The office of a local advocacy group was broken into, and the computer containing project documents and communications was stolen (cash and other valuables were left untouched). Members of a downstream village received death threats that forced them to drop out of the community needs assessment, and similar threats were issued to our community needs-assessment project coordinator. Dam-affected community leaders who signed a September 9, 2004, agreement with INDE and the Guatemalan government to develop a reparations process, following a two-day, peaceful protest at the Chixoy Dam site, were charged with trespass, vandalism, and other crimes against the state and were arrested (Amnesty International 2006). (Their legal case proceeded for three years. After much national and international advocacy and the assistance of a pro bono team of lawyers, charges were finally dismissed in 2007.)

As a scholar and scientific advisor, I found it extremely difficult to provide advice, given the real possibility that, in acting on this advice, people might find themselves in danger, or worse. What ultimately became apparent is that the science/advisor role included the responsibility not only to provide information that supported thoughtful actions by anticipating any dangers or risk, but also to ensure that all actors—be they advocates, community representatives, scholars, or other concerned parties—understood the risks associated with publicizing information and did not take independent decisive action without thorough discussion and the consensus of dam-affected communities. This need to proceed with "eyes wide open" produced, at times, painfully slow and cumbersome decision-making processes. I often found myself in a struggle to reign in the well-intended global citizen-activists, whose light-speed ways of thinking and acting especially contrasted with the day-to-day reality of the Maya communities they were attempting to assist.

I am relieved to report that this study was largely conducted within a cocoon of rights-protective space. It is my belief that because we protected the autonomous structure of the study and, more important, widely publicized the extensive array of study sponsors and supporters, we created an atmosphere that made it difficult to carry out, with impunity, the death threats. Before conducting any research or securing any funding, the conceptual approach was reviewed, and the independent status of the study was endorsed by professional organizations (the American Association for the Advancement of Science Committee on Scientific Freedom and Responsibility, the American Anthropological Association, and the Society for Applied Anthropology) and the United Nations Special Rapporteur on the Human Rights and Fundamental Freedoms of Indigenous Populations. Progress reports were delivered to these groups and to all interested parties: the World Bank and Inter-American Development Bank staffs and consultants, the Organization of American States' Inter-American Human Rights Commission, international human rights and environment groups, and the private foundations that financed the community outreach, training, participation, and scientific study. And I believe that the violence was deterred also because we pursued this case at the right moment in time. This case involved well-known aspects of Guatemala's history and drew the interest of the international community. And this history attracted critical attention within the broader context of the massive new hydro, mining, and energy development plans being proposed for the region. The Guatemalan government had much to gain if it could demonstrate, in response to this study, improvement of its human rights record.

Also important is that the notion of remedy articulated by the dam-affected communities did not call for a court trial and imprisonment of those involved in the violence, nor was it a matter of simple monetary compensation to individual victims. Rather, their vision of reparation was one that would enable their families, neighbors, and surrounding communities to again live in decent homes; gain access to fertile lands, electricity, water, education, and job opportunities; and, most of all, allow honest reconciliation with a bloody and painful past. They wanted the nation, as well as other responsible parties, to understand, acknowledge, and provide meaningful redress for the horrible human rights abuses that occurred, especially those abuses that were associated with or causally linked to hydroelectric dam development. More fundamental, they wanted the power and opportunity to "sit at the table" and help shape the scope and intent of remedial solutions.

The Chixoy Dam Legacy Issues Study was delivered to the Guatemalan government at a press conference in Guatemala City on July 13, 2005. Mayan representatives from twenty-three affected communities traveled there to attend this event. At the press conference, indigenous leaders presented to Dr. Frank LaRue, director of the Presidential Commission on Human Rights (COPREDEH), copies of the five-volume study. LaRue formally accepted the study in behalf of the Guatemalan government and announced the formation of a commission to negotiate remedy for this case, noting that Guatemala's finance minister had formally invited the Inter-American Development Bank and the World Bank to participate in a Chixoy reparations negotiations process. The event was covered (and, in some cases, carried live) by the national television networks, and all the national newspapers published articles about it. On July 26 and 27, 2005, indigenous representatives presented the study to senior staff at the World Bank and Inter-American Development Bank in Washington DC and participated in a Washington Office on Latin America–sponsored press conference held at the National Press Club. They also met with their new advisors, a pro bono team from the law offices of Holland and Knight, who agreed to act as legal advisors for the dam-affected communities in the reparations negotiations process announced by LaRue.

At this writing, there appears to be the political will on all sides to address this case. The Damages Verification Commission has been established, and a representative from the Inter-American Human Rights Commission has been appointed to monitor and facilitate. Meetings have been held to review the record of resettlement promises, actions, and consequences and to develop appropriate remedies. The Chixoy Dam Legacy Issues Study serves as a key reference piece. One of the international financial institutions issued a small grant to prepare economic development plans for each of the affected communities. Negotiations continue over the issue of who will pay for the actual implementation of remedial community and regional development projects.

I cannot argue that the act of documenting histories and their consequences caused responsible parties to acknowledge their culpability in past abuses and their resulting reparative obligations. People were pushed to the Damage Verification table for various reasons. Some of the political and economic motivations include the status of high-stakes deals involving hundreds of millions of dollars in the form of debt relief, new poverty-alleviation funds from the World Bank, and new Inter-American Development Bank financing for hydroelectric dam, energy, and mining projects in rural Mayan communities. The ability to close deals, approve contracts, release funds, and materially benefit from massive development schemes is constrained by the international attention on Guatemala's performance in protecting its citizens' humans rights and by the overall perception that the government has failed to meet the 1996 Peace Accords (see Amnesty International 2005). Therefore, public actions that reconcile past human-rights abuses and suggest progress in implementing the Peace Accords are welcomed, at this time, by this government.

LESSONS FROM THE CHIXOY STUDY

Many other Mayan groups displaced by the violence in Guatemala have returned to their former homes and begun the process of rebuilding their communities and ways of life. But the dam-displaced people cannot go home. INDE, the government of Guatemala, the World Bank, and the Inter-American Development Bank share an obligation to provide remedy for the consequences of their negligence in protecting the right to life and livelihood and the right to fair and just compensation. All share in the obligation to redress the right to remedy. No one, however, can go back in time and undo the violence that accompanied this dam development project. No amount of money can bring back to life the many who died as a result of the forced evictions and the failures to provide just compensation and create meaningful resettlement programs. But certain actions can be taken to restore the dignity, identity, and integrity of previously self-sufficient communities: helping protect sacred sites, ensuring the creation and protection of memorials and cemeteries to mark the massacres that occurred in this area, and supporting community efforts to transform the region by building an economy and society that involves all of its members in the common goal of securing a self-sustaining way of life.

At the community level, perhaps the most important lessons emerge from the earliest phases of the reparations struggle, before the formal study began. Organizing local involvement required an outreach initiated by massacre survivors who traveled to other resettlements and up and down the river valleys. This effort to organize the dam-affected communities meant meeting and learning to work with people who played indirect or

even direct roles in the violence. Such meetings were, at the most fundamental level, opportunities to confront and reconcile histories and their
consequences. Because meetings were organized around the question of
who was affected by the dam, the engagement focused on the commonalities in people's experiences with the development project. This focus on
the development intersects made visible the linkages between the micro
and the macro: between the local violence and the structural violence of
the state and its partners in the internationally financed development.
Taking on the identity of a "dam-affected community" made incredible psychosocial demands on people, and the tensions produced by these histories continue. Nevertheless, by studying and embracing their common past,
dam-affected communities are now able to envision and work towards the
possibilities of remedy.

Community reconciliation offers lessons for the nation. When the
study began, there was no mechanism for discussion of dam-development
issues among the various affected communities, let alone any evidence that
the government would support a rights-protected examination of these
issues. For some, this study and the formative negotiation process represent
an opportunity for the nation to build a mechanism that can help the many
other people who were promised reparations by the 1996 Peace Accords
yet whose problems and issues remain unaddressed. For others, the study
and its demand for remedy, which vests indigenous groups with partnership power in a development process, represent a precedent upon which
other groups might build.

This case also offers lessons for the international community. There is
most certainly a need for some sort of independent advocate mechanism
to enable project-affected communities to receive financial and technical
assistance in documenting and evaluating claims. Such a mechanism
should include a special masters court or international tribunal that functions with an advocates office, staff, and funding to conduct an investigation, develop the claim, and facilitate a negotiation process for remedy.
Also, there is a need for international financial institution and state involvement in providing information access and financing and implementing
the outcome.

CAVEAT

In documenting the many failures to address rights and resources and
the demands for reparations in the form of meaningful remedy, the Chixoy
Dam–affected communities have taken the lead in challenging the assumptions that drive development decision making. Meaningful remedy means

obtaining free, prior, and informed consent of resident peoples before approving financing and initiating dam construction. Meaningful remedy means developing scientific assessments and plans with the equitable participation of affected community members. It means that governments and financiers must respect the rights of indigenous peoples to self-determination, including the right to say no, and must not fund new projects until the outstanding legacy issues from past projects are addressed. Clearly, these actions threaten the status quo.

Resolving the legacy issues from inept, flawed, and rights-abusive development requires local, national, and international actions that give people living with the situation greater control in defining the nature of their problems, devising equitable responses, and prohibiting reoccurrence. Institutions and organizations that played a significant role in creating the problems must acknowledge their culpability and carry a greater share of the burden of resolving them. The struggle to achieve these transformations in decision-making systems requires confronting, challenging, and changing the status quo. Backlash is inevitable. Although political negotiations may produce some sort of reparative remedy, I fear that, in this case, as in far too many cases of development disaster, justice may be elusive.

Notes

1. This discussion of the evolving meaning of the term *reparation* is abstracted from a lengthier treatment of the subject (see Johnston 2000) and is further developed and illustrated in the volume *Waging War and Making Peace—Reparations and Human Rights* (Johnston and Slyomovics 2008).

2. Portions of this Chixoy case summary are abstracted from volumes 1, 2, and 3 of the Chixoy Dam Legacy Issues Study (Johnston 2005). The study is published on the web at the Center for Political Ecology (http://www.centerforpoliticalecology. org/ chixoy.html, accessed June 2008), the International Rivers Network (http:// internationalrivers.org/en/latin-america/mesoamerica/chixoy-dam-guatemala/ chixoy-dam-legacy-issues-study, accessed June 2008), and the American Association for the Advancement of Science (http://shr.aaas.org/guatemala/chixoy/chixoy.htm, accessed June 2008).

11

Routine and Dissonant Cultures

A Theory about the Psycho-socio-cultural Disruptions of Involuntary Displacement and Ways to Mitigate Them without Inflicting Even More Damage

Theodore E. Downing and Carmen Garcia-Downing

Modest advances have been made to avoid or mitigate the economic impoverishment that threatens involuntarily displaced peoples (Cernea, ed. 1999; Mejía 1999; Scudder 2005a). Less attention has been paid to the noneconomic, psycho-socio-cultural (PSC) impoverishment inflicted by involuntary displacement (Barabas and Bartolomé 1992; Cernea 2000a; de Wet 2006; Downing 1996a; Oliver-Smith 1986; Tamondong-Helin 1996). Mitigation of the economic damages has focused on restoring losses, recovering livelihoods, and—in rare instances—sharing project benefits with those displaced (Cernea 2007 and chapter 3, this volume; Downing 2002a). In contrast, mitigation of PSC damages has proven much more problematic. Few infrastructure projects consider or attempt to mitigate this risk.

Those who may benefit from these infrastructure projects avoid this untidy issue by embracing five, if not more, fallacies that conveniently block further discussions and actions, offering those who should bear responsibility a rationale, though untenable, for shirking it.

First, the compensation-is-enough fallacy holds that all moral and economic obligations to displaced peoples are met by compensation payments. Second, the strict-compliance fallacy holds that resettlement risks have been addressed when a project adheres to applicable planning, policies, and laws. Third, the blame-the-victims fallacy holds that displacees' psycho-socio-cultural problems are a consequence of their failure to take advantage of opportunities offered them. Fourth, the-clock-stops-with-construction fallacy is that external responsibilities to displaced persons end at the completion of the Resettlement Action Plan (RAP) or with termination of the construction phase of the project. And fifth, the someone-else-should-pay fallacy holds that the project designers, governments, and financiers are neither legally nor economically liable for psycho-socio-cultural changes.

This chapter reframes the psycho-socio-cultural dimension, arguing that involuntary displacement transforms routine culture into dissonant culture, which then transforms into a different routine culture. In the psycho-socio-cultural realm, it is highly improbable that a pre-displacement routine culture will be recovered, let alone restored. Although irreversible, there are ways to mitigate PSC impoverishment. Relative success, we shall argue, is determined by how well the post-displacement routine culture is able to address fundamental questions of the displaced, compared with the pre-displacement culture. If involuntary resettlement cannot be avoided, the applied question then becomes, what can be done to facilitate the reestablishment of a new routine culture so that it adequately addresses the primary cultural questions faced by the displaced peoples? We will highlight actions that might be taken to minimize PSC impoverishment and to strengthen the social and cultural capacity of displaced peoples.

IMPOVERISHMENT RISKS

Despite strong resistance and opposition to development-induced displacement, millions of people each year are unexpectedly uprooted by war, natural disasters, and infrastructure developments (Oliver-Smith 1991; Russell 2002). These events unleash widespread and, in many ways, similar psycho-socio-cultural, economic, and political changes. Chief among these is the resettlement effect, which is defined as the "loss of physical and non-physical assets, including homes, communities, productive land, income-earning assets and sources, subsistence, resources, cultural sites, social structures, networks and ties, cultural identity and mutual help mechanisms" (Asian Development Bank 1998:vi). Failure to mitigate the resettlement effect may generate "new poverty," as opposed to the "old poverty" before displacement (Cernea 2000a, 2002; Downing 2002a, 2002b; Scudder 2005a).

For more than half a century, a global struggle has been waged to discover what interventions might reduce the suffering of the displaced—unfortunate victims of other people's progress—and the likelihood of the resettlement effect (see Guggenheim 1994 for an annotated bibliography until 1993; Shami 1993). Professionals, academics, nongovernmental (NGO) and human rights activists, and a few social scientists working for key international financial institutions have shown that negative consequences of involuntary displacement extend far beyond the loss of land. They seek ways to prevent impoverishment and to reconstruct and improve the livelihoods of displacees. Despite their small numbers, their efforts have encouraged most of the international financial intermediaries (IFIs) in establishing involuntary resettlement guidelines, also known as safeguard policies (several national governments—notably, China and India—have set national policies), and have promoted research within the social sciences, including economics. More than four hundred professionals working on involuntary displacement and resettlement formed the International Network on Displacement and Resettlement in 2000. Since 2002, it has maintained a website at http://www.displacement.net and publishes an online quarterly newsletter, edited by Hari M. Mathur in India.

Risk is the possibility that a course of social action will trigger adverse effects such as loss, destruction, and deprivation for future generations (Cernea 2000a). The majority of professionals working on involuntary displacement and resettlement have focused on multidimensional impoverishment risks (homelessness, food insecurity, increased morbidity, landlessness, loss of employment, loss of access to common resources, marginalization, loss of human rights, and social disarticulation) (Cernea, ed. 1999, 2000a, 2002; Downing 2002a; Johnston and Garcia-Downing 2004; Kedia 2003; Scudder 2005a).

ROUTINE CULTURE AND PRIMARY QUESTIONS

The psycho-socio-cultural risks have been the most neglected, the most difficult to study, and the least likely to be mitigated (Cernea 2000a; Downing 1996a; Scudder 2005a; Wallace 1957). A new social poverty can be seen everywhere—in lives wrecked, social relationships realigned, social and economic assets lost, leaders toppled, people (particularly the elderly) growing ill and dying prematurely, and the diminished capacity of a society to withstand non-project-related threats (Behura and Nayak 1993; Cernea 1990, 1994, 2002, 2005a; de Wet 2006; Downing 1996a, 2002a, 2002b; Oliver-Smith 1986). A list of such impacts, however informative, does not reveal the underlying dynamics so that mitigation can be effectuated. Why are social relations realigned in one way rather than in another? Why are particular assets selected or created to replace lost assets?

An understanding of what happens when people are involuntarily displaced begins with culture. Culture is a set of constructs and rules for constructing the world, interpreting it, and adapting to it (Bock 1968; Csikszentimihalyi and Rochberg-Halton 1981; Fabian 1992; Frake 1993; Selby and Garretson 1981). The constructs and rules answer what we like to call "primary questions": Who are we? Where are we? Where are we coming from? Where are we going? Why do people live and die? What are our responsibilities to others and to ourselves? Most likely, there are more, but these cover a lot of ground.

The answers to the primary questions vary from culture to culture and within cultures. The constructs are codified in language, symbols, places endowed with meaning, kinship categories, ritual, dance, music, humor, public works, access rights to certain areas and resources, titles and job descriptions, and other socio-cultural expressions (Downing 1996a; Hirsch 1999; Lightfoot 1979; Low 1992; Pellow 1994; Riley 1994; Sutro and Downing 1988). For the most part, life is humdrum—or, to say this in another way, patterned. Day after day, individuals make tactical decisions as they navigate routine culture. People repair broken doors, meet friends, mend fences, collect firewood, and go from one place to another. Culture defines how they gain access to restricted places and situations by performing routine events such as attending school, paying admission, or working for income. These are tactical adjustments to life. Kin groups and institutions—schools, businesses, governments, and other organizations—also address primary questions and, collectively, navigate and construct routine culture (Douglas 1973). These groups and their leaders continually grapple, usually in tightly patterned fashion, with recurring questions and tactical issues such as recruitment, retirement, rewards, budget cycles, goals, arranging meetings, making announcements, opening and closing facilities, or planning an event in their annual cycle.

Routine culture is defined by *roughly* the same people, or groups, repeatedly reoccupying the same places at the same times. Negotiation is the most common way that individuals and institutions work out what is and what is not an acceptable construction of space, time, and personages. Life becomes simultaneously interesting and exasperating as people continually define and redefine their surroundings and their perceived place in those surroundings. And the PSC constructions take on value (de Pina Cabal 1994) as individuals and groups judge certain constructs to be more desirable or undesirable than others.

Life may be humdrum, but it is not static. Not everyone understands, agrees with, or accepts his or her place within the constructs, nor the constructs themselves. Institutions, individuals, and families redefine their constructed spaces, their times, and their personages. We move things around, reschedule events, make new friends, change jobs, and so on. Negotiations never end.

Occasionally, negotiated relations are more radically realigned by birth, death, divorce, or marriage. From a societal perspective, these unavoidable demographic changes cause regular *micro-disruptions* that force individuals and institutions to rearrange their routines (Behura and Nayak 1993; Lightfoot 1979). Field anthropologists take great interest in discovering the meanings associated with a new cultural landscape that may, at first glance, be devoid of recognizable meaning. Early anthropology focused on these micro-disturbances, adjustments that cultures made to changes brought about by birth, initiation, maturation, and death and its spatial-temporal manifestations. A person dies. Funerals and memorials reaffirm the primary questions. Resources controlled by the deceased are reallocated through inheritance or are destroyed, and roles and obligations, reassigned or forgotten (see anthropological works on inheritance and succession going back many years, such as Downing 1973 and Goody 1969, 1970). Memories and losses are felt and real, but life goes on. Comparable rearrangements occur when new members join the society, at birth or initiation. Weddings, funerals, and other rites of passage routinely reallocate resources, mending inescapable demographic rifts and redefining the players but not the playing field. Moreover, these rearrangements strengthen the culture as individuals reaffirm their shared values. In a comparable manner, the needs of the vulnerable—women, children, the elderly, the landless, the disabled—are met by social institutions and intrapersonal reciprocities that supply them with critical life-sustaining resources. The resiliency of peoples may be measured by their ability to mobilize resources during these micro-disruptions.[1]

Psycho-social and cultural landscapes are crowded with the results of previous, often long-forgotten, negotiations and micro-disruptions. Over time, every nook and cranny, every event, every rule is the product of intense social interactions. The landscapes take many forms, including civic calendars, time zones, property lines, zoning, parks, household gardens, buildings, and bus routes. Negotiations may be as simple as discussions about where events should be located and disputes over space or what to call something. Traditional public areas, for example, are often the product of generations-old conflicts and compromises invisible to current users (Aronsson 2002). Cultural landscapes often take on nonmaterial form, such as titles, positions, "rights," names, and kinship categories.

In the race to build infrastructure, a community that is in the way may appear to outsiders to be little more than an impoverished place, devoid of the rich meaning found in more affluent surroundings. Not true. Move closer and the layers of cultural onion seem infinite. During the senior author's four years in Arizona as a lawmaker, he spent thousands of hours refining and adding to the State of Arizona's statutory law. More than twelve thousand pages of Arizona law are the residual product of almost one hundred years of negotiations; they are the formal rules for social relationships for 6.5 million people, institutions, companies, and interests. For most Arizonans, however, the rules of routine culture are unrecorded—the product of a shared culture, an unwritten code much larger than statutory laws.

The spatial and temporal organization of routines (Downing 1996a) gives communities and individuals constructed predictability; at certain places and times, their primary questions are repeatedly addressed and answered. When is it? Christmas. Where am I? At home. Who am I with? My family. What are Christians doing? Celebrating the birth of Jesus. And so it goes, with time, place, and personages redefined according to a culture's particular constructs. The economic constructs and actions are particularly fundamental to routine culture, ensuring both identification and continuous supply or usage of resources and energy that meet the material needs of individuals and institutions. It is here that natural cycles (such as seasonal changes) intermesh with cultural constructs. Cyclical variation in food and income are predictable and are planned for accordingly.

In brief, routine culture imparts a degree of order, stability, security, and predictability in daily life, a sense of health and well-being.

DISSONANT CULTURE

Involuntary displacement drastically destabilizes routine culture by threatening it or rendering it meaningless. Then, social life becomes chaotic, uncertain, and unpredictable. Routine culture gives way to what we shall call *dissonant culture*—a temporary reordering of space, time, relationships, norms, and psycho-socio-cultural constructs. Dissonant culture, like inharmonious music that causes tension, cries out for a resolution. Tactical maneuvers of individuals and institutions become disconnected from future actions. The game cannot be played without a field. Depending on how this threat is handled, involuntary displacement may invalidate the previously constructed answers to primary culture, including associated institutions. Although the people may physically survive, culturally what was is no more.

Dissonance usually appears long before physical displacement.[2] Almost every observer of an involuntary displacement has reported that psycho-socio-cultural changes appear well before infrastructure construction or relocation actually begins. Scudder (2005a) and Scudder and Colson (1982) found in their work with the Gwenbe Tonga, in connection with the Kariba Dam, that those destined to be displaced refused, initially, to believe that they were going to be forced to relocate. The depth of the dissonance is difficult to imagine and stretches far beyond micro-disruptions. Inga-Lill Aronsson (2002) offers one of the few firsthand observations about the appearance of dissonant culture. Living with her young child among the group to be resettled, she shared with them the disbelief that everything the people knew was about to change—until the blasting began. When familiar features of the landscape were dynamited, the project-affected people realized that what they could barely imagine or not imagine was coming true.

Within the displaced population, the risks of social impoverishment usually are distributed unevenly. The vulnerable are likely to lose access to an often overburdened social safety net. Demographics, location, and income differences may inadvertently expose some parts of the population more than others. Temporal routines, such as going to work, leaving the kids at school, taking lunch breaks, getting a haircut, shopping, enjoying a morning coffee, and the like, are gone. Socially constructed relationships may be temporarily, and sometimes permanently, broken. The position of the social unit—be it a household, family, or village—relative to other non-affected social units may change (marginalization). The routine provisioning of food breaks down—not from cyclical scarcity but from unanticipated events and with an uncertain chance of replenishment.

As resettlement nears, dissonance simultaneously spreads across the culture. Productive activities are disrupted. Resources, such as land and jobs, are either irrelevant or gone. Schooling and socialization activities become difficult to sustain because what is being taught is disarticulated from present and future value. Social arrangements that allow sharing of common goods become insignificant because the common resource is insufficient, disappearing, or gone. Intensified, involuntary displacement may break a people's social geometry, the bonds that, in routine culture, were continually re-created by socially constructed time, space, and personages (Downing 1996a).

Researching the psycho-socio-cultural processes is not easy. Economic sciences have not been very useful in explaining the mega-changes unleashed by extensive socio-cultural disorganization, especially when it involves forced displacement. Part of the problem is that it is methodologically challenging: too much happens to too many people too fast.

Apart from those displaced, few have witnessed the full force of the dissonant phase of an involuntary displacement. At another place and time, we walked the streets of the new central Mexican town of Bella Vista del Rio a few weeks after its new inhabitants were involuntarily relocated to make way for the Zimapan Dam (Aronsson 2002; Greaves 1997; Guggenheim 1991, 1993). This was at dusk, usually a time of substantial activity. Children played basketball under the newly installed streetlights, but adults were not to be seen. Something was wrong. Each family sat in its house in silence. Elderly stared at the walls or rocked back and forth in chairs, gazing into space. No laughter. No radios playing. Conversations were truncated. Few tasks were being done. People just sat there, like props in a museum. A year later, the evening streets more closely resembled nonrelocated village streets.

Those fortunate enough to have never experienced dissonant culture may come close to observing spatial and temporal dissonance in the live media coverage of natural disasters.[3] On 9/11/2001 and then again during the Katrina hurricane in 2005, nonspecialists somewhat witnessed the chaos of dissonant culture—even if it was observed through the media. The familiar site of the World Trade Center was part of the routine culture of millions of Americans, including those who had never been to New York City. As repeated millions of times since, "everything changed at 9/11," and it was not as simple as the beginning of the War on Terror. What changed, in an instant, was the vulnerability of the American self-defined routine culture.

Thus far, we have identified four patterns of dissonant culture that reappear cross-culturally and in different kinds of infrastructure development. Further research will undoubtedly find more. First, dissonant culture may show the emergence of *ephemeral dissonance norms* that, to those living in routine culture, may appear to be social pathologies or unanticipated social alliances. These norms have their own situational logic, which might be unacceptable in routine culture. The news media and their viewers witnessed survivors of Hurricane Katrina searching for food, water, and security (see Button, chapter 12, this volume). Some in the media applied nondissonant culture norms, calling them looters. Others viewed them as victims.

An American television network's videotape crew followed one of the two hundred thousand families (the Locketts) left homeless by 1992 Hurricane Andrew (*ABC News* 1992). The Locketts are an extended, sixty-five-member matriarchal clan that, before the disaster, had occupied sixteen homes in Homestead, Florida. Homeless, without belongings, they were temporarily relocated in a high school auditorium. The Lockett clan's women concentrated on reestablishing a temporary order for their family, focusing on the children. The women stressed that it is important that the children be fed "three meals a day, bathe, and get to bed on time." At the shelter, each part of the family organized a small personal space. The children's behavior in their socially defined space was of considerable concern as the mothers struggled to establish where they perceived the children should and should not go within the school auditorium and yard. In the ABC interviews, the matriarch described what she felt was her (unstated) contract with the shelter workers: "If the children don't get out of line... don't go where they're not supposed to...then we won't get kicked out into the streets" (*ABC News* 1992). What normatively should have been a family micro-disruption in routine culture turned into a community ritual when the entire gymnasium of relocatees joined in celebrating a child's birthday.

A second pattern is *dissonance overload*, the overburdening of appropriate cultural responses to meet new risks. In routine culture, people draw temporarily upon their kinship and friendship networks for the extra resources during micro-disruptions. The disturbance from involuntary displacement may be so extensive and prolonged as to overload the traditional coping and support mechanisms (Scudder 2005a). Worse yet, those to whom one would turn in times of need are also seeking assistance. The threat may be not only psycho-social but also physical. Cultural responses to diseases are critical parts of a cultural inventory, and their disruption may increase mortality (see Kedia, chapter 5, this volume). Wolde-Selassie (2000) found that Ethiopians displaced by the 1984–1985 drought and famine faced new diseases, including malaria and cattle sickness. Out of 594,190 resettlers, an estimated 32,800 died. Similarly, in Orissa, India, twenty-two villages displaced by the Ramial River Project dam experienced increases in cerebral malaria, typhoid, and jaundice, as well as increases in infant and child mortality (Mahapatra and Mahapatra 2000). Developing new cultural strategies to cope with a radically changed community-health profile may take generations. In Bangladesh, the social disarticulation resulting from an involuntary, project-related displacement has also been shown to constrict a society's capacity to respond to recurring natural disasters (Hutton and Haque 2004).

Third, the disturbance of routine culture may begin an impoverishment process by *redefining access to routinely allocated resources*. Moreover, economic actions that are seemingly unrelated to the displacement may decline. In Orissa, India, Behura and Nayak (1993) noted that development-displaced peoples, irrespective of their previous economic background, underwent economic hardship. They noted that the disruption caused by resettlement not only caused economic hardship but also changed the socioeconomic configuration of their rural society (Behura and Nayak 1993). Similarly, the capacity of the displaced to protect their health and nutrition may diminish (Kedia and van Willigen 2008). In the Alto Bio Bio region of southern Chile, we interviewed people displaced by the Ralco Dam who felt that the displacement had lengthened the time and distance to their health outposts, making access to already limited resources even more difficult (Downing and Garcia-Downing 2001). The Pehuenche indigenous peoples had limited access to legal, education, and health information. The increase in distance diminished the probability of mitigating or avoiding displacement- and resettlement-induced impoverishment.

Fourth, displacees may *increase the frequency of rituals* that once reaffirmed group identity. In the Mexican project mentioned earlier, in June 1994 we observed an increase in ritual behavior by relocatees from the small Catholic community of La Vega. Before their relocation, once a year they moved their village patron saint from one private household to another and then celebrated a special annual mass. Immediately following resettlement, the saint began weekly instead of annual visits, moving from one relocated household to the next as the community struggled to reaffirm and reestablish its identity.

Apart from these four patterns, some universal psycho-social responses appear during what we are calling the dissonant period (Silove and Steel 2006). One that appears to be closely associated with the shift from routine to dissonant culture is the reports of the involuntarily displaced experiencing a dreamlike state, which seems to be some form of poorly understood *dissociation of consciousness*. Following Hurricane Andrew, the Lockett matriarch stumbled through the ruins of what, a week before, had been her home. She described her post-relocation situation as "like a dream in which you wake up." Using almost identical words, in June 1994 in central Mexico, a young wife described her loss to us. We were leaving a mountaintop where we had watched a new Zimapan reservoir slowly flooding what had been her family's home for many generations: "Like a dream. Someday I will wake up." In both cases, the women's expressions are more than metaphors. In human experience, dreams are thoughts disoriented in time and space (Friedlander 1940). We anticipate that this form of dissociation of consciousness will occur more frequently among women than men, but controlled research is necessary.

NEW ROUTINE CULTURE

Establishment of a new routine culture begins quickly, or else people have no answers to their primary questions: not only where am I and where are we, but also, more fundamentally, who am I and who are we? Some elements of a new routine culture begin to rearticulate almost immediately. Relationship by relationship, decision by decision, block by block, group by group, new routines crystallize. New organizations appear. In Orissa, India, at the Ramial Resettlement and Rehabilitation operation, Mahapatra and Mahapatra (2000) found that ten years after relocation, displacees had formed new conflict-resolution committees, youth and women's clubs, lending societies, and ritual organizations to cope with relocation challenges.

The emergence of what we are calling a new routine culture is not well understood and depends on the degree of disruption (de Wet 2005, 2006). Temporally, not everything comes together at once. It is as if different "articulation clocks" are ticking in different places for different groups. As displacees attempt to reestablish a new routine, Scudder (1981b, 2005a) reports, they favor incremental change over transformational change. They build on their familiar, earlier routines. He observed people maintaining ties to kin, replicating former house types, and transferring crops and productive techniques to the new area, regardless of their compatibility. The changes, in turn, followed their own patterns.

Let us call the time between the appearance of dissonant culture and the appearance of a new routine culture as the "dissonant interval." In essence, this measures the lifespan of the transition from routine, to dissonance, to new routine (R→D→R'). Methodologically, there are simultaneous, multiple R→D→R' cycles. The R→D→R' model we are proposing complements the temporal sequencing of changes in the celebrated stage model developed by Scudder and Colson (1982; see a summary of Scudder's life work in Scudder 2005a and chapter 2, this volume). Scudder (1981b) found that his stage two of involuntary resettlement, the adjustment and coping phase, lasted at least a year and usually ended after stage three.

New social articulations, the onset of a new routine culture, may also begin and end at different times within a population. People may reestablish a new routine for their children's education but remain in dissonance over how they make a living. Some families or communities within the same involuntary resettlement may develop a new routine; others may be slower in doing so. Because the shift from routine, to dissonance, to a new routine may begin and end at different times, our R→D→R' model is not a stage model.

Certain new socio-cultural articulations may not be sustainable. A new routine may surface and then revert back to dissonant culture. In southern Chile, we observed the routine, deeply impoverished herding-and-gathering economy of Pehuenche Indians disrupted by the construction and relocation of the Ralco and Pangue dams (Downing 1996b; Downing and Garcia-Downing 2001). Initial dissonance from loss of daily and seasonal agricultural activities was replaced by a new, temporary routine for those who found employment at the construction site (Johnston and Garcia-Downing 2004). When construction ended, many Pehuenche plunged into a new dissonant culture. In our simple notation, this would be R→D→R'→D' until a new, more lasting routine, R'', takes hold.

In a comparable fashion, dissonant culture dreams may morph into economic delusions. Returning to Zimapan, we witnessed three communities being forcefully resettled from highly productive riverside and irrigated farmland to an arid plateau high above their villages. In meeting after meeting with the Mexican Federal Electric Commission responsible for the displacement, the displaced demanded an economically impractical irrigation scheme that would pump water thousands of feet up to their poor-quality land. This unrealistic expectation influenced their decision to forego more economically rational alternatives (Aronsson 2002). They unexpectedly sold highly productive, irrigated land they had received in restitution, anticipating a future that would never be. Almost fifteen years later, an impressive community infrastructure rests on a high, arid mountain plateau, sustained by remittances from the United States, and the arid-land agriculture yields a fraction of what the rich, now submerged river bottomland yielded.

Creative, unstable tension emerges. Does the new routine culture align with the old answers to the primary questions? If not, the answers to the primary questions must change, or dissonance will persist. The dynamics of psycho-socio-cultural change during the involuntary resettlement process are quite distinct from the patterns observed in economics. In economics, it is possible to recover lost income or property. Restoration is feasible. In the psycho-socio-cultural realm, it is highly unlikely. Humpty-Dumpty cannot be put back together again.

STEPS TO FACILITATE THE TRANSITION

What can be done, if anything, to avoid or limit cultural dissonance induced by involuntary resettlement and, if unavoidable, to facilitate the establishment of a new routine culture? The first two of seven steps are (1) to recognize fallacies that may become excuses for inaction in avoiding or mitigating PSC risks and (2) to ensure that the appropriate laws and policies and financing are in place. (3) There must also be clear objectives with respect to desired PSC outcomes. The chances for smooth articulation to a new routine may be improved by (4) strengthening baseline studies, (5) ensuring that vulnerable peoples are protected, (6) providing procedures that encourage displaced persons to participate actively in displacement decisions that affect their destiny, and (7) actively promoting socio-cultural and psychological innovations that directly address the rebuilding of a new routine.

National laws and policies, as they presently stand, are economically underdesigned and do not address PSC disruptions. The lack of attention to PSC risks and mitigation is partially a consequence of misunderstandings about the socio-cultural changes that we have just described. In particular, several fallacies impede action to address the moral and legal obligations of governments, owners, and financiers for PSC disruptions and the articulation of new, meaningful routine culture.

Rejecting Fallacies

The *compensation-is-enough fallacy* holds that the moral and economic obligations to displaced persons are met by compensation payments. This assumption is deeply embedded in national laws, that compensation is, a priori, assumed by the taking party to include all the costs of involuntary resettlement, including financing of PSC recovery. Not so. Cernea and his colleagues have successfully argued that, from an economic perspective, involuntary resettlement policy has not incorporated critical knowledge from scores of empirical studies, project evaluations, and theoretical works that confirm that compensation alone cannot provide a financial platform for the recovery of the economic losses occurring in involuntary resettlement (Cernea 2008c; Cernea and Mathur 2008).

Involuntary resettlement specialists insist that compensation is not enough for restoration of lost livelihoods. This fallacy was incorporated into the World Bank's involuntary resettlement policies despite early warnings that the planned benefits should be higher than their previous standard of living and that displaced persons must be made better off and beneficiaries of a project (Scudder 2005a:279, quoting correspondence of May 17, 1979). The fallacy has persisted through subsequent policy updates in the different international institutions and is part of an ongoing controversy over the updating of the Asian Development Bank's involuntary resettlement policy (Downing and Scudder 2008).

Let there be no misunderstanding. Resources are a necessary precondition for social recovery (Cernea, chapter 3, this volume; Oliver-Smith 2005a). Without viable livelihoods—which mean sustainable income streams better than those before displacement—articulation of a new routine culture is more difficult. Scarce human energy and capital must be triaged in favor of basic survival.

It is naïve to assume that social recovery occurs when the material needs—such as income, housing, livelihood, productive systems, jobs, compensation, and social infrastructure—are met (de Wet 2006; Oliver-Smith 2005a; Tamondong-Helin 1996). Nor can economic gains, rare as they may be, be used as a surrogate for judging post-displacement social success (Partridge 1993) because even the opposite may occur. For example, Hirschon (2000) found that a refugee settlement in Greece suffered a decline in economic welfare but developed a higher degree of social integration and community than it had before displacement. And to make matters worse, both national laws and international safeguards may constrain successful recovery (Scudder 2005a). It is not simply a matter of getting it right— having a law or policy— but also not getting it wrong.

The *strict-compliance fallacy* holds that resettlement risks have been addressed if a project follows applicable planning, policies, private agreements, or laws. The World Bank's and other international financial intermediaries' approach to involuntary resettlement is heavily front-loaded towards planning. The IFIs and their public- and private-sector clients have prepared several thousand Resettlement Action Plans (RAPs) as part of the routine social and environmental due diligence for project appraisal.[4] The World Bank RAP guidelines are detailed in Annex A of OP (Operational Policy) 4.12. The annex requires social and economic studies, not simply a compilation of information. The studies should include a 100 percent census of current occupants of the affected area; standard characteristics of displaced households (including production system, labor, and household organization); baseline information on livelihoods and standards of living; the magnitude of expected loss; and information on vulnerable groups (World Bank Operational Policy on Involuntary Resettlement, OP 4.12, the World Bank, Annex A, par. 6). In August 2008 we measured more than 28 feet of RAPs on the shelves of the World Bank's Info Shop in Washington DC. After the respective boards approve RAPs, the IFI staff supervises and evaluates their implementation. In reality, supervision is often limited to a few weeks or less than a year on relatively large projects, and the focus is on checking compliance with the RAP.[5]

The strict-compliance fallacy may become inappropriately folded into legal agreements, financial negotiations, or project documents that unfairly limit future claims of displaced persons. Unaware of the full extent of their risks, displaced persons are asked to sign compensation agreements to make no further claims regarding damages or loss of assets. Not only the displaced, but in the case of private-sector projects, even governments may be unaware of agreements that may require public commitments to address project-induced impoverishment among the displaced persons. These agreements wilt when exposed to the bright sunlight of international human rights standards (Johnston and Garcia-Downing 2004). At question is not whether an agreement is necessary, which it may well be, but the coercive, nontransparent nature of such agreements and whether they are being made with full, informed consent of the displaced. Technically, the resulting compensation agreements may limit the project sponsor's liability, but from the perspective of economics, science, and social justice, the documents are coerced works of fiction.

On the project sponsor's or owner's side, unresolved economic and social impacts of involuntary resettlement may cause problems. Project sponsors and financiers want to avoid leaving a project's ledger with unspecified liabilities—real or perceived. As scientific research has uncovered livelihood risks, apart from the value of lost land or housing, the possibility arises that a project's ledger may show unspecified and lingering uncompensated liabilities to the displaced.

A third, the *blame-the-victims fallacy*, holds that the displacees' PSC or economic problems are a consequence of their failure to take advantage of the opportunities offered to them. This fallacy is most common when baseline studies of displaced persons are poorly done or missing altogether. It also tends to surface when projects involve indigenous, traditional peoples or ethnic minorities. The fallacy derives from, and feeds, stereotypes that portray indigenous, traditional, or powerless peoples as irrational or custom bound or as obstacles to national development. On more than one occasion, we have listened to sponsors and financiers argue that it is better to compensate displaced peoples in cash because, if they were given land for land, they would just turn around and sell it. Instead of assumptions, the preferences of even the poorest, most illiterate peoples should be measured and reported, even if culturally unexpected results appear. In Chile, we designed methodological instruments that enabled indigenous, mostly illiterate peoples to define and choose between alternative investments (Downing 1996b). Our work proved that Chile's poorest indigenous group, the Pehuenche, was willing to forego short-term cash rewards in favor of long-term investments in the group's survival, even at the risk of hunger (Downing 1996b).

The fourth, the *someone-else-should-pay fallacy*, is that the project designers, governments, and financiers are not legally or economically responsible for PSC disruptions and changes. The questions of "who is and who is not liable" and "liable for what" turn out to be highly dynamic areas of modern jurisprudence in international displacement policy and, to a lesser extent, in national and subnational laws. Elsewhere, we distinguish liabilities that are widely acknowledged from those that appear weakly articulated with a project (possible liabilities) and those that seem probable (Downing 2002a). This liability line shifts back and forth as new research becomes available.

Fifth and last, *the-clock-stops-with-construction fallacy* is that external responsibilities to the displaced end with the completion of the RAPs or construction phase of projects. Crystallization of a new routine is likely to take time and most likely will extend beyond infrastructure construction. RAPs are frequently prepared and, unfortunately, approved with budgets and timelines coterminous with the completion of the physical infrastructure or tranches of a loan. The fallacy is that the economics or socio-cultural and economic dynamics of an involuntary resettlement end when project construction ends.

Ensuring Adequate Legal and Policy Frameworks

An effective struggle to work past these fallacies and secure social justice for displaced persons should not begin, a nova, with each project. Sustainable social justice that ensures that displaced persons will improve their livelihoods, benefit from development, and have viable societies and cultures requires that entitlements be formalized, literally embedded in laws, policies, bureaucratic procedures, and project financing. Sustainability is further strengthened by aligning these formalized laws and policies with the socio-cultural dynamics of involuntary resettlement.

The R→D→R' indicates that the ability of displaced peoples to articulate their new routine culture may be improved or hindered by external actions—including the stimulus causing the displacement and the legal and policy frameworks defining the rights of the displaced. Globally, advocates for social justice, involuntary resettlement specialists, NGOs, and allies within international organizations have worked together to ensure due diligence of IFIs in the area of involuntary resettlement. Specifically, they have pressured and helped prepare involuntary resettlement policy frameworks that detail avoidance, risk, and mitigation measures for people who are in the way of a specific development project. Comparable struggles occur at the national and subnational levels but are weakly, if not totally, unarticulated with the international efforts.

Obligations of those benefiting from a development project to those they displace are expressed in both hard and soft laws. Hard laws refer to legally binding obligations that are precise (or can be made precise through adjudication or the issuance of detailed regulations) and that delegate authority for interpreting and implementing the laws (Abbott and Snidal 2000). Hard laws are codified and subject to courts and enforcement actions. In most nation-states, the laws related to the involuntary takings of assets are well defined. Sovereign governments gain the allegiance of their subjects by creating, recognizing, and regulating property rights (Oliver-Smith 2008). To protect their integrity, sovereign governments or their designated jurisdictions define situations and compensation systems in which these rights may be withdrawn (for example, eminent domain, compulsory acquisition, and takings).

Soft laws begin when legal arrangements are weakened along the dimensions of obligation, precision, and delegation (Abbott and Snidal 2000). Consequently, there are differing degrees of "softness." Abbott and Snidal point out that soft legalization is becoming increasingly used by financial actors, firms, activist groups, and non-state-based groups to mitigate loss of sovereignty and contracting costs of working through a legal framework and to provide a tool of compromise in bargaining, particularly between weak and strong parties.

This is certainly true in the area of involuntary resettlement. Over the past thirty years, an emerging body of standards and principles is redefining the responsibilities of governments, financial intermediaries, and owners to people being displaced by development projects over and above those in national or subnational law. These soft laws include financial lenders' safeguard policies, international covenants between lenders or corporations, corporate social responsibility policies, contracts, and informal agreements. The World Bank (1990, 1994, and 2001) has revised its involuntary resettlement policies for its lending portfolios, along with procedural guidelines for its staffs (see the World Bank's Involuntary Resettlement Policy and Procedures OP/BP 4.12 and the International Finance Corporation PS5). Other international financial intermediaries (IFIs) with involuntary resettlement policies include the Organization for Economic Co-operation and Development (1991), the Inter-American Development Bank (1998), and the Asian Development Bank (1998). Recently, sixty of the world's leading financial institutions and the International Finance Corporation (IFC, the private sector arm of The World Bank Group) agreed on involuntary resettlement guidelines within the Equator Principles (IFC 2006b) and have tried to use their syndicated financial leverage to encourage national governments and private partners to move beyond simple, legalistic, cash compensation of taken land to a more comprehensive approach (Clark, Fox, and Treakle 2003; Kardam 1993; see Clark, chapter 9, this volume). The World Commission on Dams (WCD) has also developed criteria and guidelines for addressing the involuntary resettlement risks facing peoples displaced by large dams (WCD 2000b; also see Scudder 2005a).

National and subnational laws tend to focus on the level, form, and timing of compensation; eligibility for compensation; notification; and grievance and appeal procedures. Psycho-socio-cultural impacts are largely ignored. In contrast, the emerging safeguard policies move beyond arrangements for compensation for forced takings. The central focus is on economic restoration and development for the displaced. Benefiting from experience, criticism, evaluation, and research, most of the IFIs are gradually strengthening these safeguard policies to address multiple livelihood risks (Cernea, ed. 1999). It appears that soft law on involuntary resettlement is changing faster than hard law, probably because revision of hard law is more deeply ensconced in political and legislative processes.[6] Specifically, the soft laws include remedies that may not be evident in national laws, including preferences of land-for-land replacement for lost assets, compensation at replacement value, restoration of housing, provisions for income losses (usually, local jobs during construction), infrastructure reconstruction, special consideration for vulnerable groups, and some efforts to restore damaged livelihoods (Cernea, ed. 1999, 2000a, and chapter 3, this volume). Conversely, safeguard policies fall short of specifying legal procedures that displaced persons might use within national laws to contest the arrangements offered to mitigate their losses.[7]

By now, these policies and the associated entitlements for displaced persons, including the requirement for RAPs, are becoming embedded in soft international laws and are routinely incorporated into international lending agreements, particularly in infrastructure projects financed by syndicated loans involving a broad mix of private and public investors. As a result, displaced persons sometimes face multiple, contradictory levels of soft and hard laws, international standards, and national legal and regulatory frameworks. The situation becomes even more complex because of divergent expectations among the displaced over what is and is not an appropriate quid pro quo for the forceful taking of their properties and other rights (see Danielson 2004 for a general review of standards in the natural resource industries). The senior author's recent analysis of an involuntary resettlement complaint to the World Bank's Inspection Panel (2008a) provides a glimpse of this complexity. The Yoruba of southwestern Nigeria were having their lands taken to make way for the West African Gas

Pipeline (WAGP). As we investigated complaints about unfair compensation, we found three layers of soft laws overlaying the compulsory acquisition laws of what was an appropriate payment to displaced persons as defined by Nigeria law (hard). The soft law included a Nigeria oil-industry standard, a WAGP project interpretation of the World Bank standard of replacement value (soft, but higher entitlement), and a World Bank policy-defined standard based on livelihood restoration (soft, but even higher entitlement) (World Bank Inspection Panel 2008a:ch. III, 27–81). The entitlements calculated in these frameworks, measured by compensation per unit of land, differed by a factor of more than 10. Thus, the WAGP pipeline owners and the displaced persons made different claims and counterclaims within these four frameworks.

The processes for changing hard and soft law differ. More lasting changes in the rights of the displaced come from changes at the national and subnational levels. However, change at this level is the most difficult. Historically, priorities favor provisioning of infrastructure over livelihood restoration, and livelihood restoration over PSC issues. The battle over IFI policy formation involves an often intense dialogue between the IFI boards, their staff, and major social and environmental NGO stakeholders. It is seldom subject to public scrutiny. In sharp contrast, the changes in hard laws on eminent domain or takings require full immersion in a political process.

Having been elected to two terms in the Arizona legislature, the senior author can testify that even incremental changes in law in the United States may take several years, considerable organization, and money. The process involves dealing with lawmakers and other stakeholders. And, in the political arena, unlike in science, logical and economic rationality may not have a seat at the table. The upside of this effort is that after changes become formalized, they have a broader impact than dealing with individual cases. Moreover, reversal of gains is equally, if not more, difficult than their achievement. Social scientists and civil society organizations (CSOs) in Asia, particularly India and China, have taken more interest in national changes. In sharp contrast, social scientists or social justice advocates in developed countries have not taken an active role in comparable issues such as the firestorm that erupted over displacement (phrased as property rights) in almost every state following the US Supreme Court decision *Kelo v. City of New London* 545 US 469 (2005).[8]

The ingenuity of the legislative process is that it has "rules for making rules" that all stakeholders may follow, that is, majority votes, committee hearings, notification times, and the like. In contrast, the rule-making processes for changing involuntary resettlement policies of IFIs are ambiguous.[9] In the World Bank, the involuntary resettlement policy has the status of an operational procedure (OP) and a bank procedure (BP) for due diligence on investments that carry the disclaimer that they are "prepared for use by World Bank staff and are not necessarily a complete treatment on the subject" (World Bank 2001:1). Consequently, civil society must simultaneously battle social justice policy issues and attempt to negotiate its place within an idiosyncratic policy-making process (Downing et al. 2003). From 2006 through fall 2008, the Asian Development Bank and the Asian Forum were engaged in a contentious dialogue over the consultation procedure for updating the Asian Development Bank's involuntary resettlement policy, as well as the issue of the policy itself (Downing and Scudder 2008). After a failed attempt at public consultation that was boycotted by the major NGOs, the Asian Development Bank had to negotiate a new consultation.

Despite these obstacles, the involuntary resettlement policies have undergone progressive changes. Agencies and advocates have made incremental progress that has increased the opportunities for displaced persons to articulate a new routine culture. Progress can be measured in the realm of both procedural and distributive justice (Paavola and Adger 2002). Our remaining discussion focuses on the World Bank's Operational Policy/ Bank Procedures on Involuntary Resettlement OP/BP 4.12 because the World Bank has been the progenitor of other IFI and private-sector involuntary resettlement policies.

Setting a Psycho-socio-cultural Objective

The R→D→R' theoretical framework argues that preservation of a routine culture is unrealistic, if not impossible. Current World Bank involuntary resettlement policy is ambivalent and generalized, requiring that "to the extent possible, the existing social and cultural institutions of resettlers and any host communities are preserved" (OP 4.12, par. 13[a]). Whereas preservation, restoration, rehabilitation, and recovery may be feasible, albeit inadequate, targets for discussions of livelihood or living standards, these concepts are nearly meaningless in the socio-cultural and psychological realm. An objective more attuned to the social dynamics of involuntary resettlement would be that a meaningful, new articulation occurs when displaced persons can once more answer their primary questions: Who are we? Where are we? Where are we coming from? Where are we going? Why do people live and die? What are our responsibilities to others and to ourselves? The articulation consists of a network of interlocking routines and institutions to which people are willing to dedicate their time and resources. The answers may differ from those of the preceding routine culture. When a new articulation begins, people regain the ability to define their temporal, spatial, and social order—their social geometry—in ways comparable to those of people around them who were not displaced (excluding host communities whose routines may also be disrupted by the displacement).

Enhancing Baseline Analysis

IFI and national policies require collection of baseline information on the properties and population to be affected. The technical annex of OP 4.12 requires a RAP assessing the impoverishment risks and mitigation measures to be based on socio-economic studies conducted early on in project preparation and with the involvement of the displaced persons (OP 4.12, Annex A, par. 6). Specifically, these studies require a census survey of current occupants of the affected area, standard characteristics of displaced households (including production system, labor, and household organization), information on livelihoods and standards of living, the magnitude of expected loss, and information on vulnerable groups (OP 4.12, Annex A, 2001, par. 6[v]). The studies should also describe the patterns of social interaction in the affected communities, including social networks and support systems, as well as other socio-cultural characteristics of the displaced communities. These characteristics include their formal and informal institutions that may be relevant to the consultation strategy and to designing and implementing the resettlement activities (OP 4.12, par. 6[b]ii, iv). All the above are to be prepared with the participation of the potentially affected people and to be updated at regular intervals (OP 4.12, Annex A, 2001, par. 6[v]). Although these policies do not explicitly require studies of routine-dissonant culture, if done by a competent socio-economic specialist, they fit within the policy framework, particularly if included within the RAP's terms of reference. Unfortunately, RAPs seldom move past a cursory examination of socio-cultural issues, particularly of the spatial-temporal order and routines. Participation is almost cynically defined as answering questionnaires, listening to information, or being given promotional presentations on the benefits of the project (World Bank Inspection Panel 2008a, 2008b). Consequently, the policy should be strengthened by making explicit reference to describing the spatial and temporal organization of the displaced persons and their communities.

When socio-economic studies pay attention to the full socio-cultural domain, the results have proven positive not only for the people but also for the project sponsors. During an appraisal for World Bank financing, social science consultants discovered that the Aguamilpa Hydroelectric

Dam in Western Mexico would inundate a highly sacred ceremonial site of the Huichol Indian water goddess Nakahue at the convergence of the Santiago and Huaynamota rivers (Downing 1987; Maltos Sandoval 1995). Bank and Mexican anthropologists and the chief engineer consulted and negotiated with groups of shamans for movement of the site to a new location on the edge of the reservoir. The relocation ran coterminously with the construction and took several years. The result was a successful mitigation, without loss of the cultural ceremonial routine. Traditional ceremonies punctuated the dam construction up to, and including, its inauguration in 1995 by the president of Mexico. Unanticipated at the time, the Huichol were later to view the entire reservoir as sacred (Nahmad-Sitton, personal communication, August 2008).

Active participation of the displaced peoples in the socio-economic study may help them anticipate and begin to mitigate PSC disruptions. At Zimapan Dam in Central Mexico, arrangements were made for community leaders to visit a previously displaced community to review the displacement experiences of their counterparts. The initial result was disbelief, requiring subsequent confirmation visits by a larger segment of the community. This method stimulated broad community participation in the planning and execution of its own resettlement, in what has become a classic case in the involuntary resettlement literature (Aronsson 2002; Downing 1987; Greaves 1997; Guggenheim 1991, 1993).

Protecting the Vulnerable

The disruptions of involuntary resettlement fall heavier on some than others, which poses an additional challenge to building new social safety nets in a new routine culture. Studies have shown that involuntary resettlement is likely to create new poverty and often exacerbate existing inequalities within displaced communities, handicapping some people more than others as they try to recover economically and socially (Cernea 2008c; Cernea and Mathur 2008; Downing 2002a, 2002b; Pandey 1998a, 1998b, 1998c; Scudder and Colson 1980). In this regard, the involuntary resettlement policies of the IFIs are more sensitive to issues of equity and fairness than are many of the eminent domain laws of nation-states. For example, the World Bank Operational Policy on Involuntary Resettlement recognizes those with informal claims to the land, provided that such claims become recognized through a process identified in the RAP (OP 4.12, par. 15), apart from claims recognized in a country. The involuntary resettlement policies of the IFIs also call for particular attention to the needs of vulnerable groups among those displaced, especially those below the poverty line, the landless, the elderly, women and children, indigenous peoples, tenants and sharecroppers, ethnic minorities, or other displaced persons who may not be protected through national land-compensation legislation (OP 4.12, par. 8).[10] Although the US Uniform Relocation Assistance and Real Property Acquisitions Policies for Federal and Federally Assisted Programs also focus on equitable treatment, they do not pay particular attention to vulnerable peoples and exclude from eligibility persons who are not lawfully in the country (US Code Title 42, Chapter 6).

An example illustrates how critical the disturbance of routine culture may be to the future life of the vulnerable. Routines of children are often a neglected element in involuntary resettlement. Near Kampala, Uganda, the senior author interviewed people who had grown impatient waiting five years for a planned resettlement to make way for an electrical transmission line (World Bank Inspection Panel 2008b). Their willingness to relocate was mixed with concern that the move may occur after the annual school enrollment, making it difficult if not impossible for displaced children to enroll or transfer between government schools. School fees account for 23 percent of the affected households' spending, underscoring education's significance to the displaced. Thousands of children were in a comparable situation along the transmission line. The timing decision represents a substantial loss of human capital, which, according to mothers, may be irreparable for teenagers if the disruption derails their studies. Options, such as paying for full enrollment and transportation costs to private schools or adjusting the time of the move, have not yet been considered. Ironically, enrollment in school had been selected as one of the eight indicators for the involuntary resettlement's outcome evaluation, meaning that inattention to the problem threatened to skew the overall project evaluation negatively. One solution would be for the project to cover the costs of private school tuition, which is a relative small cost compared with the future value of disrupting students' lives and delaying the project.

Providing Procedural Empowerment

Displaced persons begin to articulate their new routine culture when they are able to make cumulative decisions to redefine and control their new environment to the point that they can answer, once more, primary questions and reorganize their socio-economic life. This is difficult. The displaced persons have lost control of their spatial and temporal order and of rights that most thought were inalienable. Offers are being made to monetize things around them that they never dreamt of selling. Strangers are setting timelines for meetings and relocation. And social support networks may be threatened. Leaders are trying to make decisions about the communities and simultaneously protect their own families and networks. And support networks are stressed and may now have conflicts of interest as neighbors vie for advantages.

Within this dissonant social and cultural context, the legal, policy, and procedural frameworks of the involuntary resettlement become much more than project and staff directives: they define the new, albeit temporary, routine. Within a short time, displaced persons must attempt to navigate the unfamiliar waters of planning, eligibility definition, compensation, disclosure to affected parties, impacts to be covered, exceptions to rules, reporting lines, delineation of intra-organizational responsibilities, elements to be addressed, grievance mechanisms, supervision, and monitoring requirements. When micro-disruptions occur in routine culture, specialists, such as attorneys, priests, and traditional healers, are enlisted for assistance. If this is the pattern under micro-disruptions, it is reasonable to expect that legal and other specialists be provided in the macro-disruptions of an involuntary resettlement.

In this context, national laws are procedurally detailed, compared with IFI global and regional policies, and usually administered by the state bureaucracy. National laws normally offer the displaced appellate rights, in hard law, and occasionally allow legal challenge and recovery of costs. In contrast, IFI procedural options are found in RAPs and other project-specific planning documents or contracts that should be, but seldom are, meaningfully disclosed to the affected peoples. RAPs are often administered by the infrastructure builder or sponsor, the contractor, a consultant, or a special involuntary resettlement unit formed within a government bureaucracy. The project-affected peoples cannot take the IFIs to court, and their complaints are limited to using a grievance mechanism set up by the project or to making a complaint through IFI accountability review mechanisms (the World Bank's Inspection Panel, the African Development Bank's Independent Review Mechanism, and the like). To date, no IFI has required, in policy, that its own involuntary resettlement policies be translated and meaningfully disclosed to project-affected peoples. Nor is there yet a policy requirement to include within project financing the provisioning of no-cost legal services.

The most significant involuntary resettlement objective is buried within existing policy. The framers of the World Bank policy set as one of its four principle objectives that displaced persons be meaningfully consulted and have opportunities to participate in planning and implementing resettlement programs (OP 4.12, par. 2[c]).[11] Articulation of a new routine begins with displaced persons regaining control of their own destinies. Meaningful, timely, and broadly disseminated disclosure (MTBDD) is a prerequisite to ending dissonance and articulating a new routine. Without MTBDD, each time the resettlement agency makes a new decision impacting the community, no matter how benevolent and well meaning, it reaffirms, at the PSC level, that the displaced persons and community are in dissonance, without control of their lives. In practice, MTBDD is too often misinterpreted as a way to reach the improvement of livelihoods and standards of living objectives, a means to an end, not a stand-alone objective. Failure to meaningfully disclose the policy itself to the displaced persons early in the involuntary resettlement denies the displaced persons knowledge of an entire corpus of rights that would assist in establishing a new routine. Some argue that this denial rises to the level of a possible human rights violation (Johnston and Garcia-Downing 2004).

Procedural empowerment is interlaced throughout existing policy. Procedural habilitation also begins when displaced peoples are empowered to gather and interpret information, identify pitfalls, and consider options by developing their own impoverishment-monitoring and impact-assessment capacities (Hirsch 1999). The Annex to OP 4.12 sets requirements that, if skillfully applied and aligned with the MTBDD objectives, could become methods for facilitating the emergence of a new routine. The World Bank's RAPs are supposed to provide for community participation, including an impressive list of actions that might improve the likelihood of a new and successful social articulation. Consistent with the overarching objective (OP 4.12, par. 2[b]), the policy calls for the RAP to include measures to ensure that displaced persons are informed about their options and rights pertaining to resettlement and consulted on, offered choices among, and provided with technically and economically feasible resettlement alternatives (OP 4.12, par. 6[a]ii). The RAP (OP 4.12, Annex A, par. 15) sets forth an aggressive agenda for community participation that includes the community's involvement in developing the following:

a. A description of the strategy for the hosts' consultation with resettlers and the resettlers' participation in the design and implementation of the resettlement activities.

b. A summary of the views expressed and how these views were taken into account in preparing the resettlement plan.

c. A review of the resettlement alternatives presented and the choices made by displaced persons regarding options available to them, including choices related to forms of compensation and resettlement assistance, relocating as individuals families or as part of preexisting communities or kinship groups, sustaining existing patterns of group organization, and retaining access to cultural property (for example, places of worship, pilgrimage centers, and cemeteries).

d. Institutionalized arrangements by which displaced people can communicate their concerns to project authorities throughout planning and implementation, and measures to ensure adequate representation of such vulnerable groups as indigenous people, ethnic minorities, the landless, and women.

e. Procedural empowerment means that those who feel aggrieved and mistreated should have a way to express dissent. The ability to dissent and disagree is a critical part of the reorganization process, requiring that appropriate and accessible grievance mechanisms be established for displaced people (OP 4.12, par. 13[a]).

Under normal circumstances, without an involuntary displacement, any one of these issues could keep a society busy for years. But years may not be available, as the most precious of all resources, time, usually is needlessly limited by an external project-completion schedule (normally, two to six years for large infrastructure projects). More time is available for PSC rearticulation when the involuntary resettlement component is financed apart from infrastructure construction and a revenue stream continues from project-generated revenue (Cernea 2008c). Procedural empowerment also increases when displaced persons manage and control the project benefits.

Developing Socio-cultural Innovations

We are most encouraged by the appearance of innovations that may substantively help people avoid or escape dissonant culture and establish new, meaningful cultural routines. The challenge is to find ways to fold this dispersed knowledge into policies and laws so that it is not idiosyncratic. In 2002 we visited a peri-urban farming community near Shanghai where rural peoples from the distant Three Georges Dam had been relocated. The government had arranged for each resettled family to live nearby a host family to help them adjust socially to their new urban environment.[12]

From the perspective of the R-D-R' model, the Chinese host–guest solution brilliantly ties a family caught in dissonance culture to a family ensconced in routine culture. We are uncertain whether cultural dissonance appears in the host culture in this arrangement.

Returning to the earlier example of Zimapan Dam, three villages along the river were combined into a single settlement located on an arid, river-less plateau (Aronsson 2002; Downing 1987; Greaves 1997; Guggenheim 1991, 1993). Potable water was piped in from 23 km away, and no water was available for irrigation. Early in the project, resettlers were permitted to rename the principal street in their new town. To the surprise of outside observers, they named it River Street. The local resettlement team reported serious conflicts over rival community claims of who had the right to live on the right bank of River Street in a position identical to their original location. A few months later, they selected the new name for their arid, hill-top community: Bella Vista del Rio (Beautiful View of the River). But the river is nowhere in sight! It made no difference. They were creating a new answer to one of their primary questions that was consistent, in some ways, with their old image. Where are we? We are living in Beautiful View of the River, on River Street.

Notes

1. Some cultures spend their spare time playing games that create new, tempo-rary routine cultures in which people can practice tactical moves for rewards. Gaming holds a significant place in culture, enabling individuals and groups to test and improve their agility to respond to the unexpected.

2. In some instances, dissonant culture may appear because the productive base (a fishing ground, an agricultural site, a ritual area) is lost, without any physical reloca-tion of people.

3. Three weakly articulated, scholarly discussions have focused on questions of involuntary displacement, organized on the basis of the force causing the displace-ment, that is, conflicts, disasters, and development. Noble efforts have been made to articulate these distinct traditions: Cernea 1990, 1996c; Hansen and Oliver-Smith 1982; Muggah 2003; Oliver-Smith 2005a; Scudder 1993; see Drabek 1986 and Turton 2006 for an inventory of disaster-related research.

4. Initially, Bank social scientists anticipated that these policies would form a demonstration effect, encouraging governments to incorporate the stronger IFI poli-cies into their national legal frameworks. Rarely did this happen, and adherence to the international frameworks remains problematic.

5. Evidence of noncompliance has been pervasive in the involuntary resettlement literature for decades (Cernea 2005a; Guggenheim 1994; Scudder 2005a; see Council for Social Development 2008 for examples in India). For example, Scudder (2005a:86) discovered that living conditions in his fifty-dam survey were reported improved in only three of forty-four cases and restored in another five cases. The World Bank's Inspection Panel Investigation Reports offer excellent detailed examples of compliance investigations. Recent examples are found in investigation reports on the Uganda Private Power Generation–Bujagali II Project (World Bank Inspection Panel 2008b, with resettlement compliance investigator Ted Downing); the Mumbai Urban Transportation Project in India (World Bank Inspection Panel 2005, with resettlement compliance investigators Michael Cernea and Alan Rew); and the West African Gas Pipeline Project (World Bank Inspection Panel 2008a, with resettlement compliance investigator Ted Downing), all available online at http://www.inspection panel.org under the tab "requests for inspection").

6. A persistent problem is the misalignment of both hard and soft laws. Three dynamics drive this misalignment. First, soft law is usually easier to revise than hard law, meaning that it changes more frequently. Second, IFIs adjust their safeguard policies to their governance, bureaucratic, and stakeholder needs. And third, the scientific findings and institutional experience knowledge improve. Consequently, there is global policy pressure toward inter-IFI policy harmonization, including the safeguard policies on involuntary resettlement (Paris Declaration on Aid Effectiveness, February 28–March 2, 2005, http://www.oecd.org/document, accessed August 2008, and Paris High-Level Forum, February 28–March 2, 2003, http://www.aidharmonization.org, accessed August 2008).

7. A major limitation of safeguard policies is that they are applicable only to persons who lose access to assets as a result of projects whose financiers and sponsors agree to the policies.

8. On June 23, 2005, the US Supreme Court rendered a major decision that the use of eminent domain to take private property for economic development and to displace people did not violate the public use clauses of the state and federal constitutions. The Court argued that if it generates government revenue and jobs, it is a public use. The public overwhelmingly opposed the decision, leading forty-seven states by 2007 to adopt laws to limit such takings.

9. The IFIs have not resolved the inherent conflict of interest in their rule-making processes whereby those responsible for preparing the policies and procedures also are responsible for following them. The struggle for management discretion encourages them to favor ambiguities in policy language that permit them to exercise a judgment, whereas external stakeholders focus on precise policy

language that the development bureaucracy should apply (Quarles van Ufford, Kruijt, and Downing 1988).

10. The African Development Bank's involuntary resettlement policy also recognizes the rights of vulnerable peoples and sets a broad distributional goal that displaced persons must be treated equitably and share in the benefits of projects that involve their resettlement (AfDB 2003:Section III, par. 3.1).

11. OP 4.12, par. 2, appears to list three objectives (a through c) when it actually has four. Paragraph b states that

> where it is not feasible to avoid resettlement, resettlement activities should be conceived and executed as sustainable development programs, providing sufficient investment resources to enable the persons displaced by the project to share in project benefits. Displaced persons should be meaningfully consulted and should have opportunities to participate in planning and implementing resettlement programs.

The second sentence should stand alone. We consider this a fourth policy objective and have so interpreted it, without World Bank Board objections, in our compliance analysis of involuntary resettlement policies for the World Bank Inspection Panel (2008a, 2008b) that reports to the World Bank Board. We hope that the next revision will correct the punctuation in the objectives, clarifying that there are four. The African Development Bank's involuntary resettlement policy, in contrast to the World Bank's, sets a policy goal that when people must be displaced, they be treated equitably and that they share in the benefits of the project (AfDB 2003:par. 3.1[9]). Instead of restoration, it sets an objective that displaced people receive resettlement assistance, preferably under the project, so that their standards of living, income earning capacity, and production levels are improved (AfDB 2003:par. 3.2[9]). The Asian Development Bank sets a lower objective, namely, to ensure that displaced people receive assistance, preferably under the project, so that they will be at least as well-off as they would have been in the absence of the project (Asian Development Bank 1995:par. 33[9]).

12. Further inquiry hinted at possible status differences between guest and host, with daughters of the resettled thought to be more likely to marry the sons of the hosts.

12

Family Resemblances between Disasters and Development-Forced Displacement

Hurricane Katrina as a Comparative Case Study

Gregory V. Button

My primary goal in this chapter is to narrow the gap between the seemingly different, but actually closely allied, literatures of disasters and development-forced displacement and resettlement (DFDR). By using the SAR advanced seminar papers and the case of Hurricane Katrina, I demonstrate how these two literatures may enrich each other. Indeed, the divide, especially regarding the analysis of forcibly dislocated people, is undoubtedly a social construct that inhibits a fuller understanding of the phenomenon of displacement and resettlement.

Over the past twenty-five years, colleagues from the field of development-forced displacement, refugee studies, and disaster research (Cernea 1996c; Hansen and Oliver-Smith 1982; Oliver-Smith 2006; Turton 2006) have discovered that the displaced peoples we work with share many similar challenges. The causal agents of forced migration are, as Cernea (1996c) argues, man-made and natural disasters, political conflict, persecution, and development policies (Oliver-Smith and Button 2005). Some have argued that the fragmentation of research is attributable to an overreliance on categories and concepts that are the outcome of policy instead of scientific considerations (Black 2001; Hansen 1996; Turton 2006). Indeed, a comparative analysis of the harm inflicted by development-forced displacement and by disasters readily demonstrates the unsoundness of these separations and underscores the accuracy of Johnston's term (chapter 10, this volume) *development disasters.*

Rather than recognize a sharp boundary between disaster research and development-forced displacement research, I maintain that the two domains share enough common, if not identical, similarities to bear a "family of resemblances," in the Wittgensteinian (1953) sense.

VIEWING DISASTERS AND DEVELOPMENT IN A BROADER CONTEXT

Despite technological and scientific advances in prediction and mitigation, we have seen a serious increase in mortality and economic loss from disasters since 1960, particularly in the developing world. Disasters are increasing in impact and scope through the combined effects of economic, social, demographic, ideological, and technological factors (Milleti 1999). Greater numbers of people are more vulnerable to natural and other hazards than ever before, in part because of greater population and population densities but more so because of their location in dangerous areas. In fact, disaster risks have dramatically increased in recent decades (International Federation of the Red Cross and Red Crescent Societies 2003). Growing population densities in coastal regions throughout the world contribute to the vulnerability of humans. In the United States alone, 55–60 percent of the population lives in 772 counties adjacent to coasts. It is estimated that in two decades almost 75 percent of the US population will live in coastal counties. This trend places more people in the path of coastal storm surges, hurricane winds, and flooding. Larger coastal populations also contribute to the degradation of the coastal and marine ecosystems (Hinrichsen 2005). Whatever the hazard, displacement of individuals and communities frequently results from the threat or impact of a disaster (Oliver-Smith and Button 2005).

Unlike displacement by development, most displacement by disaster tends to be temporary. Exceptions are mega disasters such as the Southeast Asian tsunami, Chernobyl, and in North America, the Dust Bowl of the Depression, the Great Mississippi Flood of 1927, and, of course, Hurricane Katrina. Given the increasing density of human coastal populations and global warming, these mega disasters may well be a harbinger of future catastrophes.

Forcible displacement may become permanent in the aftermath of disasters of smaller magnitude as well, if they destroy or seriously alter the environment or ruin a local economic base. As of this writing, it remains to be seen whether the latter effect will determine the rebuilding of New

Orleans. In the wake of a disaster, government and political decision-making processes can also adversely influence prolonged displacement. After Hurricane Andrew, the decision not to rebuild Homestead Air Force Base, a major regional employer, permanently altered the economic base of South Dade County, Florida, and may have forced some of the permanent migration that followed (Oliver-Smith, personal communication, October 2004).

If the New Orleans levees are not rebuilt to withstand Category 5 hurricane forces, many people may not choose to return. The present lack of consensus and leadership about adopting rebuilding advisory codes and new flood-elevation advisories proposed by FEMA could adversely affect federal aid to the city. Many businesses may abandon the area because of the increased costs resulting from recovery codes. The federal government's tardiness in providing the necessary funding and leadership has hampered the rebuilding process. Representative Barney Frank (D-MA) describes this inaction as "a policy of ethnic cleansing." Such inaction increases "the likelihood that most black Orleanians will never be able to return" (Davis 2006:11).

A LONGITUDINAL APPROACH TO DISASTERS

To explore some of the similarities between DFDR and disasters, we need to refine our perspective on disasters. Disasters require a more longitudinal approach, one that includes both "pre" and "post" events and sees disasters as a partial outcome of everyday life and not as exceptional occurrences. The public, the media, policy makers, and even many researchers commonly view disasters as isolates and ignore the complex processes from which these evolve. Seen in this light, disasters are thought to have "little to do with the rest of life and the environment" (Hewitt 1998:80). It is important to keep in mind Hewitt's (1983) trenchant observation that disasters are not unprecedented or isolated events but are better understood if we pay attention to the complex social processes contributing to the conditions under which they arise. In fact, it is essential to develop a political ecological approach that places disaster at the intersection of society and the environment and that explicates their mutual influences (Oliver-Smith 2002). Whereas disaster studies only in recent years have taken this long-term approach, DFDR studies seem to have paid closer attention to events along the development-forced resettlement continuum.

The 1927 Mississippi flood underscores the importance of a long-term historical approach to disaster and also shows us how development projects contribute to the formation of disaster. Barry's 1997 study, among others, helps to illustrate the linkages between DFDR and disasters. Whether a society is building a huge dam or is trying to control one of the world's largest rivers and promote major settlement patterns on that river's delta, the consequences are often similar. In both the 1927 Mississippi flood and Hurricane Katrina, the displacement and the disasters themselves were inextricably linked to the development process.

The forces that contributed to the devastating outcome of Katrina are historically located in several centuries of development along the Gulf Coast that has prevented the natural resiltation of the river delta, such as the canalization of the Mississippi River and the accompanying levees. These man-made alterations of the environment increase the annual rate of subsidence. Along with other factors, the resultant sinking of the land-mass of the delta coast makes the inland communities considerably more vulnerable to tropical storms.

The land and the people of the Gulf coastal region are made more vulnerable also by the development of oil and gas extraction, which has resulted in the dredging of tens of thousands of coastal channels. Through this maze of lace-like fingers, the saline waters of the Gulf penetrate the freshwater marshes and kill off vegetation that would protect the coast from further erosion. These factors, as well as Katrina's impacts, highlight the need to view disasters not as isolates, but as complex processes located at the intersection of society and nature.

Frequently, the societal components are the outcome of development projects both large and small, such as the development of housing in the swamps of East New Orleans, increasing population vulnerability (Colten 2006). In Katrina, many dozens of development projects ultimately made both land and people more vulnerable. The phenomena of disasters need to be seen in a more diachronic and synergistic light.

The "survival of New Orleans, scientists have noted, is dependent on the health of the Deltaic Plain coastline and the wetlands behind it" (Gramling and Hagelman 2004:114). The clear-cutting of cypress trees for garden mulch precipitated coastal erosion, and the location of hundreds of gas-and-oil rigs and pipelines along the coast further degraded the environment. Moreover, the building of transportation canals for the petrochemical industry contributed to the destruction of the coastal marshes, another source of natural protection (Laska et al. 2004). The "man-made" engineering that controls the flow of the Mississippi and the Atchafalaya rivers deprives the delta of the sediment load required to maintain it (Colten 2006; Gramling and Hagelman 2004). It is estimated that the Gulf Coast loses about thirty-five square miles each year because of these projects alone.

Another development that increased New Orleans' vulnerability was the Mississippi River Gulf Outlet ("MRGO"), built by the Army Corps of Engineers to shorten the shipping route between New Orleans and the Gulf Coast. During the early planning stages, the Department of Interior warned that its "excavation could result in major ecological change with widespread and severe ecological consequences" (quoted in van Heerden 2006:79). Unfortunately, the prediction proved to be true. The canal brought saltwater into the freshwater marshes and swamps and caused severe ecological degradation. According to van Heerden (2006:79), MRGO destroyed eleven thousand acres of cypress swamps and converted nearly twenty thousand acres of brackish marsh "into less productive saline marsh," destroying an essential nursery for shellfish and fish.

MRGO became a pathway for the storm surge from Hurricane Katrina. When the storm waters reached the Industrial Canal, they formed a funnel, "causing the storm surge to rise higher and move faster" (Williams 2005:87). Eventually, MRGO was overtopped and caused terrible flooding (which earned it a new nickname, "Hurricane Highway") that devastated St. Bernard Parish. Two thousand one hundred square miles were left underwater.

THE IMPORTANCE OF THE RECOVERY END
OF THE CONTINUUM

One way to illustrate the commonalities between development and disaster is to compare the general attributes of their long-term effects. To do this, we need to move beyond the impact stage and focus on the recovery or reconstruction period, as well as the predisposing conditions for disaster.

Although this perspective is informative, it is also problematic because there is not a rich theoretical corpus about reconstruction and recovery. Arguably, this period is as important as—and, in some cases, more important than—the initial impact period, but, to date, there is a paucity of literature that examines what constitutes true recovery and reconstruction. On the disaster continuum, recovery is the least studied, least understood process, despite its significance and the fact that it is the longest part of the continuum. A comparative analysis of development-forced displacement and disaster underscores the need for us to improve our understanding of the recovery/reconstruction process. Ted Scudder (chapter 2, this volume) has astutely observed: "Anthropology and the other social sciences are way behind the environmental sciences in carrying out the type of systematic and comparative long-term research needed for improving policy-relevant theory."

Traditionally, the process of reconstruction has been viewed in largely material terms as a physical process of rebuilding infrastructure and providing food and medical care. This is not sufficient to remedy the problem. The recovery process is far more complex than simple materiality. In our failure to study the recovery process adequately, we have failed to understand the complex interplay between materiality and culture. If we rebuild the material world without cultivating the community, "people will," as Erikson (1995:xvi) declares, "remain like refugees in their own land." Material and social reconstruction undoubtedly reinforce each other. The degree to which a basic level of materiality promotes the precondition for social reconstitution and to which cultural reconstruction helps to engender material reconstruction is little understood. Also, both approaches have the potential to hinder each other (Oliver-Smith 2005a).

As Scudder (chapter 2, this volume) and de Wet (chapter 4, this volume) observe, displacement accelerates the process of socioeconomic change for displaced people. Along with other forces, this process serves to "loosen their cultural anchors" and "lessen their material well-being" (de Wet, chapter 4). Reconstruction also has inherent potential (depending on the specificities of the event) for material and social enhancement. By rearranging the distribution of power and resources, the process of reconstruction and recovery presents an opportunity to restructure the social order and refashion the social contract to render the vulnerable less vulnerable and to break the cycle of calamity.

The post-disaster reconstruction process is a development-like process; reconstruction policies can either protect a community or make it more vulnerable to future hazards. These are important similarities we must recognize and understand to minimize displacement and to assist in the material reconstruction and social reconstitution of affected communities.

The catastrophic losses from Hurricane Katrina and other modern-day catastrophes demonstrate in horrific fashion the urgent need to develop the conceptual, strategic, and material tools to cope with natural hazards made even more potent and complex by climate change, environmental degradation, and population density on floodplains and along vulnerable coastal areas (Oliver-Smith and Button 2005).

WITH THE PASSING OF TIME, SIMILARITIES INCREASE

If there are certain dissimilarities between disasters and development in the initial stages (especially in regard to the "triggering" event and intentionality), many of these differences fall away with the passage of time. As Oliver-Smith (2005a) has observed, the commonalities between development and disasters increase the further in time from the initial event. Currently, the survivors of Hurricane Katrina are facing the same persisting challenges as development survivors: homelessness, unemployment, marginalization, loss of neighborhood and community, mental and physical health problems, and powerlessness (Cernea 1996c).

What is imperative to keep in mind is that, ultimately, development displacees, disaster victims, and refugees all confront a complex sequence of cascading events most often involving dislocation, the dismantling of families, adaptive stresses, loss of privacy, political marginalization, and the daunting task of reconstructing their ontological status, family, and community (Cernea 1996c, 1997; Colson 1971; Scudder 1981b, 1985). This litany of challenges serves as a basic outline of "family resemblances."

All of the chapters in this volume discuss issues that are salient to both DFDR and disasters. Forced dislocation is the common denominator that undergirds the bridge between the two seemingly disparate fields. Attendant to all the fundamental problems mentioned above is a myriad of interconnecting issues that challenge refugees, researchers, and policy makers alike. These issues, large and small, are not mutually exclusive; they form a connected whole that characterizes both disasters and DFDR in general.

By viewing disasters from a longitudinal perspective, we can trace, in some measure, their origins to processes of misinformed development. Moreover, the longitudinal perspective reveals certain similarities between the post-disaster reconstruction process and the development-forced displacement and resettlement process. Now I will discuss the impacts and outcomes of Hurricane Katrina to illustrate how such a disaster, which forcibly dislocated hundreds of thousands of people, shares family resemblances with "development disasters" causing involuntary migration and resettlement.

PUBLIC HEALTH IMPACTS

Kedia (chapter 5, this volume) observes that "development policies—and resettlement policies, in particular—have made minimal reference to the magnified health risks in affected communities." Furthermore, he notes that, to date, there are few comprehensive studies on the health of communities displaced and resettled by dam projects. Disaster response-and-recovery policies have been concerned with public health issues but have focused largely on the immediate response to disasters, not on the long-term recovery efforts.

In the past two decades, natural disasters alone have killed 3 million people and have harmed the lives of more than 800 million (Noji 1997).

We have no comparable figure for those disasters that could be considered "man-made" or "technological." According to Anderson (1991), 95 percent of the natural disaster deaths occur among 66 percent of the world's poorest populations.

Although Katrina's long-term damage to the environment remains unknown, there are many indications of the serious toxic contamination caused by the hurricane. The Natural Resource Defense Council's analysis of EPA (Environmental Protection Agency) data shows that most districts in New Orleans contain concentrations of arsenic, lead, diesel fuel, or cancer-causing benzo(a)pyrene "above levels that would normally trigger investigation and possible soil cleanup in the state of Louisiana" (Solomon and Rotkin-Ellman 2006:3–4). Perhaps the most pervasive problem is the high level of airborne mold contamination caused by the flooding of homes and thought to pose a "significant respiratory hazard" (Solomon et al. 2006). According to the report, the mold levels "could easily trigger serious allergic or asthmatic reactions in sensitive people" (Solomon et al. 2006:1), as well as congestion, sneezing, throat irritation, and pneumonitis. As Kedia also reports, the displaced frequently experience environmentally derived health problems.

Mental health problems accompany most disasters, just as they do DFDR. Disaster mental health studies conducted after the flooding of Buffalo Creek (Erikson 1976; Gleser, Green, and Winget 1981), the *Exxon-Valdez* oil spill (Palinkas et al. 1992), the nuclear accident at Three Mile Island (Bromet 1990), and 9/11 (Pyszczynski, Solomon, and Greenberg 2001) revealed significant levels of psychological trauma. According to the US Substance and Mental Health Services Administration, as many as one-half million Katrina survivors require some sort of psychological help. According to one major study (World Health Organization 2006), the proportion of people with mental health problems doubled in the months following the hurricane. Unfortunately, only 22 of 196 psychiatrists had returned to the New Orleans area as of 2006 (Weisler, Barbee, and Townsend 2006). In addition to a shortage of psychiatrists, the Stafford Act (the federal disaster-response legislation to assist the state and local governments) prohibits emergency funding for mental illness. The Bush administration demonstrated little interest in finding means of addressing the problem.

JOBLESSNESS

Loss of employment occurs in the wake of many disasters, just as it does as the result of DFDR. In the case of Hurricane Katrina, it is not possible to quantify unemployment precisely, even though we know that tens of thousands of people were, and in many cases still are, unemployed or underemployed. In November 2005, three months after the catastrophe, 27.9 percent of the evacuees were unemployed (Brookings Institution 2006). The Brookings Institution (2006) reported that by September 2006 the unemployment rate for the city was 5.2 percent, higher than both the state and the US average for the month. Figures for the displaced evacuees during the same period, however, show that 14.5 percent were unemployed; by October 2006 this number rose to 17.9 percent. Unfortunately, the Bureau of Labor Statistics (BLS) ceased reporting unemployment figures for displaced evacuees after October 2006, making it difficult to track this trend in the ongoing recovery period.

HOMELESSNESS AND INCREASED MARGINALIZATION

Homelessness is an inherent condition of forced displacement. In the case of Hurricane Katrina, it remains a problem today, fully three years after Katrina came ashore. Hundreds of thousands of people are still without permanent homes. Many are living in temporary homes, with no idea of how long it will be before they can return to their original homes, or rebuild their homes, or find permanent housing in their new communities. For example, in New Orleans, where the hurricane and flood damaged 175,000 homes, there is still a shortage of tens of thousands of homes.

In some of the larger urban areas, evacuees are living in temporary housing in outlying districts without transportation access to social services, medical care, or employment. This mirrors the situation Koenig (chapter 6, this volume) describes: the housing situation of urban development displacees and evacuees is likely to impoverish them further. Living on the outskirts of cities like Austin and Dallas also makes it difficult for evacuees to maintain social ties with fellow evacuees.

Ironically, many evacuees could not leave New Orleans before the storm hit because they did not own cars or had no access to public transportation. Many of these very same individuals and families are at even greater disadvantage now because they were relocated to greater metropolitan areas like Houston, Texas, cities far larger than New Orleans or the smaller Gulf Coast cities where they once lived. For Katrina, there was no resettlement plan, another important similarity between disasters and DFDR in general.

This physical marginalization is symbolic of the social and cultural marginalization that refugees and evacuees alike endure. Most Katrina evacuees had grown up in the unique cultural enclaves of New Orleans and the bayou communities along the Gulf Coast. They are, as we shall see, marginalized not only by distance from these cultures but also by race and class issues. In the Houston area, there has been extensive stigmatization of the evacuees, including allegations that they are responsible for the increase in urban crime. Disaster evacuees and development-disaster victims are often stigmatized in their new locations. In the wake of Love Canal and Seveso, children from families living near the contaminated areas were thought to be "contagious." Families and children living in FEMA trailer camps after hurricanes Andrew and Charley were stigmatized (regardless of race and class) as "FEMA kids." Refugees and disaster victims alike are typically perceived as being "sickly" and "diseased" and having "poor hygiene." Furthermore, they suffer the stigma of being among the "damned," further marginalizing them and creating a convenient cultural rationalization for their fate.

SOCIAL DISARTICULATION: THE DISMANTLING OF NEIGHBORHOOD AND COMMUNITY

Forced dislocation such as that found in development projects and in the wake of disasters on the scale of Hurricane Katrina results inevitably in what Cernea (1996c, 1997) has labeled "social disarticulation." The literal dismantling of neighborhoods and whole communities ruptures the social fabric, depriving residents of important social support networks, the cultural foundations of community, and ethnic identity, as well as the underpinnings of collective economic support. The effects of this fragmentation of social cohesion and endangered social identity underscore the significance of community. Wallace (1957) was the first to write about the cultural dissolution of community and the cultural stresses of disaster. Later, Erikson (1976) wrote about the deleterious effect of the tearing of the "social fabric" in his account of the Buffalo Creek flood in West Virginia, in which he coined the phrase "collective trauma," as opposed to the individual trauma inflicted on victims of disasters.

Collective trauma is amply illustrated in the case of Katrina and most development-forced displacement projects. Many residents of New Orleans and coastal Louisiana had lived most, if not all, of their lives in the neighborhoods destroyed by the floods. A number of families had lived in their neighborhoods for several generations. Forcibly relocated to relief centers along the Gulf Coast, many evacuees were left with no knowledge of their families and neighbors' whereabouts.

Individuals were thrust into "foreign" cultures across the nation, deprived of the cultural foundations of their way of life. Their food, everyday lifestyles, music, rituals, and celebrations were first disrupted by the storm and then by the manner in which they were relocated. At the very least, social dislocation undermines the routine of everyday life, sometimes permanently. Many evacuees mourn their loss of culture, even if they were relocated to another Southern city. They have lost the social bond of community and a sense of place. Sense of place has long been recognized as vital in the formation of individual and collective identity (Altman and Low 1992; Button 1995; Escobar 2001; Feld and Basso 1996; Tuan 1977). Place, as Oliver-Smith (chapter 7, this volume) observes, is encoded into our individual and collective memories and contributes to our ontological grounding as individuals and as communities. Downing and Garcia-Downing (chapter 11, this volume) write that the loss of place and community results in the disruption of the "social geometry."

When massive development projects and catastrophes destroy the sense of place, people are unable to return to the fountainhead of their ontological uniqueness. The loss of place in the case of indigenous societies can result in the literal death of the people and their culture (Oliver-Smith, chapter 7, this volume). Several researchers have written that grieving for home and community is tantamount to grieving for a loved one (Fried 1963; Gans 1962; Marris 1974; Wallace 1957).

With the destruction of a built environment such as the neighborhoods in New Orleans, dislocation occurs on more levels than the geographical. When I accompanied evacuees returning to their former neighborhoods for the first time, I witnessed their confusion and feelings of loss as they tried to identify street intersections and old neighborhood hangouts, once-familiar landmarks now gone. Such destruction of socially constructed spaces disrupted, as Downing (chapter 11, this volume) asserts, their sense of geophysical space, temporality, and identity. They struggled mentally to reinsert themselves into a space that was eluding them and thereby robbing them of a cherished identity. The world as they knew it had vanished, just as vast landscapes vanish from sight with the construction of a major dam. This unfamiliar landscape was baffling to them. The ontological grounding that they sought in returning home evaded them; their return had the opposite effect from what they expected. The world as they once knew it could not be found, and they had difficulty attaching meaning to what remained.

Needless to say, this dismantling has severe economic impacts on individuals and households. The informal social-support networks had provided not only psychological and cultural support but also economic assistance in the collective sharing and exchange of limited resources

(Cernea 1996c). The bartering for and exchanging of food, clothes, and labor that underpin most communities are especially vital in low-income and marginalized communities (Bott 1957; Stack 1974). As Piven and Cloward (1971) have noted, the poor in our society, and undoubtedly in other societies, are forced by the failures of the economy to improvise their own ways of coping with chronic crises and catastrophes. The loss of this social capital makes survival even more difficult. In the case of Hurricane Katrina, when the evacuees tried to improvise new mutual-support mechanisms by sharing their benefits assistance and living spaces with kin and friends, FEMA punished them, often severing their assistance for violating FEMA regulations.

LACK OF PARTICIPATION AND THE SPIRALING LOSS OF CONTROL

Victims of disasters and DFDR often report a loss of control over their lives, environment, and community. They come to question whether people inherently do have control over their own lives and whether governments exist to help people. The widespread report of loss of control increases and broadens, and events spiral downward from forced dislocation, homelessness, unemployment, marginalization, and so on. The perceived loss of control becomes a central issue in the social construction of the events and is deepened by the perception of sociocultural disorganization, or social chaos, that follows these events. Wallace (1957) speaks of how, in such circumstances, people perceive their own culture as being ineffective. The familiar maze of culture becomes disorganized and unfamiliar. Janoff-Bulman and Frieze (1987) have observed that threatening events can destroy victims' fundamental assumptions about the world and instill a sense of insecurity and loss of control. Crisis challenges people's sense of the way the world is and the way it ought to be. The familiar ways of moving about in the world to obtain their needs and alleviate stress become obscured. They perceive their own inability, and that of society as a whole, to rise to the tasks at hand. In Downing and Garcia-Downing's view (chapter 11, this volume), social disarray threatens the social geometry of the world, and a meaningful recovery occurs only when people regain mastery over their own lives.

From a political perspective, this spinning out of control is actually indicative of the fact that, as Oliver-Smith (1996:78) asserts, displacement is the ultimate expression of powerlessness. Explicitly and implicitly, the role of power and the powerlessness of forcibly dislocated populations is an inherent theme in all the chapters of this volume. This very lack of power is what makes it difficult for refugees and evacuees to regain control over their lives. Moreover, it is important for us to observe that greater vulnerability to the threat of forcible dislocation or to the ravages of disaster implies an inherent powerlessness in the everyday life of a society. In other words, people are rendered vulnerable and powerless by a social system that apportions risk unevenly among its members (Bankoff 2004; Cannon 1994; Hewitt 1998; Wisner 1993).

De Wet (chapter 4, this volume) goes beyond international, codified human-rights agreements and calls into question ethical problems surrounding forced resettlement resulting from development projects. Indeed, the central focus of his chapter is whether forced resettlement can be justified. In examining the complexities of this ethical question, he correctly points out that whatever else development is about, it is "above all, about power" (de Wet quoting Goulet, personal communication during the advanced seminar).

In my own writings (Button 2002), I have argued that disasters are not just about material phenomena but are grounded in the intensely political world of social relations. Such a perspective underscores that disasters are not merely socially and physically disruptive but also political events. By necessity, disaster and DFDR research must examine the political power relations among those affected, as well as among the various agencies and institutions involved in the event and with the victims (Button 1999). This is not to say that people are totally powerless but that "they can and do resist" (Clark, chapter 9, this volume), as Johnston's chapter 10 also attests.

In the wake of disasters and DFDR, however, some people's access to knowledge and decision making is curtailed, bringing us to the crucial contestation between local knowledge and professional knowledge that often occurs in crisis. In our highly professionalized culture, privileged arguments overwhelm the public debate over controversial topics. Civil disputes, whether they are about development projects, environmental risks, or disaster response, are seen as topics for only experts to debate; the voices of everyday people are often excluded from debates and policy formation (Button 2002). In anthropological terms, this represents the displacement of local knowledge. The bias toward professional knowledge has come to embody a high degree of information control (Brown and Mikkelsen 1990).

Access to knowledge and recognition of lay voices constitute another theme that resonates throughout all the contributions to this volume: in Johnston's chapter 10 discussion of "the lack of consultation and meaningful participation in the decision-making processes," in Clark's chapter 9 discussion of the need to address "power differentials" with respect to information and participation in decision making, in Oliver-Smith's chapter 7 discussion of the historical and contextual importance of local knowledge in the conflicts over conservation and displacement, and in de Wet's chapter 4 discussion of the lack of forums for the voices of the various stakeholders to be heard in a systematic way and equally effectively. In the case of Katrina, the evacuees have lacked access to information and effective input into the rebuilding, or demolishing, of New Orleans neighborhoods and Gulf coastal communities.

This latter point brings us to another issue that plays a central role in many of the chapters in this book. Koenig (chapter 6) writes about the desire of displaced urban residents to remain close to their original neighborhoods, which, as she notes, requires political struggle and innovative planning. In coastal Louisiana and Mississippi communities, including greater New Orleans, minorities are struggling to return to their neighborhoods and to gain a dominant voice in the preservation and rebuilding of these neighborhoods. They are concerned about the hidden agendas to which Oliver-Smith refers in his chapter 7 on conservation and displacement. The fear is that the white establishment is trying to discourage and prevent their return, in order to "gentrify" the city.

Many community officials, including those from Biloxi, New Orleans, and St. Bernard, hired outside consultants from the Congress for New Urbanism to redesign communities radically, without any effective input from community members or any recognition of their desire to retain their own sense of place and not have it redefined by architects and urban planners in Atlanta and New York. One critic has described the congress's vision of multiple parks and squares as "nostalgia for a middle-class, Middle American life that never existed" (Lewis 2006:104). Many residents complained that the new homes would be too expensive. Lack of participation is, of course, also characteristic of most DFDR projects, as many of the chapters in this volume attest.

In one sense, the new urban look is an attempt to impose a model of nature onto the urban setting, a model that is not in keeping with the residents' vision of their urban landscape. These contested visions of Nature and its symbolic representation in the city are, in some ways, analogous to the disputes between indigenous and traditional people and conservationists discussed by Oliver-Smith (chapter 7, this volume). The planned green spaces for the new urban setting impose white middle-class values about the symbolic representation of nature in modern-day life. In real terms, this means that the homes of many people will be torn down in order for a patchwork of green spaces to stand as emblems of a new urban worldview.

The political and social activism of development refugees and Katrina evacuees to gain a voice in reconstructing their lives is tied to much of the discussion in this volume about the promotion of civil society (Clark's chapter 9, Fisher's chapter 8, and de Wet's chapter 4). Fisher mentions that the testimony and personal accounts of "those who suffer" can sometimes legitimate groups' participation in the policy-making and implementation process of international organizations, although he cautions that such legitimacy is not always assured. He also notes that advocacy can sometimes be undemocratic and that agendas can be co-opted by groups to influence the decision-making process in order to achieve their own goals. De Wet cautions us about the possible negative consequences of a participatory approach that conceals several levels of power and influence. Certainly, all of these issues have arisen in the wake of controversies following Hurricane Katrina. In the contestation for meaning and control, many local and national groups have locked swords. Conflict has manifested itself in many ways as urban planners and federal and state governments try to impose their values and solutions on neighborhoods. As discussed below, the attempt of New Orleans mayor Nagin to appoint a committee of outside experts to create a recovery plan met with sharp resistance from neighborhoods that wanted to determine their own destiny. The exclusion of voices is underscored in yet another way: at the end of 2006, nearly 80 percent of former New Orleans African Americans had not returned to the city. Yet, small groups of policy planners were debating the future scope and size of the city, without any input from these voiceless evacuees.

Fisher's trenchant examination of the two ways of thinking about civil society resonates with the same tension as Johnston's presentation of the Chixoy Dam controversy in Guatemala and is as pertinent to the political struggle on the Gulf Coast as it is to the emergence of a global civil society. The first model conceives of civil society as a means by which citizens are disciplined and brought under control, a process that Foucault refers to as governmentality. The second conceives of civil society as a space where counter-hegemonic discourses become possible. Seen in this dual light, civil society is both dangerous and full of promise. These two models of civil society are most visible in New Orleans, where formal, government-sponsored civilian task forces are creating a new vision of the city's future at the same time that grassroots, neighborhood-centered organizations strive to present their own counter-hegemonic vision of a city without corruption, white domination, and social injustice. The most dramatic example is the work of the Ninth Ward (a predominantly African American community) to prevent the demolition of many of its neighborhoods. The official task forces, on municipal and state levels, heavily favor the status quo, which consists largely of pro-business and pro-development forces not necessarily indigenous to the city. Mayor Nagin basically ignored the city council and precluded it from the decision-making and advisory process by appointing mayoral commissions of predominantly white, Republican, outside experts. In turn, Governor Blanco appointed the Louisiana Recovery Authority, with a majority of corporate business leaders and not one grassroots African American leader. The authority is not merely an advisory panel; it controls the allocation of FEMA funds and congressional funding for the reconstruction process (Davis 2006).

Examples of more "promising" forms of civil society in New Orleans can be found in the organizing that ACORN (Association of Community Organizations for Reform Now) has conducted on behalf of the community to advocate for housing and for hiring evacuees, instead of outsiders, for reconstruction jobs. Other examples (of which there are many) include the community organizations that have been founded in the Ninth Ward, in East New Orleans, in the Vietnamese community, and in St. Bernard Parish. These groups promote counter-hegemonic agendas that include local people, make their voices heard in the decision-making process, and challenge the status quo.

HUMAN RIGHTS ISSUES

Human rights are at the core of many issues surrounding disasters and development projects.[1] The contributions by Johnston, Clark, and de Wet in this volume, among others, address these issues in the context of development. In chapter 9, Clark notes, "Improperly implemented development-forced displacement can violate a multiplicity of human rights." As she states, these violations result in loss of livelihood, inadequate housing, food insecurity, limited freedom of movement, impoverishment, and even death. Clark also observes that international law is intended to address the threats to the rights of forced migrants but fails to protect those populations forcibly relocated by development. Johnston's chapter 10 also addresses the injustices that result from economic development projects. Her account of the building of a hydroelectric dam in Guatemala is testimony to just how brutal human rights abuses can be in such circumstances.

In the case of Hurricane Katrina, there would appear to be many abuses of human rights. These abuses are viewed by some as violations of US jurisprudence and international law or accords or ethical violations of humanitarian standards. The right to life itself is the paramount concern among human rights activists. A House congressional investigation concluded that the failure to evacuate New Orleans fully, for instance, caused the death and suffering of thousands of people. Community and human rights activists have also stated that the failure to warn people of the levee breaks in New Orleans was gross negligence resulting in the unnecessary loss of many lives. Most of the mortality in the New Orleans metro region was caused not by the hurricane, but by the flooding due to levee failure. Research demonstrates that there was little or no warning of the flooding, even when officials were aware of the levee failures (Button 2006).

The International Covenant on Civil and Political Rights (ICCPR) states in article 6, paragraph 1: "Every human being has the inherent right to life. Law shall protect this right. No one shall be arbitrarily deprived of his or her life."[2] Furthermore, the ICCPR in article 2(1) declares that the state must carry out this obligation "without distinction of any kind, such as race, color, sex, language, religion, political or other opinion, national or social origin, property, birth or other status" (Carmalt 2006:1).[3] For instance, Carmalt argues:

> The State party failed to respect the right to life because its hurricane evacuation plan discriminated on the basis of property by only providing a policy for those residents who owned personal vehicles. In Orleans Parish, discriminating on the basis of ownership of private vehicles equated to discrimination on the basis of race, since African-Americans were [more than] twice as likely to be without a personal vehicle than whites. [Carmalt 2006:2][4]

During the initial days of the event, one of the most documented and controversial incidents occurred. Hundreds of predominately African American residents of New Orleans were prevented at gunpoint from crossing the bridge at Gretna in Jefferson Parish in order to escape the rising floodwaters. Some legal scholars consider this to be a violation of article 12 of the ICCPR (Buford 2006), which states that everyone has the right of liberty of movement within his or her own country.

Other reported abuses include the dropping of evacuees on interstate overpasses and leaving them for days without food or water. The state's failure to provide adequate humanitarian relief would seem to violate the UN accords that all internally displaced people have a right to adequate food and water (Waterman 2005). Another possible violation was of the UN accords that family members who want to remain together should be allowed and that families separated by displacement should be united as quickly as possible.

It is quite clear—from journalistic accounts, from eyewitness reports, and from testimony that I and other researchers have gathered—that many evacuees crowded together in temporary shelters or abandoned on interstate overpasses were not given a choice of remaining with their families. In fact, they were forcibly separated from their families, sometimes at gunpoint. Evacuees were dropped off at shelters in Houston, Dallas, Baton Rouge, Atlanta, and so on, without any knowledge of their immediate family members' whereabouts. Grandparents were separated from their children and grandchildren, spouses from each other; entire families were split up. Such policies only exacerbated the social disarticulation of families, neighborhoods, and communities.

Not only was there no concerted effort to reunite families quickly, but also FEMA refused evacuees, as well as social service providers, access to the computer database lists that indicated what had become of their family members. This behavior would seem to be a violation of the UN's Guiding Principles on Internal Displacement, 16(1): "All internally displaced persons have a right to know the fate and whereabouts of missing relatives" (UN 2006). Furthermore, 16(2) states: "The authorities concerned shall endeavor to establish the fate and whereabouts if internally displaced persons are reported missing, and cooperate with relevant internal organizations engaged in the task" (UN 2006).

Moreover, there was no attempt whatsoever to reunite significant groups in order to avoid individual social marginalization, which Koenig (chapter 6, this volume) states is now considered best practice in DFDR. Evacuees constantly complained that they could not find out where their immediate neighbors were, the people with whom they had had close bonds for most of their lives and who were a vital part of their social support network.

In the Houston Astrodome, during the first few days, evacuees were confined to the building in which they were housed and were not allowed to enter other buildings in the compound to search for missing relatives and friends. Neither were they allowed to look for the medical clinic. Furthermore, the compound was run like a vast paramilitary complex, with excessive police and military presence, including mounted police, hovering helicopters, and on-site swat teams. Many evacuees complained of being treated like second-class citizens or prisoners of war. On one occasion, evacuees were forced in the middle of the night to move en masse to another shelter without explanation. Evacuees whom we interviewed were frightened by the experience, and one elderly woman likened it to being in a Nazi concentration camp.

This treatment seemed to intensify the evacuees' trauma and appeared to be a violation of the UN Guiding Principles on Internal Displacement, specifically, the injunction that "every human being has the right to dignity and physical and moral integrity" (UN 2006). The difficult problem faced by Hurricane Katrina evacuees (and many people displaced by DFDR projects) is how to get the international accords and covenants recognized and enforced. In the case of development, Clark (chapter 9, this volume) cites as one example the behavior of the World Bank; its policy framework is supposed to protect the rights of displaced persons but is rarely enforced. In the case of Hurricane Katrina, the US government has also failed in many instances to uphold and protect evacuees' civil rights.

CONCLUSION

Cernea's (1997) eight impoverishment risks model provides us with a template by which to compare the deleterious effects of disasters and DFDR, but it is not a perfect fit in the case of Hurricane Katrina. Three elements are demonstrably absent: food insecurity, landlessness, and loss of access to common property. In particular, the first two elements are barely relevant to our case study. Certainly, in the immediate days after Hurricane Katrina, there was food insecurity; many stranded residents lacked potable water and food of any kind. However, as critical as these shortages were during the initial crisis period, in most cases these were short-lived. Landlessness was a factor in some of the more rural areas along the outer coast where the storm surge destroyed land, but this loss cannot be said to have played a critical role. Nor was loss of access to common property the case in the wake of Hurricane Katrina. These three elements, however, do play a vital role in other disasters.

For example, in the reconstruction process after the Asian tsunami of 2005, Thai fishermen were displaced from their homes on the coast by authorities favoring the tourism industry in the reconstruction process (Gunewardena 2006). Loss of access to common property was a large factor in the *Exxon-Valdez* oil spill. Significantly large areas of the coast and ocean were contaminated, thereby depriving native and non-native residents of marine harvesting activities essential to their livelihoods and their culture.

No doubt, there is as much variability among disasters as there is between disasters and development-forced resettlement projects. Moreover, the specificities surrounding events in both domains vary from case to case, as do their cultural settings and the economic, political, and global forces that drive them. However, as Turton (2006) asserts, empirical observation alone suggests that the separation between development-forced displacement literature and disaster studies (specifically in regard to forced displacement) is "scientifically unsound." There are enough shared traits between the two research endeavors to constitute a "family of resemblances" that we cannot afford to ignore. If anthropology is to carry out (in the words of Scudder, chapter 2, this volume) the "systematic and comparative long-term research required for improving a policy-relevant theory," it is imperative that we view these family resemblances as the ground on which to build such a theory.

Notes

1. Barutciski (2006:74–75) cautions us on the term *rights*: "The meaning of the term 'rights' may be varied, so a certain amount of caution is necessary when dealing with this term in a legal sense. For example some 'rights' are meant to be enforceable binding commitments, whereas others only indicate a desire to achieve certain types of behavior in the future."

2. International Covenant on Civil and Political Rights. Adopted and open for signature, ratification, and accession by General Assembly resolution 2200A (XXI), December 16.

3. International Covenant on Civil and Political Rights, GA res. 2200A (XXI), 21 UN GAOR Supp. (no. 16) at 52, UN Doc. A/6316 (1966), 999 UNTS 171, entered into force March 23, 1976.

4. State of Louisiana Emergency Operations Plan Supplement 1A: Southeast Louisiana Evacuation and Sheltering Plan (revised January 2000) at III-2, par. 5. Available at http://www.letxa.com/katrina/EOPSupplement1a.pdf (as cited in Carmalt 2006), accessed July 2008.

Declaration on Disaster Recovery

Santa Fe, New Mexico
September 30, 2005

The School for Advanced Research invited internationally recognized experts to examine knowledge about and lessons derived from the study of development projects relevant to population displacement and post-disaster reconstruction.

Too often, large-scale development projects meant to spur economic growth have increased ecological and social vulnerability, leaving local people displaced, disempowered, and destitute. Drawing on the work of the participants over the last fifty years, the seminar focused on the known links between involuntary displacement and impoverishment. The group identified strategies for assisting displaced people in rebuilding their lives and communities. Lessons from development-forced displacement and resettlement are relevant to recovery efforts following Hurricane Katrina (2005) and an effective, ethical, and democratic process of reconstruction.

Hurricane Katrina is a horrific example of the effects of a powerful storm intensified by poorly designed, inequitable economic development. The human experience with natural disaster reflects a history of short-sighted development driven by economic interests. This has increased environmental degradation and social vulnerability. We are now confronted with a disaster of historic magnitude that is having disproportionate impacts on vulnerable people because of race and class divisions. This catastrophe has led to massive displacement of people from the gulf region.

Disasters on the scale of Katrina demand thoughtful responses that address the root causes of vulnerability and impoverishment. Successful recovery will require:

- Incorporating existing knowledge on development and disaster displacement into policy, planning, implementation, and monitoring;

- Enabling the meaningful participation of all affected people in the decisions about and planning processes for recovery and reconstruction, including public forums that provide opportunities to set the agenda for rebuilding communities and improving livelihoods;

- Marshalling the political will, institutional capacity, and adequate financial resources, including systems to minimize corruption and ensure maximum benefits to affected people;

- Making a social investment to reduce vulnerability and impoverishment risks by moving beyond capital and infrastructure investment to an emphasis on job creation, job training, support for and inclusion of small businesses, and credit assistance;

- Ensuring respect for culture, identity, and rights (including rights to adequate housing, a safe environment, livelihood, and health and nutrition);

- Establishing independent bodies that include affected people to oversee the recovery processes and ensure that implementation problems are addressed as they arise;

- Applying lessons learned from this experience to reduce vulnerability to future disasters.

Findings from the School for Advanced Research Advanced Seminar on "Rethinking Frameworks, Methodologies, and the Role of Anthropology in Development-Induced Displacement and Resettlement."

Seminar Participants:
Gregory V. Button, University of Tennessee, Knoxville
Michael M. Cernea, George Washington University, Washington, DC
Dana Clark, International Accountability Project, California
Chris de Wet, Rhodes University, South Africa
Theodore E. Downing, University of Arizona
William F. Fisher, Clark University, Massachusetts
Barbara Rose Johnston, Center for Political Ecology, California
Satish Kedia, University of Memphis, Tennessee
Dolores Koenig, American University, Washington, DC
Anthony Oliver-Smith (seminar organizer), University of Florida
Thayer Scudder, California Institute of Technology

References

Abbott, K. W., and D. Snidal

2000   Hard and Soft Law in International Governance. International Organization 54(3):421–456.

ABC News

1992   Hurricane Andrew: One Family's Struggle. Videotape of *Nightline*, September 1.

Adamson, R.

2003   A Caution on Soft-Eviction Strategies. http://www.ega.org/resources/ newsletters/ win2003/softevictions.html, accessed June 2005.

ADB. *See* **Asian Development Bank**

African Development Bank (AfDB)

2003   Involuntary Resettlement Policy, November. Tunis: AfDB.

Agence France Presse

2000   Chinese Official Sentenced to Death for Three Gorges Corruption. Agence France Presse, March 10. http://www.threegorgesprobe.org/tgp/ index.cfm?DSP=content&ContentID=649, accessed July 2007.

Agrawal, A., and K. Redford

2007   Conservation and Displacement: An Overview. *In* Protected Areas and Human Displacement: A Conservation Perspective. K. Redford and E. Fearn, eds. Pp. 4–15. Working Paper 29. Bronx, NY: Wildlife Conservation Society.

Agrawal, P.

2000   Proceedings: Workshop on Urban Resettlement (Assisting Informal Dwellers), July 25–26. Manila: Social Development Division, Office of Environment and Social Development, Asian Development Bank.

2003   Technical Guidelines for Resettlement and Compensation. Draft. Vientiane, Lao PDR: Science, Technology, and Environment Agency, Lao People's Democratic Republic.

References

Ahmad, N.

2003   Women, Mining, and Displacement. New Delhi: Indian Social Institute.

Alfalit International

1993   Madre Tierra: Vida y Esperanza Indigenas (Memoria del 1 encuentro indigena sobre vivencias y practicas de conservacion de la naturaleza. Hone Creek-Talamanca) Alajuela, Costa Rica: Alfalit International.

Altman, I., and S. Low

1992   Place Attachment. Vol. 8 of Human Behavior and Environment: Advances in Theory and Research. I. Altman and J. Wohl, eds. New York: Plenum.

American Psychiatric Association (APA)

1994   Diagnostic and Statistical Manual of Mental Disorders (DSM-IV). 4th edition. Washington DC: APA.

Amnesty International

2005   Amnesty International's Concerns Regarding the Current Human Rights Situation. Memorandum to the government of Guatemala, April 20. http://web.amnesty.org/library/pdf/AMR340142005ENGLISH/$File/AMR34 01405.pdf, accessed July 2007.

2006   Guatemala: Politically Motivated Charges Get in the Way of Justice for Massacre Survivors. Press release, February 8. http://web.amnesty.org/library/index/engAMR340052006?open&of=eng-GTM, accessed July 2007.

Anderson, D. L.

N.d.   Avian Diversity in the Rio Platano Biosphere Reserve, Honduras: The Influence of Indigenous Agricultural Practices. http://rrc.boisestate.edu/Abstracts/D%20Anderson%20abstract.htm, accessed August 2005.

Anderson, M. B.

1991   Which Costs More? Prevention or Recovery? *In* Managing Natural Disasters and the Environment. Selected Materials from the Colloquium on the Environment and Disaster Management, June 27–28. A. Kreimer and M. Munasinghe, eds. Pp. 17–27. Washington DC: World Bank.

Arnold, D.

1996   The Problem of Nature: Environment, Culture, and European Expansion. Oxford: Blackwell.

Aronsson, I.-L.

2002   Negotiating Involuntary Resettlement: A Study of Local Bargaining during the Construction of the Zimapan Dam. Occasional Paper 17. Uppsala, Sweden: Department of Anthropology and Ethnology, Uppsala Universitet.

Asian Development Bank (ADB)

1992   Guidelines for the Health Impact Assessment of Development Projects. Environment Paper 11. Manila: Office of the Environment, ADB.

1995   Involuntary Resettlement Policy, August. Manila: ADB.

1998   Summary of the Handbook on Resettlement. Manila: ADB.

2003   Operations Manual F2 on Involuntary Resettlement. Manila: ADB.

Aspelin, P., and C. Coelho dos Santos

1981   Indian Areas Threatened by Hydroelectric Projects in Brazil. Copenhagen: IWGIA (International Work Group for Indigenous Affairs).

Balon, E. K.

1974   Fishes of Lake Kariba, Africa. Neptune City, NJ: T. F. H. Publications.

Bankoff, G.

2004   The Historical Geography of Disaster: "Vulnerability" and "Local Knowledge" in Western Discourse. *In* Mapping Vulnerability: Disasters, Development, and People. G. Bankoff, G. Frerks, and D. Hilhorst, eds. Pp. 25–36. London: Earthscan.

Barabas, A., and M. Bartolomé

1973   Hydraulic Development and Ethnocide: The Mazatec and Chinantec People of Oaxaca, Mexico. Copenhagen: IWGIA (International Work Group for Indigenous Affairs).

1992   Antropología y relocalizaciones. Alternidades 2(4):5–15.

Barry, J. M.

1997   Rising Tide: The Great Mississippi Flood of 1927 and How It Changed America. New York: Simon and Schuster.

Bartolomé, L.

1984   Forced Resettlement and the Survival Systems of the Urban Poor. Ethnology 23(3):177–192.

1993   The Yacyretá Experience with Urban Resettlement: Some Lessons and Insights. *In* Anthropological Approaches to Resettlement: Policy, Practice, and Theory. M. M. Cernea and S. E. Guggenheim, eds. Pp. 109–132. Boulder, CO: Westview.

Bartolomé, L. J., C. de Wet, H. Mander, and V. K. Nagraj

2000   Displacement, Resettlement, Rehabilitation, Reparation, and Development. Thematic Review 1.3. Cape Town: World Commission on Dams (WCD). http://www.dams.org/kbase/thematic/tr13.htm, accessed June 2008.

Barutciski, M.

2002   Addressing Legal Constraints and Improving Outcomes in DIDR Projects. *In* Improving Outcomes in Development-Induced Displacement and Resettlement Projects. C. de Wet, ed. Forced Migration Review 12:6–9. http://www.fmreview .org/FMRpdfs/FMR12/fmr12.2.pdf, accessed August 2008.

2006   International Law and Development-Induced Displacement and Resettlement. *In* Development-Induced Displacement: Problems, Policies, and People. C. de Wet, ed. Pp. 71–104. Oxford and New York: Berghahn Books.

Behura, N. K., and P. K. Nayak

1993   Involuntary Displacement and the Changing Frontiers of Kinship: A Study of Resettlement in Orissa. *In* Anthropological Approaches to Resettlement: Policy, Practice, and Theory. M. M. Cernea and S. E. Guggenheim, eds. Pp. 283–306. Boulder, CO: Westview.

References

Beiser, M.

1982   Migration in a Developing Country: Risk and Opportunity. *In* Uprooting and Surviving: Adaptation and Resettlement of Migrant Families and Children. R. C. Nann, ed. Pp. 119–146. Dordrecht, Holland: D. Reidel.

Ben-Achour, M. A.

2000   Human Cost of Agricultural Land Privatization in the South of Yemen. Paper presented at the Symposium on Involuntary Resettlement, Xth World Congress of Rural Sociology, International Rural Sociology Association (IRSA), Rio de Janeiro, July 30–August 5.

Bernard, H. R.

1995   Research Methods in Anthropology: Qualitative and Quantitative Approaches. 2nd edition. Walnut Creek, CA: AltaMira.

Bilharz, J. A.

1998   The Allegheny Senecas and Kinzua Dam: Forced Relocation through Two Generations. Lincoln: University of Nebraska Press.

Bird-David, N.

1990   The Giving Environment: Another Perspective on the Economic System of Gatherer-Hunters. Current Anthropology 31(2):183–196.

Black, R.

2001   Fifty Years of Refugee Studies: From Theory to Policy. International Migration Review 35(2):57–78.

Blaser, M., H. A. Feit, and G. McRae, eds.

2004   In the Way of Development: Indigenous Peoples, Life Projects, and Globalization. London and New York: Zed Books.

Bock, P. K.

1968   Modern Cultural Anthropology. New York: Alfred A. Knopf.

Bodmer, R., and P. Puertas

2007   Impacts of Displacement in the Pacaya-Samiria National Reserve, Peru. *In* Protected Areas and Human Displacement: A Conservation Perspective. K. Redford and E. Fearn, eds. Pp. 29–33. Working Paper 29. Bronx, NY: Wildlife Conservation Society.

Bolaños, O.

2008   Constructing Indigenous Ethnicities and Claiming Land Rights in the Lower Tapajos and Arapiuns Region, Brazilian Amazon. PhD. Dissertation, University of Florida.

Bott, E.

1957   Family and Social Networks: Roles, Norms, and External Relationships in Ordinary Urban Families. London: Tavistock.

Bradley, D. J.

1993   Human Tropical Diseases in a Changing Environment. *In* Environmental Change and Human Health, CIBA Foundation Symposium 175. Proceedings of the European Environmental Research Organisation's Symposium on Environmental Change and Human Health, Wageningen, Netherlands, September 1–3, 1992. J. V. Lake, G. Bock, and K. Ackrill, eds. Pp. 146–170. Chichester, NY: John Wiley.

Brandt, S. A., and F. A. Hassan, eds.
In press   Damming the Past: Cultural Heritage Management and Dams in Global Perspective. Lanham, MD: Lexington Books.

Bray, D. B., and A. B. Anderson
2005   Global Conservation Non-governmental Organizations and Local Communities: Perspectives on Programs and Project Implementation in Latin America. Working Paper 1, Conservation and Development Series, Institute for Sustainability Science in Latin America and the Caribbean. Miami: Latin American and Caribbean Center, Florida International University.

Brechin, S. R., P. R. Wilshusen, C. L. Fortwangler, and P. C. West
2002   Beyond the Square Wheel: Toward a More Comprehensive Understanding of Biodiversity Conservation as Social and Political Process. Society and Natural Resources 15(1):41–64.

2003   Contested Nature: Promoting International Biodiversity with Social Justice in the Twenty-first Century. Albany: State University Press of New York.

Bridgeland, F.
2005   Bushmen to Be Denied Homeland. Africa Reports 32. Institute for War and Peace Reporting. http://www.minesandcommunities org/action/press16htm, accessed August 2005.

Brockington, D.
2002   Fortress Conservation: The Preservation of Mkomazi Game Reserve, Tanzania. Bloomington: Indiana University Press; Oxford: James Currey.

Brockington, D., and J. Igoe
2006   Eviction for Conservation: A Global Overview. Conservation and Society 4(3):424–470.

Brokensha, D.
1963   Volta Resettlement and Anthropological Research. Human Organization 22(3):286–290.

Brokensha, D., and T. Scudder
1968   Resettlement. *In* Dams in Africa. N. N. Rubin and W. M. Warren, eds. Pp. 20–62. London: Frank Cass.

Bromet, E.
1990   The Nature and Effects of Technological Failures. *In* The Psychosocial Aspects of Disaster. R. Gist and B. Lubin, eds. Pp. 120–139. New York: John Wiley.

Brookings Institution
2006   Katrina Index: Tracking Variables of Post Katrina Construction (November 2006). Issued February 1. Washington DC: Brookings Institution.

References

Brosius, J. P.

2007   Reflections on Conservation, Displacement, and Exclusion. *In* Protected Areas and Human Displacement: A Conservation Perspective. K. Redford and E. Fearn, eds. Pp. 106–112. Working Paper 29. Bronx, NY: Wildlife Conservation Society.

Brown, A. W. A., and J. O. Deom

1973   Summary: Health Aspects of Man-Made Lakes. *In* Man-Made Lakes: Their Problems and Environmental Effects. W. C. Ackerman, G. F. White, and E. B. Worthington, eds. J. L. Even, assoc. ed. Pp. 755–764. Washington DC: American Geophysical Union.

Brown, C.

1985   Mode of Subsistence and Folk Biological Taxonomy. Current Anthropology 26(1):43–64.

Brown, P., and E. Mikkelsen

1990   No Safe Place. Berkeley: University of California Press.

Bryceson, D., C. Kay, and J. Mooij, eds.

2000   Disappearing Peasantries? Rural Labour in Africa, Asia, and South America. London: Intermediate Technology.

Buford, J.

2006   Memo to Members of UN Human Rights Committee. Presented May 31 on behalf of Meiklejohn Civil Liberties Union, Peoples Institute, and Allen Temple.

Butcher, D.

1971   An Organizational Manual for Resettlement: A Systematic Approach to the Resettlement Problem Created by Man-Made Lakes, with Special Reference for West Africa. Rome: Food and Agriculture Organization.

Button, G. V.

1995   What You Don't Know Can't Hurt You: The Right to Know and the Shetland Islands Oil Spill. Human Ecology 23(2):224–258.

1999   Negation of Disaster: The Media Response to Oil Spills in Great Britain. *In* The Angry Earth: Disaster in Anthropological Perspective. A. Oliver-Smith and S. M. Hoffman, eds. Pp. 113–132. New York: Routledge.

2002   Popular Media Reframing of Man-Made Disasters: A Cautionary Tale. *In* Catastrophe and Culture: The Anthropology of Disaster. S. M. Hoffman and A. Oliver-Smith, eds. Pp. 142–158. Santa Fe, NM: School of American Research Press.

2006   Voices from the Astrodome and Beyond: Counternarrative Accounts of Disasters. *In* Learning from Catastrophe: Quick Response in the Wake of Hurricane Katrina. Produced by the National Hazards Center under National Science Foundation Grant CMS0408499. Pp. 299–311. Boulder, CO: Institute of Behavioral Science, University Press of Colorado.

Byrne, D.

2001   Understanding the Urban. New York: Palgrave.

Byrne, J. P.

2005   Supreme Court's Ruling on Land. June 24, 2 p.m., online discussion of *Kelo v. City of New London* ruling. http://www.washingtonpost.com, accessed July 2005.

Cannon, T.

1994   Vulnerability Analysis and Disasters. *In* Floods (Hazards and Disasters). D. Parker, ed. Pp. 13–29. London: Routledge.

Carmalt, J.

2006   Hurricane Katrina Violations of ICCPR Articles 6 and 26: A Response to the Third Periodic Report of the United States of America, November. http://www .nesri.org/media_updates/Katrina%20shadow%20report%20submitted%20by %20the%20US%20Human%20Rights%20Network.pdf, accessed December 2006.

Cauchon, D.

2004   Pushing the Limits of Public Use. USA Today, April 1: 3A.

CEH. *See* **Comisión para el Esclarecimiento Histórico**

Center for World Indigenous Studies. *See* **CWIS**

Cernea, M. M.

1990   Poverty Risks from Population Displacement in Water Resource Development. HIID (Harvard Institute for International Development) Discussion Paper 355. Cambridge, MA: Harvard University Press.

1991   Involuntary Resettlement: Social Research, Policy, and Planning. *In* Putting People First: Sociological Variables in Rural Development. M. M. Cernea, ed. Pp. 188–215. Oxford: Oxford University Press.

1993   The Urban Environment and Population Relocation. World Bank Discussion Paper 152. Washington DC: World Bank.

1994   Poverty Risks from Population Displacement in Water Resource Development. ICA-94, Uppsala, Sweden, July 6.

1996a   Eight Main Risks: Impoverishment and Social Justice in Resettlement. Washington DC: Environment Department, World Bank.

1996b   Understanding and Preventing Impoverishment from Displacement. *In* Understanding Impoverishment: The Consequences of Development-Induced Displacement. C. McDowell, ed. Oxford: Berghahn Books.

1996c   Bridging the Research Divide: Studying Refugees and Development Oustees. *In* In Search of Cool Ground: War, Flight, and Homecoming in Northeast Africa. T. Allen, ed. Pp. 293–317. London: James Currey; Trenton: Africa World Press.

1997   The Risks and Reconstruction Model for Resettling Displaced Populations. World Development 25(10):1569–1588.

1999   Why Economic Analysis Is Essential to Resettlement: A Sociologist's View. *In* The Economics of Involuntary Resettlement: Questions and Challenges. M. M. Cernea, ed. Pp. 5–49. Washington DC: World Bank.

References

2000a   Risks, Safeguards, and Reconstruction: A Model for Population Displacement and Resettlement. *In* Risks and Reconstruction: Experiences of Resettlers and Refugees. M. M. Cernea and C. McDowell, eds. Pp. 11–55. Washington DC: World Bank. http://www.his.com/~mesas/irr_model/irr_model.htm, accessed November 2007.

2000b   Impoverishment Risks and Reconstruction: A Model for Population Displacement and Resettlement. *In* Risks and Reconstruction: Experiences of Resettlers and Refugees. M. M. Cernea and C. McDowell, eds. Pp. 127–143. Washington DC: World Bank.

2002   For a New Economics of Resettlement: A Sociological Critique of the Compensation Principle. International Social Science Journal, no. 175:47–53. Paris: UNESCO.

2005a   Concept and Model: Applying the IRR Model in Africa to Resettlement and Poverty. *In* Displacement Risks in Africa: Refugees, Resettlers, and Their Host Population. I. Ohta and Y. D. Gebre, eds. Pp. 195–258. Kyoto: Kyoto University Press; Melbourne: Trans Pacific Press.

2005b   Restriction of Access Is Displacement: A Broader Concept and Policy. Forced Migration Review 23:48–49.

2007   Financing for Development: Benefit-Sharing Mechanisms in Population Resettlement. Economic and Political Weekly 42(12):1033–1044, India.

2008a   Compensation and Investment in Resettlement: Theory, Practice, Pitfalls, and Needed Policy Reform. *In* Can Compensation Prevent Impoverishment? Reforming Resettlement through Investments and Benefit-Sharing. M. M. Cernea and H. M. Mathur, eds. Pp. 15–98. London and New Delhi: Oxford University Press.

2008b   Reforming the Foundations of Involuntary Resettlement. *In* Can Compensation Prevent Impoverishment? Reforming Resettlement through Investments and Benefit-Sharing. M. M. Cernea and H. M. Mathur, eds. Pp. 1–10. London and New Delhi: Oxford University Press.

2008c   Can Compensation Prevent Impoverishment? Reforming Resettlement through Investments and Benefit-Sharing. M. M. Cernea and H. M. Mathur, eds. London and New Delhi: Oxford University Press.

Cernea, M. M., ed.

1985   Putting People First: Sociological Variables in Rural Development. New York: Oxford University Press for the World Bank.

1991   Putting People First: Sociological Variables in Rural Development. 2nd edition, revised and expanded. New York: Oxford University Press for the World Bank.

1999   The Economics of Involuntary Resettlement: Questions and Challenges. Washington DC: World Bank.

Cernea, M. M., and S. E. Guggenheim, eds.

1993   Anthropological Approaches to Resettlement: Policy, Practice, and Theory. Boulder, CO: Westview.

Cernea, M. M., S. E. Guggenheim, W. van Wicklin, and D. Aronson

1994 Resettlement and Development: Report on the Bank-Wide Review of Projects Involving Involuntary Resettlement. Washington DC: World Bank.

Cernea, M. M., and H. M. Mathur, eds.

2008 Can Compensation Prevent Impoverishment? Reforming Resettlement through Investments and Benefit-Sharing. London and New Delhi: Oxford University Press.

Cernea, M. M., and C. McDowell

2000 Risks and Reconstruction: Experiences of Resettlers and Refugees. Washington DC: World Bank.

Cernea, M. M., and K. Schmidt-Soltau

2006 National Parks and Poverty Risks: Policy Issues in Conservation and Resettlement. World Development 34(10):1808–1830.

Chambers, R.

1970 The Volta Resettlement Experience. New York: Praeger; Accra: Volta River Authority; Kumasi: University of Science and Technology.

Chambers, R., ed.

1969 Settlement Schemes in Africa. London: Routledge and Kegan Paul.

Chape, S., J. Harrison, M. Spalding, and I. Lysenko

2005 Measuring the Extent and Effectiveness of Protected Areas as an Indicator for Meeting Global Biodiversity Targets. Philosophical Transactions of the Royal Society B 360(1454):443–455.

Chapin, M.

1990 Introduction: The Value of Biological and Cultural Diversity. Cultural Survival Quarterly 14(4):2–3.

2004 A Challenge to Conservationists. World Watch (November–December):17–21.

Chatty, D., and M. Colchester

2002 Introduction: Conservation and Mobile Indigenous Peoples. *In* Conservation and Mobile Indigenous Peoples: Displacement, Forced Settlement, and Sustainable Development. D. Chatty and M. Colchester, eds. Pp. 1–21. Oxford and New York: Berghahn Books.

Chicchon, A.

2007 Working with Local People to Conserve Nature in Latin America. *In* Protected Areas and Human Displacement: A Conservation Perspective. K. Redford and E. Fearn, eds. Pp. 16–19. Working Paper 29. Bronx, NY: Wildlife Conservation Society.

Clark, D.

2002a World Bank Resettlement Policy Compromised. World Rivers Review 17(1):10.

2002b The World Bank and Human Rights: The Need for Greater Accountability. Harvard Human Rights Journal 15(Spring):205–226.

2006   Overview of Performance Standard 5: Land Acquisition and Involuntary Resettlement. *In* One Step Forward, One Step Back: An Analysis of the International Finance Corporation's Sustainability Policy, Performance Standards, and Disclosure Policy. Halifax Initiative Coalition, ed. Pp. 16–17. Ottawa: Halifax Initiative Coalition. http://www.halifaxinitiative.org/updir/ IFCAnalysis-HalifaxFINAL.pdf, accessed September 2007.

2009   An Overview of Revisions to the World Bank Resettlement Policy. *In* Displaced by Development: Confronting Marginalisation and Gender Injustice. L. Mehta, ed. Pp. 195–224. Delhi: Sage.

Clark, D., J. Fox, and K. Treakle
2003   Demanding Accountability: Civil Society Claims and the World Bank Inspection Panel. Lanham, MD: Rowman and Littlefield.

Cleaver, F.
1999   Paradoxes of Participation: Questioning Participatory Approaches to Development. Journal of International Development 11(4):597–612.

Cliggett, L.
2005   Grains from Grass: Aging, Gender, and Famine in Rural Africa. Ithaca, NY: Cornell University Press.

Colchester, M.
1994   Salvaging Nature: Indigenous Peoples, Protected Areas, and Biodiversity Conservation. Discussion Paper 55. Geneva: United Nations Research Institute for Social Development (UNRISD).

Colchester, M.—Forest Peoples Programme
2000   Dams, Indigenous People, and Vulnerable Ethnic Minorities. Thematic Review 1.2. Cape Town: World Commission on Dams (WCD). http://www.dams.org/ kbase/thematic/tr12.htm, accessed June 2008.

Colchester, M., and A. Gray
1999   Towards Conclusions. *In* Indigenous Peoples and Protected Areas in South and Southeast Asia. M. Colchester and C. Erni, eds. Pp. 300–307. IWGIA document 97. Copenhagen: IWGIA (International Work Group for Indigenous Affairs).

Colson, E. F.
1971   The Social Consequences of Resettlement: The Impact of the Kariba Resettlement upon the Gwembe Tonga. Manchester, UK: Institute for African Studies, University of Zambia / Manchester University Press.

1999   Gendering Those Uprooted by "Development." *In* Engendering Forced Migration: Theory and Practice. D. Indra, ed. Pp. 23–39. Oxford and New York: Berghahn Books.

2003   Forced Migration and the Anthropological Response. Journal of Refugee Studies 16(1):1–18.

Colten, C. E.
2006   An Unnatural Metropolis: Wrestling New Orleans from Nature. Baton Rouge: Louisiana State University Press.

Comisión para el Esclarecimiento Histórico (CEH)

1999   Informe de la Comisión para el Esclarecimiento Histórico, Guatemala: Memoria del silencio. 12 vols. Guatemala City: Oficina de Servicios para Proyectos de las Naciones Unidas. The Río Negro case is detailed in Caso ilustrativo número 10: Masacre y eliminación de la comunidad de Río Negro, Capítulo VI, Casos ilustrativos—Anexo 1, Volumen 1, p. 48.) http://shr.aaas.org/guatemala/ceh/report/english/toc.html, accessed July 2007.

Community Rights Counsel

2005   Amici Curiae brief to the Supreme Court, no. 04-108, filed by the National League of Cities, National Conference of State Legislatures, US Conference of Mayors, Council of State Governments, National Association of Counties, International Municipal Lawyers Association, and International City/County Management Association. http://www.communityrights.org/PDFs/Briefs/Kelo.pdf, accessed September 2007.

CONAIE (Confederación de Nacionalidades Indígenas del Ecuador)

2004   Ley de Biodiversidad. Quito: CONAIE.

Convention on Biological Diversity (CBD)

1992   Preamble. Convention on Biological Diversity, June 5. http://www.cbd.int/convention/articles.shtml?a=cbd-00, accessed June 2008.

Corruccini, R. S., and S. Kaul

1983   The Epidemiological Transition and Anthropology of Minor Chronic Non-infectious Diseases. Medical Anthropology 7(3):36–50.

Council for Social Development

2008   India: Development and Displacement. Social Development Report 2008. New Delhi: Oxford University Press.

Coura, J. R., A. C. V. Junqueira, C. M. Giordano, and R. K. Funatsu

1994   Chagas Disease in the Brazilian Amazon. Revista de Instituto de Medicina Tropical de Sao Paulo 36(4):363–368.

Craik, B.

2004   The Importance of Working Together. *In* In the Way of Development: Indigenous Peoples, Life Projects, and Globalization. M. Blaser, H. A. Feit, and G. McRae, eds. Pp. 166–185. London and New York: Zed Books.

Crankshaw, O., and S. Parnell

2004   Johannesburg: Race, Inequality, and Urbanization. *In* World Cities beyond the West: Globalization, Development, and Inequality. J. Gugler, ed. Pp. 348–370. New York: Cambridge University Press.

Cronon, W., ed.

1995   Uncommon Ground: Reinventing Nature. New York: W. W. Norton.

Csikszentimihalyi, M., and E. Rochberg-Halton

1981   The Meaning of Things: Domestic Symbols and the Self. New York and Cambridge: Cambridge University Press.

Cumanzula, F.

2000   Zimbabwe: The Resettlement of the Tonga Community Will Never Be Justified. *In* Once There Was a Community. Southern African Hearings for Communities Affected by Large Dams, Cape Town, November 11–12, 1999. Final Report. Cape Town: Environmental Monitoring Group (EMG).

CWIS (Center for World Indigenous Studies)

1994   International Covenant on the Rights of Indigenous Nations. Geneva: CWIS. http://www.cwis.org/icrin-94.htm, accessed August 2005.

Daly, H. E.

2008   Forced Displacement: Allocative Externality or Unjust Redistribution? *In* Can Compensation Prevent Impoverishment? Reforming Resettlement through Investments and Benefit-Sharing. M. M. Cernea and H. M. Mathur, eds. Pp. 121–128. London and New Delhi: Oxford University Press.

Danielson, L.

2004   Sustainable Development in the Natural Resources Industries: New Perspectives, New Rules, and New Opportunities. 50 Rocky Mt. Min. L. Inst. 14-1.

Declaration of Curitiba

1997   Electronic document. http://www/irn/org/programs/curitiba.html, accessed August 2006.

Davis, G. J.

1976   Parigi: A Social History of Balinese Movement to Central Sulawesi, 1907–1964. PhD dissertation, Stanford University.

Davis, M.

2006   Who Is Killing New Orleans? The Nation, April 10: 11–20.

de Wet, C.

1995   Moving Together, Drifting Apart: Betterment Planning and Villagisation in a South African Homeland. Johannesburg: Witwatersrand University Press.

2003   Why Do Things Often Go Wrong in Resettlement Schemes? *In* People, Space, and the State: Migration, Resettlement, and Displacement in Ethiopia. A. Pankhurst and F. Piguet, eds. Pp. 50–70. Addis Ababa: Ethiopian Society of Sociologists, Social Workers, and Anthropologists.

2005   Some Socio-economic Risks and Opportunities Relating to Dam-Induced Resettlement in Africa. *In* Displacement Risks in Africa. I. Ohta and Y. D. Gebre, eds. Pp. 259–281. Kyoto: Kyoto University Press.

2006   Risk, Complexity, and Local Initiative in Forced Resettlement Outcomes. *In* Development-Induced Displacement: Problems, Policies, and People. C. de Wet, ed. Pp. 180–202. Oxford and New York: Berghahn Books.

D'Monte, D.

2005   Mumbai (India): The Tough Way to a Slum-Free Mumbai. S-Dev Geneva 05: International Platform on Sustainable Urban Development. http://www.s-dev .org/en/decouvrir/villes/villes.php?idContent-88, accessed April 2006.

Dobby, E. H.

1952   Resettlement Transforms Malaya: A Case History of Relocating the Population of an Asian Plural Society. Economic Development and Cultural Change 50(3):163–189.

Douglas, M.

1973   Rules and Meaning. Harmondsworth, UK: Penguin.

Dove, M.

1983   Theories of Swidden Agriculture and the Political Economy of Ignorance. Agroforestry Systems 1(2):85–99.

Downey, K.

2005   Fighting the Power to Take Your Home. Washington Post, May 7: F1.

Downing, T. E.

1973   Zapotec Inheritance. PhD dissertation, Stanford University.

1987   Appraisal of the Zimapan and Aguamilpas Dams, July 2, 1987. Washington DC: World Bank. http://www.ted-downing.com, accessed August 2008.

1996a   Mitigating Social Impoverishment When People Are Involuntarily Displaced. In Understanding Impoverishment: The Consequences of Development-Induced Displacement. C. McDowell, ed. Pp. 33–48. Oxford and New York: Berghahn Books.

1996b   A Participatory Interim Evaluation of the Pehuen Foundation: Executive Summary. IFC Report 2067 of the Pangue Project. Washington DC: International Finance Corporation (IFC). (Note: This report was prepared by Downing for the IFC. It was held secret from 1995 to 1997 and became the subject of international controversy. The full report is available at http://www.ted-downing.com, accessed August 2008.)

2002a   Avoiding New Poverty: Mining-Induced Displacement and Resettlement. Report commissioned by the Mining, Minerals, and Sustainable Development Project of the International Institute for Environment and Development (IIED) and World Business Council for Sustainable Development. http://www.iied.org, accessed June 2007.

2002b   Creating Poverty: The Flawed Logic of the World Bank's Revised Involuntary Resettlement Policy. Forced Migration Review 12:13–14.

Downing, T. E., and C. Garcia-Downing

1996   Methodology for the Participatory Evaluation of the Pehuen Foundation. Annex to IFC Report 2067. http://www.ted-downing.com, accessed August 2008.

2001   Plan B: What Is Going to Happen to My People? Cultural Survival Quarterly 25(3):8–19.

Downing, T., C. Garcia-Downing, J. Moles, and I. McIntosh

2003   Mining and Indigenous Peoples: Stakeholder Strategies and Tactics. In Finding Common Ground: Indigenous Peoples and Their Association with the Mining Sector. L. Danielson, ed. Pp. 11–46. London: World Business Council for Sustainable Development/International Institute for Environment and Development.

Downing, T., and C. McDowell

1996 Oxford Statement on Reconstructing Livelihoods of Displaced People. Statement from the First International Conference on Development-Induced Displacement and Impoverishment, Oxford University, January 1995. http://fmo.qeh.ox.ac.uk/FMO/Reader/Viewdoc.asp?Path=Oxford/1610/06/ 06&BookKey=Oxford/1610/06/06/1/Ar00100.xml&BookCollection=FMO, accessed November 2007.

Downing, T., and J. Moles

2002 The World Bank Denies Indigenous Peoples Their Right to Prior Informed Consent. Cultural Survival Quarterly 25(4):68–69.

Downing, T. E., and T. Scudder

2008 Open Letter to the Asian Development Bank's Board of Directors, 20 March 2008. http://www.ted-downing.com, accessed August 2008.

Drabek, T. E.

1986 Human System Responses to Disaster: An Inventory of Sociological Findings. New York: Springer-Verlag.

Drèze, J., M. Samson, and S. Singh

1994 Resettlement of Narmada Oustees. Economic Times, February 22.

Drydyk, J.

2001 Towards Ethical Guidelines for Displacement-Inducing Development: Filling the Gaps. Unpublished paper, Ethics of Development-Induced Displacement Project, Centre for Refugee Studies, York University, Toronto.

2002 Ethical Standards and Limits for Displacement-Inducing Development. Unpublished paper, Ethics of Development-Induced Displacement Project, Centre for Refugee Studies, York University, Toronto.

Dupont, V.

2003 Urban Development and Population Redistribution in Delhi: Implications for Categorizing Population. In New Forms of Urbanization: Beyond the Urban–Rural Dichotomy. T. Champion and G. Hugo, eds. Pp. 170–190. Aldershot, UK: Ashgate.

Dwivedi, R.

1999 Displacement, Risks, and Resistance: Local Perceptions and Actions in the Sardar Sarovar. Development and Change 30(1):43–78.

EarthRights International

1996 Total Denial: A Report on the Yadana Pipeline Project in Burma. http://www .earthrights.org/files/Reports/TotalDenial96.pdf, accessed September 2007.

Égré, D., V. Roquet, and C. Durocher

2002 Benefit Sharing from Dam Projects: Phase 1: Desk Study. Final Report. Montreal: Vincent Roquet and Associates.

2008 Benefit Sharing to Supplement Compensation in Resource Extractive Activities: The Case of Multipurpose Dams. In Can Compensation Prevent Impoverishment? Reforming Resettlement through Investments and Benefit-

Sharing. M. M. Cernea and H. M. Mathur, eds. Pp. 318–356. London and New Delhi: Oxford University Press.

Environmental Defense

2003 Amazon Indians to Protect the Rainforest: Panará Tribe Wins Precedent-Setting Lawsuit. http://www.environmentaldefense.org/article.cfm?contentid=1640, accessed July 2007.

The Equator Principles

2003 The Equator Principles: A Framework for Banks to Manage Environmental and Social Issues in Project Financing. http://www.equator-principles.com, accessed December 2003.

Equipo de Antropología Forense de Guatemala (EAFG)

1997 Las massacres en Rabinal. Estudio histórico-antrológico de las massacres de Plán de Sánchez, Chichupac y Río Negro. Guatemala City: EAFG.

Eriksen, J. H.

1999 Comparing the Economic Planning for Voluntary and Involuntary Resettlement. *In* The Economics of Involuntary Resettlement: Questions and Challenges. M. M. Cernea, ed. Pp. 83–146. Washington DC: World Bank.

Erikson, K.

1976 Everything in Its Path: Destruction of Community in the Buffalo Creek Flood. New York: Touchstone.

1995 Forward. *In* A Poison Stronger Than Love: The Destruction of an Ojibwa Community, by Anastasia Shkilnyk. New Haven, CT: Yale University Press.

Escobar, A.

1999 After Nature: Steps to an Antiessentialist Political Ecology. Current Anthropology 40(1):1–30.

2001 Culture Sits in Places: Reflections on Globalism and Subaltern Strategies of Localization. Political Geography 20(2):139–174.

Espelund, W. N.

1998 The Struggle for Water: Politics, Rationality, and Identity in the American Southwest. Chicago: University of Chicago Press.

European Centre for Health Policy (ECHP)

1999 Health Impact Assessment: Main Concepts and Suggested Approach. Gothenburg consensus paper, December. Brussels: WHO Regional Office for Europe. http://www.euro.who.int/document/PAE/Gothenburgpaper.pdf, accessed November 2007.

Extractive Industries Review (EIR)

2003a Striking a Better Balance: The Extractive Industries Review, Final Report. Consultation on the Future of the World Bank Group in the Extractive Industries. http://www.eirview.org/eir/eirhome.nsf/englishmainpage/about?opendocument, accessed December 2004.

2003b Striking a Better Balance: The Extractive Industries Review, Executive Summary. Washington DC: EIR. http://www.eireview.org, accessed September 2007.

Fabian, S. M.

1992   Space–Time of the Bororo of Brazil. Gainesville: University Press of Florida.

Fabricius, C., and C. de Wet

2002   The Influence of Forced Removals and Land Restitution on Conservation in South Africa. *In* Conservation and Mobile Indigenous Peoples: Displacement, Forced Settlement, and Sustainable Development. D. Chatty and M. Colchester, eds. Pp. 142–157. Oxford and New York: Berghahn Books.

Fahim, H.

1983   Egyptian Nubians: Resettlement and Years of Coping. Salt Lake City: University of Utah Press.

Farmer, P.

2004   An Anthropology of Structural Violence. Current Anthropology 45(3):305–326.

Feit, H., and A. F. Penn

1974   The Northward Diversion of the Eastmain and Opinaca Rivers as Proposed: An Assessment of Impacts on the Native Community at Eastmain Village. Montreal: Grand Council of the Crees (Quebec).

Feld, S., and K. H. Basso, eds.

1996   Senses of Place. Santa Fe, NM: School of American Research Press.

Fernandes, W.

2004   Rehabilitation as a Right: Where Is the Policy? Paper presented at the International Seminar on Development and Displacement: Afro-Asian Perspectives, Osmania University, Hyderabad, November 27–28.

Fernandes, W., and E. G. Thukral

1989   Development, Displacement, and Rehabilitation. New Delhi: Indian Social Institute.

Fisher, W. F.

1997   Doing Good? The Politics and Antipolitics of NGO Practices. Annual Review of Anthropology 26:439–464.

Fisher, W. F., ed.

1995   Toward Sustainable Development: Struggles over India's Narmada River. Armonk, NY, and London: M. E. Sharpe.

Fisher, W. F., and T. Ponniah

2003   Another World Is Possible: Popular Alternatives to Globalization at the World Social Forum. London: Zed Books.

Flyvbjerg, B., N. Bruzelius, and W. Rothengatter

2003   Megaprojects and Risk: An Anatomy of Ambition. Cambridge: Cambridge University Press.

Fortwangler, C.

2003   The Winding Road: Incorporating Social Justice and Human Rights into Protected Area Policies. *In* Contested Nature: Promoting International Biodiversity with Social Justice in the Twenty-first Century. S. R. Brechin,

P. R. Wilshusen, C. L. Fortwangler, and P. C. West, eds. Pp. 25–40. Albany: State University Press of New York.

Fox, J.
2003   Introduction: Framing the Inspection Panel. *In* Demanding Accountability: Civil Society Claims and the World Bank Inspection Panel. D. Clark, J. Fox, and K. Treakle, eds. Pp. xi–xxxi. Lanham, MD: Rowman and Littlefield.

Fox, J. A., and L. D. Brown, eds.
1998   The Struggle for Accountability: The World Bank, NGOs, and Grassroots Movements. Cambridge, MA: The MIT Press.

Frake, C.
1993   Seafaring and the Medieval Construction of Time. Stanford, CA: Stanford University Press.

Fried, M.
1963   Grieving for a Lost Home. *In* The Urban Condition: People and Policy in the Metropolis. L. Duhl, ed. Pp. 151–171. New York: Basic Books.

Friedlander, K.
1940   On the "Longing to Die." International Journal of Psychoanalysis 16(3):416–468.

Gaitán, G. A.
1979   Las Communidades de la Cuenca del Río Negro y Chixoy: Resultados de la encuesta socioeconomica levanyada en parajes, caserios, fincas y aldeas se con-struye el embalse de la hidroelectrica del Proyecto Pueblo Viejo-Quixal. Comité de Reconstrucción Nacional. Informe presentado por el Dr. Gustavo Adolfo Gaitán Sanchez, Guatemala, March de 1978 (date submitted), February 1979 (date released).

Gans, H. J.
1962   The Urban Villagers: Group and Class in the Life of Italian Americans. Glencoe, IL: The Free Press.

Gardener, G., and J. Perry
1995   Big-Dam Construction Is on the Rise. World Watch 8(5):36–37.

Gebre, Y.
2003   Resettlement and the Unnoticed Losers: Impoverishment Disasters among the Gumz in Ethiopia. Human Organization 62(1):50–61.

Geisler, C., and R. de Sousa
2001   From Refuge to Refugee: The African Case. Journal of Public Administration and Development 21(2):159–170.

Ghimire, K.
1994   Parks and People: Livelihood Issues in National Parks Management in Thailand and Madagascar. Development and Change 23(2):195–229.

Gleser, G. C., B. L. Green, and C. Winget
1981   Prolonged Psychological Effects of Disaster: A Study of Buffalo Creek. New York: Academic Press.

Gomide, F. L. S.

2004   Benefit Sharing: Experiences from Brazil. Presented at the United Nations Symposium on Hydropower and Sustainable Development, Beijing, October.

GNCTND. *See* **Government of National Capital Territory of New Delhi**

Goodall, H.

2006   Exclusion and Re-emplacement: Tensions around Protected Areas in Australia and Southeast Asia. Conservation and Society 4(3):383–395.

Goodland, R.

2000   Social and Environmental Assessment to Promote Sustainability. Environmental Paper 74. Washington DC: World Bank.

2004   Prior Informed Consent and the World Bank Group. Paper presented at the Prior Informed Consent conference, American University Center for International Environmental Law, Washington College of Law, Washington DC, March 2.

Goody, J.

1969   Inheritance, Marriage, and Property in Africa and Eurasia. Sociology 3:55–76.

1970   Sideways or Downwards? Lateral and Vertical Succession, Inheritance, and Descent in Africa and Eurasia. Man 5(4):627–638.

Gorenflo, L. J., and K. Brandon

2005   Agricultural Capacity and Conservation in High-Biodiversity Forest Ecosystems. Ambio 34(3):199–204.

Goulet, D.

1985   The Cruel Choice—A New Concept in the Theory of Development. Lanham, MD: University Press of America.

Government of National Capital Territory of New Delhi (GNCTND)

2000   Economic Survey of Delhi, 1999–2000. http://delhiplanning.nic.in/ Planning.htm, accessed November 2007.

Gramling, R., and R. Hagelman

2004   A Working Coast: People in the Louisiana Wetlands. Special issue, Journal of Coastal Research 44:112–133.

Gray, A.

1996   Indigenous Resistance to Involuntary Relocation. *In* Understanding Impoverishment: The Consequences of Development-Induced Displacement. C. McDowell, ed. Pp. 99–122. Providence, RI, and London: Berghahn Books.

Greaves, P.

1997   La intervención del Banco Mundial y la CFE en los proyectos hidroeléctricos de Aguamilpa y Zimapán: Los límites de una política social de reacomodos. Tesis de Maestría en Antropología Social, ENAH, Mexico.

Greene, K.

2002   The Cultural Form of Saving as a Group: Flexible Savings Group Strategies in the New South Africa. PhD dissertation, American University.

Guggenheim, S. E.

1991   Salvaging the Damned: Resettlement in Mexico. *In* Anthropological Approaches to Involuntary Resettlement: Policy, Practice, and Theory. M. M. Cernea and S. E. Guggenheim, eds. Pp. 14–15. Boulder, CO: Westview.

1993   Peasants, Planners, and Participation: Resettlement in Mexico. *In* Anthropological Approaches to Involuntary Resettlement: Policy, Practice, and Theory. M. M. Cernea and S. E. Guggenheim, eds. Pp. 201–228. Boulder, CO: Westview.

1994   Involuntary Resettlement: An Annotated Reference Bibliography for Development Research. Environment Working Paper 64. Washington DC: World Bank.

Guggenheim, S. E., and M. M. Cernea

1993   Anthropological Approaches to Involuntary Resettlement: Policy, Practice, and Theory. *In* Anthropological Approaches to Resettlement: Policy, Practice, and Theory. M. M. Cernea and S. E. Guggenheim, eds. Pp. 1–13. Boulder, CO: Westview.

Gugler, J.

2004   Introduction. *In* World Cities beyond the West: Globalization, Development, and Inequality. J. Gugler, ed. Pp. 1–24. New York: Cambridge University Press.

Guha, A.

2007   Land, Law, and the Left: The Saga of Disempowerment of the Peasantry in the Era of Globalization. New Delhi: The Concept Publishing Company.

Guha, R.

1997   The Authoritarian Biologist and the Arrogance of Anti-humanism: Wildlife Conservation in the Third World. The Ecologist 27(1):14–20.

Gunewardena, N.

2006   Peddling Paradise, Rebuilding Serendib: The 100-Meter Refugees versus the Tourism Industry in Post-tsunami Sri Lanka. The Applied Anthropologist 26(2):149–169.

Guo Xiaohong and Li Jingrong

2000   Construction Safety Guaranteed on the Dam Site. Beijing: China Internet Information Center (CIIC). http://www.china.org.cn/english/2000/Oct/3240.htm, accessed November 2007.

Hamilton, L. A.

2003   The Political Philosophy of Needs. Cambridge: Cambridge University Press.

Hanna, J. M., and M. H. Fitzgerald

1993   Acculturation and Symptoms: A Comparative Study of Reported Health Symptoms in Three Samoan Communities. Social Science and Medicine 36(9):1169–1180.

Hansen, A.

1996   Future Directions in the Study of Forced Migration. Keynote address at the fifth International Research and Advisory Panel, Center for Refugee Studies, Moi University, Eldoret, Kenya.

Hansen, A., and A. Oliver-Smith, eds.

1982   Involuntary Migration and Resettlement: The Problems and Responses of Dislocated People. Boulder, CO: Westview.

Hastrup, K.

1995   A Passage to Anthropology: Between Experience and Theory. London: Routledge.

Hayes, T. M.

2006   Parks, People, and Forest Protection: An Institutional Assessment of the Effectiveness of Protected Areas. World Development 34(12):2064–2075.

Health Canada

2004   Canadian Handbook on Health Impact Assessment. Ottawa: Public Works and Government Services Canada.

Heap, S. H.

1992   Planning. In The Theory of Choice—A Critical Guide, by S. H. Heap, M. Hollis, B. Lyons, R. Sugden, and A. Weale. Pp. 238–248. Oxford: Blackwell.

Heckenberger, M. J., A. Kuikuru, U. T. Kuikuru, J. C. Russell, M. Schmidt, C. Fausto, and B. Franchetto

2003   Amazonia 1492: Pristine Forest or Cultural Parkland? Science 301(5640):1710–1714.

Heggelund, G.

2004   Environment and Resettlement Politics in China: The Three Gorges Project. Hants, UK: Ashgate.

Heilongjiang Provincial Project Office (HPPO)

2001   Resettlement Plan for Qunli Dyke Core Subproject. Harbin City, China: HPPO.

Hewitt, K.

1983   Interpretations of Calamity. Winchester, MA: Allen and Unwin.

1998   Excluded Perspectives in the Social Construction of Disaster. In What Is a Disaster? E. Quarentelli, ed. Pp. 75–91. New York and London: Routledge.

Heyneman, D.

1979   Dams and Disease. Human Nature 2(2):50–57.

Hinrichsen, D.

2005   The Coastal Population Explosion. http://www.oceanservice.noaa.gov/websites/retiredsites/natdia_pdf/3hinrichsen.pdf, accessed October 2006.

Hirsch, P.

1999   Dams in the Mekong Region: Scoping Social and Cultural Issues. Cultural Survival Quarterly 23(3):37–40. http://www.cs.org/publications/csq/csq-article.cfm?id=1371, accessed June 2008.

Hirschon, R.

2000   The Creation of Community: Well-being without Wealth in an Urban Greek Refugee Locality. In Risks and Reconstruction: Experiences of Resettlers and Refugees. M. M. Cernea and C. McDowell, eds. Pp. 393–411. Washington DC: World Bank.

Hitchcock, R. K.
2001 Hunting Is Our Heritage: The Struggle for Hunting and Gathering Rights among the San of Southern Africa. *In* Parks, Property, and Power: Managing Hunting Practice and Identity within State Policy Regimes. D. G. Anderson and K. Ikeya, eds. Pp. 139–156. Seri Ethnological Studies, vol. 59, no. 59. Osaka: National Museum of Ethnology.

Hitchcock, R. K., M. Biesele, and R. B. Lee
2003 The San of Southern Africa: A Status Report. Committee for Human Rights, American Anthropological Association. http://www.aaanet.org/committees/cfhr/san.htm, accessed August 2005.

Holling, C. S.
1994 An Ecologist View of the Malthusian Conflict. *In* Population, Economic Development, and the Environment. K. Lindahl-Kiessling and H. Landberg, eds. Pp. 79–103. New York: Oxford University Press.

Hong, E.
1987 Natives of Sarawak: Survival in Borneo's Vanishing Forest. Pulau Pinang, Malaysia: Institut Masyarakat.

HPPO. *See* **Heilongjiang Provincial Project Office**

Hughes, C. C., and J. M. Hunter
1970 Disease and "Development" in Africa. Social Science and Medicine 3(4):443–493.

Humphrey, C.
2003 Rethinking Infrastructure: Siberian Cities and the Great Freeze of January 2001. *In* Wounded Cities: Destruction and Reconstruction in a Globalized World. J. Schneider and I. Susser, eds. Pp. 91–107. New York: Berg.

Hutton, D., and C. E. Haque
2004 Human Vulnerability, Dislocation, and Resettlement: Adaptation Processes of River-Bank Erosion-Induced Displacees in Bangladesh. Disasters 28(1):41–62.

ICOLD. *See* **International Commission on Large Dams**

IFC. *See* **International Finance Corporation**

Igoe, J.
2004 Conservation and Globalization: A Study of National Parks and Indigenous Communities from East Africa to South Dakota. Belmont, CA: Wadsworth.

Imhoff, A.
1999 We Will Not Be a Party to Our Own Death: Philippine Dam Draws Fire from Indigenous People. San Roque campaign articles. Berkeley, CA: International Rivers Network (IRN). http://irn.org/programs/sanroque/wrr.html, accessed November 2007.

Imhoff, A., S. Wong, and P. Bosshard
2002 Citizen's Guide to the WCD. Berkeley, CA: International Rivers Network (IRN).

Inter-American Development Bank
1998 Involuntary Resettlement Policy, GN-1979-3, July.

International Commission on Large Dams (ICOLD)

2003   World Register of Dams. Paris. http://www.icold-cigb.org/registre/ index.php?lang=en, accessed November 2007.

International Federation of the Red Cross and Red Crescent Societies

2003   World Disasters Report. Bloomfield, CT: Kumarian.

International Finance Corporation (IFC)

2006a   Sustainability Policy and Performance Standards. Washington DC: World Bank and IFC. http://www.ifc.org, accessed September 2007.

2006b   Performance Standard 5. Washington DC. http://www.equator-principles.com, accessed July 2008.

International Union for the Conservation of Nature / World Commission on Protected Areas (IUCN/WCPA)

2004   The Durban Action Plan. http://www.iucn.org/themes/wcpa/wpc2003/ english/outputs/durban/durbactplan.htm, accessed August 2005.

Jacoby, K.

2001   Crimes against Nature: Squatters, Poachers, Thieves, and the Hidden History of American Conservation. Berkeley: University of California Press.

Janoff-Bulman, R., and I. Frieze

1987   A Theoretical Perspective for Understanding Reactions to Victimization. Journal of Social Sciences 39(2):1–17.

Jayewardene, R. A.

1995   Cause for Concern: Health and Resettlement. *In* Development, Displacement, and Resettlement: Focus on Asian Experiences. H. M. Mathur and M. M. Cernea, eds. Pp. 39–73. New Delhi: Vikas.

2008   Can Displacement Be Turned into Development by Compensation Alone? The South Asian Experience. *In* Can Compensation Prevent Impoverishment? Reforming Resettlement through Investments and Benefit-Sharing. M. M. Cernea and H. M. Mathur, eds. Pp. 253–259. London and New Delhi: Oxford University Press.

Jobin, W.

1999   Dams and Disease: Ecological Design and Health Impacts of Large Dams, Canals, and Irrigation Systems. London: E&FN Spon.

Johnston, B. R.

2000   Reparations and the Right to Remedy. Briefing paper prepared for the World Commission on Dams (WCD), July. http:// www.dams.org/thematic/ contrib._papers.php, accessed December 2000.

2005   Chixoy Dam Legacy Issues Study, vol. 1: Executive Summary Consequential Damages and Reparation: Recommendations for Remedy; vol. 2: Document Review and Chronology of Relevant Actions and Events; vol. 3: Consequential Damage Assessment of Chixoy River Basin Communities. Center for Political Ecology, March 17. http://www.centerforpoliticalecology.org/chixoy.html, accessed July 2007.

Johnston, B. R., and C. Garcia-Downing

2004   Hydroelectric Development on the Bio-Bio River, Chile: Anthropology and
         Human Rights Advocacy. *In* In the Way of Development: Indigenous Peoples,
         Life Projects, and Globalization. M. Blaser, H. A. Feit, and G. McCrae, eds.
         Pp. 211–231. London and New York: Zed Books.

Johnston, B. R., and S. Slyomovics, eds.

2008   Waging War and Making Peace: The Anthropology of Reparations. *In* Waging
         War and Making Peace—Reparations and Human Rights. B. R. Johnston and
         S. Slyomovics, eds. Pp. 11–28. Walnut Creek, CA: Left·Coast Press.

Jordan, L., and P. van Tuijl

2000   Political Responsibility in NGO Advocacy. World Development
         28(12):2051–2065.

Josephson, P. R.

2002   Industrialized Nature: Brute Force Technology and the Transformation of the
         Natural World. Washington DC: Island.

Kanbur, R.

2002   Development Economics and the Compensation Principle. *In* An Exchange on
         the Compensation Principle in Resettlement, by M. M. Cernea and R. Kanbur.
         Pp. 4–19. Working Paper 2002-33. Ithaca, NY: Department of Applied
         Economics and Management, Cornell University.

2008   Development Economics and the Compensation Principle. *In* Can
         Compensation Prevent Impoverishment? Reforming Resettlement through
         Investments and Benefit-Sharing. M. M. Cernea and H. M. Mathur, eds.
         London and New Delhi: Oxford University Press.

Kardam, N.

1993   Development Approaches and the Role of Policy Advocacy: The Case of the
         World Bank. World Development 21(11):1773–1789.

Keck, M. E., and K. Sikkink

1998   Activists beyond Borders: Advocacy Networks in International Politics. Ithaca,
         NY: Cornell University Press.

Kedia, S.

1992   Accounting for Sociocultural Impacts of Involuntary Resettlement: Lessons
         from the Sardar Sarovar Dam Projects in India. Paper presented at the annual
         meeting of the International Association for Impact Assessment (IAIA),
         Washington DC, August 19–22.

2003   Assessing and Mitigating the Health Impacts of Involuntary Resettlement: The
         Tehri Hydroelectric Dam Project. Advances in Science and Technology of
         Water Resources 23(2):65–68.

2004   Changing Food Production Strategies among Garhwali Resettlers in the
         Himalayas. Ecology of Food and Nutrition 43(6):421–442.

REFERENCES

Kedia, S., and J. van Willigen

2008   Nutrition and Health Impacts of Involuntary Resettlement: The Tehri Dam Experience. *In* India: Development and Displacement. Social Development Report 2008 of the Council for Social Development. Pp. 116–126. New Delhi: Oxford University Press.

Khagram, S.

1999   Dams, Democracy, and Development: Transnational Struggles for Power and Water. PhD dissertation, Stanford University.

Kirby, D. G.

1989   Immigration, Stress, and Prescription Drug Use among Cuban Women in South Florida. Medical Anthropology 10(4):287–295.

Kloos, H.

1990   Health Aspects of Resettlement in Ethiopia. Social Science and Medicine 30(6):643–656.

Kloos, H., G. DeSole, and A. Lemma

1981   Intestinal Parasitism in Seminomadic Pastoralists and Subsistence Farmers in and around Irrigation Schemes in the Awesh Valley, Ethiopia, with Special Emphasis on Ecological and Cultural Associations. Social Science and Medicine 15B(4):457–469.

Koenig, D.

1995   Women and Resettlement. *In* The Women and International Development Annual, vol. 4. R. Gallin and A. Ferguson, eds. Pp. 21–49. Boulder, CO: Westview.

2006   Enhancing Local Development in Development-Induced Displacement and Resettlement Projects. *In* Development-Induced Displacement: Problems, Policies, and People. C. de Wet, ed. Pp. 105–140. Oxford and New York: Berghahn Books.

Kroll-Smith, S., and H. H. Floyd

1997   Bodies in Protest: Environmental Illness and the Struggle over Medical Knowledge. New York: New York University Press.

Kupperman, K. O.

1993   Providence Island, 1630–1641: The Other Puritan Colony. Cambridge: Cambridge University Press.

Lane, C.

2005   Justices Affirm Property Seizures. Washington Post, June 24: A1.

Langholz, J.

2003   Privatizing Conservation. *In* Contested Nature: Promoting International Biodiversity with Social Justice in the Twenty-first Century. S. R. Brechin, P. R. Wilshusen, C. L. Fortwangler, and P. C. West, eds. Pp. 117–136. Albany: State University Press of New York.

Lansing, S. J., P. S. Lansing, and J. S. Erazo
1998   The Value of a River. Journal of Political Ecology 5. http://dizzy.library
        .arizona.edu/ej/jpe/vol5~1.htm, accessed June 2008.

Lari, Y.
1982   The Lines Area Resettlement Project. *In* Urban Housing. M. Sevcenko, ed.
        Pp. 56–64. Cambridge, MA: Aga Khan Program for Islamic Architecture.

Laska, S., G. Woodell, R. Hagelman, R. Gramling, and M. Teets Farris
2004   At Risk: The Human Community and Infrastructure of Resources in Coastal
        Louisiana. Special issue, Journal of Coastal Research 44:90–111.

La Torre López, L.
1999   All We Want Is to Live in Peace. Lima: IUCN.

Leighton, A.
1945   The Governing of Men: General Principles and Recommendations Based on
        Experiences at a Japanese Refugee Camp. Princeton, NJ: Princeton University
        Press.

Levey, B., and J. Freundel Levey
2000   End of the Roads. Washington Post Magazine, November 26: 10–26.

Lewis, J.
2006   Battle for Biloxi. New York Times Magazine, May 21: 100–108.

Lightfoot, R. P.
1979   Spatial Distribution and Cohesion of Resettled Communities. *In* Population
        Resettlement in the Mekong River Basin. L. A. P. Gosling, ed. Pp. 40–53.
        Studies in Geography 10. Chapel Hill: University of North Carolina.

Lipschultz, R.
1992   Restructuring World Politics: The Emergence of Global Civil Society.
        Millennium: Journal of International Studies 21(3):389–420.

Little, P. E.
1999   Political Ecology as Ethnography: The Case of Ecuador's Aguarico River Basin.
        Serie Antropologia 258. Brasilia: Departamento de Antropologia, Universidade
        de Brasilia.

Lohmann, L.
1999   Forest Cleansing: Racial Oppression in Scientific Nature Conservation. Corner
        House Briefing 13. Dorset: The Corner House.

Lomnitz, C.
2003   The Depreciation of Life during Mexico City's Transition into "the Crisis." *In*
        Wounded Cities: Destruction and Reconstruction in a Globalized World. J.
        Schneider and I. Susser, eds. Pp. 47–69. New York: Berg.

Lopez, G. A., J. Smith, and R. Pagnucco
1995   The Global Tide. Bulletin of Atomic Scientists 51(July/August):33–39.

REFERENCES

Low, S. M.

1992   Symbolic Ties That Bind: Place Attachment in the Plaza. *In* Place Attachment. I. Altman and S. M. Low, eds. Pp. 165–187. New York: Plenum.

Lusambili, A.

2007   Environmental Sanitation and Gender among the Urban Poor: A Case Study of the Kibera Slums, Kenya. PhD dissertation, American University.

Mabeus, C. B.

2005   Getting a Head Start on Owning: Young Buyers Are Focusing Their Energies on Fixer-Uppers in DC. Washington Post, July 2: F1.

MacKay, F.

2002   Addressing Past Wrongs—Indigenous Peoples and Protected Areas: The Right to Restitution of Lands and Resources. October 2002–January 2003. Moreton-in-Marsh, UK: Forest Peoples Programme. http://www.forestpeoples.org/documents/law_hr/ips_restitution_protected_areas_oct02a_eng.pdf, accessed July 2007.

Mahapatra, L. K.

1999   Resettlement, Impoverishment, and Reconstruction in India: Development for the Deprived. New Delhi: Vikas.

Mahapatra, L. K., and S. Mahapatra

2000   Social Re-articulation and Community Regeneration among Resettled Displacees. *In* Risks and Reconstruction: Experiences of Resettlers and Refugees. M. M. Cernea and C. McDowell, eds. Pp. 431–444. Washington DC: World Bank.

Maisels, F., T. Sunderland, B. Curran, K. von Loebenstein, J. Oats, L. Usongo, A. Dunn, S. Asaha, M. Balinga, L. Defo, and P. Telfer

2007   Central Africa's Protected Areas and the Purported Displacement of People: A First Critical Review of Existing Data. *In* Protected Areas and Human Displacement: A Conservation Perspective. K. Redford and E. Fearn, eds. Pp. 75–89. Working Paper 29. Bronx, NY: Wildlife Conservation Society.

Maltos Sandoval, M. H.

1995   La CFE y El Desplazamiento Involuntario de Poblaciones. ¿Una Nueva Politia? Relation de lo Acontecido en el P.H. Aguamila. Tesis de Licenciatura en Antropologia Social, Universidad Autonoma Metropolitana, Unidad Iztapalapa, Mexico, DF.

Marris, P.

1974   Loss and Change. New York: Pantheon.

Mathur, H. M., and D. Marsden

1998   Development Projects and Impoverishment Risks: Resettling Project-Affected People in India. Oxford: Oxford University Press.

McClean, J., and S. Straede

2003   Conservation, Relocation, and the Paradigms of Park and People

Management—A Case Study of Padampur Villages and the Royal Chitwan National Park, Nepal. Society and Natural Resources 16(6):509–526.

McCully, P.

1998   Silenced Rivers: The Ecology and Politics of Large Dams. London: Zed Books.

2001   Silenced Rivers: The Ecology and Politics of Large Dams. 2nd edition. Atlantic Highlands, NJ, and London: Zed Books.

McElwee, P. D.

2006   Displacement and Relocation Redux: Stories from Southeast Asia. Conservation and Society 4(3):396–403.

McMillan, D. F.

1995   Sahel Visions: Planned Settlement and River Blindness Control in Burkina Faso. Tucson: University of Arizona Press.

Meakins, R. H.

1981   Development, Disease, and the Environment. Lesotho, South Africa: Robin Press.

Meffe, G. K., and C. R. Carroll

1997   Principles of Conservation Biology. Sunderland, MA: Sinauer Associates.

Meikle, S., and J. Walker

1998   Resettlement Policy and Practice in China and the Philippines. ESCOR Research Scheme R6802. London: Development Planning Unit, University College London.

Meikle, S., and Zhu Youxuan

2000   Employment for Displacees in the Socialist Market Economy of China. *In* Risks and Reconstruction: Experiences of Resettlers and Refugees. M. M. Cernea and C. McDowell, eds. Pp. 127–143. Washington DC: World Bank.

Mejía, M. C.

1999   Economic Dimensions of Urban Involuntary Resettlement: Experiences from Latin America. *In* The Economics of Involuntary Resettlement: Questions and Challenges. M. M. Cernea, ed. Pp. 147–188. Washington DC: World Bank.

Menon, G.

2001   Gender in Displacement and Resettlement: A Study of World Bank Aided Projects in India. Report to Social Development Cell, World Bank, New Delhi.

Menon, M., N. Vagholikar, K. Kohli, and A. Fernandes

2003   Large Dams in the North East: A Bright Future? The Ecologist in Asia 11(1):3–8.

Merten, M.

2005   Richtersveld Claimants Demand State Aid. Mail and Guardian Online, November 28. http://www.mg.co.za/articlePage.aspx?articleid=255833&area=/insight/insight_national/, accessed July 2007.

Messer, E.

2004   Hunger and Human Rights: Old and New Roles for Anthropologists. *In* Human Rights: The Scholar as Activist. C. Nagengast and C. G. Velez-Ibanez, eds. Pp. 43–63. Oklahoma City, OK: Society for Applied Anthropology.

Milewski, J., D. Égré, and V. Roquet

1999 Dams and Benefit Sharing. Contributing paper prepared for World Commission on Dams (WCD) Thematic Review 1.1: Social Impacts of Large Dams: Equity and Distributional Issues.

Milleti, D.

1999 Disasters by Design: A Reassessment of Natural Hazards in the United States. Washington DC: Joseph Henry.

Milton, K.

1996 Environmentalism and Cultural Theory. London: Routledge.

Mines and Communities

2006 Africa Update, October 27. http://www.minesandcommunities.org/Action/press1261.htm, accessed July 2007.

Morgen, S., and J. Maskovsky

2003 The Anthropology of Welfare "Reform": New Perspectives on US Urban Poverty in the Post-welfare Era. Annual Review of Anthropology 32:315–338.

Muggah, R.

2003 A Tale of Two Solitudes: Comparing Conflict and Development-Induced Internal Displacement and Involuntary Resettlement. International Migration 41(5):5–31.

Mulder, M. B., and P. Coppolillo

2005 Conservation: Linking Ecology, Economics, and Culture. Princeton, NJ: Princeton University Press.

Mullings, L.

2003 After Drugs and the "War on Drugs": Reclaiming the Power to Make History in Harlem, New York. *In* Wounded Cities: Destruction and Reconstruction in a Globalized World. J. Schneider and I. Susser, eds. Pp. 173–199. New York: Berg.

Mumbai Metropolitan Region Development Authority (MMRDA)

2009 Projects: Mumbai Urban Transport Project. http://www.mmrdamumbai.org/projects_mutp.htm, accessed December 2009.

Nakayama, M., and K. Furuyashiki

2008 From Expropriation to Land Renting: Japan's Innovations in Compensating Resettlers. *In* Can Compensation Prevent Impoverishment? Reforming Resettlement through Investments and Benefit-Sharing. M. M. Cernea and H. M. Mathur, eds. Pp. 357–374. London and New Delhi: Oxford University Press.

Naughton-Treves, L., M. B. Holland, and K. Brandon

2005 The Role of Protected Areas in Conserving Biodiversity and Sustaining Local Livelihoods. Annual Review of Environmental Resources 30:219–252.

Nelson, M.

1973 Development of Tropical Lands: Policy Issues in Latin America. Baltimore: Johns Hopkins University Press.

New York Times

2005 Unloved, but Not Unbuilt. New York Times, Week in Review, June 5: 3.

Noji, E. K.

1997 The Nature of Disaster: General Characteristics and Public Health Effects. *In* The Public Health Consequences of Disasters. E. Noji, ed. Pp. 3–20. New York: Oxford University Press.

Oates, J. F.

1999 Myth and Reality in the Rain Forest: How Conservation Strategies Are Failing in West Africa. Berkeley: University of California Press.

O'Connor, J.

1998 Natural Causes: Essays in Ecological Marxism. New York: Guilford.

Oliver-Smith, A.

1986 The Martyred City: Death and Rebirth in the Andes. Albuquerque: University of New Mexico Press.

1991 Involuntary Resettlement, Resistance, and Political Empowerment. Journal of Refugee Studies 4:132–149.

1994 Resistance to Resettlement: The Formation and Evolution of Movements. Research in Social Movements, Conflict, and Change 17:197–219.

1996 Fighting for a Place: The Policy Implications of Resistance to Development-Induced Resettlement. *In* Understanding Impoverishment: The Consequences of Development-Induced Displacement. C. McDowell, ed. Pp. 77–97. Providence, RI, and Oxford: Berghahn Books.

2001 Displacement, Resistance, and the Critique of Development: From the Grass Roots to the Global. Working Paper 9. Oxford: Refugee Studies Centre, University of Oxford.

2002 Theorizing Disasters: Nature, Power, and Culture. *In* Catastrophe and Culture: The Anthropology of Disaster. S. M. Hoffman and A. Oliver-Smith, eds. Pp. 23–47. Santa Fe, NM: School of American Research Press.

2005a Communities after Catastrophe: Reconstructing the Material, Reconstituting the Social. *In* Community Building in the Twenty-first Century. S. E. Hyland, ed. Pp. 45–70. Santa Fe, NM: School of American Research Press.

2005b Applied Anthropology and Development-Induced Displacement and Resettlement. *In* Applied Anthropology: Domains of Application. S. Kedia and J. van Willigen, eds. Pp. 189–219. Westport, CT: Praeger.

2006 Displacement, Resistance, and the Critique of Development: From the Grass Roots to the Global. *In* Development-Induced Displacement: Problems, Policies, and People. C. de Wet, ed. Pp. 141–179. Oxford and New York: Berghahn Books.

2008 Behind the Economics of Displacement: Challenging the Philosophical Assumptions. Paper presented at the annual meeting of the Society for Applied Anthropology, Memphis, TN, March 26.

Oliver-Smith, A., and G. V. Button

2005   Forced Migration as an Index of Vulnerability in Hurricane Katrina. Paper presented at the sixth open meeting of the Human Dimensions of Global Environmental Change Research, Bonn, October 11–14.

Organization for Economic Co-operation and Development (OECD)

1991   Guidelines for Aid Agencies on Involuntary Displacement and Resettlement in Development Projects. CODE/GAD (91) 201. Paris: Development Assistance Committee, OECD.

Osun, M.

1999   Zapatista Report. First presented as a speech at the Indigenous Struggles panel at the Second National Conference on Mexico–US Relations, Mexico Solidarity Network, Chicago. http://www.thirdworldtraveler.com/Latin_America/Zapatista_Report_Z.html, accessed August 2005.

Oviedo, G., L. Maffi, and P. B. Larsen

2000   Indigenous and Traditional Peoples of the World and Ecoregion Conservation. Gland, UK: WWF International / Terralingua.

Oxfam

1996   A Profile of European AID II: Northern Corridor Transport Project. Adverse Social and Environmental Impacts Caused by the Rehabilitation of the Westlands–St. Austins and Kabete-Limuru Roads, Kenya. Nairobi: Kituo Cha Sheria; Oxford: Oxfam United Kingdom and Ireland.

Paavola, J., and W. N. Adger

2002   Justice and Adaption to Climate Change. Tyndall Centre for Climate Change Research. Working Paper 23. Norwich, UK: University of East Anglia.

Palinkas, L. A., M. A. Downs, J. S. Peterson, and J. Russell

1992   Social, Cultural, and Psychological Impacts of the *Exxon-Valdez* Oil Spill. Human Organization 51(1):1–13.

Panchal, P.

2005   Citizens' Rage Makes SPARC Fly. Daily News and Analysis, October 18. http://www.dnaindia.com/dnaPrint.asp?NewsID=16302&CatID-1, accessed April 2006.

Pandey, B.

1998a   Depriving the Underprivileged for Development. Bhubaneswar: Institute for Socio-economic Development.

1998b   Impoverishing Effects of Coal Mining Projects: A Case Study of Five Villages in Orissa. *In* Development Projects and Impoverishment Risks: Resettling Project-Affected People in India. H. M. Mathur and D. Marsden, eds. Pp. 174–192. New Delhi: Oxford University Press.

1998c   Displaced Development: Impact of Open Cast Mining on Women. New Delhi: Friedrich Ebert Stiftung.

Paranjpye, V.

1988   Evaluating the Tehri Dam: An Extended Cost Benefit Appraisal. New Delhi: Indian National Trust for Art and Cultural Heritage.

1990   High Dams on the Narmada: A Holistic Analysis of the River Valley Projects. New Delhi: Indian National Trust for Art and Cultural Heritage.

Partridge, W. L.

1993   Successful Involuntary Resettlement: Lessons from the Costa Rican Arenal Hydroelectric Project. *In* Anthropological Approaches to Resettlement: Policy, Practice, and Theory. M. M. Cernea and S. E. Guggenheim, eds. Pp. 351–374. Boulder, CO, San Francisco, and Oxford: Westview.

Partridge, W. L., A. B. Brown, and J. B. Nugent

1982   The Papaloapan Dam and Resettlement Project: Human Ecology and Health Impacts. *In* Involuntary Migration and Resettlement: The Problems and Responses of Dislocated People. A. Hansen and A. Oliver-Smith, eds. Pp. 245–263. Boulder, CO: Westview.

Patel, A.

1997   What Do the Narmada Valley Tribals Want? *In* Toward Sustainable Development? Struggling over India's Narmada River. W. F. Fisher, ed. Pp. 179–200. Armonk, NY: M. E. Sharpe.

Pearce, D.

1999   Methodological Issues in the Economic Analysis for Involuntary Resettlement Operations. *In* The Economics of Involuntary Resettlement: Questions and Challenges. M. M. Cernea, ed. Pp. 50–82. Washington DC: World Bank.

Pearce, D., and T. Swanson

2008   The Economic Evaluation of Projects Involving Forced Population Displacements. *In* Can Compensation Prevent Impoverishment? Reforming Resettlement through Investments and Benefit-Sharing. M. M. Cernea and H. M. Mathur, eds. Pp. 99–120. London and New Delhi: Oxford University Press.

Pellow, D.

1994   Spaces That Teach. *In* Place Attachment. I. Altman and S. M. Low, eds. Pp. 187–210. New York: Plenum.

Peluso, N.

1993   Coercing Conservation: The Politics of State Resource Control. *In* The State and Social Power in Global Environmental Politics. R. D. Lipschutz and K. Conca, eds. Pp. 46–70. New York: Columbia University Press.

Penz, G. P.

1992   Development Refugees and Distributive Justice: Indigenous Peoples, Land, and the Developmentalist State. Public Affairs Quarterly 6(1):105–131.

1995   The Ethics of Development-Induced Displacement. Refuge 16(3):37–41.

Perlman, J.

1982   Favela Removal: The Eradication of a Lifestyle. *In* Involuntary Migration and Resettlement: The Problems and Responses of Dislocated People. A. Hansen and A. Oliver-Smith, eds. Pp. 225–243. Boulder, CO: Westview.

PESC-KSP. *See* **Philippine European Solidarity Centre**

Peters, J. D.

1997   Seeing Bifocally: Media, Place, Culture. *In* Culture, Power, Place: Explorations in Critical Anthropology. A. Gupta and J. Ferguson, eds. Durham, NC: Duke University Press.

PHAC. *See* **Public Health Advisory Committee**

Philippine European Solidarity Centre (PESC-KSP)

2001   News Summaries on Selected Topics: San Roque Dam Project, April–May 2000. The Netherlands: PESC-KSP. http://www.philsol.nl/news/01/SRDP-apr01 .htm, accessed November 2007.

Picciotto, R., W. van Wicklin, and E. Rice

2001   Involuntary Resettlement: Comparative Perspectives. World Bank Series on Evaluation and Development, vol. 2. Washington DC: World Bank.

de Pina Cabal, J.

1994   The Valuation of Time among the Peasant Population of the Alto Minho, Northwestern Portugal. *In* Who Needs the Past? Indigenous Values and Archaeology. R. Layton, ed. Pp. 59–69. London and New York: Routledge.

Piven, F. F., and R. Cloward

1971   Regulating the Poor: Functions of Public Welfare. New York: Vintage.

Power, M.

2003   Rethinking Development Geographies. London and New York: Routledge.

Price, S.

2008   Copensatino, Restoration, and Development Opportunities: National Standards on Involuntary Resettlement. *In* Can Compensation Prevent Impoverishment? Reforming Resettlement through Investments and Benefit-Sharing. M. M. Cernea and H. M. Mathur, eds. Pp. 147–179. London and New Delhi: Oxford University Press.

Public Health Advisory Committee (PHAC)

2005   A Guide to Health Impact Assessment: A Policy Tool for New Zealand. 2nd edition. Wellington, New Zealand: Public Health Commission. http://www.phac.health.govt.nz/moh.nsf/indexcm/phac-guide-hia-2nd, accessed November 2007.

Pyszczynski, T., S. Solomon, and J. Greenberg

2001   In the Wake of 9/11: The Psychology of Terror. Washington DC: American Psychological Association.

Quarles van Ufford, P., D. Kruijt, and T. E. Downing, eds.

1988   The Hidden Crisis in Development: Development Bureaucracies. Tokyo: United Nations University Press; Amsterdam: Free University Press.

Raina, V., A. Chowdhury, and S. Chowdhury

1997   The Dispossessed: Victims of Development in Asia. Hong Kong: Arena.

Rajagopal, B.

2000   Human Rights and Development. Contributing paper prepared for World Commission on Dams (WCD) Thematic Review, vol. 4: Regulation,

Compliance, and Implementation Options. http://www.dams.org/docs/
kbase/contrib/ins206.pdf, accessed May 2008.

Ramanathan, U.

2008   Eminent Domain, Protest, and the Discourse on Rehabilitation. *In* Can
Compensation Prevent Impoverishment? Reforming Resettlement through
Investments and Benefit-Sharing. M. M. Cernea and H. M. Mathur, eds. Pp.
208–230. London and New Delhi: Oxford University Press.

Rangarajan, M., and G. Shahabuddin

2006   Displacement and Relocation from Protected Areas: Towards a Biological and
Historical Synthesis. Conservation and Society 4(3):359–378.

Recovery of Historical Memory Project (REMHI)

1999   Guatemala: Never Again! The Official Report of the Human Rights Office,
Archdiocese of Guatemala. New York: Maryknoll. (English translation of *Nunca
Más*, Oficina de Derechos Humanos del Arzobispado de Guatemala, 4 tomos,
1998.)

Reddy, I. U. B.

2000   Restoring Housing under Urban Infrastructure Projects in India. *In* Risks and
Reconstruction: Experiences of Resettlers and Refugees. M. M. Cernea and
C. McDowell, eds. Pp. 167–183. Washington DC: World Bank.

Rede Brasil

2005   Rede Brasil Statement on Agreement between the IDB and Tractebel Energy
Company. Press release, June 3. http://www.bicusa.org/en/Article.2138.aspx,
accessed September 2007.

Redford, K.

1991   The Ecologically Noble Savage. Cultural Survival Quarterly 15(1):46–48.

1992   The Empty Forest. Bioscience 42(6):412–422.

Redford, K., and E. Fearn, eds.

2007   Protected Areas and Human Displacement: A Conservation Perspective.
Working Paper 29. Bronx, NY: Wildlife Conservation Society.

Redford, K. H., and M. Painter

2006   Natural Alliances between Conservationists and Indigenous Peoples. Working
Paper 25. Bronx, NY: Wildlife Conservation Society.

Redford, K., and S. Sanderson

2000   Extracting Humans from Nature. Conservation Biology 14(5):1362–1364.

2006   No Roads, Only Directions. Conservation and Society 4(3):379–382.

REMHI. *See* **Recovery of Historical Memory Project**

Rew, A. W.

1996   Policy Implications of the Involuntary Ownership of Resettlement Negotiations:
Examples from Asia of Resettlement Practice. *In* Understanding Impoverishment:
The Consequences of Development-Induced Impoverishment. C. McDowell, ed.
Pp. 201–221. Oxford: Berghahn Books.

2003   Tapping the Bell at Governance Temple. *In* A Moral Critique of Development. P. Quarles van Ufford and A. K. Giri, eds. Pp. 118–136. London and New York: Routledge.

Rew, A. W., and P. A. Driver
1986   Evaluation of the Social and Environmental Impact of the Victoria Dam Project. Overseas Development Administration (ODA) Evaluation Report EV 392. London: Evaluation Department, ODA.
1987   Resettlement Implications. *In* Evaluation of Victoria Project in Sri Lanka, 1978–1985: vol. 1, main report. P. L. Owen, T. C. Muir, A. W. Rew, and P. A. Driver, eds. Overseas Development Administration Evaluation (ODE) Study EV392. London: ODE.

Rew, A., E. Fisher, and B. Pandey
2000   Addressing Policy Constraints and Improving Outcomes in Development-Induced Displacement and Resettlement Projects. Final report prepared for ESCOR R7644 and the research programme on development-induced displacement and resettlement, DFID, UK Department for International Development. Oxford: Refugee Studies Centre, University of Oxford.
2006   Policy Practices in Development-Induced Displacement and Rehabilitation. *In* Development-Induced Displacement: Problems, Policies, and People. C. de Wet, ed. Pp. 38–70. Oxford and New York: Berghahn Books.

Riley, R. B.
1994   Attachment to the Ordinary Landscape. *In* Place Attachment. I. Altman and S. M. Low, eds. Pp. 13–35. New York: Plenum.

Rio Tinto
2001   Murowa Project Newsletter. Harare: Rio Tinto.

Robinson, K.
1986   Stepchildren of Progress: The Political Economy of Development in an Indonesian Mining Town. Albany, NY: SUNY.

Robinson, W. C.
2003   Risks and Rights: The Causes, Consequences, and Challenges of Development-Induced Displacement. Occasional Paper. Washington DC: The Brookings Institution–SAIS Project on Internal Displacement.

Rodman, M.
1992   Empowering Place: Multilocality and Multivocality. American Anthropologist 94(3):640–656.

Rodríguez, J. P., A. B. Taber, P. Daszak, R. Sukumar, C. Valladares-Padua, S. Padua, L. F. Aguirre, R. A. Medellin, M. Acosta, A. A. Aguirre, C. Bonacic, P. Bordino, J. Bruschini, D. Buchori, S. González, T. Mathew, M. Mendez, L. Múgica, L. F. Pacheco, A. P. Dobson, and M. Pearl
2007   Globalization of Conservation: A View from the South. Science 317(5839):755–756.

Rothman, M.

2000   Measuring and Apportioning Rents from Hydroelectric Developments. Washington DC: World Bank.

Roy, A., and D. Barsamian

2004   The Checkbook and the Cruise Missile. Boston: South End.

Russell, J. W.

2002   Land and Identity in Mexico: Peasants Stop an Airport. Monthly Review 54(9):14–25. http://www.monthlyreview.org/0203russell.htm, accessed June 2008.

Santos, L. A. de O, and L. M. M. de Andrade

1990   Hydroelectric Dams on Brazil's Xingu River and Indigenous Peoples. Cambridge, MA: Cultural Survival.

Sapkota, N.

2001   Impoverishment Risks and Reconstruction on Kali Gandaki Dam, Nepal. High Plains Applied Anthropologist 21(2):147–156.

Schmidt-Soltau, K.

2005   The Environmental Risks of Conservation-Related Displacement in Central Africa. *In* Displacement Risks in Africa. I. Ohta and Y. D. Gebre, eds. Pp. 282–311. Kyoto: Kyoto University Press; Melbourne: Trans Pacific Press.

Schuh, G. E.

1993   Involuntary Resettlement, Human Capital, and Economic Development. *In* Anthropological Approaches to Resettlement: Policy, Practice, and Theory. M. M. Cernea and S. E. Guggenheim, eds. Pp. 55–62. Boulder, CO: Westview.

Schwartzman, S., A. Moreira, and D. Nepstad

2000   Rethinking Tropical Forest Conservation: Perils in Parks. Conservation Biology 14(5):1351–1357.

Scudder, T.

1973a   The Human Ecology of Big Projects: River Basin Development and Resettlement. Annual Review of Anthropology 2:45–61.

1973b   Summary: Resettlement. *In* Man-Made Lakes: Their Problems and Environmental Effects. W. C. Ackerman, G. F. White, and E. B. Worthington, eds. J. L. Even, assoc. ed. Pp. 707–719. Washington DC: American Geophysical Union.

1975   Resettlement. *In* Man-Made Lakes and Human Health. N. F. Stanley and M. P. Alpers, eds. Pp. 453–471. London: Academic Press for the Institute of Biology.

1981a   The Development Potential of New Land Settlement in the Tropics and Subtropics: A Global State of the Art Evaluation with Specific Emphasis on Policy Implications. Binghamton, NY: Institute for Development Anthropology.

1981b   What It Means to Be Dammed: The Anthropology of Large-Scale Development Projects in the Tropics and Subtropics. Engineering & Science 54(4):9–15.

1985   A Sociological Analysis for New Land Settlements. *In* Putting People First: Sociological Variables in Rural Development. M. M. Cernea, ed. Pp. 149–184. New York: Oxford University Press.

REFERENCES

1993   Development-Induced Relocation and Refugee Studies: 37 Years of Change
            and Continuity among Zambia's Gwembe Tonga. Journal of Refugee Studies
            6(2):123–152.

1997   Chapters on Social Impacts and on Resettlement. In Water Resources:
            Environmental Planning, Management, and Development. A. K. Biswas, ed.
            Pp. 623–710. New York: McGraw Hill.

2005a   The Future of Large Dams: Dealing with Social, Environmental, Institutional,
            and Political Costs. London: Earthscan; Sterling, VA: James and James.

2005b   The Kariba Case Study. Social Science Working Paper 1227. Pp. 1–64.
            Pasadena: California Institute of Technology.

Scudder, T., and E. Colson

1980   Secondary Education and the Formation of an Elite: The Impact of Education
            on Gwembe District, Zambia. London: Academic Press.

1982   From Welfare to Development: A Conceptual Framework for the Analysis of
            Dislocated People. In Involuntary Migration and Resettlement. A. Hansen and
            A. Oliver-Smith, eds. Pp. 267–288. Boulder, CO: Westview.

Scudder, T., and J. Habarad

1991   Local Responses to Involuntary Relocation and Development in the Zambian
            Portion of the Middle Zambezi Valley. In Migrants in Agricultural Develop-
            ment. J. A. Mollet, ed. Pp. 178–205. London: MacMillan.

Selby, H., and L. Garretson

1981   Cultural Anthropology. Dubuque, IA: W. C. Brown.

Seymour, F. J.

2008   Conservation, Displacement, and Compensation. In Can Compensation
            Prevent Impoverishment? Reforming Resettlement through Investments and
            Benefit-Sharing. M. M. Cernea and H. M. Mathur, eds. Pp. 286–314. London
            and New Delhi: Oxford University Press.

Shami, S.

1993   The Social Implications of Population Displacement and Resettlement: An
            Overview with a Focus on the Arab Middle East. International Migration
            Review 27(1):4–33.

Shi Guoqing and Hu Weisong

1996   Comprehensive Evaluation and Monitoring of Displaced Persons' Standards of
            Living and Production. In Papers on Resettlement and Development. Pp.
            56–62. Nanjing, China: National Research Centre for Resettlement.

Shi Guoqing, Zhou Jian, and Chen Shaojun

2006   China: Improvements in Resettlement Policies and Practices: Compensation
            Norms, Institutions, and Development. Presented at the IAPS (International
            Association for Population Studies) Conference, Alexandria, Egypt,
            September.

Shihata, I. F. I.

1993   Legal Aspects of Involuntary Population Displacement. *In* Anthropological
         Approaches to Involuntary Resettlement: Policy, Practice, and Theory.
         M. M. Cernea and S. E. Guggenheim, eds. Pp. 39–54. Boulder, CO: Westview.

Sigaud, L.

1986   Efeitos Sociais de Grades Projetos Hidroeletricos: As Barragens de Sobradinho
         y Machadinho. Comunicacao 9. Rio de Janeiro: Programa de Pos-Graduacao en
         Antropologia Social, Museo Nacional.

Silove, D., and Z. Steel

2006   Understanding Community Psychosocial Needs after Disasters: Implications for
         Mental Health Services. Journal of Postgraduate Medicine 52(2):121–125.

Simon, D.

1999   Development Revisited: Thinking about, Practicing, and Teaching
         Development after the Cold War. *In* Development as Theory and Practice. D.
         Simon and A. Narman, eds. Pp. 17–54. Harlow, UK: Longman.

Simone, A.

2004   For the City Yet to Come: Changing African Life in Four Cities. Durham, NC:
         Duke University Press.

Singh, M.

1992   Displacement by Sardar Sarovar and Tehri: A Comparative Study of Two Dams.
         New Delhi: MARG.

Skifter Andersen, H.

2003   Urban Sores: On the Interaction between Segregation, Urban Decay, and
         Deprived Neighbourhoods. Burlington, VT: Ashgate.

Smart, A., and J. Smart

2003   Urbanization and the Global Perspective. Annual Review of Anthropology
         32:263–285.

Smith, J., C. Chatfield, and R. Pagnucco

1997   Transnational Social Movements and Global Politics: Solidarity beyond the
         State. Syracuse, NY: Syracuse University Press.

**Soils Incorporated (Pty) Ltd and Chalo Environmental and Sustainable Development
Consultants**

2000   Kariba Dam Case Study. Prepared as input to the World Commission on Dams
         (WCD). http://www.dams.org, accessed April 2008.

Solomon, G. M., M. Hjelmroos-Koski, M. Rotkin-Ellman, and S. K. Hammond

2006   Airborne Mold and Endotoxin Concentrations in New Orleans, Louisiana, after
         Flooding, October–November 2005. Environmental Health Perspectives.
         Washington DC: The National Institute of Environmental Health Sciences.

Solomon, G. M., and M. Rotkin-Ellman

2006   Contaminants in New Orleans Sediment: An Analysis of EPA Data. New York:
         National Resource Defense Council. http://www.nrdc.org/health/effects/
         katrinadate/ contents.asp, accessed February 2006.

Sonohara, T.
1997   Toward a Genuine Redress for an Unjust Past: The Nibutani Dam Case.
E Law—Murdoch University Electronic Journal of Law 4(2):1–43.

Squires, G. D., L. Bennett, K. McCourt, and P. Nyden
1987   Chicago: Race, Class, and the Response to Urban Decline. Philadelphia:
Temple University Press.

Stack, C.
1974   All Our Kin: Strategies for Survival in a Black Community. New York: Harper
Torchbook.

State Council of the PRC (People's Republic of China)
2004   Decision on Deepening Reform and Strictly Enforcing Land Administration.
Document 28.

2006   Circular on Relevant Issues of Land Control, August 31.

Stevens, S.
1997   Conservation through Cultural Survival: Indigenous Peoples and Protected
Areas. Washington DC: Island.

Stokstad, E.
2003   "Pristine" Forest Teemed with People. Science 301(5640):1645–1646.

Sugden, R.
1992   Social Justice. In The Theory of Choice—A Critical Guide, by S. Heap,
M. Hollis, B. Lyons, R. Sugden, and A. Weale. Pp. 259–285. Oxford: Blackwell.

Surrallés, A., and P. García Hierro
2005   The Land Within: Indigenous Territory and the Perception of Environment.
Copenhagen: IWGIA (International Work Group for Indigenous Affairs).

Sutro, L., and T. E. Downing
1988   A Step toward a Grammar of Space in Zapotec Villages. In House and
Household in the Mesoamerican Past. R. R. Wilk and W. Ashmore, eds.
Pp. 29–48. Albuquerque: University of New Mexico Press.

Suttles, G.
1968   The Social Order of the Slum: Ethnicity and Territory in the Inner City.
Chicago: University of Chicago Press.

Tamondong-Helin, S. D.
1996   State Power as a Medium of Impoverishment: Case of Pantabangan
Resettlement in the Philippines. In Understanding Impoverishment: The
Consequences of Development-Induced Displacement. C. McDowell, ed.
Pp. 169–186. Providence, RI: Berghahn Books.

Tankha, S., J. Burtner, and J. Schmandt
1998   Relocation and Resettlement in Ceará: Second Interim Report on Findings to
the Secretary of Water Resources, State of Ceará. The Woodlands, TX: Center
for Global Studies, Houston Advanced Research Center.

Tanner, L.

2005   Broken Promises and Loss of Trust: The Corruption Stemming from the Use of the Development Resettlement Policy at the Three Gorges Dam Site. Contemporary Topics in Forced Migration, Working Paper 3. San Diego: Forced Migration Laboratory, Center for Comparative Immigration Studies, University of California.

Terborgh, J.

1999   Requiem for Nature. Washington DC: Island.

Trembath, B. P.

2008   Beyond Compensation: Sharing Rents Arising from Hydropower Dams. *In* Can Compensation Prevent Impoverishment? Reforming Resettlement through Investments and Benefit-Sharing. M. M. Cernea and H. M. Mathur, eds. Pp. 375–393. London and New Delhi: Oxford University Press.

Tuan, Y.-F.

1977   Sense and Place: The Perspective of Experience. Minneapolis: University of Minnesota Press.

Turner, T.

1991   Representing, Resisting, Rethinking: Historical Transformations of Kayapo Culture and Anthropological Consciousness. *In* Colonial Situations: Essays on the Contextualization of Ethnographic Knowledge, vol. 7: History of Anthropology. G. W. Stocking Jr., ed. Pp. 285–313. Madison: University of Wisconsin Press.

Turton, D.

2002   Forced Displacement and the Nation-State. *In* Development and Displacement. J. Robinson, ed. Pp. 19–75. Milton Keynes, UK: The Open University in association with Oxford University Press.

2006   Who Is a Forced Migrant? Risk, Complexity, and Local Initiative in Forced Resettlement Outcomes. *In* Development-Induced Displacement: Problems, Policies, and People. C. de Wet, ed. Pp. 13–37. Oxford and New York: Berghahn Books.

Udall, L.

1997   The International Narmada Campaign: A Case of Sustained Advocacy. *In* Toward Sustainable Development? Struggling over India's Narmada River. W. F. Fisher, ed. Pp. 201–227. Armonk, NY: M. E. Sharpe.

UNEP/WCMC/WCPA/IUCN

2003   2003 United Nations List of Protected Areas. Gland, UK: IUCN; Cambridge, UK: UNEP World Conservation Monitoring Centre.

United Nations (UN)

1948   Universal Declaration of Human Rights.

1986   Declaration on the Right to Development. G.A. res. 41/128. New York: United Nations. http://www.unhchr.ch/html/menu3/b/74.htm, accessed September 2007.

REFERENCES

1991   Committee on Economic, Social, and Cultural Rights, General Comment No. 4, The Right to Adequate Housing (Art. 11[1]). New York: United Nations.

1993   Forced Evictions. UN Commission on Human Rights, Resolution 77a.

1997   Committee on Economic, Social, and Cultural Rights, General Comment No. 7, The Right to Adequate Housing. New York: United Nations.

1999   Guiding Principles on Internal Displacement. New York: Office for the Coordinator of Humanitarian Affairs.

2005   Basic Principles and Guidelines on the Right to a Remedy and Reparation for Victims of Violations of International Human Rights and Humanitarian Law, E/CN.4/2005/L.48.

2006   United Nations Guiding Principles on Internal Development. http://www.unhchr.ch/html/menu2/7/b/principles.htm, accessed July 2006.

United Nations Development Programme (UNDP)

2006   Human Development Report 2006. Beyond Scarcity: Power, Poverty, and the Global Water Crisis. New York: UNDP.

United Nations Environment Programme (UNEP)

2006   Dams and Development Projects. Proceedings of the Fifth Dams and Development Forum Meeting, UNEP-DDP Secretariat, Nairobi, Kenya, November 23–24.

US Department of the Interior Bureau of Reclamation (USDI)

2006   Dams, Projects, and Power Plants: Fatalities during Construction of Hoover Dam. Washington DC: Bureau of Reclamation. http://www.usbr.gov/dataweb/dams/hoover_fatalities_table.htm, accessed November 2007.

US Supreme Court

2005   *Kelo v. New London*, 125 S.Ct. 2655.

van Heerden, I.

2006   The Storm: What Went Wrong and Why during Hurricane Katrina: The Inside Story from One Louisiana Scientist. New York: Viking.

van Wicklin, W. A., III

1999   Sharing Project Benefits to Improve Resettlers' Livelihoods. *In* The Economics of Involuntary Resettlement: Questions and Challenges. M. M. Cernea, ed. Pp. 231–256. Washington DC: World Bank.

Vigil, J. D.

2003   Urban Violence and Street Gangs. Annual Review of Anthropology 32:225–242.

Villa Rojas, A.

1955   Los Mazatecos y el Problema Indígena de la Cuenca del Papaloapan. México, DF: Instituto Nacional Indigenista.

Waddy, B. B.

1973   Health Problems of Man-Made Lakes: Anticipation and Realization, Kainji, Nigeria, and Koussou, Ivory Coast. *In* Man-Made Lakes: Their Problems and

Environmental Effects. W. C. Ackerman, G. F. White, and E. B. Worthington, eds. J. L. Even, assoc. ed. Pp. 765–768. Washington DC: American Geophysical Union.

Waldram, J. B.

1980   Relocation and Political Change in a Manitoba Native Community. Canadian Journal of Anthropology 1(2):173–178.

1985   Hydroelectric Development and Dietary Delocalization in Northern Manitoba, Canada. Human Organization 44(1):41–49.

Wali, A.

1989   Kilowatts and Crisis: Hydroelectric Power and Social Dislocation in Eastern Panama. Boulder, CO: Westview.

Wallace, A. F. C.

1957   Mazeway Disintegration: The Individual's Perception of Sociocultural Disorganization. Human Organization 16(2):23–27.

Wallington, T., R. J. Hobbs, and S. A. Moore

2005   Implications of Current Ecological Thinking for Biodiversity Conservation: A Review of the Salient Issues. Ecology and Society 10(1):15. http://www .ecologyandsociety.org/vol10/iss/art15, accessed August 2005.

Ward, P.

2004   Mexico City in an Era of Globalization and Demographic Downturn. *In* World Cities beyond the West: Globalization, Development, and Inequality. J. Gugler, ed. Pp. 151–188. New York: Cambridge University Press.

Ward, R. H., and I. A. Prior

1980   Genetic and Sociocultural Factors in the Response of Blood Pressure to Migration of the Tokelau Population. Medical Anthropology 4(3):339–366.

Waterman, S.

2005   Cops Trapped Survivors in New Orleans. UPI, September 9: 31.

WB. *See* **World Bank**

Webster, M. H.

1975   Medical Aspects of the Kariba Hydro-electric Scheme. *In* Man-Made Lakes and Human Health. N. F. Stanley and M. P. Alpers, eds. Pp. 69–88. London: Academic Press.

Weisler, H. R., J. G. Barbee IV, and M. H. Townsend

2006   Mental Health and Recovery in the Gulf Coast after Hurricanes Katrina and Rita. Journal of the American Medical Association 296:585–588.

Werner, D.

1985   Psychosocial Stress and the Construction of Flood-Control Dams in Santa Catarina, Brazil. Human Organization 44(2):161–167.

West, P., J. Igoe, and D. Brockington

2006   Parks and Peoples: The Social Impact of Protected Areas. Annual Review of Anthropology 35:251–277.

REFERENCES

WHO. *See* **World Health Organization**

Wilgoren, D.

2005   At Each Hurdle, Stronger Resolve. Washington Post, December 15: B1.

Williams, L.

2005   Eastern N.O. Residents Call for MRGO to Close. Times-Picayune, January 29.

Wilshusen, P. R.

2003   Exploring the Political Contours of Conservation. *In* Contested Nature: Promoting International Biodiversity with Social Justice in the Twenty-first Century. S. R. Brechin, P. R. Wilshusen, C. L. Fortwangler, and P. C. West, eds. Pp. 41–58. Albany: State University Press of New York.

Wilson, A.

2003   Bangkok, The Bubble City. *In* Wounded Cities: Destruction and Reconstruction in a Globalized World. J. Schneider and I. Susser, eds. Pp. 203–226. New York: Berg.

Wines, M.

2005   In Zimbabwe, Homeless Belie Leader's Claim. New York Times, November 13. http://www.nytimes.com/2005/11/13/international/africa/13zimbabwe, accessed November 2005.

Wirsing, R. L.

1985   The Health of Traditional Societies and the Effects of Acculturation. Current Anthropology 26(3):303–322.

Wisner, B.

1993   Disaster Vulnerability: Scale, Power, and Daily Life. GeoJournal 30(2):127–140.

Wittgenstein, L.

1953   Philosophical Investigations. Oxford: Blackwell.

Wolde-Selassie, A.

2000   Social Re-articulation after Resettlement: Observing the Beles Valley Scheme in Ethiopia. *In* Risks and Reconstruction: Experiences of Resettlers and Refugees. M. M. Cernea and C. McDowell, eds. Pp. 412–430. Washington DC: World Bank.

World Bank (WB)

1985   The Experience of the World Bank with Government-Sponsored Land Settlement. Operations Evaluation Department. Report Number 5625. Washington, DC: The World Bank.

1990   Operational Directive 4.30: Involuntary Resettlement. The World Bank Operational Manual. Washington DC: World Bank.

1994   Resettlement and Development: The Bankwide Review of Projects Involving Involuntary Resettlement, 1986–1993. Washington DC: Environment Department, World Bank.

1996a   The World Bank Experience with Large Dams—A Preliminary Review of Impacts: Profiles of Large Dams. Background document. Washington DC: World Bank.

1996b   Resettlement and Development: The Bankwide Review of Projects Involving
         Resettlement, 1986–1993. Report of Task Force, prepared by M. Cernea,
         S. Guggenheim, D. Aronson, and W. van Wicklin III. Washington DC: World
         Bank.

1999   Meeting India's Energy Needs (1978–1999). Report 19972. Washington DC:
         Operations Evaluation Department, World Bank.

2001   Operational Policies/Bank Procedures (OP/BP) 4.12: Involuntary
         Resettlement. Washington DC: World Bank. http://www.worldbank.org,
         accessed December 2003.

2003   Stakeholder Involvement in Options Assessment: Promoting Dialogue in
         Meeting Water and Energy Needs. Washington DC: Energy Sector Management
         Assistance Programme (ESMAP), World Bank.

World Bank Inspection Panel

2005   India: Mumbai Urban Transport Project (IBRD Loan 4665-IN; IDA Credit
         3662-IN). Investigation Report. Washington DC: World Bank Inspection Panel.
         http://www.inspectionpanel.org, accessed August 2008.

2008a   Ghana: West African Pipeline Project: Investigation Report of Inspection Panel
         42644-GH, April 25. Washington DC: World Bank. http://www.inspectionpanel
         .org, accessed August 2008.

2008b   Uganda: Private Power Generation Project—The Bujagali Project: Investigation
         Report of Inspection Panel 44977-UG, August 29. Washington DC: World Bank.
         http://www.inspectionpanel.org, accessed December 2008.

World Commission on Dams (WCD)

2000a   Dams and Development: A New Framework for Decision-Making—Overview.
         Sterling, VA, and London: Earthscan. http://www.dams.org//docs/overview/
         wcd_overview.pdf, accessed November 2007.

2000b   Dams and Development: A New Framework for Decision Making. http://
         www.dams.org//docs/report/wcdreport.pdf, accessed August 2008.

World Health Organization (WHO)

2000   Human Health and Dams. The World Health Organization's submission to the
         World Commission on Dams (WCD). Geneva: WHO. http://www.who.int/
         docstore/water_sanitation_health/documents/dams/damsfinal.pdf, accessed
         November 2007.

2006   Mental Illness and Suicidality after Hurricane Katrina, by R. Kessler, S. Galea,
         R. T. Jones, and H. A. Parker. http://www.who.int/bulletin/volumes/84/12/
         06-03301ab/en, accessed June 2008.

**World Health Organization and the Centre for Environmental Management and
Planning (WHO and CEMP)**

1992   Environmental and Health Impact Assessment of Development Projects: A
         Handbook for Practitioners. R. G. H. Turnbull, ed. London: Elsevier Applied
         Science.

REFERENCES

World Parks Congress (WPC)

2003   Recommendations (1–32). http://www.iucn.org/themes/wcpa/wpc2003/ english/outputs/recommendations.htm, accessed August 2005.

World Wildlife Fund for Nature (WWF) and Terralingua

2000   Indigenous and Traditional Peoples of the World and Ecoregion Conservation. Gland, UK: WWF International.

Yambayamba, E. S. K., A. S. Mweene, D. J. Banda, and S. Kang'omba

2001   Investigation into Groundwater Pollution in the Gwembe Valley: The Case of Lusitu. September Report. Lusaka: Ministry of Environment and Natural Resources.

Index

School for Advanced Research Advanced Seminar Series

PUBLISHED BY SAR PRESS

CHACO & HOHOKAM: PREHISTORIC
REGIONAL SYSTEMS IN THE AMERICAN
SOUTHWEST
Patricia L. Crown & W. James Judge, eds.

RECAPTURING ANTHROPOLOGY: WORKING IN
THE PRESENT
Richard G. Fox, ed.

WAR IN THE TRIBAL ZONE: EXPANDING
STATES AND INDIGENOUS WARFARE
*R. Brian Ferguson &
Neil L. Whitehead, eds.*

IDEOLOGY AND PRE-COLUMBIAN
CIVILIZATIONS
*Arthur A. Demarest &
Geoffrey W. Conrad, eds.*

DREAMING: ANTHROPOLOGICAL AND
PSYCHOLOGICAL INTERPRETATIONS
Barbara Tedlock, ed.

HISTORICAL ECOLOGY: CULTURAL
KNOWLEDGE AND CHANGING LANDSCAPES
Carole L. Crumley, ed.

THEMES IN SOUTHWEST PREHISTORY
George J. Gumerman, ed.

MEMORY, HISTORY, AND OPPOSITION UNDER
STATE SOCIALISM
Rubie S. Watson, ed.

OTHER INTENTIONS: CULTURAL CONTEXTS
AND THE ATTRIBUTION OF INNER STATES
Lawrence Rosen, ed.

LAST HUNTERS–FIRST FARMERS: NEW
PERSPECTIVES ON THE PREHISTORIC
TRANSITION TO AGRICULTURE
*T. Douglas Price &
Anne Birgitte Gebauer, eds.*

MAKING ALTERNATIVE HISTORIES:
THE PRACTICE OF ARCHAEOLOGY AND
HISTORY IN NON-WESTERN SETTINGS
Peter R. Schmidt & Thomas C. Patterson, eds.

SENSES OF PLACE
Steven Feld & Keith H. Basso, eds.

CYBORGS & CITADELS: ANTHROPOLOGICAL
INTERVENTIONS IN EMERGING SCIENCES AND
TECHNOLOGIES
Gary Lee Downey & Joseph Dumit, eds.

ARCHAIC STATES
Gary M. Feinman & Joyce Marcus, eds.

CRITICAL ANTHROPOLOGY NOW:
UNEXPECTED CONTEXTS, SHIFTING
CONSTITUENCIES, CHANGING AGENDAS
George E. Marcus, ed.

THE ORIGINS OF LANGUAGE: WHAT
NONHUMAN PRIMATES CAN TELL US
Barbara J. King, ed.

REGIMES OF LANGUAGE: IDEOLOGIES,
POLITIES, AND IDENTITIES
Paul V. Kroskrity, ed.

BIOLOGY, BRAINS, AND BEHAVIOR: THE
EVOLUTION OF HUMAN DEVELOPMENT
*Sue Taylor Parker, Jonas Langer, &
Michael L. McKinney, eds.*

WOMEN & MEN IN THE PREHISPANIC
SOUTHWEST: LABOR, POWER, & PRESTIGE
Patricia L. Crown, ed.

HISTORY IN PERSON: ENDURING STRUGGLES,
CONTENTIOUS PRACTICE, INTIMATE
IDENTITIES
Dorothy Holland & Jean Lave, eds.

THE EMPIRE OF THINGS: REGIMES OF VALUE
AND MATERIAL CULTURE
Fred R. Myers, ed.

CATASTROPHE & CULTURE: THE
ANTHROPOLOGY OF DISASTER
*Susanna M. Hoffman &
Anthony Oliver-Smith, eds.*

URUK MESOPOTAMIA & ITS NEIGHBORS:
CROSS-CULTURAL INTERACTIONS IN THE ERA
OF STATE FORMATION
Mitchell S. Rothman, ed.

REMAKING LIFE & DEATH: TOWARD AN
ANTHROPOLOGY OF THE BIOSCIENCES
Sarah Franklin & Margaret Lock, eds.

TIKAL: DYNASTIES, FOREIGNERS,
& AFFAIRS OF STATE: ADVANCING
MAYA ARCHAEOLOGY
Jeremy A. Sabloff, ed.

GRAY AREAS: ETHNOGRAPHIC ENCOUNTERS
WITH NURSING HOME CULTURE
Philip B. Stafford, ed.

PLURALIZING ETHNOGRAPHY: COMPARISON
AND REPRESENTATION IN MAYA CULTURES,
HISTORIES, AND IDENTITIES
John M. Watanabe & Edward F. Fischer, eds.

PUBLISHED BY CAMBRIDGE UNIVERSITY PRESS

THE ANASAZI IN A CHANGING ENVIRONMENT
George J. Gumerman, ed.

REGIONAL PERSPECTIVES ON THE OLMEC
Robert J. Sharer & David C. Grove, eds.

THE CHEMISTRY OF PREHISTORIC HUMAN
BONE
T. Douglas Price, ed.

THE EMERGENCE OF MODERN HUMANS:
BIOCULTURAL ADAPTATIONS IN THE LATER
PLEISTOCENE
Erik Trinkaus, ed.

THE ANTHROPOLOGY OF WAR
Jonathan Haas, ed.

THE EVOLUTION OF POLITICAL SYSTEMS
Steadman Upham, ed.

CLASSIC MAYA POLITICAL HISTORY:
HIEROGLYPHIC AND ARCHAEOLOGICAL
EVIDENCE
T. Patrick Culbert, ed.

TURKO-PERSIA IN HISTORICAL PERSPECTIVE
Robert L. Canfield, ed.

CHIEFDOMS: POWER, ECONOMY, AND
IDEOLOGY
Timothy Earle, ed.

RECONSTRUCTING PREHISTORIC PUEBLO
SOCIETIES
William A. Longacre, ed.

PUBLISHED BY UNIVERSITY OF NEW MEXICO PRESS

NEW PERSPECTIVES ON THE PUEBLOS
Alfonso Ortiz, ed.

STRUCTURE AND PROCESS IN LATIN AMERICA
Arnold Strickon & Sidney M. Greenfield, eds.

THE CLASSIC MAYA COLLAPSE
T. Patrick Culbert, ed.

METHODS AND THEORIES OF
ANTHROPOLOGICAL GENETICS
M. H. Crawford & P. L. Workman, eds.

SIXTEENTH-CENTURY MEXICO:
THE WORK OF SAHAGUN
Munro S. Edmonson, ed.

ANCIENT CIVILIZATION AND TRADE
*Jeremy A. Sabloff &
C. C. Lamberg-Karlovsky, eds.*

PHOTOGRAPHY IN ARCHAEOLOGICAL
RESEARCH
Elmer Harp, Jr., ed.

MEANING IN ANTHROPOLOGY
Keith H. Basso & Henry A. Selby, eds.

THE VALLEY OF MEXICO: STUDIES IN
PRE-HISPANIC ECOLOGY AND SOCIETY
Eric R. Wolf, ed.

DEMOGRAPHIC ANTHROPOLOGY:
QUANTITATIVE APPROACHES
Ezra B. W. Zubrow, ed.

THE ORIGINS OF MAYA CIVILIZATION
Richard E. W. Adams, ed.

EXPLANATION OF PREHISTORIC CHANGE
James N. Hill, ed.

EXPLORATIONS IN ETHNOARCHAEOLOGY
Richard A. Gould, ed.

ENTREPRENEURS IN CULTURAL CONTEXT
*Sidney M. Greenfield, Arnold Strickon,
& Robert T. Aubey, eds.*

THE DYING COMMUNITY
Art Gallaher, Jr. & Harlan Padfield, eds.

SOUTHWESTERN INDIAN RITUAL DRAMA
Charlotte J. Frisbie, ed.

LOWLAND MAYA SETTLEMENT PATTERNS
Wendy Ashmore, ed.

SIMULATIONS IN ARCHAEOLOGY
Jeremy A. Sabloff, ed.

CHAN CHAN: ANDEAN DESERT CITY
Michael E. Moseley & Kent C. Day, eds.

SHIPWRECK ANTHROPOLOGY
Richard A. Gould, ed.

ELITES: ETHNOGRAPHIC ISSUES
George E. Marcus, ed.

THE ARCHAEOLOGY OF LOWER CENTRAL
AMERICA
Frederick W. Lange & Doris Z. Stone, eds.

LATE LOWLAND MAYA CIVILIZATION:
CLASSIC TO POSTCLASSIC
Jeremy A. Sabloff & E. Wyllys Andrews V, eds.

Participants in the School for Advanced Research advanced seminar "Rethinking Frameworks, Methodologies, and the Role of Anthropology in Development Induced Displacement and Resettlement," Santa Fe, New Mexico, September 25 to 29, 2005. Standing (left to right): Theodore Downing, Satish Kedia, Thayer Scudder, Gregory Button, Michael Cernea, Chris de Wet, William Fisher, Barbara Rose Johnston. Seated (left to right): Dolores Koenig, Anthony Oliver-Smith, Dana Clark.